PROGRESS IN INFANCY RESEARCH, VOLUME 2

PROGRESS IN INFANCY RESEARCH, VOLUME 2

Edited by

Jeffrey W. Fagen
St. John's University

Harlene Hayne
The University of Otago

LEA
2002

LAWRENCE ERLBAUM ASSOCIATES, PUBLISHERS
Mahwah, New Jersey   London

Lawrence Erlbaum Associates, Inc., Publishers
10 Industrial Avenue
Mahwah, NJ   07430

Cover design by Kathryn Houghtaling Lacey

Library of Congress ISSN: 1527-5884
ISBN: 0-8058-3944-5

Books published by Lawrence Erlbaum Associates are printed on
acid-free paper, and their bindings are chosen for strength and durability.

Printed in the United States of America

10   9   8   7   6   5   4   3   2   1

Contents

List of Contributors

Karen E. Adolph, Department of Psychology, New York University, New York, NY.

Marion A. Eppler, Department of Psychology, East Carolina University, Greenville, NC.

Lewis P. Lipsitt, Department of Psychology, Brown University, Providence, RI.

Denis Mareschal, Department of Psychology, Birbeck College, London, U. K.

David S. Moore, Pitzer College and Claremont Graduate University, Claremont, CA.

Yuko Munakata, Department of Psychology, University of Denver, Denver, CO.

Elaine Reese, Department of Psychology, University of Otago, Otago, New Zealand.

Ann M. Skoczenski, Smith-Kettlewell Eye Research Institute, San Francisco, CA.

Melanie J. Spence, School of Human Development, University of Texas at Dallas, Dallas, TX.

Jennifer Merva Stedron, Department of Psychology, University of Denver, Denver, CO.

Preface

We are very pleased to present the second volume of the series *Progress in Infancy Research*. The Progress series was originally edited by Carolyn Rovee-Collier and Lewis P. Lipsitt. Their vision was to establish a book series dedicated to the presentation of innovative and exciting research on infants, both human and animal. Our goal is to continue this tradition. Each volume is designed to stand alone; there is no intention to represent any subject area exclusively or to integrate the contributions with one another. Rather, we aim to publish autonomous chapters that are based on high quality, cutting-edge research programs. Work that deviates from conventional approaches, or that challenges or modifies traditional perspectives, is especially welcomed. We also attempt to strike a balance between well established and emerging researchers. We hope this series will be a forum for the presentation of technological breakthroughs, methodological advances, and new integrations that might create platforms for future programmatic work on the complexities of infant behavior and development.

Appearance in these volumes is principally by invitation. Nonetheless, we consider uninvited manuscripts, which may be submitted initially in outline form and with an abstract. All manuscripts are critically reviewed. Our judgment as to the appropriateness of a manuscript for these volumes depends partly on the extent to which authors inform other researchers whose expertise is not central to the topic of the manuscript but whose own research may be affected beneficially by the manuscript.

The editors are happy to acknowledge with gratitude the aid of their home institutions, St. John's University in New York and The University of Otago in Dunedin, New Zealand. We are grateful for the time and facilities provided by our home institutions for the preparation of this volume.

We also express our gratitude to the several editorial advisors whose service and wisdom have helped us to begin this series with such high quality contributions:

Susan Galvin
Scott Adler
Julien Gross
Joyce Prigot
Melissa Welch-Ross
Thomas Keenan
Richard Bogartz
Barbara Younger-Rossman
Philippe Rochat
Lorraine Bahrick

Each volume in this series is dedicated to an outstanding investigator whose research has illuminated the nature of infant behavior and development and whose contributions to the field have been of seminal importance. We are pleased and proud to dedicate this volume to one of the forefathers of infant research, Emeritus Professor of Psychology, Medical Science, and Human Development, Lewis P. Lipsitt of Brown University.

Jeffrey W. Fagen, St. John's University
Harlene Hayne, The University of Otago

Dedication

It is only fitting that as we take over the editorship of *Progress in Infancy Research*, we dedicate our first volume to Dr. Lewis P. Lipsitt, who qualifies more than anyone as the "intellectual grandfather" to both of us. Lew Lipsitt, "Mr. Infancy," has had, and continues to have, a distinguished career in psychological science, particularly in the field of infancy. His pioneering work in the early 1960s at Brown University laid the foundation for the work of numerous investigators from various areas within the broad field of infancy research. Although he is probably best known for his work in infant conditioning, Dr. Lipsitt's research interests have been quite broad. In his own words:

> I have come to understand in recent years that in different phases of my scientific life I have been especially concerned with and have focused my attention on behavioral and developmental phenomena that have been of special concern to me in rather personal ways: (1) the effect of birth risk factors on later development; (2) the instrumental role of behavioral factors in survival, even of babies; (3) the effects of delayed reward on performance; (4) the origins and consequences of prejudicial behavior, including false accusations; (5) the hedonic origins of basic approach and avoidance behaviors; (6) the life-span consequences of the pleasures and annoyances of sensation; (7) the origins of developmental delays and debilities, particularly learning disabilities, and, do I dare say it; (8) the ontogeny of danger-seeking and risk-taking behavior. (Lipsitt, 1996, p. 137)

Lewis Paeff Lipsitt was born on June 28, 1929 in New Bedford, Massachusetts, in a hospital where his uncle was the head of pediatrics. He was named after his maternal grandfather, Louis Paeff, and it was not until he was around 2 years of age that it was discovered that the name on his birth certificate had incorrectly been listed as "Lewis" rather than "Louis." Lewis was the third son of Joseph Lipsitt, an attorney, and Anna Naomi Paeff, a homemaker and musician with a degree from the New England Conservatory of Music. Joseph and Anna Lipsitt were both of Eastern European descent. They went on to have two more boys, the last being born when Anna was almost 50 years of age. Seven years separated Lew from his younger brother Cy and until Cy was born, his parents and relatives referred to him as "Baby Lou." Perhaps this fact, coupled with his uncle being a pediatrician, had something to do with his fascination with babies.

As with many parents of Eastern European origin, the Lipsitts stressed the value of education to their children. All of the Lipsitt boys are college graduates: Paul, the oldest, is a lawyer and clinical psychologist who was a founder of the American Board of Forensic Psychology; Don, the next oldest, is a psychiatrist; and the two younger Lipsitts, Cy and Peter, are artists. Lew's first love was writing and he admits that, had he not become a psychologist, he probably would have become a journalist. His first "job" was as the "dog editor" for *The Sippian Compass*, a town newspaper begun in 1939 by his father in their new hometown of Marion, Massachusetts. As his title implies, Lew's job was to write interesting stories about dogs in the community. Lew has been writing interesting "stories" ever since!

Lewis Lipsitt graduated high school in 1947. He did his undergraduate work at the University of Chicago and graduated with a degree in liberal arts in 1950. One of the turning points in his professional life occurred at Chicago when he went to hear a talk by a McGill University psychology professor named Donald O. Hebb. Not knowing what he wanted to do with his life after graduation, Lipsitt went to Boston after college to be nearer his family and, being interested in hedonics even back then, to simply have fun. While in Boston, Lew enrolled for a semester and a summer of advanced undergraduate courses in psychology and he soon decided on clinical psychology as a career. He wanted to help people and he was intrigued by Freud and psychoanalysis. Strange as it may seem for such an esteemed scientist, he admits that, at the time, "the scientific aspects of psychology seemed to me rather dry and laboratory work a bit of a drudge" (Lipsitt, 1996, p. 146).

More important than the knowledge of psychology that he gained at Boston is the fact that it was here that he met Edna Duchin, the woman who was to become his wife and lifelong partner. Together they moved to Amherst, Massachusetts, where Lew enrolled in a master's program at the University of Massachusetts. Although he still wanted to be a clinician, Lew was fascinated, while doing his thesis, that numbers could be assigned to attributes of people's personalities, and that the scientific method of hypothesis generation and testing could be applied to something as complex as the behavior and attitudes of human beings. Massachusetts was also the place where Lew first made contact with animal research, investigating first how rats reacted when switched from solvable to unsolvable tasks and then back again, and then the designing interventions to reverse the animals' "learned helplessness." In his own words:

My fascination with these systematic studies of extreme effects of unsatisfying experiences was enormous and galvanized my understanding, even insistence for the rest of my career, that (1) developmental experiences have profound effects, (2) adverse conditions can debilitate, (3) organisms can recover from terribly stressful experiences if given rehabilitative opportunities, and (4) the processes involved in these psychodynamic changes can be observed systematically, can be quantified, and are verifiable. Life destinies may be profoundly altered by changing the environmental context and the expectations of the organism. (Lipsitt, 1996, p. 148)

After receiving his Master's degree in clinical and social psychology, Lew joined the Air Force, where he was assigned to a unit at Lackland Air Force Base doing follow-up psychological testing of airmen who had done poorly on the Air Force Qualifying Test. It was here that Lew's career as a clinical and developmental psychologist really began: "I enjoyed learning about patients' problems and about the diverse treatment plans of well-trained professionals for fixing these problems. At the same time, I had a rising suspicion that my real interests, and perhaps my best talents, resided not so much in diagnosing (labeling, as I saw it) people in distress, but rather in *trying to figure out what the processes were by which they came to be the way they were*" (Lipsitt, 1996, p. 150, emphasis added).

In 1954, Lew left the Air Force and, at the urging of David Palermo, his friend from graduate school days at Massachusetts, enrolled in the newly established doctoral program in experimental child psychology at the University of Iowa. Here, Lew's desire to use empirical approaches to understand behavioral development were fueled by the likes of Boyd McCandless, Charles Spiker, and Alfredo Castenada. His lifelong interest in learning principles also began in earnest at Iowa, where he was exposed to such notables as Kenneth Spence and Don Lewis, both of whom were on Lew's dissertation committee. His dissertation, under the directorship of Professor Castenada, was entitled, "Effects of differential (delayed reward) instrumental training on subsequent performance of children in a discrimination task."

Like many other individuals at the time, Lew did not actually interview for his first (and only) academic position. "One morning in my last year at Iowa before graduating with the PhD, Boyd McCandless, on the way to his usual coffee break in the East Hall lounge, walked the hallway waving a letter he had just received from Brown University. He asked as he walked by the graduate student offices: 'Anyone want to go to Brown?' I replied, 'Yes, please'" (Lipsitt, 1996, p. 152). Lipsitt was not only smart but he was polite! And so began a vibrant and productive academic career that has spanned more than 40 years, all of which have been spent as a faculty member at Brown University. He currently holds the title of Professor of Psychology and Medical Science.

Early in his career at Brown, Lipsitt established a laboratory at the nearby Providence Lying-In Hospital to systematically study infant behavior and development. It was here that he conducted the first and now classic systematic studies of newborn learning. Lipsitt's neonatal laboratory is still one of the leading laboratories for newborn research in the world. This is the research that led to Professor Lipsitt being recognized around the world as the founder of the scientific study of infant behavioral development. Hence the title "Mr. Infancy." At Brown, Lipsitt also continued three lines of research on children that he had begun at Iowa: studies on the effects of delayed reward on children's discrimination learning, the interaction of habit and drive factors on children's learning performance, and the role of verbal mediation in children's paired-associates learning. Several Brown students who are now themselves distinguished developmental psychologists worked with Lipsitt, including Carolyn Rovee-Collier (our mentor and hence our earlier reference to Professor Lipsitt as our intellectual grandfather), Dan Ashmead, Carol Nagy Jacklin, and Juarlyn Gaiter, to name just a few. Lipsitt's early work with infants and children was heavily influenced by Thorndike's Law of Effect, Skinner's behavior analytic approach, and the then popular Hull-Spence theory of learning. In 1967, Lipsitt founded the Child Study Center at Brown, which he directed for the next 25 years. The Center was involved in a systematic study of children from birth to 7 years of age as part of the National Collaborative Perinatal Project. Although the actual study ended in 1973, Lipsitt and his colleagues have continued to follow a group of original study participants who were characterized as "learning disabled," trying to determine why some have managed to succeed in spite of their disability whereas others have not.

Dr. Lipsitt's interest in the importance of the infancy period in development led him to found and edit four publications in this area: *Infant Behavior and Development*, an international, interdisciplinary journal; *Advances in Infancy Research*, an annual publication that highlights the programmatic research of investigators at the cutting edge of the infancy field; the *Monographs in Infancy* series; and, with Carolyn Rovee-Collier and Harlene Hayne, the current *Progress in Infancy Research* annual publication. Lew and his wife Edna were also instrumental in organizing the first International Conference on Infant Studies, which met in Providence in 1978 and has met in various cities in North America and Europe every other year since. Dr. Lipsitt also was instrumental in the formation of the International Society for Infant Studies, which adopted the journal he founded, *Infant Behavior and Development*, as the official journal of the Society.

From 1986 to 1987, Dr. Lipsitt was a visiting scientist at the National Institute of Mental Health, where he studied psychopathological aspects of risk-taking behavior and began work on a coedited volume entitled, "Self-regulatory and risk taking behavior: Causes and consequences" published in 1991. He is the editor of the *Brown University Child and Adolescent Letter*, a newsletter about the development of children and adolescents. He has been a Guggenheim Fellow, and a Fellow of the Tavistock Institute of Human

Relations and at St. Mary's Hospital in London. In 1979, he was a fellow at the Center for Advanced Study in the Behavioral Sciences at Stanford University, for which he received a prestigious James McKeen Cattell Fellowship Award. In 1990, the American Psychological Association honored him with the Nicholas Hobbs Award for "science in the service of children." Lipsitt was the president of the Eastern Psychological Association from 1992 to 1993. He has dedicated much of his time and effort to the American Psychological Association (APA), serving a term as president of the Division on Developmental Psychology, two terms on the Council of Representatives, as chair of the Board of Scientific Affairs, and as the Association's Executive Director for Science. He ran twice for the presidency of APA, in 1993 and 1994, running second among five candidates both times.

We would like to close with a quote from a letter that Dr. Lipsitt's student and our mentor, Carolyn Rovee-Collier, recently wrote in support of his nomination for the New England Psychological Association Distinguished Contribution Award:

> Finally, as one of his first graduate students at Brown University, I would like to comment on Lew's singular qualities as a mentor and role model. Besides the many facts he taught and integrative ideas he encouraged, Lew taught us candor, humility, an appreciation of our intellectual predecessors, to follow where our data led us, and to have the courage to confront and overcome conventional attitudes and biases through our Science. He encouraged us to grasp the past and look with hope to the future, to ask the important unanswered questions, to challenge the status quo. Most of all, through daily example, he taught us the importance of compassion—the importance of using our knowledge, not just for our own self-satisfaction, but for improving the lot of those we study. I think that all of our lives will reflect that, in our individual and often meager ways, we have attempted to follow these teachings and to communicate them to our own students as well. Those he has touched, both directly and indirectly, will forever be indebted for these lessons.

We thank Lew (and Carolyn) for instilling these qualities in us and we humbly dedicate this, our first volume as editors, to Lewis Paeff Lipsitt.

—Jeffrey Fagen, St. John's University
—Harlene Hayne, University of Otago

REFERENCE

Lipsitt, L. P. (1996). Lewis P. Lipsitt. In D. Thompson & J. D. Hogan (Eds.), *A history of developmental psychology in autobiography* (pp. 137–160). Boulder, CO: Westview Press.

Dr. Lewis P. Lipsitt

Reminiscence and Rumination

I selected this article because it contains several of my scientific fascinations, even passions. Of special importance to me is the basic research from my infant behavior and development laboratory on the oral behavior and "savoring mechanisms" of the newborn, which led to my appreciation more generally of babies' approach and avoidance behaviors. In particular, I was impressed with the way in which babies, while engaged avidly in feeding, could simultaneously and with equal enthusiasm, defend themselves against respiratory occlusion. This work led me to believe that the pleasures and annoyances of sensation are at the core of a human's *being* and provide the context in which, probably, all early childhood learning occurs.

It was while studying infants' sensory and learning processes that I came to believe that many crib deaths are attributable to behavioral processes, and not exclusively to an organic defect or disease. The essence of the argument was first proposed in Lipsitt (1976). It is elaborated in chapter 1 and, with more detail, in later pieces (Lipsitt, 1979), fortified by my increasing acquaintance with and enthusiasm for the research and writings of Myrtle McGraw (1943). My scholarly investment in my initial thinking about the sudden infant death syndrome (SIDS) remains for me as intense today as it was in my first conceptualization of it in the early 1970s. Ironically, my experience with the hypothesis constitutes one of the more disappointing aspects of my career.

Let me amplify. The chapter reproduced here was written about 20 years after I went to Brown University from my graduate study in experimental child psychology at the University of Iowa, and appeared in a volume edited by two good friends in the field of child behavior and development. I wasn't yet 50 years old. My laboratory was thriving on ample, if not lavish, grant resources. I had excellent students and colleagues collaborating with me in the study of infant sensory and learning processes and in my other work on older children. I had founded and was editing publications that many colleagues regarded as pioneering in a field that had not yet reached the level of careful industry and respect for which it is known today. In every aspect of my career except one, I felt fulfilled.

My disappointment, explicated in Lipsitt (1996), was that I was not able to prevail on the crib death research dynasty and powerful money granters that the *behavior* of infants is critically important for the preservation of their lives and well-being. My theory, with strong presumptive evidence, has been presented to the SIDS research community at two very visible Eisenhower Medical Center conferences on SIDS, and at other meetings, but has rarely received more than polite acknowledgement as one among many hypotheses. There was enormous resistance to, even denial of, the critical importance of behavioral defense mechanisms in infants' viability.

A prevailing hypothesis for many years was that a "condition" of apnea (fortuitous, mostly unexplained, and sometimes lethally prolonged, interruption of respiration) was the root cause of crib death. Eventually, however, lack of empirical support for this hypothesis brought the research community to its knees and to its senses. Revelation of medical misadventures, owing partly to a persevering team of legal persecutors, medical pathologists, and nurses in upstate New York finally called into serious question the veracity of apnea as "the cause" or even "a major cause" of crib deaths. (See the volume by Firstman & Talan [1997] for an undisputed recitation of events concening this unfortunate era in the history of SIDS research.)

When the apnea hypthosis was in the ascendancy, I prepared a grant proposal, based on an assumption of neurobehavioral deficit that could be ameliorated by training. My proposal was to test the behavioral hypothesis by training vulnerable infants to engage in life-saving postural (motoric) adjustments. Infant survivors do this all the time. The proposal was turned down by the government granting agency. This left me very discouraged, and I turned my attention to other venues. I have spent a lot of my career energy, nonetheless, trying to find a perch from which to encourage greater acceptance of the importance of behavior in the preservation of life.

More young people die or are dibilitated by *behavioral acts* that involve essentially *remediable insufficiencies*—accidents, suicide, homicide, excessive drinking, drug taking, and other failures of defensive self-regulation—than from all other causes combined. SIDS has been reduced in the last 10 years to half its previous prevalence, through the "back-to-sleep" movement designed to prevent respiratory occlusion. That a simple adjustment in behavioral caretaking, preventing the baby from smothering, makes such a great difference is clear testimony to the importance of behavioral interventions in saving babies' lives. For the sake of babies passed over, I do wish that this had been appreciated much earlier.

Lewis Lipsitt

REFERENCES

Firstman, R., & Talan, J. (1997). *The death of innocents: A true story of murder, medicine and high-stakes science*. New York: Bantam Books.

Lipsitt, L. P. (1976). Developmental psychobiology comes of age. In L. P. Lipsitt (Ed.), *Developmental psychobiology: The significance of infancy* (pp. 109–127). Mahwah, NJ: Lawrence Erlbaum Associates.

Lipsitt, L. P. (1979). Critical conditions in infancy: A psychological perspective. *American Psychologist, 34,* 973–980.

Lipsitt, L. P. (1996). Lewis P. Lipsitt. In D. Thompson & J. D. Hogan (Eds.), *A history of developmental psychology in autobiography* (pp. 109–127). Boulder, CO: Westview Press.

McGraw, M. B. (1943). *The neuromuscular maturation of the human infant*. New York: Columbia University Press.

1

▼▼▼▼▼▼▼

The Newborn as Informant

Lewis P. Lipsitt
Brown University

The newborn's psychobiological status is a product of congenital, prenatal, and birth conditions. Hereditary factors interact with intra-uterine biochemical factors, and both sets of conditions can be further complicated by obstetrical circumstances. By capitalizing on clinical–pediatric and behavioral assessment procedures, we should be able to carry out psychophysiological assessments on the newborn that will clearly reflect the course of and hazards inherent in embryonic and fetal development. Because specific prenatal hazards often have enduring effects, the newborn should be able to tell us whether things have gone badly or well. The neonate could become our collaborator in helping to forecast future developmental problems, and under the best of such circumstances might provide information about the probable success of various remedial interventions. The behavior of the newborn, in short, might provide the best, most valid indices of the "condition of the organism" that can be obtained. This dream is possible because so many advances have been made over the past two decades in the recording and understanding of sensory functioning, central nervous system integrity, and behavioral plasticity.

It is not too early for the behavioral scientist to apply already existing technologies for the benefit of infants born following a hazardous pregnancy. We should be better able to detect the character of the insufficiencies incurred and to plan the best possible remediation procedures for the problems discovered through close studies of sensory and learning processes in the young infant.

1

Many neonatal laboratories now use polygraphic recording procedures to document impairments due to prematurity, oxygen deprivation, and other perinatal conditions that tend to place infants in developmental jeopardy. Although it is well known that prematurity and anoxia contribute heavily to various developmental anomalies, including cerebral palsy, mental retardation, epilepsy, and school problems (Drillien, 1964; Sameroff & Chandler, 1975), much research remains to be done to develop the best clues for the early detection and amelioration of these conditions (Gluck, 1974; Lipsitt, 1977).

This chapter reviews several areas of behavioral investigation of the newborn, with emphasis on those procedures that have shown special promise for the eventual better detection of neonatal aberrations and their sequelae. The promising techniques to be considered are those that have yielded interesting and stable individual-difference data in groups of normal infants and provided some preliminary findings suggesting that they may have special use in detecting early deficits related to later cognitive functioning. The propositions to be considered are:

1. Careful measurement of sucking behavior in the normal newborn, when appropriated for use with premature, small for dates, and otherwise stressed infants can have special value, particularly if questions are asked about patterns of response, rather than merely about whether the infant has a particular response in its repertoire. It should be more illuminating to ask not only whether the infant can hear or suck, but also whether the psychophysical curve relating the baby's response to various stimulus intensities matches that for other infants of the same age. We thus not only ask whether the infant detects a new taste, but also whether its adaptation to the new taste resembles that of normal infants who show an orderly accommodation of responses to different concentrations of sweet fluid.
2. The detection of sensory and behavioral deficit will probably be facilitated by the intensive study of habituation, which capitalizes upon the organism's accommodation to external stimuli. The infants are asked not only to detect a light of moderate intensity, but to report on changes in their defensive or orienting "attitude" toward repetitive presentations of the same stimulus. The inability of infants to show psychophysiological change to such redundant stimulation has been shown in preliminary studies to be a mark of nervous-system (probably cortical) immaturity or central nervous system (CNS) damage.
3. Stimulation of premature infants with special procedures for providing extra experience has suggested that infants who may be predicted on an actuarial basis to be retarded or to show some deficit later in life might benefit from compensatory stimulation. Such extra

input, in anticipation of the predicted deficit, could succeed in mitigating the loss.

4. There are presently some indications that the so-called "sudden infant death syndrome" (crib death) is a disorder of development that might have some anticipatory components detectable during the earliest days of life. The early leads into an understanding of this matter require much additional work, because we cannot know the possibilities until the plausible existing hypotheses have been pursued. The supposition is put forward here that at least some crib deaths, which occur mostly between 2 and 4 months of age, may be due to a failure to undergo critical experiences during the first 2 months of life. By the age of 2 to 4 months, many responses that were initially unconditioned or obligatory become executed on an operant or more "voluntary" basis. During the early months, the infant must learn to engage in "respiratory retrieval responses" in order to respond properly to potentially lethal threats of respiratory occlusion.

POLYGRAPHIC STUDIES OF THE NEWBORN'S SUCKING AND HEART RATE

Recent advances in the use of polygraphic recording in infant research, and the exquisite sensitivity and responsivity of the newborn to exteroceptive stimulation, have led to considerable progress in our understanding of the sensory and learning capabilities of the newborn. The developmental psychologist's capability for conducting refined assessments of the neonate's sensorium has brought us closer to doing informative longitudinal studies, both short- and long-term. These investigations are necessary not only to discover whether certain very early experiences may have a lasting effect upon the behavior and well being of the baby, but also to find whether stimulus interventions may have salubrious consequences for a child who might otherwise manifest a later developmental deficit. It is not too early for us to hope that it might be possible to provide immunity, through behavioral techniques, against some sorts of developmental anomalies. First, however, it is necessary to seek solid documentation of the sensory capacities and behavioral repertoire of the very young infant (Lipsitt, 1977).

In this spirit, a number of studies have been carried out in my laboratory at Women and Infants Hospital of Rhode Island to find out, for example, about the neonate's capacity for discriminating odors and tastes. Through both of these senses the newborn relates closely with the world in the first hours following birth. Our studies have generated some data relating to the approach and avoidance style of the newborn, the differ-

ences among newborns in such styles, and the reactions of babies to stimuli that adults would regard as pleasant and unpleasant. In this section,
several studies are reviewed from which the inexorable conclusion is
drawn that the baby is keenly sensitive in the first few hours of life to subtle
changes in gustatory stimulation.

The baby acts on its discrimination of these taste changes either to promote the perpetuation of the taste or to suppress it, depending largely
upon sweetness. In short, the newborn is a hedonic creature who responds
to the incentive-motivational properties of reinforcers with both motor
changes in behavior, such as in sucking and swallowing, and autonomic
behavioral changes. The autonomic aspects of these behavioral consequences of pleasant and unpleasant stimulation, such as the accompany-
ing heart-rate changes, are, of course, the rudiments of affect. There is no
mistaking the most avid manifestations of such affect, as when the infant
goes quickly quiet when offered a sweet fluid. Mothers do indeed respond
sympathetically and reciprocally to these behaviors in their newborns by,
for example, moving to promote the baby's search for the nipple and the
sweet taste or by helping the baby to escape momentary respiratory occlusion when awkwardly positioned. Mothers and fathers usually respond
quickly with looking, touching, and lifting when the baby cries; this is,
in fact, a good example of the infant and its caretakers "pleasuring" each
other.

Our studies of neonatal taste are carried out in a special crib, housed in
a white, sound-attentuated chamber with temperature about 80° Fahren-
heit. Ambient light is about 50 foot-candles. Breathing is monitored by a
Phipps and Bird infant pneumobelt around the abdomen and respiration
and body activity recorded continuously on a Grass polygraph. Hewlett-
Packard electrodes are placed on the chest and leg, permitting polygraphic
monitoring of the primary heart rate, which is then integrated by a Hewlett-
Packard cardiotachometer and recorded on another channel.

Sucking is recorded on one of the polygraph channels, using a "suck-
ometer," which consists of a stainless-steel housing with a pressure trans-
ducer, over which a commercial nipple is pulled. A polyethylene tube runs
into the nipple from a pump source and delivers fluid under the experimenter's control and, in most of our studies, on demand of the subject.
When delivering, the pump ejects into the nipple-end a tiny drop of fluid
contingent upon the execution of a sucking response of preset amplitude.
The size of this drop for each criterion suck is usually 0.02 ml although in
some studies in which the effect of the magnitude of the drop is under
study, the drop amount may be varied from 0.01 ml to 0.04 ml. See Figs.
1.1 and 1.2.

The situation is arranged such that the infant may receive no fluid for
sucking, or might receive a fluid such as sucrose or dextrose in any desired

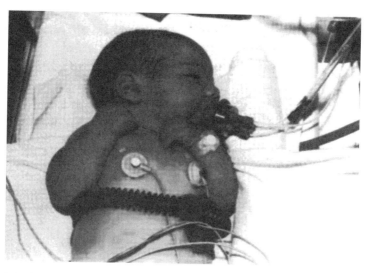

FIG. 1.1   Two-day-old infant prepared for recording of respiration, heart rate, and sucking.

concentration. Contingent upon sucking, one drop of fluid is ejected into the baby's mouth for each suck. A polygraph event marker records fluid ejections during fluid delivery periods or the occurrence of a criterion suck during no-fluid conditions. A 74 dB background white noise assures a fairly constant acoustical environment in the infant chamber.

The laboratory nurse initially makes contact with the mother to explain the research program and obtain informed consent. When the infant is brought to the laboratory for testing, the electrodes and pneumobelt are applied and the infant is swaddled and placed on its left side. The nipple is inserted, supported by a cushion to enable recording without touching the baby. During the first few sucking bursts on the nipple, no fluid is delivered, and the experimenter calibrates the equipment. Preamplifier sensitivity is adjusted for each infant so that the average sucking amplitude results in a 5 cm excursion of the polygraph pen. The threshold criterion is then set at half this excursion, and only those responses exceeding that minimum are considered as criterion responses.

Newborns characteristically suck in bursts of responses separated by rests. Burst length and rest length both constitute individual-difference variables under no-fluid conditions, i.e., some newborns engage in reliably longer bursts and pauses than others. Both of these parameters, as well as the sucking rate within bursts, however, are significantly influenced by the conditions that are prearranged as the consequences of an infant's behavior. With a change from a no-fluid condition to a fluid-sucking

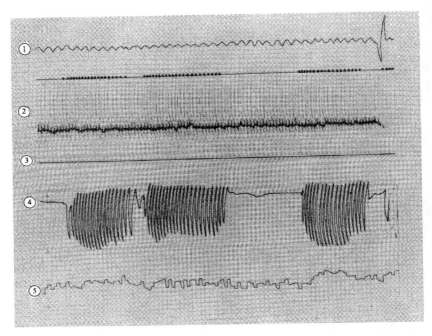

FIG. 1.2. Polygraph recording of (1) respiration, (2) electrocardiogram, (3) blank channel, (4) sucking, and (5) electrocardiotachometer, with digital representation between channels 1 and 2 of the sucking responses recording in channel 4.

condition or from sucking for a less-sweet solution to a sweeter solution, several behavioral consequences characteristically occur. There is a tendency for the sucking bursts to become longer, for the inter-burst intervals to become shorter, and for the inter-suck intervals to become longer. Thus, sucking rate within bursts becomes slower with increasing sweetness of the fluid, and the infant takes fewer and shorter rest periods.

Contrast Effects

The aforementioned regularities of response in relation to the incentive-reinforcement conditions imposed upon the infants during polygraphic testing make it possible (a) to explore the effects of a previous taste experience upon the infant's response during a subsequent taste experience and (b) to investigate the interrelationships of these various sucking-response parameters and their relationship to certain other response measures, such as heart rate. Kobre and Lipsitt (1972) tested infants for 2 minutes on the nipple without any fluid delivery whatever. Subjects in this study were rejected for further study if they had a mean sucking rate lower than 30 per minute during the 2 minute period. The 25 subjects remaining were divided into five groups. A total of 20 minutes of responding was recorded for each subject in four successive 5-minute periods. Between each period the nipple was removed for 1 minute to allow the tube to be flushed with water and the child to be picked up.

These 25 infants, most 3 days old, received one of five reinforcement regimens for the 20-minute period. One group received only sucrose. A second group received water throughout, and a third received sucrose and water, alternated twice, in 5-minute units. A fourth group received no fluid throughout the four 5-minute periods and was compared with a group that received sucrose alternated with no fluid in 5-minute periods.

Frequency polygons of the inter-response times, or inter-suck intervals, were printed out on the console of an on-line PDP-8 computer. Comparison of the first three groups revealed that sucking rate within bursts slows down for a fluid-sucking condition relative to no-fluid sucking and that sucking rate becomes still slower for sweet-fluid sucking relative to sucking for plain distilled water. Thus, there is an orderly progression from no fluid to plain water to 15% sucrose sucking, with sucking response becoming slower and slower as the incentive value of the reinforcement delivered consequent upon the response increases. Also, under the sucrose condition, the infants invested a larger number of responses during a comparable period of time than under either the water or no-fluid condition. This effect, which was a consequence of the infant taking fewer rest periods under the higher incentive condition, also occurred in the comparison of responses emitted for water compared with no fluid.

In this study, the infants who sucked for sucrose throughout the 20-minute testing period emitted significantly more responses per minute than did the group that received water throughout the 20-minute period. Moreover, both groups showed stable response rates for their respective fluids through the four blocks of 5 minutes each. The most interesting finding in this experiment, however, concerned subjects who were alternated from one 5-minute period to another between sucrose and water, or between sucrose and no fluid. These groups showed marked effects attributable to the alternating experiences. For example, when sucking for sucrose, the sucrose/water group was essentially comparable to the group sucking for sucrose throughout. When switched to water, however, response rate during each of those 5-minute periods was significantly lower than in their counterpart controls in the water-throughout group. Thus, when newborns have experience in sucking for sucrose, an immediately subsequent experience with water "turns them off." They display their apparent "aversion" for the water by a marked reduction in instrumental behavior that would put that fluid in their mouths. When the consequence of the response is changed, as from water to sucrose, response rate goes back to a normal level. The infant thus optimizes taste-incentive experiences by modulating oral behaviors pertinent to their occurrence.

The same type of effect occurred in the sucrose/no-fluid group, which showed lower response rates when sucking for no fluid after experience in sucking for sucrose. These negative contrast effects were reliable, and there is no reason to suppose that the phenomenon is not widespread throughout the range of incentive conditions to which neonates would be normally subjected. We would expect such effects to occur whenever the infant is called upon to "compare and contrast" two levels of incentive, such as formula vs. plain water or breast-milk vs. a sweeter formula.

Newborns, then, seem strikingly affected in their subsequent behavior by experiences within the immediately previous 5 minutes. The negative contrast effect demonstrated here is one of the most rudimentary types of behavioral alteration due to experiential circumstances. As with neonatal habituation to olfactory stimulation (Engen & Lipsitt, 1965), the suggestion is that memorial processes are already working in the newborn, such that there is a lasting impression made, admittedly of unknown duration, of the experience endured. These are the beginnings of learning processes.

Relations Between Sucking Behavior and Heart Rate

We now know that at least some aspects of the motor behavior of the newborn are modulated to accord with the incentive conditions to which the baby is exposed. Several studies have reinforced this impression and have further provided us with data on the rudiments of affect in the neonate in the form of changes in autonomic responding depending on incentive conditions.

A study of 44 normal full-term newborns, 24 males and 20 females, was conducted on two consecutive days using the same polygraphic techniques (Lipsitt, Reilly, Butcher, & Greenwood, 1976). On the first day of testing, the mean age of the infants was 54 hours and, on the second day, 78 hours. Eleven of the infants were breast-fed and the remainder bottle-fed.

Immediately following calibration of the apparatus, a period of 10 minutes of sucking was recorded for each infant in five successive periods, each of 2 minutes duration. Three of these periods were spent sucking for no fluid, followed by two periods of 15% sucrose-sucking. About 35 seconds intervened between periods, during which time a computer printed out the inter-response time data (IRT) for the preceding period. The nipple was not removed between periods, and the infant continued sucking under the same condition as in the preceding period. The beginning of a period, following the 35-second print-out, was initiated after the infant stopped sucking for at least 2 seconds and after the end of a burst. Following the second sucrose period, the nipple was removed. A 2-minute period of polygraph recording then ensued during a "resting" state, defined as quiescent and with regular respiration, in which the infant neither sucked nor was stimulated in any way.

The results suggest a very interesting interplay between the sucking response and heart rate. They further substantiate a process supporting our supposition that a "savoring mechanism" seems to be operative in the earliest days or even minutes of life.

The computer print-out at the end of each 2-minute period provided a frequency distribution of sucking IRTs in 100 msec bins for inter-suck intervals under 2 seconds. The mean IRT could be calculated from the print-out, using the midpoint of the bin as its numerical representation.

The sucking data from this study essentially replicated those of the previously reported study in showing that under no-fluid sucking, significantly more rest periods (defined as IRTs greater than 2 seconds) were engaged in than for 15% sucrose sucking, fewer responses per burst occurred for no-fluid sucking, and both the modal and mean IRT for no-fluid sucking were reliably shorter than for sucrose sucking. In addition, more responses per minute were emitted for sucrose than under the no-fluid condition.

A feature of the data that was rather a surprise was the seemingly paradoxical increase in heart rates during sucrose-sucking conditions where the sucking rate within bursts was slower. This effect, like all of the sucking-parameter effects, occurred on both the first and second days of the study. During basal recording, the heart-rate mean was approximately 116 beats per minute. When sucking for no fluid, the rate rose to 124, and when sucking for sucrose the rate rose further to 147. Thus, although sucking rate within burst was *reduced* when the infant sucked for sucrose, heart rate nevertheless increased reliably. Moreover, correlations from first to second day of testing indicated that heart rate is a stable individual difference variable under all three conditions but, interestingly, the correlation coefficient rose from 0.29 to 0.46 to 0.71 in going from basal to no fluid to sucrose-sucking, respectively. (An incidental suggestion from this finding is that heart rate as an individual difference variable will have greater utility when measured under a high-incentive sucking condition.)

One interpretation of the increased heart rate during the sucrose period over the water-sucking period could be that while sucking under the higher incentive condition, more sucks per minute are emitted and fewer rest periods occur even though sucking rate is slower within bursts; thus, there could be greater over-all energy expenditure during the high-incentive condition, accounting for the higher heart rates as secondary to this energizing phenomenon. Inspection of the polygraph records from the Lipsitt et al. (1976) study indicated quite clearly that the enhanced heart rate during sucrose-sucking bursts, relative to no-fluid bursts, could not be attributed to a generalized increase in heart rate over the entire period of sucrose sucking. The fact is that within a few sucks of the switch in conditions from no fluid to sucrose or from water to sucrose, the enhanced heart rate could already be seen. That is, it takes only a few seconds or a few sucks for the effect of the sweet taste on the tongue to be reflected in the higher heart rate. This observation was substantiated in a subsequent study by Crook and Lipsitt (1976) who showed that the enhanced heart-rate effect under sweet-sucking conditions can be documented even when length of the sucking burst is controlled and heart rates are considered only during actual sucking and not during inter-burst intervals. A detailed analysis in the Crook and Lipsitt study of heart rate and sucking was made possible by tape recording each interbeat interval and each intersuck interval for subsequent processing by a small computer. Because heart rate accelerates to a stable level at the start of a sucking burst, this period of acceleration was excluded from analysis. Thus, only bursts of 12 or more sucks were considered, and for any such burst the heart rate within it was taken as the mean rate between the eighth and final suck. This method of analysis concentrates upon the asymptotic heart-rate level under differential incentive conditions.

In the Crook and Lipsitt study, half of the 22 full-term newborns sucked for 9 minutes in three blocks of 3 minutes, first receiving a 0.02 ml drop of 5% sucrose for each criterion suck, then no fluid contingent upon such sucks, and finally a 0.02 ml drop of 15% sucrose for each suck. The other half received these conditions in reverse order. Regardless of the order in which the two nutrient conditions were administered, inter-suck intervals were longer under the sweeter condition, but heart rate was also higher.

In another recent study, Crook (1976) carefully documented the effects of quantity of the response-contingent fluid upon sucking rhythm and heart rate to complement the extensive data now available on sweetness. The temporal organization of neonatal nutritive sucking and heart rate were studied in two consecutive 4-minute periods to analyze the effects of two quantities of response-contingent fluid. In this study of 53 full-term infants with uncomplicated delivery (23 males and 30 females between 48 and 72 hours old), one group experienced only the larger amount (0.03 ml per suck), a second experienced the smaller (0.01 ml per suck), and two other groups experienced both in counterbalanced order. Crook found that cumulative pausing time and inter-suck intervals were both affected by the amount of fluid delivered at each response, just as with variations in sweetness. At the start of sucking bursts, heart rate accelerated to a stable level, and within-burst heart rates were higher with increased quantity of contingently delivered fluid.

Thus, sweetness and amount of fluid operate upon the baby in essentially identical ways, and it might be said that sweetness and amount of fluid are essentially collapsible incentive-motivational variables. It is tempting to infer further that the "pleasures of sensation" (Pfaffmann, 1960) control certain features of the newborn's motor behavior and autonomic nervous system processes.

HABITUATION IN THE NEWBORN

Habituation involves the gradual diminution of response, where response decrement due to sensory or motor fatigue can be ruled out, to an initially effective stimulus under conditions of repetitive stimulation. Through habituation, the infant can inform us not only that a given stimulus has been perceived, but that repetition of the stimulus is of no vital consequence, i.e., poses no threat calling for continued alerting or other defensive behavior. Moreover, response to a novel stimulus following habituation to a now-familiar stimulus yields information about the infant's discriminative capacities (Engen & Lipsitt, 1965). It has been shown that various responses, such as heart-rate acceleration and deceleration, bodily motility, sucking interruption, and respiratory disruption are subject to progressive response decrement under the habituation procedure. Frequently, several response systems may simultaneously habituate. Habituation can be demonstrated in human newborns, very likely in all sensory modalities, although there does remain trace of controversiality about it.

Recovery from habituation is demonstrable with the passage of time since last stimulation and under conditions involving the introduction of a stimulus that is discrepant from the habituating stimulus. This response to novelty, combined with the capacity of the neonate to disregard innocuous stimulation after several repetitions, clearly reveals the neonate as a competent processor of stimulation and as an organism that benefits from experience. It is likely that the relative novelty of stimuli, to which the newborn is sensitive, is pertinent to the ease with which conditioning takes place. It is therefore of considerable interest for developmental psychologists to explore the effects of different types of stimulus familiarization (habituation training) or subsequent conditioning processes. Too little of that sort of work has been done (Cantor, 1955; Cantor & Cantor, 1964, 1965).

In a series of experiments in my laboratory (Engen & Lipsitt, 1965; Engen, Lipsitt, & Kaye, 1963), we delivered olfactory stimuli to the newborn simply by placing before the infant's nostrils a Q-tip dipped in one or another odorant such as anise oil or asafetida. The newborn child does respond respiratorily and with changes in heart rate to such olfactory stimulation. Under most circumstances, the infant's response includes respiratory disruption, heart-rate acceleration, and bodily movement measured on a stabilimeter. When stimulation by these odorants is repeated, the response declines markedly in even as few as 10 trials. The newborn habituates quickly to olfactory stimuli. These infants, all within the first 4 days of life, are first habituated to a given odorant, whereupon we present an alternate odorant without violation of the temporal sequencing of the stimuli. This procedure results in dishabituation or response recovery. Thus, the newborns can tell us which odorants they are sensitive to, both by their initial reactions to stimuli and by their recovery behavior after habituation. The infants "report" to us when they can discriminate the difference between two stimuli. If habituation to anise oil occurs and we then switch to asafetida, the habituated response will recover, informing us that the discrimination has been made.

In an elaboration of this procedure, we have administered mixed odorants to the newborns. After habituation to the mixture, we administer either component separately in the same diluent. In this situation, dishabituation does occur, indicating that the baby discriminates between the component odors and the mixture of both odorants combined. This latter study suggests that we are dealing not with a peripheral phenomenon, but rather with a central nervous system function or sensory integration.

It needs to be added that there may be some odorants, particularly those that are especially critical to the infant's early interactions with the mother, that do not easily habituate. Indeed, there is the suggestion that the odor of the mother herself may continue to draw orienting response and visual gaze from the infant as early as 10 days of age (Macfarlane, 1975).

Habituation relates to memory functions that are mediated by the brain. It should be possible, therefore, to improve our armamentarium of psychometric and psychophysical procedures for identifying deficiencies of the central nervous system by incorporating measures of habituation in our test battery. Lewis (1967) has in fact shown that impaired infantile habituation is related to low Apgar scores obtained in the delivery room and that poor habituation performance is related to other indices of possible brain damage. Similarly, hydrocephalic and anencephalic infants may show no habituation at all (Brackbill, 1971; Wolff, 1969). Thus, it seems reasonable to suppose that cognitive functioning is first affected by adverse perinatal circumstances and second, that it is closely associated with the ability of the very young infant to habituate to repetitive stimulation. One of the earliest and most systematic studies of habituation processes of infants, especially with relevance to the infant born at risk, was conducted in the Soviet Union (Bronshtein, Antonova, Kamenetskaya, Luppova, & Sytova, 1960). In these studies, a habituation technique involving the sucking response was used to document that infants born under conditions of excessive cranial pressure or with the umbilical cord around the neck display deficiencies in habituation. The infants were presented with stimuli while sucking. In normal infants momentary interruptions of sucking behavior occur with the intrusion of stimuli such as sounds or lights, and with repetitive presentations of the same stimulus, a reduction of interruptions in sucking occurs. With infants born at risk, however, many more trials of the interruptive stimulus were required to habituate the sucking-suppression response. Similarly, a study of average evoked responses in Down's syndrome infants, age 8 days to 1 year, showed that relative to normal infants matched in age, no significant response decrement occurred.

Bowes, Brackbill, Conway, and Steinschneider (1970) have shown that maternal anesthesia has a definite effect upon the capacity of the infant for habituation. Infants were tested at 2 and 5 days of age. Those whose mothers received relatively high dosages of anesthesia required as many as four times the number of trials to habituate as those who received little medication. Interestingly, these differences persisted at least to 1 month of age. It is challenging for child developmentalists to explore the mechanisms whereby such early effects of perinatal conditions manifest themselves at later ages. It may be that later developmental conditions are affected indirectly rather than directly by perinatal conditions, such as amount of maternal anesthesia. A baby that is lethargic and unresponsive at birth might inhibit the "natural" responsiveness of the mother in such a way that subsequent mother–infant interactions will have been cumulatively delimited by the infant's initial under-responsiveness.

Of special interest is the fact that infants and mothers are reciprocally interactive with one another. The early habituation process, which is so natural to normal infants and which seems to be deficient in infants with birth stresses or nervous-system anomalies, can be exceedingly important in the early interactions between the infant and mother. It is through the process of mutual stimulation that familiar and novel events are experienced. Novel stimulation is typically introduced by the adult after habituation to some stimulus has occurred. In the case of infants deficient in habituation, all stimuli tend to be experienced similarly; there is no distinction between familiar and novel stimulation.

TEACHING THE LOW BIRTH-WEIGHT BABY

It is a commonplace assumption today that infants born prematurely, small for gestational age, or otherwise at risk within the first days and weeks of life can be stimulated in special ways to optimize cognitive and adaptive behavioral development (Barnard, 1976). This assumption is due in part to the considerable advances made over the past 20 years in the understanding of normal infant behavior and development (Lipsitt, 1977; Lipsitt, Mustaine, & Zeigler, 1977). It also stems from the heroic empirical efforts of a rather small number of behavioral investigators who have been fortunate to be productively associated with neonatal intensive care units. These observers called attention to the possibly injurious aspects of the nursery environment, such as the isolation of the baby from normal environmental stimulation often for weeks (Rothschild, 1967), the lack of opportunity for physical contact with a human caretaker (Klaus & Kennell, 1970), the prevailing loud and monotonous roar of the incubator (Lipsitt, 1971), and the diminished handling and other opportunities for stimulation from which learning to cope might follow (Hasselmeyer, 1969; Siqueland, 1969; Solkoff, Yaffe, Weintraub, & Blase, 1969). The best indications from this now-burgeoning literature on experiential effects in premature infants is that it is not a waste of time to arrange reciprocating interactions between small babies and their caretakers. Sensory-motor advances beyond the usual seem to be made in infants provided with extra stimulation in the high-risk nursery, and these gains are reflected in later developmental tasks and tests.

Some of the studies conducted with small babies have demonstrated that rather minimal exposure to extra stimulation during the neonatal period can have prolonged and profound effects on later behavior (e.g., Klaus & Kennell, 1976), so much that one must wonder about the mechanisms by which such large effects are mediated. There are indications in this regard that the introduction of special regimens of handling and other types of stimulation for the small baby has an immediate effect in altering the baby's behavior and may in addition change the caretaker's own behavior in relation to the child. The infant that is more alert and responsive will undoubtedly call forth more attention, caressing, and playing activities from the caretaker than the listless, lethargic, disinterested, and uninteresting baby. A model of child–caretaker interaction assuming that reciprocating relationships do occur at all developmental levels is appropriate. Such a model would predict that even a minor advance in the behavior of a young infant might evoke ever more complicated and curious behaviors in the caretaker. Thus, both immediately and perhaps a week later, the caretaker would attempt to elicit somewhat more sophisticated responses from the infant than would otherwise have been the case. One behavior recruits another, and each developmental advance in the baby provides the caretaker with the impetus to promote still further advances at later ages. It is of interest that most adults in their interactions with infants tend to operate at the frontiers of the baby's capabilities, often seeking to promote the occurrence of behaviors that are at the moment just below the threshold of the infant's capabilities. It is this natural tendency on the part of parents and other adults in the infant's environment that keeps most infants "on their toes," i.e., attuned to novel stimulation and in a state of readiness to benefit from experience. Unfortunately, it is only quite recently that these natural tendencies of adults have been capitalized upon in the newborn nursery.

Among the studies that have thus far demonstrated that some extra added attention to the stimulus needs of the newborn can have felicitous effects upon developmental outcome are those of Kennell, Klaus, and their colleagues (Kennell et al., 1974; Klaus et al., 1972). They arranged for mothers of newborns to have close physical contact with their infants for 1 hour after delivery and many times in the ensuing days of hospitalization. Control mothers were simply subjected to the usual routine of the hospital with regard to mother–infant contact: "a glance at their baby shortly after birth, a short visit 6 to 12 hours after birth for identification purposes, and then 20- to 30-minute visits for feeding every four hours during the day" (Kennell et al., 1974, p. 173). One month later observations of the mothers and their infants confirmed that those mothers who had had extra interaction during the period of hospitalization engaged in more demonstrative affection and generally showed more attention to their infants than did the control mothers. Follow-up data of a sort that has been all too rare after such manipulative studies showed that the mother–infant pairs with the neonatal head-start still interacted more when the children were 2 years of age, and the mothers tended even to speak differently to their youngsters!

Such follow-up studies as those by Klaus, Kennell, and their colleagues should help to illuminate more clearly the processes by which long-term gains of modest experiential enrichment are achieved. In all likelihood, the positive and sometimes even startling effects that have been achieved in this area will appear less like magic under closer scrutiny. As previously suggested, early stimulation of an infant may produce a more interested and inquisitive infant who then essentially calls for more stimulation as he or she matures. Solkoff et al. (1969) examined immediate and subsequent effects of handling premature infants during the earliest days of life. Both behavioral and physical measures were taken on 10 low birth-weight infants. Five of these infants were stroked in their incubators 5 minutes in every hour of the day over a period of 10 days. The five controls simply received routine nursery care. The researchers found that the handled infants became more active and alert, regained their birth weights faster, and were rated as healthier in terms of indices of growth and development than were the control babies. When the experimenters obtained information about the 10 infants at 7 to 8 months of age, the handled infants were described as more interested in stimulation than were the controls.

Another such study (Solkoff & Matuszak, 1975) involved the use of the Neonatal Behavioral Assessment Scale (Brazelton, 1973) administered to 11 premature infants (mean gestational age 31 weeks) who were still in the intensive care unit of the hospital in which they were born. Six of these infants received a short period of extra handling during each 16-hour nursing shift over a period of 10 days. The five control babies received only routine care. Both groups were administered the assessment scale on a before and after basis. Although there were no differences in the mean weight gain of the two groups, the handled infants showed positive changes (i.e., toward maturational improvement on 11 of the scale's items) whereas the control infants showed such changes on only 2 such items.

DEVELOPMENTAL JEOPARDY AND CRIB DEATH

We have seen the considerable recent successes in exploring the sensory capabilities and response repertoire of the newborn. Spurred on by these successes, developmental psychologists, psychophysiologists, and pediatricians have taken an increasing interest in using the new information about infant behavior and individual differences for the better detection of developmental deficits. A considerable literature has begun to appear on the assessment of perinatal risk and the determination of the sequelae of such risk. The issue of risk has become of more intense concern in part because of medical and technological advances that have enabled the fetologist and neonatologist to rescue for prolonged survival an infant that, only a few short years ago, would have been likely to die. The continuum of reproductive casualty (Pasamanick & Knobloch, 1961), then, still exists, but the cutoff point for survival has shifted sharply. There is great concern today that the very small, very premature babies that are now saved for survival may be in very special jeopardy for non-fatal developmental anomalies, such as learning disabilities and behavior disorders.

Psychologists are especially interested in high-risk infants whose futures may be marked for developmental jeopardy, because it is quite possible that behavioral interventions and compensations may help to avoid the hazards for which these infants seem destined.

It is my purpose here to elaborate upon a specific group of at-risk infants; those who are victims of the sudden infant death syndrome. Some infants show an apparent deficiency in their response to the threat of respiratory occlusion or the blockage of respiratory openings. I believe this problem may be related to crib death, but not directly through an inadequate unconditioned response. Instead, it may be due to a congenital aberration leading to an experiential deficiency that puts the infant in special danger with respect to the sudden infant death syndrome.

Normal newborn infants have a well-organized and readily elicited constellation of defensive responses that are made when aversive stimulation becomes intolerable or when there is even the suggestion of a threat to the blockage of the respiratory passages. This response, which has been incorporated as a test item in both the Graham (1956) and Brazelton (1973) scales, can be critical for survival. It is present on a reflexive basis in the very young infant, although indeed there are striking individual differences in the rapidity and vigor with which the response is elicited. My intention here is only to make the point that behavioral reciprocity between the infant and its environment must work in such a way that between birth and 2 months of age the infant must gain experience in retrieving its respiratory passages for breathing freely. If this is not done, at the critical age between 2 and 4 months of age, when so many basic biological reflexes begin to evolve into voluntary and operant behaviors, the infant may be in special jeopardy through not "knowing how" to adjust its posture and clear its respiratory passages for the continuation of breathing. If the response deficiency lasts a sufficiently long period of time, as in cases of repetitive apnea, especially during "rapid eye movement" (REM) sleep (Steinschneider, 1976), the baby may become anoxic and ultimately comatose before the appropriate defensive behavior is executed.

Although the contention espoused here is largely speculative, there is considerable presumptive evidence suggesting that babies at risk for crib death do have such a deficiency that, if not compensated for, could conceivably provide a pathway to the sudden infant death syndrome. The remaining remarks in this section are relevant to this notion.

The idea of behavioral reciprocity is, as stated, not limited to the communication of one psychobiological system of the infant with another of its systems. It also involves reciprocating relationships between the infant and another person in its life. The mother–infant interaction especially is a two-way affair, and this entire subject of reciprocating relationships deserves much greater attention than it has received. English pediatrician Mavis Gunther (1955, 1961) made some close observations of the fascinating ways in which the nursing mother and her infant affected each other reciprocally, immediately after birth and quite possibly with lasting effects. The nursing couple is comprised of a pair of persons that happen to be, so it seems, excellent operant conditioners of one another. Gunther has described the situation in which the nursing newborn often finds itself. When the newborn is suckling at the breast, its nostrils periodically and fortuitously become occluded. This results in an aversive reaction on the part of the infant, involving various manifestations of withdrawal from the nipple and breast. The newborn ordinarily sucks with a secure pressure seal between its lips and the nipple. Unlatching from the breast is not accomplished easily, particularly by a hungry infant. When threatened with nasal occlusion, therefore, the baby first engages in minor head movements, swaying the head from side-to-side and pulling its head backwards. Sometimes these actions succeed in freeing the nasal passages for breathing. If these maneuvers do not succeed, however, the normal infant executes a more vigorous pattern of behavior, such as arm waving and pushing against the mother's breast, this being often accompanied by facial vasodilation. Ultimately, if none of these maneuvers succeeds in wrestling the infant free of the offending object, crying occurs. Under such circumstances, the baby is reinforced for retreating from the breast rather than remaining at it. Gunther described some instances in which the infant was observed to show reluctance when put to the breast after such an apparently aversive experience. Although Gunther does not phrase the sequence of activities as such, the stimulating event, the resulting reaction, and the subsequent aversion to the feeding situation may be easily conceptualized as one of the operant learning.

Aversive behavior occurs in human infants under conditions in which biological threat exists. In its milder forms, such behavior is manifested in the autonomic and withdrawal responses to intense stimulation, such as bright lights, noxious tactile stimuli, unpleasant odorants and tastes, trigeminal stimulants, and loud noises. The amount of active response to such stimulation is directly proportional to stimulus intensity, with very intense stimulation culminating in crying.

Angry behavior may be defined in terms of the presence and vigor of autonomic and withdrawal response to noxious stimulation. Aggressive behavior, in contrast, may be taken to refer to responses of the baby, in the presence of anger, that have the function of thwarting perpetuation of the instigating noxious stimulation. In ordinary feeding circumstances, such defensive behavior can be fortuitously directed against the mother. Stimulation that supports or threatens respiratory occlusion tends to elicit a response pattern consisting of five components, which may be viewed as a fixed action pattern beginning with mild responsivity and proceeding toward extreme arousal if the stimulus condition is not removed. The five steps involved, as noted earlier, are (a) side-to-side head waving; (b) head withdrawal, with backward jerks and grimacing; (c) facial vasodilation; (d) arm jabbing; and (e) crying. The continuum of response is here defined as angry behavior, which can be seen to abate when the threatening or noxious stimulation is reduced.

Such behavior often occurs in the natural course of infant feeding. When anger in the newborn results from respiratory occlusion, the action pattern has the effect of freeing the respiratory passages by displacing the offending object or by impelling the mother to adjust her feeding position. The freeing from occlusion constitutes a reinforcement condition that can increase the probability of its occurrence under this and similar future conditions. The anger response may occur subsequently with a shorter latency, or even anticipatorily to less intense but similar stimulating conditions. Still later in ontogeny, it may occur without direct (exteroceptive) instigation at all. Moreover, such "aggressive" behavior may be mediated by anger generated from circumstances entirely different from those in which the behavior has been first learned. The learning mechanisms involved in the acquisition of aggressive behavior are those presumed to be implicated in other forms of instrumental learning. Initially, a congenital response pattern (anger) is elicited by experiential circumstances conducive to its expression. Components of that action pattern are selectively reinforced, following which these behaviors (now called aggressive) are learned and perpetuated through periodic practice, with reinforcement renewed on subsequent occasions.

The foregoing comments are, as must be appreciated, entirely speculative and theoretical, except for their evidential basis in the observations of Gunther and others who have documented the infantile response to brief respiratory occlusion in the natural feeding situation. The thesis relating this type of behavior to the possible development of aggression is presented as a heuristic model of reciprocating relationships between mother and infant as well as for the "content," the verification of which is largely wanting. The following elaborations are presented in the same spirit.

From the earliest moments after birth, newborns engage in systematic, replicable, congenital patterns of behavior, which enter immediately into a reciprocating relationship with the environment. The moment a baby is born, stimuli impinge on its receptors, producing changes in the infant's behavior that in turn alter the effective stimulation from the environment. Experience has an immediate effect on the baby, and the baby immediately alters the world in which it lives.

Part of the newborn's behavioral repertoire is an important tendency to divert threats to its biological safety. Numerous aversive responses can be observed to noxious stimulation. A sudden increase in illumination occurring in the vicinity of the infant's open eyes, for example, causes the lids to close. If the skin surface is touched with great pressure or is pricked by a pointed object, the infant withdraws the offended part of its anatomy from the stimulus. If a noxious trigeminal stimulant is presented, the baby turns its head from the locus of the stimulation and shows by facial expression and vocalization that the experience is disturbing. On stimulation with bitter quinine, withdrawal of the tongue occurs. Each of the sensory modalities of the newborn can be excessively stimulated to produce its own aversive style of response, always culminating in crying when lesser manifestations of aversion fail to enable escape.

The absence of or deficiency in the respiratory occlusion response may be related to the occurrence of the still unexplained "crib death" that takes the lives of a large number of infants at around 2 and 3 months of age. Many infants who succumb to crib death are known to have had a mild cold, usually described as "sniffles," for a day or several days prior to their death. Still others have been diagnosed on autopsy as having pneumonitis, presumably not so serious as to cause death. It is an empirical problem for developmental psychologists and psychobiologists to determine whether respiratory occlusion, and the failure to make appropriate adjustive responses to such occlusion, are pertinent factors in such deaths. Throat-clearing responses in the older child and adult are so prevalent and facile that, as with so many mature and fairly universal behaviors, we do not concern ourselves much with their ontogeny. It is possible, however, that just as learning (and failure to learn) are important antecedents of lifesaving responses (and their absence) in other spheres of human activity, so also is the learning of maneuvers to prevent respiratory occlusion necessary for the survival of the infant.

It is not inconceivable that a modicum of early practice is required for the infant to achieve a suitable level of "respiratory retrieval" when faced with the threat of occlusion. The infants who achieve the required minimum of practice are perhaps those whose experience at retrieval has been most frequent and most vigorous. These would be the infants who at birth and shortly thereafter have vigorous responses to the threat of a respiratory occluding stimulus; i.e., most practice in this situation is probably self-administered, as the baby lies in the crib, especially in the prone position, and moves around among blankets, hands, and other objects that are so readily brought to the mouth by the infant's own arms. In this connection, one wonders whether the lethargy of response displayed by the "failure-to-thrive infant" may not have had its earliest representation in a deficiency of this and similar neonatal response patterns or in the failure of opportunity to practice early congenital patterns of behavior.

SUMMARY

I have presented the thesis that newborn children may be considered to be informants about their own developmental condition. As when capitalizing upon information theoretically available from any informant, it is important to formulate the important questions and to pose them in such a way as to facilitate a response. Newborn infants can report upon their own condition by being asked to respond to environmental challenges. We can find out in this way that the neonate can see, hear, taste, smell, and feel. By presenting a challenge, we can also find out whether the child is capable of responding defensively.

The introduction of a taste on the tongue reveals much about the ability of the infant to suck, swallow, and discriminate one taste from another. Monitoring heart rate may even reveal whether the infant enjoys an experience. Thus, the study of diverse psychological processes of infants, including habituation, conditioning, discrimination, and all types of sensory and motor functions, can help to identify babies whose early behavior and development may have been compromised by perinatal hazards. It is important to study offspring resulting from adverse conditions of pregnancy in order to better understand the causes of fetal and neonatal aberrations. It is perhaps of even greater urgency that we understand better the psychobiological nature and significance of infancy in order to identify as early as possible those deficiencies that can best be compensated for at earlier ages. Our strongest ally in this endeavor is the infant, who should be observed closely and asked smart questions.

ACKNOWLEDGMENTS

Much of the research reported here was supported by the W. T. Grant Foundation. The author is indebted to Bernice Reilly, for her inestimable help in the design and execution of our neonatal studies over a 10-year period, and to Patricia Daniel and Helen Haeseler for helpful readings of an earlier draft of this manuscript.

REFERENCES

Barnard, K. E. Nursing: High risk infants. In T. D. Tjossem (Ed.), *Intervention strategies for high risk infants and young children.* Baltimore: University Park Press, 1976.

Bowes, W. A., Brackbill, Y., Conway, E., & Steinschneider, A. Obstetrical medication and infant outcome: A review of the literature. *Monographs of the Society for Research in Child Development*, 1970, *35*, 3–25.

Brackbill, Y. The role of the cortex in orienting: Orienting reflex in an anencephalic human infant. *Developmental Psychology*, 1971, *5*, 195–201.

Brazelton, T. B. *Neonatal Behavioral Assessment Scale.* Philadelphia: William Heinemann Medical Books, 1973.

Bronshtein, A. T., Antonova, T. G., Kamenetskaya, N. H., Luppova, V. A., & Sytova, V. A. On the development of functions of analyzers in infants and some animals at the early stage of ontogenesis. In *Problems of evolution of physiological functions.* USSR: Academy of Science (U.S. Department of Health, Education, and Welfare, Translation Service), 1960.

Cantor, G. N. Effects of three types of pretraining on discrimination learning in preschool children. *Journal of Experimental Psychology*, 1955, *49*, 339–342.

Cantor, G. N., & Cantor, J. H. Effects of conditioned-stimulus familiarization on instrumental learning in children. *Journal of Experimental Child Psychology*, 1964, *1*, 71–78.

Cantor, G. N., & Cantor, J. H. Discriminative reaction time performance in preschool children as related to stimulus familiarization. *Journal of Experimental Child Psychology,* 1965, *2,* 1–9.

Crook, C. K. Neonatal sucking: Effects of quantity of the response-contingent fluid upon sucking rhythm and heart rate. *Journal of Experimental Child Psychology,* 1976, *21,* 539–548.

Crook, C. K., & Lipsitt, L. P. Neonatal nutritive sucking: Effects of taste stimulation upon sucking rhythm and heart rate. *Child Development,* 1976, *47,* 518–522.

Drillien, C. M. *The growth and development of the prematurely born infant.* Baltimore: Williams & Wilkins, 1964.

Engen, T., & Lipsitt, L. P. Decrement and recovery of responses to olfactory stimuli in the human neonate. *Journal of Comparative and Physiological Psychology,* 1965, *59,* 312–316.

Engen, T., Lipsitt, L. P., & Kaye, H. Olfactory responses and adaptation in the human neonate. *Journal of Comparative and Physiological Psychology,* 1963, *56,* 73–77.

Gluck, L. Perinatology: State of the art. *Contemporary Obstetrics and Gynecology,* 1974, *3,* 125–159.

Graham, F. K. Behavioral differences between normal and traumatized newborns. I. The test procedures. *Psychological Monographs,* 1956, *70,* (20, Whole No. 427).

Gunther, M. Instinct and the nursing couple. *Lancet,* 1955, *1,* 575.

Gunther, M. Infant behavior at the breast. In B. Foss (Ed.), *Determinants of infant behavior.* London: Methuen & Co., 1961.

Hasselmeyer, E. G. *Behavior patterns of the premature infant* (PHS Doc. No. 840). Washington, D.C.: U.S. Department of Health, Education, and Welfare, Public Health Service, Division of Nursing, 1969.

Kennell, J. H., Jerauld, R., Wolfe, H., Chesler, D., Kreger, N. C., McAlpine, W., Steffa, M., & Klaus, M. H. Maternal behavior one year after early and extended postpartum contact. *Developmental Medicine and Child Neurology,* 1974, *16,* 172–179.

Klaus, M. H., Jerauld, R., Kreger, N. C., McAlpine, W., Steffa, M., & Kennell, J. H. Maternal attachment: Importance of the first post-partum days. *New England Journal of Medicine,* 1972, *286,* 460–463.

Klaus, M. H. & Kennell, J. H. Mothers separated from their newborn infants. *Pediatric Clinics of North America,* 1970, *17,* 1015–1037.

Klaus, M. H., & Kennell, J. H. *Maternal–infant bonding.* St. Louis: C. V. Mosby, 1976.

Kobre, K. R., & Lipsitt, L. P. A negative contrast effect in newborns. *Journal of Experimental Child Psychology,* 1972, *14,* 81–91.

Lewis, M. The meaning of a response, or why researchers in infant behavior should be oriental metaphysicians. *Merrill-Palmer Quarterly,* 1967, *13,* 7–18.

Lipsitt, L. P. Learning ability and its enhancement. In J. H. Menkes & R. J. Schain (Eds.), *Learning disorders in children. Report of the Sixty-First Ross Conference on Pediatric Research.* Columbus, Ohio: Ross Laboratories, 1971.

Lipsitt, L. P. The study of sensory and learning processes of the newborn. In J. Volpe (Ed.), *Clinics in perinatology* (Vol. 4, No. 1) Philadelphia: W. B. Saunders, 1977.

Lipsitt, L. P., Mustaine, M. G., & Zeigler, B. Effects of experience on the behavior of the newborn. *Neuropadiatrie*, 1977, *8*, 107–133.

Lipsitt, L. P., Reilly, B. M., Butcher, M. J., & Greenwood, M. M. The stability and interrelationships of newborn sucking and heart rate. *Developmental Psychobiology*, 1976, *9*, 305–310.

Macfarlane, A. Olfaction in the development of social preference in the human neonate. *Parent–infant interaction*. London: CIBA Foundation Symposium 33, 1975.

Pasamanick, B., & Knobloch, H. Epidemiological studies on the complications of pregnancy and the birth process. In G. Caplan (Ed.), *Prevention of mental disorder in children*. New York: Basic Books, 1961.

Pfaffmann, C. The pleasures of sensation. *Psychological Review*, 1960, *67*, 253–268.

Rothschild, B. F. Incubator isolation as a possible contributing factor to the high incidence of emotional disturbance among prematurely born persons. *Journal of Genetic Psychology*, 1967, *110*, 287–304.

Sameroff, A. J., & Chandler, M. J. Reproductive risk and the continuum of caretaking casualty. In F. D. Horowitz (Ed.), *Review of child development research*. Chicago: The University of Chicago Press, 1975.

Siqueland, E. R. *The development of instrumental exploratory behavior during the first year of human life*. Paper presented at the meeting of the Society for Research in Child Development, Santa Monica, California, 1969.

Solkoff, N., & Matuszak, D. Tactile stimulation and behavioral development among low-birthweight infants. *Child Psychiatry and Human Development*, 1975, *6*, 33–37.

Solkoff, N., Yaffe, S., Weintraub, D., & Blase, B. Effects of handling on the subsequent developments of premature infants. *Developmental Psychology*, 1969, *1*, 765–768.

Steinschneider, A. *Implications of the sudden infant death syndrome for the study of sleep in infancy*. Paper presented at a symposium on crib death at the meeting of the American Psychological Association, Washington, D.C. 1976.

Wolff, P. H. What we must and must not teach our young children from what we know about early cognitive development. In *Planning for better learning*. Philadelphia: William Heinemann Medical Books. 1969.

2

Memory for Hidden Objects in Early Infancy: Behavior, Theory, and Neural Network Simulation

Yuko Munakata
Jennifer Merva Stedron
University of Denver

Why study infants' memory for hidden objects? As an undergraduate student in an introductory psychology course, the first author remembers wondering why anyone would. After all, infants seemed to do pretty much what you would expect them to do in this domain: They succeeded at some simple memory tasks relatively early in life, and got better at more and more complex tasks as they got older. It seemed pretty intuitive and not particularly engaging. Of course, this perspective overlooked the ingenuity of the experimental methods that allowed researchers to determine anything at all about the nature of infants' memory for hidden objects, as well as many of the subtleties of infant behavior in these tasks. I can now better appreciate (after taking a few twists and turns and eventually coming to research infants' memory for hidden objects myself) that this perspective also missed two fundamental contributions of research in this domain: advances in thinking about exactly what it means to remember something, and how success in some memory tasks, together with failure in other tasks, can provide a window onto the nature of our memory systems. These contributions are the focus of this chapter.

We first describe some key behavioral findings on memory for hidden objects in the first year of life. We then discuss how these findings have helped to advance theorizing about memory development and about the implications of success in one task versus another. We cover a range of theoretical approaches to memory development and a number of interpretations of infants' behavior with hidden objects. We explore two approaches in depth, employing a paradigm that we believe has the potential to clearly delineate and test hypotheses regarding fundamental issues in memory development: neural network (aka connectionist or parallel distributed processing) models. As we show, these models allow for the instantiation and testing of specific ideas on what it means to remember something, and they lead to novel empirical predictions. We close with a discussion of future directions for work within the modeling paradigm, and the broader implications of empirical and modeling work in the exploration of memory development.

BEHAVIOR

One of the hallmarks of infants' memory for hidden objects is that it depends heavily on how the infants are tested—infants can appear wildly precocious in the first few months of life in violation-of-expectation paradigms, but seem to possess an "out of sight, out of mind" mentality for several months longer when tested in searching for hidden objects. It might seem uninteresting that infants appear simply to get better at harder tasks as they get older in this way. In fact, such seemingly intuitive task-dependent progressions raise fundamental questions about cognitive development, which we return to after reviewing some of the behavioral data. For example, what do task-dependent behaviors reveal about the structure of the mind? What does it really mean to remember something? Are different types of memory required by different tasks? What are the implications of infants' task-dependent progression with hidden objects for the origins of our knowledge about the permanence of objects?

Piagetian Tasks

When Piaget (1954) measured the extent to which infants possess a concept of object permanence, he observed several limitations in their memory for hidden objects. For example, infants fail to retrieve completely hidden objects until around 8 months. Prior to this age, in simple search tasks in which a toy is hidden in one location, infants appear to have an "out of sight, out of mind" mentality; they will often look away as soon as a toy is completely hidden. Even when infants begin to retrieve hidden objects, they still show apparent limitations in their memory for hidden objects in the A-not-B task. When an object is hidden in one location (A), infants can retrieve it. However, when the object is then hidden in a new location (B), infants perseverate in reaching to the original A location (committing the A-not-B error).

Looking Measures

In contrast, more recent studies demonstrated a greater sensitivity to hidden objects in much younger infants. Violation-of-expectation studies yielded some of the earliest signs of infants' memory for hidden objects. Such studies build on the assumption that infants look longer at events that they find novel or unnatural (Fantz, 1964; Spelke, 1985). When the novelty or unnaturalness of such events arises based on the presence of objects that have been occluded, infants' longer looking times to these events are taken as an indication of their memory for the hidden objects.

For example, in a series of studies (Baillargeon, 1987a, 1987b, 1991; Baillargeon, Spelke, & Wasserman, 1985), infants viewed a drawbridge-like stimulus rotating back and forth. Infants were presented with this event until they habituated to it, that is, until their looking times to the display declined, indicating that they had become familiar with the drawbridge motion and were no longer particularly interested in it. Then, a block was placed in the path of the drawbridge. In the "possible" event, the drawbridge rotated back to the point where it would touch the block and then rotated back to its starting point. In the "impossible" or novel/unnatural event, the drawbridge appeared to rotate through the space occupied by the block before rotating back to its starting point. In both conditions, the drawbridge occluded the block as it rotated toward it. Infants as young as 3.5 months looked longer at the impossible event, indicating some apparent memory for the occluded block's continued existence. A number of labs have similarly employed the violation-of-expectation paradigm to demonstrate an apparent memory for hidden objects in infants in their first few months of life (Baillargeon, 1993; Spelke, Breinlinger, Macomber, & Jacobson, 1992; Wynn, 1992).

Infants have also demonstrated greater memory for hidden objects in violation-of-expectation and gaze variants of the A-not-B task (Ahmed & Ruffman, 1998; Hofstadter & Reznick, 1996; Lecuyer, Abgueguen, & Lemarie, 1992; Matthews, 1992). In the violation-of-expectation studies (Ahmed & Ruffman, 1998), 8- to 12-month-old infants watched an experimenter hide an object at A, and after a delay the experimenter revealed the object at A or allowed infants to retrieve the object from A. The object was then hidden at B and, after a delay, was revealed at B (the possible event) or A (the impossible event). Infants looked longer at the impossible event, following delays at which they nonetheless searched perseveratively at A in the standard search version of the A-not-B task. The gaze variants of the A-not-B task built on Diamond's (1985) observation that infants occasionally reach to the wrong location while looking at the correct location, and often reach to the wrong location without looking in it and then immediately reach to the correct location. Hofstadter and Reznick (1996) confirmed that when infants' gazing and reaching behaviors differ in the A-not-B task, the gazing response is more accurate. Also, infants make fewer errors in gaze variants of the A-not-B task in which they observe hidings at A and B without ever reaching (Hofstadter & Reznick, 1996; Lecuyer et al., 1992; Matthews, 1992). Thus, what infants appear to remember about hidden objects can depend critically on the response tested, whether reaching, looking time, or direction of gaze.

Additional Task Differences and Similarities

Moreover, such task-dependent demonstrations of memory for hidden objects are observed even when testing modalities are equated across tasks. For example, infants appear to reach for objects hidden by room darkening (Clifton, Muir, Ashmead, & Clarkson, 1993; Clifton, Rochat, Litovsky, & Perris, 1991; Hood & Willatts, 1986) more than a month before they will reach for objects occluded by visible covers in the light. In both cases the response measure is reaching, but the two tasks yield different results. Such findings indicate that task-dependent behaviors with hidden objects cannot be due simply to differences in testing modalities. Instead, other factors must play a role, as discussed in the next section.

In contrast, some tasks yield similar results even when response measures are not equated. For example, infants appear to perseverate in some violation-of-expectation studies much as they do in the standard manual A-not-B task. If presented repeatedly with an event such as a ball falling into a container, infants appear to perseverate by expecting balls to fall into containers even when the balls are too large to fit into the containers (Baillargeon & Aguiar, 1998).

THEORY

What then, can we conclude about infants' memory for hidden objects? What do their task-dependent behaviors reveal about the structure of the developing mind? What do infants really remember, and what does it really mean to remember something? Answers to these kinds of questions depend critically on how one interprets infants' task-dependent behavior because different tasks paint such strikingly different pictures of infants' memory. Theorists have approached this issue in various ways, arguing for one or more of the following:

1. Apparent limitations in infant memory are artifacts of invalid assessment methods.

2. Apparent precocities in infant memory are artifacts of invalid assessment methods.
3. Task-dependent behaviors arise due to separate memory pathways.
4. Task-dependent behaviors arise due to distinct types of memory.
5. Task-dependent behaviors arise due to gradedness of memory.

The first two approaches treat certain methods as more valid than others; infants show task-dependent behaviors because only certain methods provide a valid assessment of what infants remember. The other three approaches treat different methods as equally valid; infants show task-dependent behaviors due to the nature of the memories underlying performance across the different testing methods. We consider each of these approaches in turn, and then explore graded and distinct types of memory in more detail through neural network simulations.

Apparent Limitations in Infant Memory Are Artifacts of Invalid Assessment Methods

This argument takes two distinct forms. The first makes a competence–performance distinction, claiming that infants have object permanence competence (i.e., they remember that hidden objects continue to exist) but fail search tasks due to performance deficits. The second form of the argument is that hidden toys are actually irrelevant to certain tasks demonstrating limitations, indicating that such tasks do not measure memory for hidden objects. We critically evaluate these two forms of the argument and conclude that they cannot fully explain infants' limitations away, such that these limitations remain as important constraints on theorizing about infants' memory for hidden objects.

Competence–Performance. Several researchers have discounted simple search tasks as measures of infant memory for hidden objects by arguing that infants fail such tasks due to deficits in performance factors such as means–ends analysis and problem-solving abilities (Baillargeon, Graber, DeVos, & Black, 1990; Diamond, 1991; Willatts, 1990). For example, infants may fail to retrieve hidden objects because they cannot act on one object (e.g., a cloth cover) as a means to retrieving another (e.g., a toy; Diamond, 1991). Similarly, researchers have argued on the basis of violation-of-expectation and gaze variants of the A-not-B task that infants know about hidden objects, but search perseveratively due to deficits in performance factors such as inhibition (Ahmed & Ruffman, 1998; Diamond, 1985; Hofstadter & Reznick, 1996) and problem-solving abilities (Baillargeon, DeVos, & Graber, 1989; Baillargeon & Graber, 1988). According to the inhibition account, infants make the A-not-B error because they cannot inhibit a conditioned reaching response to A.[1] According to the problem-solving account, A-not-B errors may be understood in terms of a distinction between reactive problem solving (responding immediately and without conscious reasoning) and planful problem solving (based on active reasoning or computation); younger infants tend to be more reactive, which leads them to "run off" previous solutions and respond perseveratively. According to each of these accounts, infants' failures in search tasks result from factors unrelated to their memory for hidden objects, so search tasks provide invalid assessments of infant memory for hidden objects.

Some findings appear to be consistent with these accounts, suggesting a role for performance factors in infants' increasing abilities to demonstrate memory for hidden objects; however, there are some contrary findings that indicate that such performance factors alone cannot fully explain infants' behaviors with hidden objects. For example, Diamond's (1985) inhibition theory of the A-not-B error seems to be supported by the finding that infants occasionally search at A even when the object is visible at B (Bremner & Knowles, 1984; Butterworth, 1977; Harris, 1974). However, Sophian and Yengo (1985) showed that such errors reflected random incorrect responses rather than true A-not-B errors: In an experiment including a third, control location, infants were as likely to err when the toy was visible at B by searching at the control location and at the A location. Other findings further challenge the inhibition and problem-solving accounts. For example, if infants make A-not-B errors because they are conditioned or reactive, they should not perseverate as they do in A-not-B task variants in which they merely observe hidings at A without establishing reaching to A as a solution (Butterworth, 1974; Diamond, 1983; Evans, 1973). If infants make A-not-B errors because they are reactive, allowing more time before they are permitted to search should make them less reactive and so less likely to perseverate, but longer delays between hiding and search instead lead to more perseverative errors (Diamond, 1985; Wellman, Cross, & Bartsch, 1986).

Similarly, means–ends and problem-solving accounts of infants' failures in simple search tasks at first appear consistent with some existing data. For example, such accounts seem consistent with the finding that infants begin searching for hidden objects around the same age that they demonstrate other means–ends behaviors, such as pulling a cloth to retrieve a distant toy on the cloth (Piaget, 1954; Willatts, 1990). In addition, such accounts seem consistent with the finding that infants reach for

---

[1]Although Diamond's (1991) account also stressed the importance of memory demands in the standard A-not-B task, it focused on inhibition to explain the discrepancies between infants' gazing and reaching.

objects in the dark at least a month before reaching for objects occluded in the light (Clifton et al., 1991; Hood & Willatts, 1986). Infants can reach for objects directly in the dark, so means–ends and problem-solving abilities are presumed to be less taxed. However, a number of studies indicate that means–ends/problem-solving deficits alone cannot fully explain infants' failures to search for hidden objects.

In one set of studies (Munakata, McClelland, Johnson, & Siegler, 1997), 7-month-old infants were trained on the abilities required for retrieving toys. The infants were then tested on the retrieval of visible and occluded toys, in tasks in which the means–ends/problem-solving demands were equated. If infants were simply missing the relevant retrieval abilities, then they should have performed similarly in the visible and occluded conditions. Across three studies, infants consistently performed better under visible conditions, indicating that their difficulties with occluded objects could not be attributed simply to means–ends or problem-solving deficits.

In the first experiment, infants were trained to pull a towel to retrieve a distant toy. Infants were then tested on trials with an opaque or transparent screen moved in front of the toy. Trials without toys were also included, and the difference between toy and no-toy trials in number of retrieval responses was used as a measure of toy-guided retrieval. The means–ends abilities required for toy-guided retrieval in the transparent and opaque conditions were identical, yet toy-guided retrieval was more frequent in the transparent condition (Fig. 2.1, left panel).

Subsequent experiments with different means–ends behaviors yielded similar results. Infants were trained to push a button either to cause a distant shelf to drop (Experiment 3) or to retrieve a toy (Experiment 2); pushing the button caused the shelf supporting the toy to drop, so that the toy slid down a ramp to within reach. At test, infants again completed more toy-guided retrievals in the transparent condition (Fig. 2.1, middle and right panels). This series of studies demonstrates that infants fail to carry out the same behaviors required to retrieve occluded toys that they employ in the retrieval of visible toys; thus, infants' difficulties with occluded objects cannot be attributed solely to means–ends or problem-solving deficits.

In another set of studies (Munakata, Spelke, Jonsson, von Hofsten, & O'Reilly, in preparation), 6-month-old infants were presented with visible toys moving within their reach. The infants were then tested with moving toys that were briefly hidden by one of three things: an obliquely placed occluder that did not block manual access to the toys, a blacking out of the lights during the same period that the occluder would have blocked sight of the toy, or a combination of the occluder and the blackout. If infants fail to retrieve occluded objects due to means–ends or problem-solving deficits alone, they should have showed improved performance in all

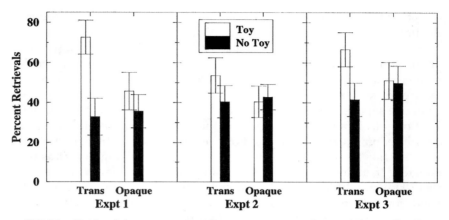

FIG. 2.1.   Retrievals by screen type and toy presence across three training studies. In each study, 7-month-old infants completed more toy-guided retrievals (Toy–No Toy) in the Transparent Condition than in the Opaque Condition, indicating that their retrieval failures with hidden objects could not be attributed solely to means–ends or problem-solving deficits (adapted from Munakata et al., 1997).

three of these occlusion conditions in which they could reach for the objects directly, and they should have performed similarly across the three conditions with equated retrieval demands. Instead, our preliminary work indicates that infants performed poorly in the visible occluder condition, and better in the blackout and occluder+blackout conditions. The poor performance in the visible occluder condition, despite direct access to the toy, is consistent with other findings in this moving-object paradigm (von Hofsten, Spelke, Feng, & Vishton, 1994). Together with infants' better performance in the blackout and occluder+blackout conditions, despite similar direct access to the toys, these results argue against means–ends/problem-solving deficit accounts of infants' failures to search for hidden objects.

Infants also fail to reach for occluded objects in other conditions when they could reach for the objects directly (Shinskey, 1999). For example, 6-month-old infants failed to reach directly for objects submerged in and occluded by milk, despite succeeding in reaching directly for visible objects submerged in water, and appearing equally comfortable reaching into water and milk. Similarly, 6-month-old infants failed to reach directly through a slit in an opaque curtain to retrieve a toy hidden by the curtain, despite succeeding in reaching directly through a slit in a transparent curtain to retrieve a visible toy. Infants' failures to retrieve the occluded objects thus appeared to reflect memory deficits rather than means–ends or problem-solving deficits.

Taken together, these experiments demonstrate the insufficiency of means–ends and problem-solving accounts to fully explain infants' failures to search for hidden objects. Thus, one cannot discount search tasks as invalid methods of assessing infant memory by arguing that infants fail them due to deficits in performance factors; infants demonstrate proficiency with such factors when objects are not hidden by visible occluders, so their difficulties with occluded objects cannot be attributed solely to such performance factors.

Irrelevance of Hidden Toys. Other researchers have discounted search tasks by arguing that infants behave similarly regardless of whether an object is hidden, indicating that the tasks do not measure memory for hidden objects. For example, 8- and 10-month-old infants make the A-not-B error without hidden toys, when simply reaching to visible covers over empty containers (Smith, Thelen, Titzer, & McLin, 1999). In these studies, an experimenter directed infants' attention to one of two identical covers over empty containers and allowed infants to reach following a short delay. Nothing was ever placed inside the containers, and nothing was ever hidden. On A trials, infants tended to reach to the cover to which the experimenter had directed their attention. On B trials, in which the experimenter directed attention to the other cover, infants tended to perseverate in reaching to A. That is, infants made the A-not-B error with completely visible objects. On the basis of these studies, Smith et al. (1999) argued that the A-not-B paradigm may be understood in terms of infants' motor histories rather than their memory for hidden objects.

However, Smith et al.'s (1999) studies demonstrated only that repeated exposure to a stimulus—hidden toy under cover or cover alone—at A led to perseveration when the same stimulus was presented at B; infants may have nonetheless remembered covers with and without toys underneath in different ways. This possibility was confirmed in two experiments (Munakata, 1997). In the first, the experimenter presented A trials as in Smith et al. (1999), with only a visible cover at A. On B trials, the experimenter presented at B either a visible cover (cover condition) or a toy that was then hidden under the cover (toy condition). Infants reached perseveratively to A in the cover condition (replicating Smith et al., 1999), but not in the toy condition, indicating that infants can distinguish covers with and without toys underneath on B trials (left side of Fig. 2.2). The second study was identical except that on all A trials the experimenter presented a toy and then hid it under the A cover. Infants made similar A-not-B errors on B trials in the cover and toy conditions (right side of Fig. 2.2). The difference in B-trial performance between the two experiments indicated that infants distinguished covers with and without toys underneath on A trials, although their motor histories were the same in the two cases.

Thus, although Smith et al. (1999) showed that infants perseverate with and without hidden toys, these studies demonstrate that infants nonethe-

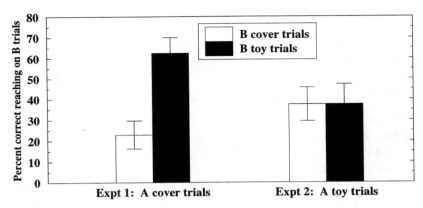

FIG. 2.2.   Correct reaching on B trials across two A-not-B studies. Ten-month-old in-fants distinguished B cover and B toy trials after A cover trials, indicating that infants can distinguish covers with and without toys underneath on B trials (Experiment 1). Ten-month-old infants did not distinguish B cover and B toy trials after A toy trials (Experiment 2). The difference in B-trial performance between the two experiments in-dicated that infants distinguished covers with and without toys underneath on A tri-als, although their motor histories were the same in the two cases (adapted from Mu-nakata, 1997).

less remember hidden toys differently from visible covers alone, on both A and B trials. Thus, one cannot discount the A-not-B task as an invalid method for assessing infant memory for hidden objects by arguing that hidden objects are irrelevant to infants' perseveration.

Evaluation of Discounting Infants' Limitations.   In summary, we have considered two forms of the argument against methods demonstrating infants' limitations. Neither can fully explain infants' limitations away sim-ply as performance deficits or as toy-irrelevant, so these limitations remain as important constraints on theorizing about infants' memory for hidden objects.

Apparent Precocities in Infant Memory Are Artifacts of Invalid Assessment Methods

Instead of discounting infants' limitations in search tasks, other researchers discounted infants' apparent successes in violation-of-expectation studies. According to this approach, infants demonstrate an apparent memory for hidden objects in violation-of-expectation studies without actually repre-senting the continued existence of the hidden objects (Bogartz, Shinskey,

& Schilling, 2000; Thelen & Smith, 1994). That is, infants look longer at impossible events with occluded objects than at possible events due to the operation of fairly basic perceptual processes, without actually continuing to remember the objects after occlusion.

Dynamic Systems. For example, dynamic systems theorists have reinterpreted infant behavior in violation-of-expectation studies in terms of "attractors" created in the infant by habituation events (Thelen & Smith, 1994). Test events that are similar enough to the habituation events will be pulled into these attractors, shaping expectations about what will happen next. Infants' looking times might be driven by these attractor dynamics, rather than by their memories for hidden objects. In this way, dynamic systems theorists have reinterpreted Baillargeon's (1986) study in which infants were habituated to a cart rolling along a track; at test, a block was placed on the track (impossible event) or behind it (possible event), an occluder was lowered in front of the block, and then the cart rolled along the track, passed behind the occluder, and reemerged on the other side of the occluder. Infants looked longer at the impossible event, which was taken as evidence that they remembered the occluded block and realized that the cart should not pass through it. In contrast, according to the dynamic systems reinterpretation (Thelen & Smith, 1994), the repeated presentation of the rolling cart created an attractor that led infants to expect events to end soon after they saw something on the track near its end. In the impossible event, the block was placed in this location, leading infants to expect the event to end shortly thereafter. The event instead continued for some time, violating infants' expectations, leading to longer looking. In the possible event, the block was placed behind the track, an occurrence that was not similar enough to the habituation event to be pulled into its attractor. Infants thus did not form strong expectations, and so did not perceive a violation-of-expectation such as that in the impossible event. In this way, dynamic systems accounts may explain infants' behavior in violation-of-expectation studies without positing memory for hidden objects.

However, many steps remain for a thorough evaluation of such dynamic systems reinterpretations. For example, the dynamic systems account of Baillargeon's (1986) rolling-cart study relies on the fact that the possible and impossible events differed at the start, leading one event to be pulled into the habituating attractor whereas the other was not. In other violation-of-expectation studies, however, the possible and impossible events begin in exactly the same way (e.g., with the placement of a block in the path of a drawbridge). It is not clear how naturally the dynamic systems framework could account for such cases, or how carefully crafted each explanation would need to be to explain each finding. The possibility remains that such dynamic systems reinterpretations, when applied to the broad range of findings using the violation-of-expectation paradigm, will seem more ad hoc than explanations that posit memory for hidden objects. A related challenge is that the imprecision of dynamic systems constructs may make it inherently difficult for the framework to yield specific, testable predictions (Aslin, 1993).

Novelty/Familiarity Preferences.   Other researchers posited that infants' looking times in violation-of-expectation studies are determined by the novelty of presented events, together with infants' preferences for novelty versus familiarity (Bogartz et al., 1999). According to this account, infants in Baillargeon and colleagues' (Baillargeon, 1987a, 1991; Baillargeon, Spelke, & Wasserman, 1985) drawbridge studies may have looked longer at the full rotation of the drawbridge in the impossible event not because it was impossible, but because it was more familiar (to the habituated motion), and infants preferred this familiarity to the relatively unfamiliar partial rotation of the possible event. Familiarity and possibility were thus confounded, and so existing data cannot tease apart this alternative familiarity account from the more standard possibility account. According to this argument, the violation-of-expectation paradigm may in theory serve as a tool to test infants' memory for hidden objects, but in practice familiarity and possibility have typically been confounded, making it unclear whether infants' looking times were based on memory for hidden objects. Proponents of the familiarity account argue that proper deconfounding may be achieved using an "event set × event set" design, in which all events serve as both familiarization and test events across different conditions of a study (Bogartz, Shinskey, & Speaker, 1997). Familiarity and possibility accounts then make different predictions about infants' looking times; proponents of the familiarity account argue that it better fits the observed data, for both the drawbridge study (Bogartz et al., 1999) and other violation-of-expectation studies (Bogartz & Shinskey, 1998; Bogartz et al., 1997).

However, proponents of the familiarity account have failed to replicate earlier findings (Baillargeon, 1987a, 1987b, 1991; Baillargeon et al., 1985), making it difficult to interpret their data and evaluate their claims. For example, in their work on the drawbridge experiment, Bogartz et al. (1999) ran three different types of habituation events (between subjects), and four different types of test trials (within subjects). A critical pairing corresponded to the original studies: habituation to a 180° motion, followed by test with a block in the path and either a 180° motion (impossible) or a 120° motion (possible). Overall, infants looked longer at the possible event than at the impossible, failing to replicate the original studies. Bogartz et al. (1999) claimed that this pattern can be explained by their familiarity account; infants that showed a novelty preference on other trials looked longer at the novel 120° possible motion in the critical pairing, whereas infants that showed a familiarity preference on other trials looked longer at the familiar 180° impossible motion in the critical pairing. In other words, infants' looking patterns could be explained in terms of the familiarity of events and the familiarity preferences of infants. However, Bogartz et al. (1999) failed to explain why they did not replicate the original finding, raising questions about the methods of their studies. For example, the block was two-dimensional in Bogartz et al.'s (1999) studies rather than three-dimensional as in the original studies, and infants received one of each of four types of test trials in Bogartz et al.'s (1999) studies rather than more than one of each of two types of test trials as in the original studies. Such factors might lead familiarity to be a better predictor than possibility in Bogartz et al.'s (1999) studies, but not necessarily in the original studies. That is, Bogartz et al. (1999) showed only that when they fail to replicate the original findings, familiarity is the best predictor of infants' looking, not that familiarity explains the looking times in the original results.

Evaluation of Discounting Infants' Successes. In summary, these accounts suggest that infants need not actually remember that hidden objects are present to demonstrate an apparent memory for them in violation-of-expectation studies. Although we believe it is important to continue to explore this possibility, there are reasons to be cautious about these basic perceptual process accounts. Such accounts have not yet explained the full range of infant behaviors currently interpreted as evidence for memory for hidden objects. And some of the purported empirical support for such accounts demonstrates only the importance of factors other than memory for hidden objects (e.g., familiarity), not the unimportance of memory for hidden objects. A variety of factors presumably influence infant behavior; demonstrating one does not negate another.

Each of the three remaining approaches to infants' task-dependent behaviors—separate pathways, distinct types of memory, and graded memory—views different methods as providing equally valid assessments of infant memory for hidden objects, and explores why memories may be evidenced on different tasks at different points in development.

Task-Dependent Behaviors Arise Due to Separate Memory Pathways

According to this argument, infants demonstrate sensitivity in violation-of-expectation studies using one relatively early developing neural pathway, whereas they demonstrate sensitivity in search studies using a separate, later developing pathway (Bertenthal, 1996; Spelke, Vishton, & von Hofsten, 1995). For example, anatomical, physiological, and behavioral evidence suggests that the visual processing system comprises two distinct cortical pathways (Goodale & Milner, 1992; Maunsell & Newsome, 1987; Ungerleider & Mishkin, 1982), which have been characterized as differentially subserving perception (the ability to understand what is seen) versus action (the ability to physically interact with what is seen; Goodale & Milner, 1992). Such a division of labor might contribute to infants' task-dependent behaviors if the perception pathway developed earlier than the action pathway, and violation-of-expectation tasks differentially tapped the perception pathway whereas search tasks differentially tapped the action pathway.

Evaluation of Separate Pathways. Distinct pathways for perception and action may contribute to infants' task-dependent behavior across violation-of-expectation and manual search paradigms. One outstanding question is whether certain pathways do in fact develop before others (and if so why). Another question is whether any such distinct pathways map cleanly onto the distinct behaviors they are posited to support. For example, both violation-of-expectation and search studies require infants to make actions to demonstrate their knowledge, so it is not clear that search studies would tap an action pathway whereas violation-of-expectation studies would tap a perception pathway. In addition, the considerable range of task-dependent behaviors observed (e.g., search in the dark vs. under a cover vs. with multiple hiding locations) suggest the operation of other factors, which are explored in the two remaining approaches.

Task-Dependent Behaviors Arise Due to Distinct Types of Memory

Several theories posit that infants demonstrate sensitivity in violation-of-expectation studies using one relatively early developing type of memory, whereas they demonstrate sensitivity in action tasks using a distinct, later developing type of memory (Diamond, 1998; Meltzoff & Moore, 1998; Munakata, 2001; Schacter & Moscovitch, 1984). A variant of this idea posits that some tasks require the coordination of distinct types of representations (a relatively late development), whereas other tasks do not require such coordination (Mareschal, Plunkett, & Harris, 1995).

Although in some cases these distinct types of memories may be localized to different neural pathways (blurring the distinction between distinct-memory and separate-pathway theories), this is not always the case. A single neural system may be hypothesized to support distinct types of memories, and different neural pathways may be hypothesized to support the same type of memory (Munakata, 2001). Alternatively, distinct-memory theories may be agnostic with respect to their neural implementation.

Identity Versus Permanence. Meltzoff and Moore (1998), for example, distinguished several representational abilities that may tap different types of memory, including representations of identity (e.g., knowing that a currently visible object is the same object as one previously viewed and now represented) and object permanence (e.g., knowing that a persisting representation in mind is linked to an object that is now hidden but continues to exist). Representations subserving identity may develop relatively early and suffice for success in violation-of-expectation studies, whereas representations subserving permanence may develop later and be required for success in search tasks. For example, according to this account, infants could succeed in Baillargeon and colleagues' (1991, 1987a; Baillargeon, Spelke, & Wasserman, 1985) drawbridge studies by representing the identity of the occluded box but not its permanence. Representations of identity include location information, such that infants' identity representations could lead them to expect to see the box in its location whenever the location was visible, independent of any beliefs regarding the permanence of the box. These identity-based expectations would be violated in the impossible condition but not the possible, leading to the observed patterns of looking times.

Active Versus Latent. This chapter explores in more detail another distinction, between "active" and "latent" memories (Munakata, 1998a, 1998b, 2001). These types of memory have been distinguished at the neural level and have been shown to support different types of behaviors, so they may contribute to task-dependent behaviors observed in infants.

Active memories take the form of sustained neuronal firing that can influence behavior in the absence of external memory cues, whereas latent memories take the form of changes in firing thresholds or neuronal connections that influence neuronal activity and behavior only in subsequent processing of memory cues. For example, Miller and Desimone (1994) presented monkeys with sequences of visual stimuli and trained them to respond when the first stimulus of a sequence was repeated. Inferotemporal neurons showed no sign of maintained firing for the target stimulus during the intervening stimuli; however, roughly half of the neurons recorded responded differently to the target stimulus on its second presentation. Monkeys appeared to simply observe the first stimulus and as a result, formed a latent memory trace for this stimulus, resulting in facilitated processing (usually suppressed activity) to the memory cue of the repeated stimulus. Suppression of neuronal responses to familiar spatial locations has also been demonstrated in the parietal cortex (Steinmetz, Connor, Constantinidis, & McLaughlin, 1994).

Miller and Desimone (1994) next altered their stimuli so sequences contained internal repeats, and the same monkeys were trained to respond to the match to the first stimulus in the sequence. Early in training, monkeys often responded to the internal repeat, supporting the idea that monkeys were not responding based on active maintenance of the target stimulus but instead on latent facilitated processing that occurred for any repeat. In contrast, when monkeys eventually learned to respond to the match-to-first only, sustained neuronal firing to the target was observed in prefrontal cortex, indicating a more active form of representation that could influence behavior in the absence of memory cues. Such active memory is consistent with a number of neural recording and imaging experiments in the prefrontal cortex (e.g., Cohen et al., 1997; Fuster, 1989; Goldman-Rakic, 1987).

Active memories of hidden objects may be required for search tasks, whereas latent memories may suffice for violation-of-expectation studies (Munakata, 2001). In this chapter, we explore the idea that a competition between active and latent memories leads to task-dependent behavior across simple search and A-not-B tasks, as well as within the A-not-B task (Munakata, 1998a).

Evaluation of Distinct Types of Memory.   The simulation section of this chapter further evaluates the active–latent account of task-dependent behavior. Relevant questions for any version of this distinct-memory approach include: Why does one type of memory develop before another? What develops to subserve these types of memory? Why do certain types of memory suffice for certain tasks but not others?

For example, one might ask of Meltzoff and Moore's (1998) identity-permanence distinction: Why do identity representations lead to success in violation-of-expectation studies but not search tasks? If infants succeed in Baillargeon's drawbridge studies (1987a, 1987b, 1991; Baillargeon et al., 1985) because they expect to see the box in its location whenever that location is visible, why wouldn't they use such identity representations to remove an occluding cover so that a hidden toy could be viewed in its location (and then retrieved)?

Task-Dependent Behaviors Arise Due to Gradedness of Memory

The final theoretical approach we consider posits that different tasks rely on the same, shared memory for hidden objects (rather than requiring distinct types or pathways of memory), and infant behavior across different tasks can be understood in terms of the gradedness of these shared memories of objects. According to this approach, infants gradually acquire the ability to remember hidden objects, rather than maintaining representations of hidden objects in an all-or-nothing manner. Different tasks require different strengths of these underlying memories, and infants' graded abilities to remember become stronger with development, allowing infants to demonstrate sensitivity across an increasing number of tasks (Fischer & Bidell, 1991; Haith & Benson, 1997; Munakata, 1998a; Munakata et al., 1997). Piaget (1954) should perhaps be included in this theoretical grouping. He noted both precocities and limitations in infants' memory for hidden objects, suggesting that infants develop an understanding of object permanence over a protracted period. A full object permanence concept was attributable to infants only around 18 to 24 months.

The notion of graded representations has proven useful for understanding task-dependent behavior following brain damage (Farah, Monheit, & Wallace, 1991; Farah, O'Reilly, & Vecera, 1993). For example, patients with a deficit known as *extinction* make accurate same/different judgments about pairs of stimuli, although they are impaired in reporting the identity of the stimulus opposite the side of their brain lesion (Volpe, LeDoux, & Gazzaniga, 1979). This task-dependent behavior may be based on the poor perception of extinguished stimuli, with identification requiring more visual information than same/different judgments, as suggested by the finding that such task-dependent behaviors can be induced in normal subjects presented with degraded visual images (Farah et al., 1991). Similar arguments have been made to explain task-dependent behaviors in *prosopagnosia* (Farah et al., 1993), the selective deficit in the overt recognition of faces. Although prosopagnosics show impairments on a variety of overt measures of face recognition, they are nonetheless able to show signs of covert recognition, for example, in consistently relearning correct face–name and face–occupation pairings more quickly than learning incorrect pairings (De Haan, Young, & Newcombe, 1987). Farah et al. (1993) proposed that degraded representations following brain damage are only strong enough to support covert recognition, and demonstrated how a computational model could simulate such dissociations based on graded representations.

The notion of graded representations may also be useful for understanding why infants search for objects hidden by darkness earlier than they will search for objects occluded in the light. A somewhat weak memory of an occluded object might not be able to overcome the interference produced by the visual stimulus of an occluder where the object used to be. This same memory, however, might be strong enough to guide a reach in the dark, when there is no direct visual information conflicting with the weak memory. This interpretation is consistent with the data reported earlier, indicating that infants searched more in an occluder+blackout condition than with a visible occluder (Munakata et al., in preparation). The strength of infants' memory for hidden objects may vary with the strength of interference provided by occlusion events (with interference stronger for a visible occluder than for a blackout or occluder+blackout).

In this section, we explore the idea that search tasks require stronger memories for hidden objects than do violation-of-expectation studies (Munakata et al., 1997).

Evaluation of Gradedness of Memory. The simulation section of this chapter further evaluates the graded memory account of task-dependent behavior. Relevant questions for any version of this account include: What develops to strengthen memories? Why do certain tasks require stronger memories than other tasks?

Summary of Theories

Why do infants seem so smart in violation-of-expectation studies in the first few months of life, but so oblivious in search tasks for many months afterward? We considered five distinct approaches to such task-dependent behaviors with hidden objects.

Two of these approaches treat certain methods as invalid for assessing memory for hidden objects, and so try to discount either infants' failures or their successes with hidden objects. Based on the available evidence, we concluded that we can discount neither failures nor successes. It seems unlikely that infants' failures can be explained away as merely performance deficits, or as unrelated to hidden toys. Further evidence is needed to determine whether infants' successes could occur in the absence of any ability to represent occluded objects. Thus, both infants' successes and their failures should provide important constraints on theorizing about infants' memory for hidden objects.

Of the remaining three approaches, we next focus on two: graded memory and distinct types of memory. We believe that there may be promise in the third approach, separate pathways of knowledge (e.g., perception–action). However, direct challenges to this type of approach remain, and the wide range of task-dependent behaviors suggest that other factors are likely to play a role. Thus, it should be productive to explore other approaches.

SIMULATION

Through the discussion of neural network simulations, this section further explores two of the accounts of infants' task-dependent behavior with hidden objects described in the preceding section: accounts based on graded memories and distinct types of memories (active vs. latent). We review three of our neural network simulations (Munakata, 1998a; Munakata et al., 1997), exploring performance in violation-of-expectation studies, simple search tasks, and the A-not-B task (for reviews of contributions of neural network simulations to understanding other developmental phenomena, see Elman, Bates, Karmiloff-Smith, Johnson, Parisi, & Plunkett, 1996; Munakata & Stedron, 2001).

There has been extensive debate on the role of simulations in general in cognitive theorizing, as well as of neural network simulations in particular (e.g., McCloskey, 1991; Seidenberg, 1993). We view our models as serving as the following: (a) explicit instantiations of theories (in this case on the effects of graded and distinct memories on task-dependent behavior), (b) demonstrations of nonintuitive yet principled ways in which behaviors may arise, and (c) the source of novel empirical predictions. We therefore view computational models as a complement to behavioral work, allowing for the exploration of potential mechanisms underlying behavior.

In neural network simulations, processing occurs through the propagation of activation among simple processing units. These units typically represent groups of neurons, with activation of the units representing neuronal firing rates. Activation is propagated from one unit to another via connection weights, which represent the strength of synapses between neurons. These weights thus influence the activity of units, and in turn, the ability of neural networks to solve tasks. As experience or maturation leads to gradual changes in these weights, networks can become increasingly able to solve tasks. (For introductory textbooks on neural network modeling, see Elman et al., 1996; O'Reilly & Munakata, 2000; Rumelhart & McClelland, 1986.)

Both the gradedness of memory and the distinction between active and latent memory are captured very naturally in the neural network framework. The activation of neural network units is graded in nature (activation values typically fall between 0 and 1), reflecting the gradedness inherent in neural activity (in terms of neuronal firing rates, number of contributing neurons, etc.). The gradedness of memory can be captured in such graded patterns of activation, when such patterns represent information no longer present in the environment. Further, neural networks can represent information in two related but distinct ways: in weights and in activations. Changes to the connection weights may be viewed as latent memories that can influence subsequent processing, whereas the sustained activations of units may be viewed as active memories that can influence ongoing behavior. Active and latent memories influence one another; the activity of a unit depends on the weights coming into it, and weights can change based on patterns of activity.

In the first two models we consider, active and latent memories go hand in hand, so for simplification we focus on active memories in the analyses. In contrast, in the third model, active and latent memories compete, and so we consider them separately. These models demonstrate how graded memories might lead infants to succeed in violation-of-expectation studies before succeeding in search tasks, and how the A-not-B task may require even stronger memories than simple search tasks due to a competition between active and latent memories. We then consider future directions for the modeling work, including the integration of mechanisms that are currently present only in separate models.

Violation-of-Expectation

The first simulations (Munakata et al., 1997) explored the memories that might underlie infants' longer looking times to impossible events in violation-of-expectation studies, and how these memories might develop gradually through experience with the world. These simulations demonstrated that networks could gradually improve their ability to retain information about occluded objects based on experiences with objects that conformed to the principle of object permanence (i.e., experiences in which objects that disappear when occluded reappear when the occluder is removed). Such abilities allowed networks to form predictions about events in their world; discrepancies between these predictions and actual events (as might arise in "impossible" events) could lead to observed patterns of looking times in violation-of-expectation studies.

Architecture and Environment. The simulations involved simple recurrent networks (Elman, 1990; Jordan, 1986) that viewed simple events as sequences of patterns of activity (Fig. 2.3). These patterns of activity were presented to the network's percept layer and then propagated to the network's internal representation layer, which the network could use to form meaningful representations of its environment. The internal representation layer also received input from its own earlier activity, such that the activity of the internal representation layer reflected both the perceptual input at a given time and the network's representation of the world on preceding time steps. Thus, the network's representation of the world was not driven simply by what was perceptually visible at a given time, but also by what the network represented prior to that time. That is, the network's memories were reflected in the activity of the internal representation layer.

The network's goal at each time step was to use its internal representations to predict what it would see next. For example, at "time 0" in Fig. 2.3, the network's goal was to predict the pattern of activity that appeared at "time 1," its goal at "time 1" was to predict the pattern of activity at "time 2," and so on. If there were discrepancies between what the network predicted and what was actually visible on the next time step, these discrep-

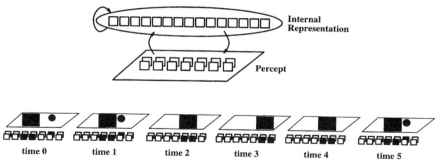

FIG. 2.3.   Recurrent network (top) and an occlusion event shown in schematic and activation form (bottom; adapted from Munakata et al., 1997): Events were presented as patterns of activity on the percept layer. In this event, an occluder moved from left to right, occluding a ball, and then from right to left, revealing the ball. This activity was propagated to the internal representation layer, which the network could use to form meaningful representations of its world. These internal representations fed back to themselves, so that they were influenced by representations on previous time steps. The network used these representations to form perceptual predictions.

ancies provided a signal to the network to adjust its weights appropriately (i.e., to learn). Thus, with repeated exposure to events conforming to basic principles such as object permanence, the network could learn to reliably predict the behavior of the objects in its world.

The corresponding processes in infants might be understood as follows: Infants view events in their world, with the goal of predicting what will happen next. To form accurate predictions, they must not only represent the current state of the world, they must also remember what came before. Infants appear to develop such predictive abilities over the first 3 months of life, that allow them to visually track objects (Aslin, 1981; Rosander & Hofsten, 1994) and to predict sequences (Haith, Hazan, & Goodman, 1988). As explored in the following network, such processes, combined with events conforming to the principle of object permanence, could lead infants to learn to remember the continued existence of hidden objects.

Performance.   One measure of the network's memory for hidden objects was its prediction just prior to the reappearance of an occluded object (e.g., at "time 4" in Fig. 2.3). Would the network remember the hidden object sufficiently to predict that it would reappear? Would it distinguish this case from one in which no object should reappear (e.g., at "time 4" in Fig. 2.4)? To quantify this measure, the network's prediction about the ball at "time 4" (the extent to which it activated the relevant ball unit in its prediction) was measured for both types of events, and the prediction activity in the nonocclusion event was subtracted from the prediction activity

FIG. 2.4   A nonocclusion event shown in schematic and activation form (adapted from Munakata et al., 1997): An occluder moved from left to right and then from right to left.

in the occlusion event. The length of the occlusion period varied from three time steps (as shown in Fig. 2.3) to seven time steps, so the ball did not always reappear on the same time step. The network's prediction was always measured on the time step just prior to the ball's reappearance, as the occluder began to move back. The maximum activity of a unit was 1, and the minimum activity of a unit was 0. Perfect performance on this subtraction measure would thus equal 1, corresponding to the network predicting that the ball should reappear when in fact it should, and that it should not reappear when in fact it should not.

The subtraction measure of sensitivity to occluded objects showed that the network gradually learned to predict an occluded object's reappearance (Fig. 2.5). Further simulations indicated that the network could generalize such predictions to novel objects. If an occluded object did not reappear, there would thus be a discrepancy between the network's prediction and the observed event. Discrepancies of this kind might provide the signal that causes infants to look longer at impossible events in violation-of-expectation studies.

We note two important aspects of the network's development. First, the network's sensitivity to occluded objects was graded in nature. There was no discrete point in time at which the network abruptly became sensitive to hidden objects without demonstrating any sensitivity prior to that point. Instead, the progression was more gradual, with the network becoming increasingly sensitive to hidden objects with experience. Moreover, at any point in development, the network exhibited more sensitivity to occluded objects when tested with shorter occlusion periods. These graded aspects of the network's development are consistent with the idea that looking times in violation-of-expectation studies might reveal sensitivity to hidden objects at a relatively early age, even though the full development of memories for hidden objects may span a much longer period.

Second, the network learned about occluded objects without receiving any explicit training that occluded objects continued to exist. When objects were occluded in the network's world, the network received no signal that the objects were still there; the perceptual input consisted only of the occluding stimulus. That is, there was no object permanence signal in the network's input. Instead, the network had to learn about the permanence of objects based on the fact that objects that became occluded later reap-

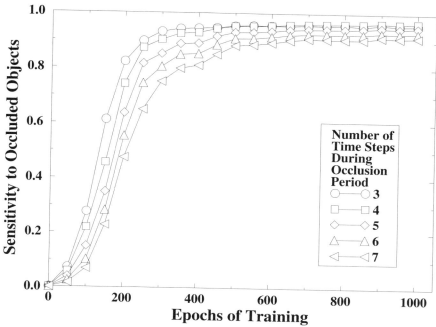

FIG. 2.5. Learning curves indicating the network's increasing sensitivity to the reappearance of occluded objects (from Munakata et al., 1997): The network's sensitivity was computed as the difference between the network's predictions for events with and without occluded objects.

peared. At first, the network's connections did not support meaningful predictions about occluded objects, but with the experience of seeing occluded objects reappear and with the goal of predicting what it will see next in the world, the network came to have the appropriate expectations.

The next section explores the memories subserving the network's predictions. These memories, like the network's sensitivity to hidden objects, were graded in nature. The subsequent simulation demonstrates how such gradedness in memories can lead to task-dependent behaviors of the sort observed in infants.

Internal Representations. How did the network learn to predict the reappearance of occluded objects? It learned to remember objects that were no longer visible in the form of patterns of activation in its internal representation units. These patterns of activation for occluded objects resembled the patterns for the objects when they were visible.

The network's learning was subserved by changes to its connection weights, and was evident in its activity patterns, which we focus on here. To evaluate the network's memories of occluded objects, we recorded the patterns of activity across the network's internal representation units during various events. To isolate the network's representation of the ball from other things (e.g., the time step of the event), we computed differences between particular pairs of patterns (Fig. 2.6). For example, to isolate the network representation of a visible ball, we recorded the pattern of activity for a "ball-only" event and subtracted from it the pattern of activity recorded for the analogous "nothing" event. Similarly, to isolate the network representation of the ball during occlusion events, we recorded the pattern of activity across the network's internal representation units in a "ball-occluder" event and subtracted from it the pattern of activity from the corresponding time step in the corresponding "occluder-only" event. When we compared these various representations for the object, we saw that the network gradually learned to represent the object in similar ways when it was visible (whether alone, or prior to or following occlusion) and when it was occluded.

The network's representations for the visible ball after 100 epochs of training are shown in Fig. 2.7. The relevant event subtraction ("ball-only" minus "nothing") is shown on the left, with the absolute magnitudes of the resulting subtractions for each of the 15 internal representation units represented on the right by the size of the white boxes. Large boxes (e.g., for unit 1) indicate units that code for the ball's presence, because these units are activated differentially for stimuli that are similar in all regards except

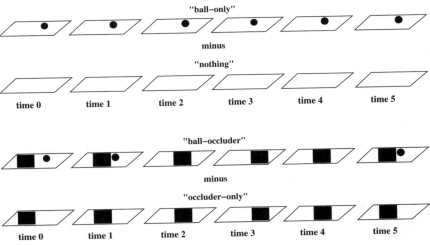

FIG. 2.6 Events to isolate the network's representation of the ball (adapted from Munakata et al., 1997): The pattern of activity across the network's internal representation units was recorded for these events. The "nothing" pattern was subtracted from the "ball-only" pattern to isolate the network's representation of a visible ball, and the "occluder-only" pattern was subtracted from the "ball-occluder" pattern to isolate the network's representation of the ball during occlusion.

FIG. 2.7. The network's internal representation of a visible ball on one time step, after 100 epochs of training (adapted from Munakata et al., 1997): The relevant event subtraction is shown on the left. The resulting values of the subtractions for each of the internal representation units are represented by the size of the white boxes. The network showed similar representations for the visible ball across other time steps and with additional epochs of training (not shown).

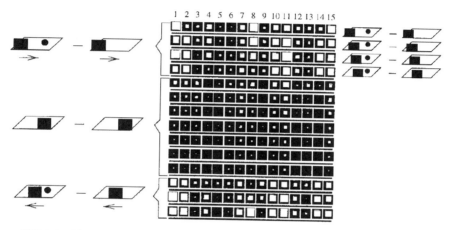

FIG. 2.8. The network's internal representation of a ball preceding, during, and after occlusion, after 100 epochs of training (adapted from Munakata et al., 1997): The fifteen units in the internal representation layer are represented across each row, with each row corresponding to a particular time step in the event subtraction. The individual events subtracted for the first four time steps are shown to the right. The three general classes of event subtractions are shown to the left (occluder moving right while ball is visible, occluder occluding ball, and occluder moving left while ball is visible). The same units that coded for the visible ball alone coded for the ball preceding and after occlusion. However, the signal from those units was only weakly maintained during the occlusion period.

for the presence or absence of the ball. The network showed similar representations for the visible ball across other time steps, and with additional epochs of training.

In contrast, consider the network's representations for the ball during an occlusion event at this same point in development (Fig. 2.8). Recall that the network demonstrated limited sensitivity to occluded objects at this time (as shown previously in Fig. 2.5). The fifteen units in the internal representation layer are represented across each row in Fig. 2.8, with each row corresponding to a particular time step in the event subtraction. The individual events subtracted for the first four time steps are shown to the right. The three general classes of event subtractions are shown to the left (oc-

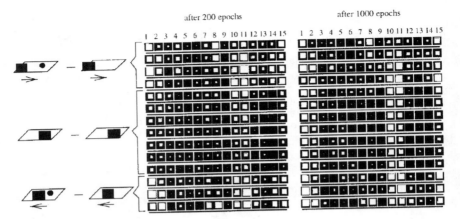

FIG. 2.9.   The network's internal representation of a ball preceding, during, and after occlusion, after 200 and 1000 epochs of training (adapted from Munakata et al., 1997): The network became increasingly able to maintain the signal for the ball during the occlusion period.

cluder moving right while ball is visible, occluder occluding ball, and occluder moving left while ball is visible). The same units that coded for the visible ball alone (Fig. 2.7) coded for the ball preceding and after occlusion. However, this signal for the ball was only weakly maintained during the occlusion period.

With experience, the network gradually developed the ability to maintain representations over the occlusion period (Fig. 2.9). The network's representation of the occluded ball became more similar to its representation of the visible ball. At any time point in the network's development, the longer the period of occlusion, the weaker the representation became.

Summary of Violation-of-Expectation Simulation.   This simulation demonstrated how a network could learn to remember occluded objects to support perceptual predictions, which could in turn support longer looking times to events that violate such predictions, like those presented in violation-of-expectation studies. The network learned on the basis of events in its world that conformed to the principle of object permanence, in the absence of any explicit signal that hidden objects continued to exist. The network's memory for hidden objects was graded in nature, gradually becoming both more like the network's representations of the objects when visible and better able to sustain delays.

The graded memories approach posits that such gradedness may lead to task-dependent behaviors, with relatively weak memories sufficing for some tasks but not others. The next simulation explored this possibility by incorporating a separate, reaching output system to the perceptual prediction model.

Simple Reaching Tasks

This simulation (Munakata et al., 1997) explored the idea that search tasks require stronger memories than violation-of-expectation studies. Search tasks might require stronger memories due to a number of possible factors, including a greater complexity of reaching, a greater physical effort required for reaching, a lower frequency of reaching behaviors, or the later development of the reaching system. Infants fixate interesting stimuli from birth (Banks & Salapatek, 1983), indicating some level of development of the systems that might underlie looking at interesting events in violation-of-expectation studies, whereas they first reach consistently only around 3 to 4 months of age (Hofsten, 1984; Thelen, Corbetta, Kamm, Spencer, Schneider, & Zernicke, 1993).

To explore the role of graded memories in violation-of-expectation and simple search tasks, Munakata et al. (1997) added a second output system to their perceptual prediction model. This second output system corresponded to a reaching system, although it did not incorporate any details of the reaching process. Instead, two manipulations of the reaching system served as proxies for the mechanisms responsible for the later mastery of reaching behaviors. These proxies allowed for the evaluation of the role of graded memories on separate output systems.

Architecture and Environment.   These simulations involved the recurrent network used in the initial violation-of-expectation simulation, with an additional reaching output layer (Fig. 2.10). The task structure of the reaching system was basically the same as the task structure of the prediction system, but two manipulations delayed the development of the reaching system. The first manipulation reduced the rate of learning within the reaching system to one tenth the rate of learning in the looking system. The second manipulation was in the onset of training; the reaching system began developing only after the network had partially learned to form predictions. These manipulations allow the reaching system to capture the assumption that reaching behaviors are delayed relative to perceptual predictions, without specifying the detailed mechanistic basis for this delay. These manipulations lead to the obvious prediction that the model will be better at forming perceptual predictions than at reaching, all else being equal. However, the model allows for the further and more interesting exploration of how the development of different output systems might interact with the strength of representations.

Reach

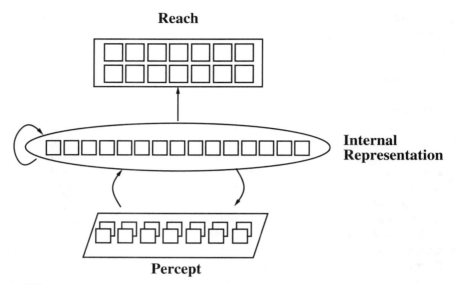

**Internal
Representation**

Percept

FIG. 2.10. Recurrent network (adapted from Munakata et al., 1997): The reaching system was identical to the standard perceptual prediction system, but training of the weights in the reaching system began after the network had begun to make predictions, and the learning rate for these weights was smaller than for the prediction weights.

The two output systems were each trained with the same events used in the original set of simulations. The network's sensitivity to occluded objects was computed in the same way as in the original model, based on the network's ability to form different predictions (in both the perceptual system and in reaching) for events involving occluders with and without balls.

Performance.   The reaching system showed the expected delayed course of development with occluded objects, due to its reduced learning rate and delayed onset of training (Fig. 2.11). However, the reaching system showed sensitivity to visible objects fairly early in development, around the time that the perceptual prediction system began showing sensitivity to occluded objects. That is, the network's insensitivity in reaching for occluded objects was not simply a result of deficits in its reaching system; it could reach just fine to visible objects. This confluence of behaviors corresponds to that observed in infants; within the first few months of life, they show sensitivity to occluded objects in violation-of-expectation studies and to visible objects in their reaching behavior, but for several more months they show little or no sensitivity to occluded objects in their reaching (i.e., no discrimination in their reaching given an occluder with and without an object behind it).

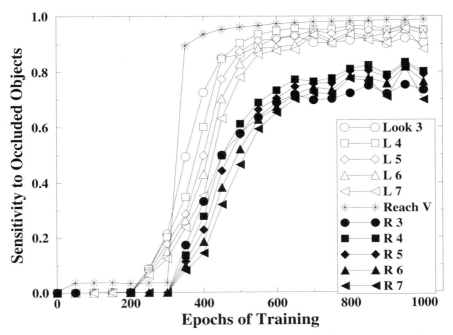

FIG. 2.11. Learning curves indicating the network's increasing sensitivity to the reappearance of occluded objects (from Munakata et al., 1997): The development of the reaching system was slowed, so that the looking system showed greater sensitivity to occluded objects (the numbers in the legend indicate the number of time steps during the occlusion period). However, the reaching system responded appropriately to visible objects early in learning ("Reach V"), suggesting that the strengthening of memories for occluded objects played a role in improvements in reaching behavior.

Representational and Output Contributions. Analyses of the units in the internal representation layer revealed the same developmental pattern shown by the original model: The network gradually learned to remember occluded objects in the form of patterns of activation that resembled the network's representations for those objects when visible. Further, additional simulations, in which different parts of the network were "frozen" during development, demonstrated that such strengthening of these memories was critical to improvements in the network's reaching for occluded objects (Munakata et al., 1997).

Summary of Simple Reaching Simulation. This simulation demonstrated how graded memories could lead to success in one task but not another. The perceptual prediction system was able to use weak memories of occluded objects to expect their reappearance, whereas the the reaching system, with a delayed and slowed timecourse of development, was unable to use the same memories of occluded objects to reach. This early inability to reach to occluded objects was not due simply to deficits in the reaching system, because this sytem was able to reach to visible objects (for which the network quickly developed strong representations). Thus, the strength of the graded representations was critical to the task-dependent behavior of the network. Moreover, the strengthening of the networks' memories alone was sufficient to allow a system to progress from initially reaching only for visible objects to then reaching for occluded objects as well. In this way, memory development may be critical to infants' increasing abilities to demonstrate sensitivity to hidden objects across a range of tasks. The next simulation explored the possibility that further memory developments are required for success in the A-not-B task, in the context of a competition between active and latent memories.

A-Not-B Task

This simulation (Munakata, 1998a, with peer commentary) explored infants' task-dependent memory for hidden objects both across different search tasks and within a task. Specifically, this model simulated the findings that infants perseverate in the A-not-B task as soon as they begin searching correctly in simple search tasks, and infants show more sensitivity to hidden objects in gaze and violation-of-expectation variants of the A-not-B task than in the standard manual search version. The simulation demonstrated how the A-not-B error might arise based on a competition between latent memories of A and active memories of B, and how the inherent gradedness of active memory again allows for the support of certain behaviors but not others.

To focus on the dynamics of active and latent memory and the gradedness of memory within this task, the network architecture and environment were greatly simplified for this exploration. For example, this network focused on infants' experiences within search tasks, with less attention than Munakata et al.'s (1997) model to infants' experiences across development. Further, the full A-not-B simulation evaluated many variants of the A-not-B task not covered here, so we simplify the presentation of the network architecture to include only those elements covered in the simulations described in this section.

Architecture and Environment. The network was comprised of two input layers that encoded information about the location and identity of objects, an internal representation layer, and two output layers for gaze/expectation and reach (Fig. 2.12).

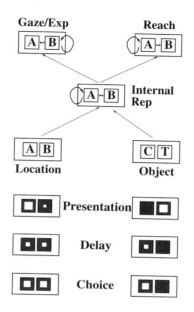

FIG. 2.12. Simplified version of the A-not-B network and the elements of an A trial (adapted from Munakata, 1998a): The activation level of the input units for the three segments of the trial is shown by the size of the white boxes. The "Object" input indicated whether a cover ("C") or toy ("T") was visible.

The gaze/expectation layer responded (i.e., updated the activity of its units) to every input during the A-not-B task, whereas the reaching layer responded only to inputs corresponding to a stimulus within "reaching distance." This updating constraint was meant to capture the fact that infants' reaching is permitted at only one point during each A-not-B trial, when the apparatus is moved to within the infant's reach, whereas nothing prevents infants from forming expectations (that may underlie longer looking to impossible events) throughout each trial.[2]

---

[2]The model simplifies over nuances in infants' gazing and reaching. For example, infants' gaze is sometimes restricted during A-not-B experiments so that they cannot gaze continuously at a recent hiding location, whereas the model gazes continuously. And, infants may plan or imagine reaching movements prior to the point when they can reach to the A-not-B apparatus, so that they may activate brain areas relevant for reaching to some degree prior to the actual reach, whereas the model cannot activate its reaching units until the actual reach. Nevertheless, the model captures an essential difference between gaze/expection and reach in the A-not-B task—infants have many more opportunities to gaze and to form expectations than to execute reaching responses.

The network's feedforward connectivity included an initial bias to respond appropriately to location information, and also developed further biases based on the network's experience during the A-not-B task. The initial bias allowed the network, for example, to look to location A if something were presented there. Infants appear to enter A-not-B experiments with such biases, so this manipulation may be viewed as a proxy for experience prior to the A-not-B study. The network's feedforward weights changed based on its experience during the study according to a Hebbian learning rule, such that connections between units that were simultaneously active tended to be relatively strong. The network's latent memory thus took the form of these feedforward weights; they reflected the network's prior experiences and influenced its subsequent processing.

Each unit in the hidden and output layers had a self-recurrent excitatory connection back to itself. These recurrent connections were largely responsible for the network's ability to maintain representations of a recent hiding location; units that are active tend to remain active when they receive their own activity as input through sufficiently large weights. The network's active memory thus took the form of maintained representations on the network's hidden and output layers, as supported by its recurrent connections. To simulate gradual improvements with age in the network's active memory, the strength of the network's recurrent connections was manipulated, with "older" networks having higher recurrence. This manipulation might be viewed as a proxy for the experience-based weight change process of the original simulations (Munakata et al., 1997).

The simulated A-not-B task consisted of four pretrials (corresponding to the "practice" trials typically provided at the start of an experiment to induce infants to reach to A), two A trials, and one B trial. Each trial consisted primarily of three segments: the presentation of a toy at the A or B location, a delay period, and a choice period (Fig. 2.12). During each segment, patterns of activity were presented to the input units corresponding to the visible aspects of the stimulus event. The levels of input activity represented the salience of aspects of the stimulus, with more salient aspects producing more activity. For example, the levels of input activity for the A and B locations were higher during choice than during delay, to reflect the increased salience of the stimulus when it was presented for a response.

Performance. For all analyses of the network's performance, the network's percent correct response was computed as the activation of the appropriate output unit divided by the sum of activation over all possible output units. For example, the network's percent correct reaching on A trials was computed as the activity of A/(A+B) for the reaching layer. The model simulated the A-not-B error (successful reaching on A trials with perseverative reaching on B trials), improvements with age, and the earlier sensitivity of gaze/reach measures (Fig. 2.13). Further, the model led to the novel prediction that under certain conditions, infants may perseverate more in gaze/expectation than in reach. Each of these behaviors could be understood in terms of model's underlying graded, active and latent memories, as discussed in the next section.

Internal Representations. Why did the network perseverate, improve with age, and show earlier sensitivity in gaze/expectation than in reach?

The network performed well on A trials at all ages because latent changes to the feedforward weights, built up over previous trials in which the network represented and responded to A, favored A over B. These latent memories thus supported enough activity at A that the network's ability to maintain activity at A had little effect on performance. The internal representations of a relatively young network during an A trial (Fig. 2.14) showed that even with relatively weak recurrent weights to support the active maintenance of the most recent hiding location, the network was

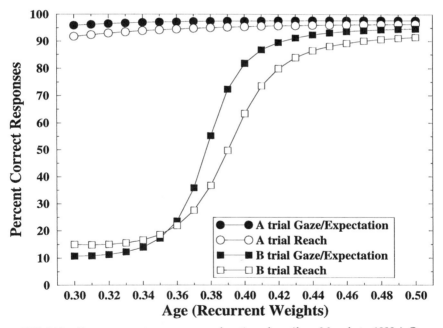

FIG. 2.13.   Percent correct responses as a function of age (from Munakata, 1998a): On A trials, the network is accurate across all levels of recurrence shown. On B trials, the network responds nonperseveratively only as the recurrent weights get stronger. The gaze/expectation system shows nonperseverative responding earlier than the reach system.

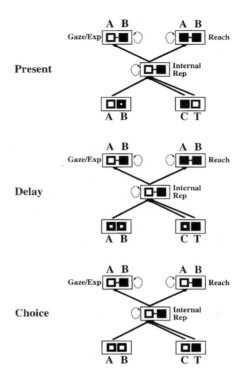

FIG. 2.14. A young network's representations during an A trial (adapted from Munakata, 1998a): The network responds correctly to A in gaze/expectation and in reach.

able to strongly represent A during all three segments of the trial. Thus, the latent memories in the network's weights, biasing it toward A, allowed it to respond correctly toward A even with only a weak ability to actively hold the most recent hiding location in mind.

In contrast, the network's ability to maintain activity for the most recent hiding location was critical to its performance on B trials, because the network had to maintain a representation of B in the face of the latent bias to respond to A. The activity of the units of the young network during a B trial (Fig. 2.15) indicated that the network appropriately represented and responded to B in gaze/expectation during the presentation of the toy at B, when the B input unit was strongly activated. Infants in the A-not-B task similarly look to B when an object is hidden there. However, the memory for B faded during the delay, when the A and B input units were equally activated, so that the internal representation activity showed little evidence of which location was recently attended. If judged at that time on the basis of active traces alone, the network showed little memory of prior events. However, the network showed strong evidence of memory for the previous trials by making the A-not-B error at choice, indicating the influence of latent traces. In particular, the network's connection weights had learned to favor activity at A over B, based on the preceding pretrials and A trials. Thus, by repeatedly attending and responding to one location, the network became increasingly likely to attend and respond there.

The activity of the units of a slightly older network during a B trial (Fig. 2.16) indicated why the network improved with age, and why it showed earlier sensitivity in gaze/expectation than in reach. The stronger recurrent weights allowed the network to maintain an active memory of B during the delay. That is, the network was better able to hold recent information about a recent location in mind, rather than simply falling back to its biases for previous locations. The gaze/expectation system was able to take advantage of this information with its constant updating, showing

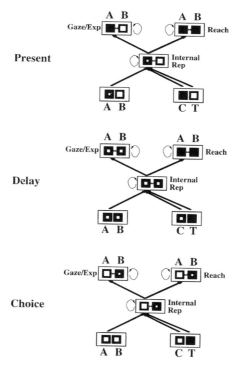

FIG. 2.15.   A young network's representations during a B trial (adapted from Munakata, 1998a): The network responds perseveratively to A in gaze/expectation and in reach.

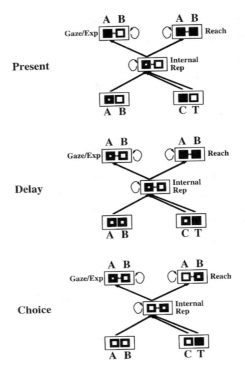

FIG. 2.16. A slightly older network's representations during a B trial (adapted from Munakata, 1998a): The network responds correctly to B in gaze/expectation, but reaches perseveratively to A.

correct responding during presentation and delay, which carried over to choice. In contrast, the reach system was only able to respond at choice. Because the network's active memory for the most recent location faded with time, by the choice point the network's internal representation reflected more of the network's latent memory of A.

Similarly, infants may show earlier success in gaze/expectation variants of the A-not-B task because they can constantly update their gazing and their expectations. As a result, they can counter perseverative tendencies on B trials by gazing at B and forming expectations about B during the presentation, delay, and choice trial periods. In contrast, infants can only reach at the choice point, by which time their memories have become more susceptible to perseverative biases.

Unexpectedly, Fig. 2.13 demonstrated that very young networks showed slightly more perseveration in gaze/expectation than in reach. The basis for this difference was again the different rates of updating in the two output systems. Networks with relatively weak recurrent weights tended to default to the prepotent response, in which case the continual updating of the gaze/expectation system led it to show more of this prepotent response than the reach system. In effect, when recurrence was high enough to keep the right location (B) in mind, then "repeating" it, as the gaze/expectation system did, helped performance; in contrast, when recurrence was low so that the wrong, prepotent location (A) came to mind, then repeating hurt performance. The simulation thus yielded the novel empirical prediction that infants may perseverate more in gaze/expectation than in reaching early in development, a prediction that we are now testing.

Summary of A-Not-B Simulation. The A-not-B simulation demonstrated how the continued strengthening of memories could lead infants to progress from succeeding in simple single-location search tasks to succeeding in search tasks requiring infants to overcome prepotent biases. In the simulation, stronger memories took the form of maintained activity on the network's internal representation units, which competed with prepotent biases in the form of latent memories in the connection weights. Again, weaker memories sufficed for success in some tasks but not others.

Summary of Simulations and Future Directions

The preceding sections described how networks progressed from succeeding in violation of expectation to simple search, and from gaze/expectation variants of the A-not-B task to the standard reaching version of the A-not-B task, all based on the same process of gradual strengthening of active memories. We stress that these results run counter to approaches that invoke new ancillary deficits to explain each infant failure (as described earlier in the competence–performance section). Instead, the simulations suggest that a common process—the development of the ability to maintain active memories—may underlie infants' task-dependent progression for demonstrating sensitivity to hidden objects. Apparent improvements in infants' abilities to solve problems or to inhibit inappropriate responses may result from their increasing maintenance abilities.

We next consider issues that arise in the comparison of simulations reviewed in this chapter, primarily: factors distinguishing looking and reaching processes, relevance of the active–latent distinction to the dissociation between violation-of-expectation and simple search, and underlying learning mechanisms.

First, the violation-of-expectation/simple-search and A-not-B simulations employed different manipulations to contrast the looking and reaching systems. In the violation-of-expectation/simple-search simulations, the greater sensitivity of the looking system to graded memories resulted from delayed and slowed learning in the reaching system. In the A-not-B simulations, the greater sensitivity of the looking system to graded memories resulted from the more frequent updating of this system relative to the reaching system. Why the different manipulations for the different simulations? Although the later mastery of the reaching system might also play a role in the looking–reaching task-dependency in the A-not-B task, this factor may contribute less because infants tested in the A-not-B task are typically older (and thus have more experience reaching) than infants in the single-location looking and reaching tasks. However, it does seem possible that different frequencies of reaching versus expectation-formation during single-location tasks might also contribute to this looking–reaching task-dependency. For example, infants in Baillargeon and colleagues (1987a, 1987b, 1991; Baillargeon et al., 1985) drawbridge studies might make use of fairly weak memories for the hidden block to continually update the expectation that the block will remain and the drawbridge will stop. In contrast, such continual updating is rarely possible in reaching behaviors; infants are usually too far to reach or are prevented from reaching while a toy is hidden, and must then generate the reach after the toy is fully occluded. Finally, it is interesting to note that the different frequencies of looking and reaching in general (outside of experimental tasks) may contribute to their differential sensitivity in early development, so the two explanations of different frequencies of behaviors in particular tasks and differential sensitivities of behaviors may be closely related.

Second, in the discussion of the active–latent distinction, we focused on the dissociation between simple search and A-not-B tasks; however, it also seems possible that this distinction may contribute to the dissociation observed in violation-of-expectation and simple-search tasks. Specifically, in ongoing work, we are exploring the possibility that infants succeed in some violation-of-expectation studies using latent memories, whereas search tasks may require later developing active memories (Munakata, 2001). Infants may use their well-documented predictive abilities to form predictions about upcoming events in violation-of-expectation tasks (e.g., the visible drawbridge will follow its habituated course of motion, hit the block in its path, and stop). The formation of these predictions leads to changes in the processing system, so that the predictions result in latent memories. Test events can reactivate these latent memories, so that processing of possible events is facilitated although processing of impossible events is not, leading to longer looking times. In the same way that non-human primates form latent memories of visible stimuli that subserve facilitated processing on subsequent presentations of the stimuli (Miller & Desimone, 1994; Steinmetz et al., 1994), infants may form latent memories of their predictions about visible stimuli that then subserve facilitated processing of events matching those predictions. Infants may thus succeed in some violation-of-expectation studies through the recognition of an event as familiar or novel (relative to a prediction formed when everything in the display was visible). In contrast, to retrieve a hidden object, infants may require a later developing active representation of the object in the form of sustained neural firing; search tasks typically do not include events that would serve to reactivate latent memories and cue infants to their earlier processing. That is, longer looking times to impossible events can be based on the recognition of earlier predictions, but reaching for hidden objects cannot rely on such recognition processes. Infants cannot simply watch occlusion events and reach based on recognition of a match, because no such match is provided.

Third, the violation-of-expectation/simple-search and A-not-B simulations employed different learning algorithms. The violation-of-expectation/simple-search algorithm was error-driven, with the network learning based on discrepancies between its perceptual predictions and what it actually saw. The A-not-B algorithm was self-organizing, with the network learning based on associations between what it saw, represented, and responded to, without any particular target response. At this point, there is little consensus in the field about *the* learning algorithm to use, or whether the ultimate goal for neural modeling should even be a single algorithm. Error-driven algorithms have typically been employed by researchers primarily concerned with solving tasks, whereas self-organizing algorithms have typically been employed by researchers primarily concerned with biological feasibility. We believe that both error-driven and self-organizing aspects of learning are likely to be important for understanding cognitive phenomena, and can be implemented in a biologically plausible manner (O'Reilly, 1996, 1998).

Ongoing and future work should help to address these issues of the factors distinguishing looking and reaching, the role of latent memories in violation-of-expectation studies, and the nature of the appropriate learning algorithm(s) for understanding memory development.

CONCLUSIONS

Why do infants get better at harder tasks with hidden objects as they get older? And why should we care? Infants' seemingly intuitive task-dependent progressions raise fundamental questions about cognitive development, as revealed by the range of accounts put forth to explain them. For example, the first two approaches we discussed (discounting either infants' limitations or their successes) have very different implications for cognitive development. If we discount infants' limitations and focus on violation-of-expectation studies as true measures of infant memory, this perspective might suggest that either infants learn about hidden objects relatively quickly and early, perhaps based on observation of the world, or they possess innate knowledge about the permanence of hidden objects. In contrast, if we discount infants' early successes and focus on search studies as true measures of infant memory, this perspective might suggest that infants learn about the continued existence of hidden objects relatively slowly or late, perhaps through manipulating objects, navigating around their environments, and so forth. These approaches clearly support very different claims about the origins of our knowledge of the permanence of objects.

We argue that these two approaches are inappropriately narrow, and that both infants' successes and failures should provide important constraints on theorizing about infant memory. Various approaches within this spirit (graded memory, distinct types of memory, and separate pathways) similarly have very different implications for cognitive development. For example, the graded memory approach allows for the possibility that very young infants remember hidden objects in violation-of-expectation studies while nonetheless requiring strengthing of these memories to reach for hidden objects. The distinct types of memory approach posits that development in qualitatively different types of memory underlies infants' performance in various tasks. The separate pathways approach makes specific, testable claims about the organization of the mind. All of these approaches challenge the notion of a single definition of infant memory for hidden objects, and of a single transition point in development when infants could be said to remember hidden objects or to know about the permanence of objects.

The study of infants' memory for hidden objects has advanced all of these important issues regarding the nature of cognitive development. Although many of the details of these issues remain unresolved, we hope that we have conveyed why puzzles of task-dependent behavior in general, and of infants' task-dependent memory for hidden objects in particular, are fascinating ones that are worth resolving (despite their ability to seem intuitive, or even uninteresting, at first blush!) Further, we hope that we have conveyed the potential of graded, active and latent memories for explaining such task-dependent behaviors, and the promise of empirical and simulation work for advancing our understanding of these windows onto the nature of cognitive development.

ACKNOWLEDGMENTS

Portions of this research were supported by McDonnell-Pew research grant 93–29. Preparation of this chapter was supported by research grants from NIMH (1RO3 MH59066–01), NICHD (1R29 HD37163–01), and NSF

(IBN-9873492). We thank Randy O'Reilly, Dick Bogartz, and Denis Mareschal for useful comments and discussions.

REFERENCES

Ahmed, A., & Ruffman, T. (1998). Why do infants make A not B errors in a search task, yet show memory for the location of hidden objects in a non-search task? *Developmental Psychology, 34,* 441–453.

Aslin, R. (1981). Development of smooth pursuit in human infants. In D. Fisher, R. Monty, & E. Senders (Eds.), *Eye movements: Cognition and visual perception* (pp. 31–51). Hillsdale, NJ: Lawrence Erlbaum Associates.

Aslin, R. (1993). Commmentary: The strange attractiveness of dynamic systems to development. In L. B. Smith & E. Thelen (Eds.), *A dynamic systems approach to development: Applications* (pp. 385–399). Cambridge, MA: MIT Press.

Baillargeon, R. (1986). Representing the existence and the location of hidden objects: Object permanence in 6- and 8-month-old infants. *Cognition, 23,* 221–41.

Baillargeon, R. (1987a). Object permanence in 3. 5- and 4. 5-month-old infants. *Developmental Psychology, 23,* 655–664.

Baillargeon, R. (1987b). Young infants' reasoning about the physical and spatial properties of a hidden object. *Cognitive Development, 2,* 179–200.

Baillargeon, R. (1991). Reasoning about the height and location of a hidden object in 4.5- and 6.5-month-old infants. *Cognition, 38,* 13–42.

Baillargeon, R. (1993). The object concept revisited: New directions in the investigation of infants' physical knowledge. In C. Granrud (Ed.), *Visual perception and cognition in infancy. Carnegie Mellon Symposia on Cognition.* Hillsdale, NJ: Lawrence Erlbaum Associates.

Baillargeon, R., & Aguiar, A. (1998). Toward a general model of perseveration in infancy. *Developmental Science, 1,* 190–191.

Baillargeon, R., DeVos, J., & Graber, M. (1989). Location memory in 8-month-old infants in a non-search AB task: Further evidence. *Cognitive Development, 4,* 345–367.

Baillargeon, R., & Graber, M. (1988). Evidence of location memory in 8-month-old infants in a non-search AB task. *Developmental Psychology, 24,* 502–511.

Baillargeon, R., Graber, M., DeVos, J., & Black, J. (1990). Why do young infants fail to search for hidden objects? *Cognition, 36,* 255–284.

Baillargeon, R., Spelke, E., & Wasserman, S. (1985). Object permanence in five-month-old infants. *Cognition, 20,* 191–208.

Banks, M., & Salapatek, P. (1983). Infant visual perception. In M. M. Haith & J. J. Campos (Eds.), *Infancy and developmental psychobiology* (pp. 435–572). New York: Wiley. 4th edition.

Bertenthal, B. I. (1996). Origins and early development of perception, action, and representation. *Annual Review of Psychology, 47,* 431–459.

Bogartz, R. S., & Shinskey, J. L. (1998). On perception of a partially occluded object in 6-month-olds. *Cognitive Development, 13,* 141–163.

Bogartz, R. S., Shinskey, J. L., & Schilling, T. (2000). Object permanence in five-and-a-half month old infants? *Infancy, 1,* 403–428.

Bogartz, R. S., Shinskey, J. L., & Speaker, C. (1997). Interpreting infant looking: The event set X event set design. *Developmental Psychology, 33*(3), 408–422.

Bremner, J. G., & Knowles, L. S. (1984). Piagetian stage IV errors with an object that is directly accessible both visually and manually. *Perception, 13,* 307–314.

Butterworth, G. (1974). *The development of the object concept in human infants.* Unpublished doctoral dissertation, University of Oxford.

Butterworth, G. (1977). Object disappearance and error in Piaget's stage IV task. *Journal of Experimental Child Psychology, 23,* 391–401.

Clifton, R. K., Muir, D. W., Ashmead, D. H., & Clarkson, M. G. (1993). Is visually guided reaching in early infancy a myth? *Child Development, 64,* 1099–1110.

Clifton, R. K., Rochat, P., Litovsky, R. Y., & Perris, E. E. (1991). Object representation guides infants' reaching in the dark. *Journal of Experimental Psychology: Human Perception and Performance, 17,* 319–323.

Cohen, J. D., Perlstein, W. M., Braver, T. S., Nystrom, L. E., Noll, D. C., Jonides, J., & Smith, E. E. (1997). Temporal dynamics of brain activation during a working memory task. *Nature, 386,* 604–608.

De Haan, E. H., Young, A. W., & Newcombe, F. (1987). Face recognition without awareness. *Cognitive Neuropsychology, 4,* 385–415.

Diamond, A. (1983). Behavior changes between 6–12 months of age: What can they tell us about how the mind of the infant is changing? *Dissertation Abstracts International, 44*(01B), 337. (University Microfilms No. AAD8311882).

Diamond, A. (1985). Development of the ability to use recall to guide action, as indicated by infants' performance on AB. *Child Development, 56,* 868–883.

Diamond, A. (1991). Neuropsychological insights into the meaning of object concept development. In S. Carey & R. Gelman (Eds.), *The epigenesis of mind* (pp. 67–110). Hillsdale, NJ: Lawrence Erlbaum Associates.

Diamond, A. (1998). Understanding the A-not-B error: Working memory vs. reinforced response, or active trace vs. latent trace. *Developmental Science, 1,* 185–189.

Elman, J., Bates, E., Karmiloff-Smith, A., Johnson, M., Parisi, D., & Plunkett, K. (1996). *Rethinking innateness: A connectionist perspective on development.* Cambridge, MA: MIT Press.

Elman, J. L. (1990). Finding structure in time. *Cognitive Science, 14,* 179–211.

Evans, W. F. (1973). The stage-IV error in Piaget's theory of object concept development: An investigation of the role of activity. *Dissertation Abstracts International, 34*(11B), 5651. (University Microfilms No. AAD74–11845).

Fantz, R. (1964). Visual experience in infants: Decreased attention to familiar patterns relative to novel ones. *Science, 146,* 668–670.

Farah, M. J., Monheit, M. A., & Wallace, M. A. (1991). Unconscious perception of "extinguished" visual stimuli: Reassessing the evidence. *Neuropsychologia, 29*(10), 949–958.

Farah, M. J., O'Reilly, R. C., & Vecera, S. P. (1993). Dissociated overt and covert recognition as an emergent property of a lesioned neural network. *Psychological Review, 100,* 571–588.

Fischer, K. W., & Bidell, T. (1991). Constraining nativist inferences about cognitive capacities. In S. Carey & R. Gelman (Eds.), *The epigenesis of mind* (pp. 199–236). Hillsdale, NJ: Lawrence Erlbaum Associates.

Fuster, J. (1989). *The prefrontal cortex* (2nd edition). New York: Raven Press.

Goldman-Rakic, P. S. (1987). Circuitry of primate prefrontal cortex and regulation of behavior by representational memory. In F. Plum & V. Mountcastle (Eds.), *Handbook of physiology: The nervous system V* (pp. 373–417). Bethesda, MD: American Physiological Society.

Goodale, M. A., & Milner, A. D. (1992). Separate visual pathways for perception and action. *Trends in Neuroscience, 15*(1), 20–25.

Haith, M. M., & Benson, J. (1997). Infant cognition. In R. Siegler & D. Kuhn (Eds.), *Cognition, perception, and language* (pp. 199–254). New York: Wiley.

Haith, M. M., Hazan, C., & Goodman, G. (1988). Expectation and anticipation of dynamic visual events by 3.5-month-old babies. *Child Development, 59,* 467–479.

Harris, P. L. (1974). Perseverative search at a visibly empty place by young infants. *Journal of Experimental Child Psychology, 18,* 535–42.

Hofstadter, M. C., & Reznick, J. S. (1996). Response modality affects human infant delayed-response performance. *Child Development, 67,* 646–658.

Hofsten, C. v. (1984). Developmental changes in the organization of prereaching movements. *Developmental Psychology, 20,* 378–388.

Hood, B., & Willatts, P. (1986). Reaching in the dark to an object's remembered position: Evidence for object permanence in 5-month-old infants. *British Journal of Developmental Psychology, 4,* 57–65.

Jordan, M. I. (1986). Attractor dynamics and parallelism in a connectionist sequential machine. *Proceedings of the Eighth Annual Conference of the Cognitive Science Society* (pp. 531–546). Hillsdale, NJ: Lawrence Erlbaum Associates.

Lecuyer, R., Abgueguen, I., & Lemarie, C. (1992). 9- and 5-month-olds do not make the AB error if not required to manipulate objects. In C. Rovee-Collier (Ed.), *Abstracts of papers presented at the eighth international conference on infant studies.* Norwood, NJ: Ablex.

Mareschal, D., Plunkett, K., & Harris, P. (1995). Developing object permanence: A connectionist model. *Proceedings of the Seventeenth Annual Conference of the Cognitive Science Society* (pp. 170–175). Hillsdale, NJ: Lawrence Erlbaum Associates.

Matthews, A. (1992). Infants' performance on two versions of AB: Is recall memory a critical factor? In C. Rovee-Collier (Ed.), *Abstracts of papers presented at the eighth international conference on infant studies.* Norwood, NJ: Ablex.

Maunsell, J. H., & Newsome, W. T. (1987). Visual processing in monkey extrastriate cortex. *Annual Review of Neuroscience, 10,* 363–401.

McCloskey, M. (1991). Networks and theories: The place of connectionism in cognitive science. *Psychological Science, 2,* 387–395.

Meltzoff, A. S., & Moore, K. M. (1998). Object representation, identity, and the paradox of early permanence: Steps toward a new framework. *Infant Behavior & Development, 21,* 201–235.

Miller, E. K., & Desimone, R. (1994). Parallel neuronal mechanisms for short-term memory. *Science, 263,* 520–522.

Munakata, Y. (1997). Perseverative reaching in infancy: The roles of hidden toys and motor history in the AB task. *Infant Behavior and Development, 20*(3), 405–416.

Munakata, Y. (1998a). Infant perseveration and implications for object permanence theories: A PDP model of the AB task. *Developmental Science, 1,* 161–184.

Munakata, Y. (1998b). Infant perseveration: Rethinking data, theory, and the role of modelling. *Developmental Science, 1,* 205–212.

Munakata, Y. (2001). Task-dependency in infant behavior: Toward an understanding of the processes underlying cognitive development. In F. Lacerda, C. v. Hofsten, & M. Heimann (Eds.), *Emerging cognitive abilities in early infancy* (pp. 29–52). Mahwah, NJ: Lawrence Erlbaum Associates.

Munakata, Y., McClelland, J. L., Johnson, M. H., & Siegler, R. (1997). Rethinking infant knowledge: Toward an adaptive process account of successes and failures in object permanence tasks. *Psychological Review, 104*(4), 686–713.

Munakata, Y., Spelke, E., Jonsson, B., von Hofsten, C., & O'Reilly, R. C. (in preparation). Graded object representations guide infants' reaching for occluded objects.

Munakata, Y., & Stedron, J. M. (2001). Neural network models of cognitive development. In C. A. Nelson & M. Luciana (Eds.), *Handbook of developmental cognitive neuroscience* (pp. 159–171). Cambridge, MA: MIT Press.

O'Reilly, R. C. (1996). Biologically plausible error-driven learning using local activation differences: The generalized recirculation algorithm. *Neural Computation, 8*(5), 895–938.

O'Reilly, R. C. (1998). Six principles for biologically-based computational models of cortical cognition. *Trends in Cognitive Sciences, 2*(11), 455–462.

O'Reilly, R. C., & Munakata, Y. (2000). *Computational explorations in cognitive neuroscience: Understanding the mind by simulating the brain.* Cambridge, MA: MIT Press.

Piaget, J. (1954). *The construction of reality in the child.* New York: Basic Books.

Rosander, K., & Hofsten, C. v. (1994). *Developing an ability to stabilize gaze during body motion and/or motion of the visual field.* Paper presented at the IXth Biennial International Conference for Infant Studies, Paris, France.

Rumelhart, D. E., & McClelland, J. L. (1986). PDP models and general issues in cognitive science. In D. E. Rumelhart, J. L. McClelland, & PDP Research Group (Eds.), *Parallel distributed processing. Volume 1: Foundations* (ch. 4, pp. 110–146). Cambridge, MA: MIT Press.

Schacter, D., & Moscovitch, M. (1984). Infants, amnesiacs, and dissociable memory systems. In M. Moscovitch (Ed.), *Advances in the study of communication and affect: Vol. 9. Infant memory* (pp. 173–216). New York: Plenum.

Seidenberg, M. (1993). Connectionist models and cognitive theory. *Psychological Science, 4*(4), 228–235.

Shinskey, J. (1999). *Why do young infants fail to search for hidden objects?* PhD thesis, University of Massachusetts, Amherst.

Smith, L. B., Thelen, E., Titzer, B., & McLin, D. (1999). Knowing in the context of acting: The task dynamics of the A-not-B error. *Psychological Review, 106*, 235–260.

Sophian, C., & Yengo, L. (1985). Infants' search for visible objects: Implications for the interpretation of early search errors. *Journal of Experimental Child Psychology, 40*, 260–278.

Spelke, E. (1985). Preferential looking methods as tools for the study of cognition in infancy. In G. Gottlieb, & N. Krasnegor (Eds.), *Measurement of audition and vision in the first year of postnatal life* (pp. 323–363). Norwood, NJ: Ablex.

Spelke, E., Breinlinger, K., Macomber, J., & Jacobson, K. (1992). Origins of knowledge. *Psychological Review, 99*, 605–632.

Spelke, E., Vishton, P., & von Hofsten, C. (1995). Object perception, object-directed action, and physical knowledge in infancy. In M. Gazzaniga (Ed.), *The cognitive neurosciences* (pp. 165–179). Cambridge: MIT Press.

Steinmetz, M., Connor, C., Constantinidis, C., & McLaughlin, J. (1994). Covert attention suppresses neuronal responses in area 7a of the posterior parietal cortex. *Journal of Neurophysiology, 72*(2), 1020–1023.

Thelen, E., Corbetta, D., Kamm, K., Spencer, J. P., Schneider, K., & Zernicke, R. F. (1993). The transition to reaching: Mapping intention and intrinsic dynamics. *Child Development, 64,* 1058–1098.

Thelen, E., & Smith, L. B. (1994). *A dynamic systems approach to the development of cognition and action.* Cambridge, MA: MIT Press.

Ungerleider, L. G., & Mishkin, M. (1982). Two cortical visual systems. In D. J. Ingle, M. A. Goodale, & R. J. W. Mansfield (Eds.), *Analysis of visual behavior* (Chap. 18, pp. 549–587). Cambridge, MA: MIT Press.

Volpe, B. T., LeDoux, J. E., & Gazzaniga, M. S. (1979). Information processing of visual stimuli in an "extinguished" field. *Nature, 282,* 722–724.

von Hofsten, C., Spelke, E., Feng, Q., & Vishton, P. (1994). *Predictive reaching for occluded objects.* Paper presented at the IXth Biennial International Conference for Infant Studies, Paris, France.

Wellman, H. M., Cross, D., & Bartsch, K. (1986). Infant search and object permanence: A meta-analysis of the A-Not-B error. *Monographs of the Society for Research in Child Development, 51*(3, Serial No. 214).

Willatts, P. (1990). Development of problem-solving strategies in infancy. In D. F. Bjorklund (Ed.), *Children's strategies: Contemporary views of cognitive development* (ch. 2, pp. 23–66). Hillsdale, NJ: Lawrence Erlbaum Associates.

Wynn, K. (1992). Addition and subtraction by human infants. *Nature, 358,* 749–750.

3

Connectionist Methods in Infancy Research

Denis Mareschal
Birkbeck College

The real challenge for developmental psychology is to explain how and why behaviors emerge. Suppose, for example, that you want to understand what causes an infant to look more at one stimulus than another, or how it is that infants develop language abilities so quickly. Perhaps you wish to know why infants appear to have sophisticated knowledge of hidden objects if tested visually but not if tested manually, or how they learn to organize the world into categories. There are many ways to tackle these questions. One long-standing approach has been to describe infant competence across different domains in great detail in the hopes that, by establishing the milestones of development, some kind of causal explanation will emerge from a synthesis of the data.

This chapter reviews a very different approach. This alternative approach consists in positing a set of mechanisms for learning, and implementing these mechanisms as a working computer model (a computer program). The model then provides a tangible tool for exploring whether behaviors can emerge or be caused by the interaction of this set of well-defined mechanisms with some equally well-defined learning environment.

Although this methodology is still relatively rare, the use of computer modeling in developmental psychology is not new (e.g., Boden, 1980; Klahr & Wallace, 1976; Mareschal & Shultz, 1996; McClelland, 1989; Papert, 1963; Shultz, Schmidt, Buckingham, & Mareschal, 1995; Simon, 1962; Young, 1976). Until recently, there have been few attempts to model infant development. This is somewhat surprising because infancy is such a rich period of development in which many behaviors are closely tied to perceptual and motor development, and there is a long history of providing computational models of perceptual and motor abilities in adults (e.g., Posner, 1989).

This chapter reviews four computational models of infant behaviors. They are all constructed using connectionist computational modeling tools. Connectionist models are loosely based on neural information processing. The four models focus on behaviors across a range of different domains. They are presented in order of complexity, from the simplest to the most complex. At each model, a new aspect of connectionist modeling is introduced. The topics covered are infant categorization, phoneme discrimination, object permanence, and the perception of object unity. Before describing the models, the computer modeling methodology is presented in more detail, and basic connectionist information processing is reviewed.

THE COMPUTER MODELING METHODOLOGY

Computer models go hand in hand with solid empirical work. They are not meant—in any way—to supercede rigorous experiments with infants. A model must be based on solid empirical data. In turn, the model can be used to guide decisions about future research. The basic methodology is as follows. First, a specific target domain (or a well-delimited set of behaviors) is identified. These behaviors form the starting point of the modeling endeavor. There is no point initially trying to model too broad a range of behaviors because the model will become so complex that it will lose any explanatory value. Second, any existing data must be collected and studied to develop a prototheory of the underlying mechanisms. Modeling is not an atheoretical activity. Models implement theories of how information is processed. Without such a theory, it is not possible to build a model.

The third step is to implement the prototheory as a working computational model. This is the richest interaction stage between the model and the data. More often than not, the initial attempt to implement a theory leads to failure. This failure signals that the theory must be revised (perhaps by changing the learning mechanisms or the environmental constraints on learning), or that further empirical work must be carried out to clarify some unforeseen point. Finally, once the existing behaviors have been captured to an acceptable level, the model can be used to predict novel behaviors in untested or untestable contexts. One further possibility is to damage the model and explore the kinds of developmental disorders that can emerge as a result of damage at different stages of development.

As a final stage, the generality of the principles embodied in the model can be evaluated. This is accomplished by trying to extend the processing principles of the specific model to different (but related) domains. Although the existing model will not be a model of behaviors in the new domains, it may provide a pointer as to how information is processed in these new domains.

Finally, it is important to remember that building a model of infant behaviors does not mean building an infant. Any model necessarily embodies a number of approximations and simplifications. The degree to which any approximation is justified depends on the nature of the task being modeled and the degree to which the task is already understood.

WHY CONNECTIONIST MODELS?

There are many computational modeling paradigms that can be used to address issues in infancy research (e.g., Drescher, 1991; Rutkowska, 1995; Simon, 1998). Throughout most of the 1970s and 1980s, it was argued that cognition and perhaps even perception could be studied independently of the neural substrate (e.g., Broadbent, 1985; Fodor, 1983; Pylyshyn, 1984). Although cognition and perception were necessarily related to neural activity, the link was believed to be so distant that it would not be fruitful to include neural constraints in any models. *What* was being computed in a task (the computational level) was separate from *how* it was being computed (the algorithmic level) and in what *physical medium* the computations were carried out (the implementational level; Marr, 1982).

However, although it is true that radically different algorithms can be implemented in identical substrates,[1] some algorithms are more naturally consistent with a neural substrate than others. Resource limitations at the lower levels of processing (the algorithmic and the implementational levels) will filter up to constrain how plausible it is to do something at the computational level. In short, there is no getting away from the fact that some things are easier to do in a neural medium than other things.

Connectionist models are computer models loosely based on the principles of neural information processing (Elman, Bates, Johnson, Karmiloff-Smith, Parisi, & Plunkett, 1996; McLeod, Plunkett, & Rolls, 1998; Rumelhart & McClellend, 1986). They are not intended to be neural models. They embody general principles such as inhibition and excitation within a distributed, parallel processing system. They attempt to strike the balance

---

[1]E.g., a rule processing system can be implemented in a neural network, or conversely, a parallel processing neural network can be simulated on a serial symbol processing machine.

between importing some of the key ideas from the neurosciences while maintaining sufficiently discrete and definable components to allow questions about behavior to be formulated in terms of a high-level cognitive computational framework.

From a developmental perspective, connectionist networks are ideal for modeling because they develop their own internal representations as a result of interacting with an environment (Plunkett & Sinha, 1992). However, these networks are not simply tabula rasa empirical learning machines. The representations they develop can be strongly determined by initial constraints. These constraints can take the form of different associative learning mechanisms attuned to specific information in the environment (e.g., temporal correlations or spatial correlations), or they can take the form of architectural constraints that guide the flow of information in the system. Although connectionist modeling has its roots in associationist learning paradigms, it has inherited the Hebbian rather than the Hullian tradition. That is, what goes on *inside* the box (inside the network) is as important in determining the overall behavior of the networks as is the correlation between the inputs (stimuli) and the outputs (responses).

CONNECTIONIST INFORMATION PROCESSING

Connectionist networks are made up of simple processing units interconnected via weighted communication lines. Units are often represented as circles, and the weighted communication lines as lines between these circles. Activation flows from unit to unit via these connection weights. Figure 3.1a shows a generic connectionist network in which activation can flow in any direction. However, most applications of connectionist networks impose constraints on the way activation can flow. These constraints are in the form of which unit can connect to which other unit.

Figure 3.1b shows a typical feedforward network. Activation (information) is constrained to move in one direction only. Some units (those units through which information enters the network) are called *input units.* Other units (those units through which information leaves the network) are called *output units.* All other units are called *hidden units.* In a feedforward network, information is first encoded as a pattern of activation across the bank of input units. That activation then filters up through a first layer of weights until it produces a pattern of activation across the band of hidden units. The pattern of activation produced across the hidden units constitutes an *internal re-representation* of the information originally presented to the network. The activation at the hidden units continues to flow through the network until it reaches the output units. The

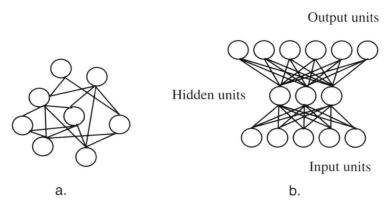

FIG. 3.1.   (a) A generic and (b) a feedforward connectionist network.

pattern of activation produced at the output units is taken as the network's response to the initial input.

Each unit is a very simple processor that mimics the functioning of an idealized neuron. The unit sums the weighted activation arriving into it. It then sets it own level of activation according to some nonlinear function of that weighted sum. The nonlinearity allows the units to respond differently to different ranges of input values. The key idea of connectionist modeling is that of collective computations. That is, although the behavior of the individual components in the network is simple, the behavior of the network as a whole can be very complex. It is the behavior of the network as a whole that is taken to model different aspects of infant development.

For a given type of unit, the network's behavior is determined by the connection weights. As activation flows through the network, it is transformed by the set of connection weights between successive layers in the network. Thus, learning (i.e., adapting one's behavior) is accomplished by tuning the connection weights until some stable state of behavior is obtained. *Supervised* networks adjust their weights until the output response (for a given input) matches a target response. That target can be obtained from an explicit teacher, or it can arise from the environment, but it must come from outside the system. *Unsupervised* networks adjust their weights until some internal constraint is satisfied (e.g., maximally different input must have maximally different internal representations). *Backpropagation* (Rumelhart, Hinton, & Williams, 1986) is a popular training algorithm for supervised networks. Backpropagation estimates the contribution of each connection weight in the network to the overall output error. It then adjusts the weights, one at a time, in a direction that is most likely to reduce the overall error. Good introductions to Backpropagation can be found throughout the literature (e.g., Plunkett & Elman, 1997; McLeod, Plunkett, & Rolls, 1998).

Through this adaptation process, the connection weights come to encode regularities in the network's environment. Networks are very sensitive to the statistical distribution of relevant features in their environment. In fact, the weight adjustment procedure in a network without any hidden units is equivalent to linear regression. These networks are implicitly finding a linear combination of the input features that best predicts each of the output values. With hidden units, the networks are implicitly computing a nonlinear function regression. A feedforward network with a single layer of hidden units can approximate arbitrarily well any finite output response function, given enough hidden units (Cybenko, 1989). Further details of the similarities between connectionist network learning and statistical learning procedures can be found elsewhere (e.g., Hertz, Krogh, & Palmer, 1991).

In some senses, there are two levels of knowledge in a network. The connection weights encode generalities about the problem that have been accumulated over repeated encounters with the environment. One can think of this as a form of long-term memory or category specific knowledge as opposed to knowledge about a particular task or object. In contrast, the pattern of activation that arises in response to inputs encodes information about the current state of the world. Internal representations are determined by an interaction between the current input (activation across the input units) and previous experience as encoded in the connection weights. A good illustration of this is Munakata's (1998) model of the A-not-B error. Munakata discussed infant reaching errors in terms of "latent memory" (connection weights) and "active memory" (activation levels) in connectionist networks.

Many connectionist networks are very simple. They may contain only some 100 units. This is not to suggest that the part of the brain solving the corresponding task has only 100 neurons! It is important to understand that most connectionist models are not intended as neural models, but rather as information processing models of behavior. The models constitute examples of how systems with similar computational properties to the brain can give rise to a set of observed behaviors. Sometimes, individual units are taken to represent pools of neurons or cell assemblies. According to this interpretation, the activation level of the units corresponds to the proportion of neurons firing in the pool (e.g., Changeux & Dehaene, 1989).

Armed with this basic outline of connectionist information processing, four connectionist models are described next. The first is a model of infant categorization. It illustrates how internal representations are driven by the distributional properties of the examples encountered by a network.

The second is a model of phoneme discrimination. It illustrates how prior learning constrains performance on subsequent tasks. The third is a model of infant responses to occluded objects. It illustrates how functional modularity can emerge through initial mechanistic constraints. The fourth is a model of the perception of object unity and it illustrates how substantial innate knowledge can be incorporated within a connectionist model.

MECHANISMS OF CATEGORIZATION IN EARLY INFANCY

This section presents a simple connectionist model of categorization in early infancy. This is one of the most basic connectionist models and illustrates the nature of information processing in these networks.

A General Model of Preferential Looking and Habituation Behaviors

Infant categorization tasks rely on preferential looking or habituation techniques based on the finding that infants direct more attention to unfamiliar or unexpected stimuli. The standard interpretation of this behavior is that infants are comparing an input stimulus to an internal representation of the same stimulus (e.g., Charlesworth, 1969; Cohen, 1973; Sokolov, 1963). As long as there is a discrepancy between the information stored in the internal representation and the visual input, the infant continues to attend to the stimulus. While attending to the stimulus, the infant updates its internal representation. When the information in the internal representation is no longer discrepant with the visual input, attention is directed elsewhere. This process is illustrated in Fig. 3.2. When a familiar object is presented, there is little or no attending because the infant already has a reliable internal representation of that object. In contrast, when an unfamiliar or unexpected object is presented, there is more attending because an internal representation has to be constructed or adjusted. The degree to which a novel object differs from existing internal representations determines the amount of adjusting that has to be done, and hence the duration of attention.

We (Mareschal & French, 1997; Mareschal, French, & Quinn, 2000) used a connectionist autoencoder to model the relation between attention and representation construction. An *autoencoder* is a feedforward connectionist network with a single layer of hidden units (Fig. 3.2b). It is called an autoencoder because it associates an input with itself. The network learns to reproduce on the output units the pattern of activation across the input units. It relies on a supervised learning algorithm, but because the input signal serves as the training signal for the output units, no teacher

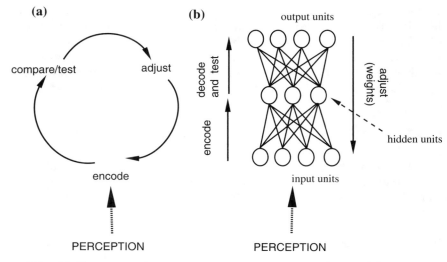

FIG. 3.2.   The process of representation construction in (a) infants and (b) autoencoder networks.

other than the environment is hypothesized. In an autoencoder, the number of hidden units is smaller than the number of input or output units. This produces a bottleneck in the flow of information through the network, forcing the network to develop a more compact internal representation of the input (at the hidden unit level) that is sufficiently rich to reproduce all the information in the original input. Information is first compressed into an internal representation and then expanded to reproduce the original input. The successive cycles of training in the autoencoder are an iterative process by which a reliable internal representation of the input is developed. The reliability of the representation is tested by expanding the representation and comparing the resulting predictions to the actual stimulus being encoded. Similar networks have been used to produce compressed representations of video images (Cottrell, Munro, & Zipser, 1988).

We suggested that during the period of captured attention, infants are actively involved in an iterative process of encoding the visual input into an internal representation and then assessing that representation against the continuing perceptual input. This is accomplished by using the internal representation to predict what the properties of the stimulus are. As long as the representation fails to predict the stimulus properties, the infant continues to fixate the stimulus and to update the internal representations (see also Di Lollo, Enns, & Rensink, 2000, for a similar account of adult object recognition).

This approach to modeling novelty preference has several implications. It suggests that infant looking times are positively correlated with the network error. The greater the error, the longer the looking time. Stimuli presented for a very short time will be encoded less well than those presented for a longer period. However, prolonged exposure after error (attention) has fallen off will not improve memory of the stimulus. The degree to which error (looking time) increases on presentation of a novel object depends on the similarity between the novel object and the familiar object. Presenting a series of similar objects leads to a progressive error drop on future similar objects. All of this is true of both autoencoders (where output error is the measurable quantity) and infants (where looking time is the measurable quantity).

The Acquisition of Perceptual Categories in Early Infancy

Categories and concepts facilitate learning and reasoning by partitioning the world into manageable units. Even 3- to 4-month-olds have been shown to categorize a range of real world images. Research by Quinn and Eimas demonstrated that these infants can categorize photographs of cats, dogs, horses, birds, tables, and chairs (see Quinn & Eimas, 1996, for a review). However, the perceptual categories do not always have the same characteristics as might be expected from the adult concepts. In particular, the extension and exclusivity of infant categories (i.e., the range of exemplars accepted or rejected as members of the category) may differ from that of adult categories.

Quinn, Eimas, and Rosenkrantz (1993) used a familiarization/novelty-preference technique to determine if the perceptual categories of familiar animals (e.g., cats and dogs) acquired by young infants would exclude perceptually similar exemplars from contrasting basic-level categories. They found that when 3- to 4-month-olds are familiarized with six pairs of cat photographs presented sequentially (12 photographs), the infants will subsequently prefer to look at a novel dog photograph rather than a novel cat photograph. Because infants prefer to look at unfamiliar stimuli (Fantz, 1964), this was interpreted as showing that the infants had developed a category of cat that included novel cats (hence less looking at the cat photograph) but excluded novel dogs (hence more looking at the dog photograph). However, if the infants are initially familiarized with six pairs of dog photographs sequentially (12 photographs), they will show no subsequent preference for looking at either a novel dog or a novel cat. Furthermore, control conditions revealed that: (a) the infants would prefer to look at a novel test bird after initial familiarization with either dogs or cats, (b) there is no a priori preference for dogs over cats, and (c) the infants are able to discriminate within the cat and dog categories. Taken together, these findings led Quinn et al. to suggest that the 3- to 4-month-olds had formed a perceptual category of dog that included novel dogs but also included novel cats. Mareschal et al. (2000) suggested that performance on these categorization tasks reflects the way in which information is stored in an associative system with distributed representations. The model described next was built to test this hypothesis.

Building the Model

The modeling results reported here are based on the performance of a standard 10–8–10 feedforward backpropagation network and are reported in more detail elsewhere (Mareschal & French, 1997; Mareschal et al., 2000). The data for training the networks were obtained from measurements of the original cat and dog pictures used by Quinn et al. (1993). There were 18 dogs and 18 cats classified according to the following ten traits: head length, head width, eye separation, ear separation, ear length, nose length, nose width, leg length, vertical extent, and horizontal extent.

Networks were trained for a fixed 250 epochs per pair of stimuli. This was done to reflect the fact that in the Quinn and Eimas studies, infants were shown pictures for a fixed duration of time. The results are averaged over 50 network replications, each with random initial weights.

Twelve items from one category were presented sequentially to the network in groups of two (i.e., weights were updated in batches of two) to capture the fact that pairs of pictures were presented to the infants during the familiarization trials. The remaining six items from each category were used to test whether the networks had formed categorical representations.

The Development of Cat and Dog Categories.   Like infants, these networks form both cat and dog categories. Figure 3.3 shows the initial error score (the *sum-squared-error* across output units), the error score after twelve presentations of either cats or dogs, and the average error score (after training) for the six remaining exemplars in either the cat or dog category. After learning, error is lower, suggesting that the network has developed a reliable internal representation of cats or dogs. The generalization error rises slightly, showing that the networks recognize these exemplars as novel. Infants are also able to distinguish individual exemplars within the category (Quinn et al., 1993). However, the generalization error remains well below the initial error, suggesting that the new exemplars are assimilated within the category representation formed by the networks across the hidden units.

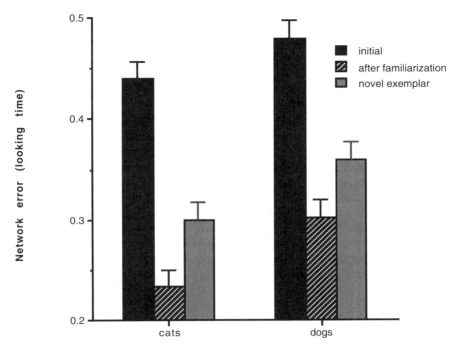

FIG. 3.3.   Network responses to CAT and DOG exemplars before and after category learning.

The Asymmetric Exclusivity of the Cat and Dog Categories.   Quinn et al. (1993) found that there was an asymmetry in the exclusivity of the cat and dog categories developed by infants. Figure 3.4 shows what happens when networks trained on cats are presented with a novel cat and a dog, and when networks trained on dogs are tested with a novel dog and a cat. When the networks are initially trained on cats, the presentation of a dog results in a large error score, corresponding to the results observed with infants in terms of a longer looking time. Dogs are not included within the category representation of cats. In contrast, when the networks are initially trained on dogs, the presentation of a cat results in only a small increase in error, suggesting that the cats have been included in the dog category.

The Source of the Asymmetry.   One advantage of building a model is that it can be taken apart to explore what causes the observed behaviors. Connectionist networks extract the correlations between features present in their learning environment. The variation of the internal representations (developed across the hidden units) reflects the variation of the corresponding categories in the environment. Figure 3.5 shows the frequency

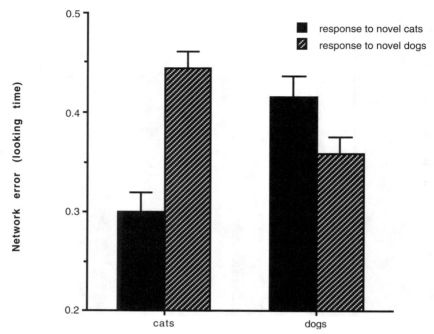

FIG. 3.4.   Asymmetric exclusivity of CAT and DOG categories.

distributions of the 10 input features for both cats and dogs. Each feature
has been fit to a normal distribution. In almost all cases the distribution for
each dog trait (represented by the dark line) subsumes the distribution
for the corresponding trait for cats. The narrower distributions for most
cat traits, on the other hand, do not subsume the range of values for
the corresponding dog traits. In other words, cats are possible dogs but the
reverse is not the case: most dogs are not possible cats.

   The key distributional feature of the data is that cat features are (in general) subsumed within the distribution of dog features. It is not just the
added variability of dogs along certain features, but the subset relationship that is crucial for explaining the asymmetry. Connectionist networks
develop internal representations that reflect the distributions of the input
features. Thus, the internal representation for cat will be subsumed within
the internal representation for dog. It is because the internal representations share this inclusion relationship that an asymmetry in error (looking
time) is observed. The behavior arises because of an interaction between
the statistics of the environment and the computational properties of the
learning algorithm.

   Mareschal et al. (2000) then used the model to explore what the effects
of learning with a mixed set of exemplars would be. They presented the

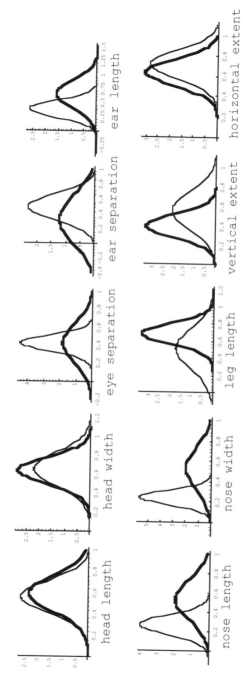

FIG. 3.5.   Normalized frequency distributions of feature values in CAT (thin line) and DOG (thick line) exemplars.

83

networks with training sets of either 8 cats and 4 dogs (the mostly-cats group), or 8 dogs and 4 cats (the mostly-dogs group). Under these conditions, the networks in the mostly-cats group developed a category that included novel cats, but excluded novel dogs. In contrast, the networks in the mostly-dog group developed a category that included novel dogs but also included novel cats. Thus, the category asymmetry was predicted to persist even when both kinds of exemplars were presented during familiarization. A further study with 48 3- to 4-month-olds revealed that this was also the case with infants, thereby confirming the model's prediction and corroborating the model as a valid mechanistic account of early infant perceptual categorizations.

In summary, this model illustrates how categorical representations of visually presented stimuli can be acquired within a testing session. An associative system that parses stimuli into distinct features and develops distributed representations will also develop categories with the same exclusivity asymmetries as 3- to 4-month-olds when presented with the same stimuli as these infants. This analysis constitutes a novel explanation of the infant data that emerges from the construction of the computational model. The model constitutes an explanation of infant categorization behaviors that can be extended to the domain of visual memory.

Developing Distinct Categories

The previous section showed how connectionist autoencoder networks can develop categories that have similar overlap structure to those developed by young infants. This section describes how that work was extended to explore the basis on which categories are developed by infants and connectionist networks given a series of exemplars. Younger (1985) showed that 10-month-olds could use the covariation between feature values to segregate items into separate categories. Although these results are based on presenting infants with line drawings of artificial animals, Younger (1990) found that these infants could still use covariation information with natural kind images. Networks similar to those in the previous section also respond to covariation information to separate categories.

These results (first reported in Mareschal & French, 2000) are based on the performance of a standard 4–3–4 (4 input units, 3 hidden units, and 4 output units) autoencoder. Networks were trained for a maximum of 200 epochs, or until all output bits were within 0.2 of their targets. This was done to reflect the fact that in the Younger (1985) studies, infants were shown pictures for a fixed duration of time rather than using a proportional looking-time criterion.

Younger (1985) examined 10-month-olds' abilities to use the correlation between the variation of attributes to segregate items into categories. In the real world, certain ranges of attribute values tend to co-occur (Rosch, Mervis, Gray, Johnson, & Boyes-Braem, 1976). Thus, animals with long necks might tend to have long legs, whereas animals with short necks might tend to have short legs. Younger examined whether infants could use such covariation cues to segment artificial animal line drawings into separate categories.

In one experiment, infants were familiarized with either (a) a set of exemplars in which any feature value could occur with any other feature value, and (b) a set of exemplars in which sets of features were constrained to covary. They were then tested with either (a) an exemplar whose attribute values were the average of all the previously experienced values along each dimension, or (b) an exemplar containing the modal attribute values (i.e., the most frequently experienced values) along each dimension. Preference for a modal versus the average stimulus was interpreted as evidence that the infants had formed a single category from all the exemplars (as evidenced by the greater familiarity of the average stimulus). Preference for the average stimulus was interpreted as evidence that the infants had formed two categories (as indicated by the lesser familiarity of the average stimulus) inasmuch as the boundary between correlated clusters lay on the average values. Younger found that 10-month-olds looked more at the modal stimuli when the familiarization set was unconstrained (i.e., all attribute values occurred with every other attribute value), suggesting that they had formed a single representation of the complete set of exemplars. However, the 10-month-olds looked more at the average stimuli when the familiarization set was constrained such that ranges of feature values were correlated, suggesting that they had formed two distinct categories.

To model infant performance in this study, the same artificial animal stimuli used by Younger were measured for presentation to the networks. The artificial animals were defined by their leg length, neck length, tail width, and ear separation. Because none of the attributes are intended to be more salient than any other attribute, each attribute was scaled to range between 0.0 to 1.0. This transformation ensures that the greater magnitude of one dimension (e.g., ear separation) does not bias the networks to attend preferentially to that dimension. Normalization was achieved by dividing each attribute value by the maximum value along that dimension.

Networks were trained in batch mode. That is, all eight familiarization items were presented as a batch to the network and the cumulative error was used to update the weights (to drive learning). This ensures that all the items in the familiarization set are weighted equally by the networks and is intended to reflect the fact that there were no significant changes in infant looking times across all familiarization trials. Batch learning also ensures that all order effects are averaged out.

Twenty-four networks were presented with eight stimuli in which the full range of values in one dimension occurred with the full range of val-

TABLE 3.1
Normalized Familiarization and Test Stimuli Used for
Training and Testing the Networks

			Familiarization Stimuli				
Broad Condition				Narrow Condition			
Legs	Neck	Tail	Ears	Legs	Neck	Tail	Ears
0.27	1.0	0.22	1.0	0.27	1.0	0.8	0.33
0.27	0.23	1.0	1.0	0.27	0.81	1.0	0.33
0.45	0.81	0.41	0.78	0.45	0.81	1.0	0.11
0.45	0.42	0.8	0.78	0.45	1.0	0.8	0.11
0.82	0.42	0.8	0.33	0.82	0.42	0.22	1.0
0.82	0.81	0.41	0.33	0.82	0.23	0.41	1.0
1.0	0.23	1.0	0.11	1.0	0.23	0.41	0.78
1.0	1.0	0.22	0.11	1.0	0.42	0.22	0.78

			Test Stimuli				
Average		0.64	0.62		0.61	0.56	
Modal1		0.27	1.0		1.0	0.11	
Modal2		1.0	0.23		0.22	1.0	

Note. Values are scaled to range from 0.0 to 1.0.

ues in the other dimension (the broad condition). Another 24 networks were presented with the eight stimuli in which restricted ranges of values were correlated (the narrow condition). The networks in both conditions were then tested with stimuli made up of the average feature values or the modal feature values. Table 3.1 shows the normalized values defining the stimuli in the broad and narrow familiarization conditions, and the three test stimuli. Figure 3.6 shows the networks' response to the average and modal test stimuli when familiarized in either the narrow or broad conditions. As with the 10-month-olds, networks familiarized in the narrow condition showed more error (preferred to look) when presented with the average test stimulus than the modal test stimuli. Similarly, as with the 10-month-olds, networks familiarized in the broad condition showed more error (preferred to look) when presented with the modal test stimuli than the average test stimuli.

Internal Representations. One advantage of computer models is that they can be taken apart to help understand what produces the observed behaviors. This section describes the internal representations developed by the networks and discusses how they lead to the observed preferential looking behaviors just described.

When an exemplar is presented to the network, activation flows from the input units to the hidden units. The pattern of activation across the

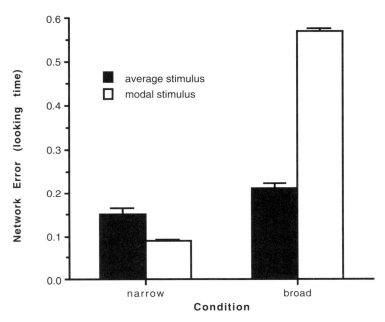

FIG. 3.6.   Network response to average and modal test stimuli when familiarized with a narrow or broad category.

hidden units is an internal representation of that input. It is the internal representation that drives the response at the output. Every exemplar produces a different activation pattern across the hidden units. One way to explore these representations is to plot them as points in a three-dimensional space. For any given input, each of the three hidden units will have some activation value. These three values can be interpreted as coordinates within that three-dimensional space. Each internal representation (arising from each separate exemplar) corresponds to a point in that space.

Figure 3.7 shows the distribution of exemplars within the hidden unit space for networks trained in the narrow and broad conditions. In the narrow condition (Fig. 3.7a), exemplars are grouped together in two distinct clusters. One cluster corresponds to those exemplars forming one category and the other cluster corresponds to those exemplars forming the second category. The test exemplars are also plotted. Note that the two modal exemplars each fall within (or very close to) one of the category clusters, whereas the average exemplar falls between the two clusters. This explains why there is more error (longer looking) to the average exemplar than to either of the modal exemplars. The modal patterns fall within areas that are well covered by the category representations, and hence, for which

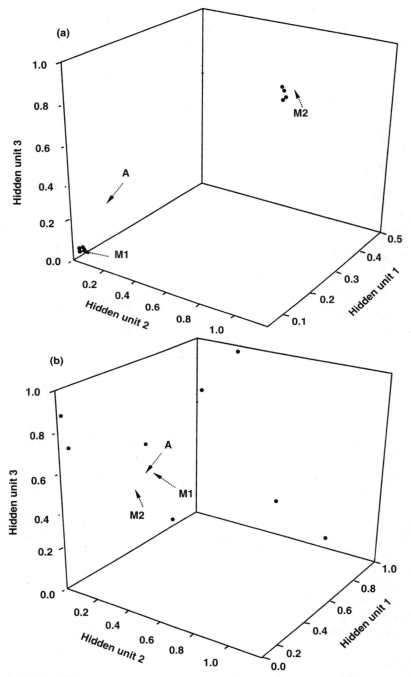

FIG. 3.7. Typical network internal representations for (a) the narrow condition and (b) the broad condition.

the network has already learned to make accurate responses. In contrast, the average pattern falls in an area that is not well covered, and hence, for which the network has no experience of making accurate responses.

Figure 3.7b shows the exemplars within hidden unit space for networks trained in the broad condition. The internal representations are spread throughout the hidden unit space, reflecting the fact that the exemplars are maximally spread out. Remember that in this condition, any feature value can occur with any other feature value. All three of the test stimuli (the average and modal stimuli) project to a similar location at the center of the space. This is because all three have comparable similarities (in terms of feature values) to all of the familiarization exemplars considered individually.

Finally, because the internal representations are located close to each other in hidden unit space, the network tends to respond to them in a similar fashion. Because they are in a sparsely populated region of the space, the network has little experience with decoding these types of internal representations. As a result, it will output an average of all the outputs it is familiar with. This is fine for the average stimulus because the correct response is precisely the average of all responses (remember that the autoencoder task requires the network to reproduce the original input values on the output units). It is completely inappropriate for the modal stimuli whose feature values lie at the ends of the possible ranges. Hence, there is more error for the modal stimuli than the average stimulus.

In summary, this set of simulations shows that connectionist autoencoder networks develop distinct categories in the same way as infants do when presented with the same stimuli as the infants. The basis for the emergence of distinct categories is the fact that connectionist networks develop internal representations that reflect the statistical distribution of features in the environment they encounter. As with infants, autoencoder networks can use feature correlation information to partition the world into distinct categories. Finally, this work introduced the notion of hidden unit space to explore the structure of the internal representations developed by a network.

PHONEME DISCRIMINATION

The models described so far demonstrate how a connectionist autoencoder extracts information in its environment and develops an internal representation. The same mechanism can be used when information arrives from different modalities or sources. For example, at some basic level, word learning consists of matching auditory input (the label) to a visual stimulus (the object). The model in this section (described in more detail in Schafer & Mareschal, 2001) explores how the integration of information from two sources impacts on the network's internal representations. The representations acquired within the context of word learning constrain the type of auditory discriminations that can subsequently be made.

A Brief Review of Phoneme Discrimination

Occasionally, development is accompanied by a reduction in a given ability rather than an improvement in that ability. This is the case with phoneme discrimination. Until the age of about 8 months, infants respond in a categorical fashion to phonemic contrasts that do not appear in their native language. However, older infants and adults find these contrasts difficult to detect (Trehub, 1976; Werker & Lalonde, 1988; Werker & Tees, 1983, 1984a, 1984b; but see Best, McRoberts, & Sithole, 1988 for a case of detection of nonnative contrasts by older infants). Werker and Pegg (1992) argued that the changes in infants' performance in such speech sound discrimination tasks are diagnostic of distinct stages in infants' speech processing.

Stager and Werker (1997) investigated the possible relationship between word learning and speech sound discrimination, using a bimodal habituation task. Infants were habituated to stimuli presented in both auditory and visual modalities—for example, a stimulus comprising a sound and an image. The authors suggested that such a task invoked the mechanisms subserving the learning of words, that is, learning that a given label (sound) goes with a given object (image). During subsequent testing, a change was made in the sound, *but not the image*. The extent to which infants dishabituated to this new sound–image combination was interpreted as an index of the specificity of the binding between the habituated sound and the (unchanged) image. Infants who have habituated to a given sound–image combination will dishabituate *only* if they perceive the difference between the sound heard during the prior habituation phase and the sound heard during the subsequent testing phase.

Stager and Werker found that within the label–object associative learning paradigm just described, 8-month-olds in an English language environment could discriminate the label [*bih*] from the label [*dih*], whereas 14-month-olds appeared unable to do so. However, the older infants *could* discriminate a more distinct pair of labels such as [*lif*] and [*neem*]. The 14-month-old infants could also discriminate [*bih*] from [*dih*] in a simple auditory discrimination task. Furthermore, the 14-month-olds were not capable of discriminating [*bih*] from [*bih*] when the task involved learning about *two* label–object tokens (i.e., [*bih*] + object 1 and [*bih*] + object 2).

Stager and Werker argued that, taken together, these data suggest a functional reorganization of the language system occurring between the ages of 8 and 14 months. As a consequence of this reorganization, infants of different ages react differently to identical stimuli. Schafer and Mareschal (in press) constructed a connectionist model to explore whether simple associative systems, whose adaptive properties do not change over time, could also account for the apparent discontinuity in processing.

Building the Model

To model infant performance, connectionist networks were taught to auto-encode labels and objects, in a homologue of looking and listening by the infant. Three-layer autoencoder networks were trained to reproduce, on their output units, the label–object pairs that had been presented at the input (Fig. 3.8). This task requires the networks to develop an internal representation across the hidden unit layer, merging the information from these two sources of information (Chauvin, 1989; Plunkett, Sinha, Møller, & Strandsby, 1992). As in the previous section, the networks were trained using the backpropagation learning algorithm. Labels were represented as consonant–vowel–consonant (CVC) strings, with each phoneme represented by six binary bits (cf. Plunkett & Marchman, 1991). The six bits

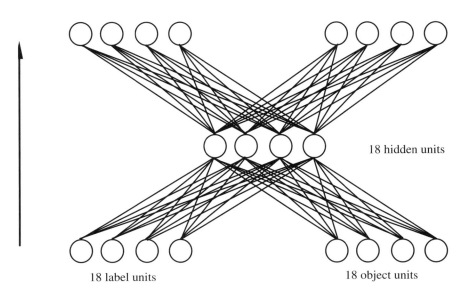

18 hidden units

18 label units   18 object units

FIG. 3.8.   Label-image autoencoder network. Not all units are shown.

represented the following features of each phoneme: consonantal (one bit), voiced (one bit), manner (two bits), place (two bits). It should be stressed that although this coding scheme is based on phonemes, it can be thought of as representing any nonarbitrary feature of words—for example, phones.

The "language" that networks were exposed to was created in the following manner: Labels were generated by randomly selecting a consonant, and then a vowel, and then a consonant, from the list of phonemes. Our artificial language comprised 240 label–object pairs. This is 5% of the $20 \times 12 \times 20 = 4800$ possible CV combinations. Object input vectors were then generated by duplicating the list of 240 18-bit label vectors, shuffling this list, and assigning each of the resultant randomly ordered object vectors to a label vector.

The networks were trained according to a two-stage procedure: a language exposure phase, and an experimental phase. Networks were initially exposed to a linguistic "environment," in which label–object pairs were successively presented to the network for a predetermined fixed period, reflecting the "age" of the network at testing. To reflect the differential language exposure of the 8- and 14-month-old infants, "older" networks received more language exposure trials before testing than did "younger" networks. Following this "language exposure" process, the experimental phase per se began. First, networks were habituated to a label–object pair. The same interpretation of habituation was used as in the previous section. Finally, after habituation, a dishabituation stimulus was presented and the error (looking time) was calculated.

"Language exposure" was modeled as follows: All the networks were trained to autoencode the same randomly generated bank of 240 label–object pairs. Following each language exposure trial, the label–object pair was returned to the bank and another pair selected at random. "Younger" networks received 1,000 such trials; older networks received 10,000 trials.

Networks were tested on a homologue of Stager and Werker's (1997) four experiments, against a background of this language exposure. The procedure for modeling Stager and Werker's Experiments 2 and 3 was as follows: During the habituation phase, a network experienced 100 habituation trials. Each habituation trial used the same label–object pair (e.g., "bih," plus a corresponding object). During the dishabituation phase, the label segment of the input vector was replaced by the to-be-tested label (e.g., "dih"). Thus, in the dishabituation phase, the network was presented with a familiar object but a novel label, as had been the case with the infants. Following Stager and Werker, we refer to this as a *switch trial*. In contrast, during a *same trial,* the label–object pair presented was the same as had been used during habituation. As described previously, the response to the novel pairing is an index of the amount of stimulus processing that has occurred during habituation, and the specificity of the binding achieved, during habituation, between label and object.

Minor modifications allowed this procedure to be used for modeling Experiments 1 and 4. In the case of Experiment 1, two label–object pairs were used in the habituation phase. In each trial, one pair was selected at random to be presented to the network. In the case of Experiment 4, all input bits coding image information were set to 0.5 (midway between the 0 and 1 binary values used to encode object information), thereby conveying no object information. These modifications correspond to analogous modifications in the procedure used by Stager and Werker for testing infants in Experiments 1 and 4.

There were 20 networks in each experimental group, all with different initial connection weights. These were randomly set at the outset to values between −1.0 and 1.0.

Model Results

Figure 3.9 illustrates the networks' performance. The model results are remarkably similar to those obtained with infants (see Stager and Werker, 1997, Fig. 1). In particular, consider the data of Experiments 2 and 3: Older networks showed poorer discrimination of the similar pair (*bih* and *dih*) than did the younger networks; the older networks were nevertheless able to discriminate the more distinct pair (*lif* and *neem*).

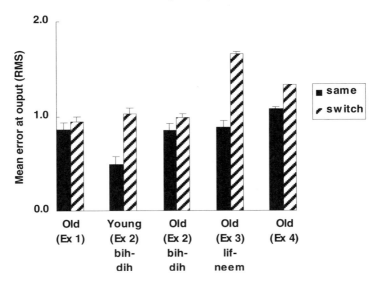

FIG. 3.9.   "Young" and "old" network performance on phoneme discrimination tasks.

To investigate the effect of language experience on the networks' responses, we compared the relative novelty preference of networks at different ages (i.e., differing degrees of language exposure) in the bih/dih and lif/neem discrimination trials. First, novelty preference was nonmonotonic with age. For both similar (bih–dih) and dissimilar pairs (lif–neem), novelty preference exhibits *two* minima in the range of language exposure evaluated. Overall, novelty preference (in the networks) reaches a minimum at around 10,000 language exposure trials, then increases again with further language exposure. This sort of nonmonotonicity is reminiscent of human behavior in the detection of nonnative speech contrasts. Young infants are initially able to make these distinctions, but lose this ability at some point before their first birthday (Werker & Tees, 1983, 1984a); nonetheless, *adults* are, in certain circumstances, able to make these distinctions (Werker & Tees, 1984b).

Second, the extent of a release from habituation in the networks follows a different time course for the two types of stimulus pairs. Assuming that release from habituation is observed when novelty preference exceeds some arbitrary but constant threshold, then there is a period during which a release from habituation will occur for dissimilar pairs but not similar pairs. We suggest that a similar mechanism may explain the difference between 8- and 14-month-olds' behavior in Stager and Werker's Experiments 2 and 3.

Further analyses suggest that the developmental profiles arise as an interaction between the computational requirements of the different test conditions (i.e., the bih–dih or nif–leem habituation tasks) and the differential language experience of the young and old networks. The representations of linguistic knowledge in the networks (in the form of connection weights) are continuously evolving in response to increasing linguistic exposure. The way in which those representations evolve is independent of the fact that the networks will subsequently be tested on bih–dih or lif–neem discriminations (as these syllables are not in the training set). The behavior on these tests will be determined by some interaction between the networks' ability to perform the task per se and its current level of linguistic representation. Because connectionist networks extract the statistical regularities of their environments, that interaction is determined by the relationship between the test syllables (bih–dih and lif–neem) and the distribution of similar syllables in the background linguistic environment.

In summary, this model showed how the representations developed by an autoencoder can integrate information from different sources or modalities. Behavior on any given task occurs within the context of prior learning. Representations developed in one learning context may determine the feasibility of subsequent learning in a different context, or even on a different (but related) task.

OBJECT-DIRECTED BEHAVIORS

This section describes a model that incorporates many more neuropsychological constraints than the models in the previous sections. The model in this section provides a mechanistic account of the infant's developing abilities to interact with objects that move in and out of sight. (It is reported in more detail in Mareschal, Plunkett, & Harris, 1999). Those models show how associative learning mechanisms can interact with the statistics of the environment to produce task appropriate internal representations. In the next sections, we show how architectural constraints gleaned from neuropsychology and neurophysiology can help shape the network architecture. The initial architecture provides added constraints on the flow of information and on the developmental profile of behaviors that emerges from the network. These constraints are one way in which innate knowledge can be built into a connectionist network. Moreover, this section describes a much more complex model than those in the previous two sections. The model is made up of a number of modules, each of which uses a different neural network technique (e.g., supervised vs. unsupervised learning). It illustrates how complex systems can be built up from relatively simple components.

A Brief Survey of Object-Directed Behaviors in Infancy

Newborns possess sophisticated object-oriented perceptual skills (Slater, 1995) but the age at which infants are able to reason about *hidden* objects remains unclear. Using *manual search* to test infants' understanding of hidden objects, Piaget concluded it was not until 7.5 to 9 months that infants understand that hidden objects continue to exist because younger infants do not successfully reach for an object hidden behind an occluding screen (Piaget, 1952, 1954). More recent studies using a violation-of-expectancy paradigm suggested that infants as young as 3.5 months do have some understanding of hidden objects. These studies rely on non-search indices such as surprise instead of manual retrieval to assess infant knowledge (e.g., Baillargeon, 1993; Baillargeon, Spelke, & Wasserman, 1985). Infants *watch* an event in which some physical property of a hidden object is violated (e.g., solidity). Surprise at this violation (as measured by increased visual inspection of the event) is interpreted as showing that the infants know (a) that the hidden object still exists, and (b) that the hidden object maintains the physical property that was violated (Baillargeon, 1993). The nature and origins of this developmental lag between understanding the continued existence of a hidden object and searching for it remains a central question of infant cognitive development.

The lag cannot be attributed to a delay in manual control because infants as young as 4.5 months reach for a moving visible object, and by 6 months can reach around or remove an occluding obstacle (Von Hofsten, 1989). Nor can it be attributed to immature planning or problem-solving abilities because infants have been shown to solve problems involving identical or more complex planning procedures (Baillargeon, 1993; Munakata, McClelland, Johnson, & Siegler, 1997).

Clues may be found in recent work on cortical representation of visual object information. Anatomical, neurophysiological, and psychophysical evidence points to the existence of two processing routes for visual object information in the cortex (Goodale, 1993; Milner & Goodale, 1995; Ungerleider & Mishkin, 1982; Van Essen, Anderson, & Felleman, 1992). Although the exact functionality of the two routes remains a hotly debated question, it is generally accepted that they contain radically different kinds of representations (Johnson, Mareschal, & Csibra, 2001). The dorsal (or parietal) route processes spatial–temporal object information, whereas the ventral (or temporal) route processes object feature information.

The dorsal and ventral routes both project into the frontal lobes (Goodale, 1993). As a whole, the frontal lobes play a crucial role in learning what responses are appropriate given an environmental context (Passingham, 1993). They have been closely tied to the development of planning and underlie the execution of voluntary actions, particularly in the context of manual search by human infants (Diamond, 1991).

Voluntary retrieval, such as manual search for an occluded object, must involve the integration of spatial–temporal information concerning the location of the occluded object with surface feature information concerning its identity. The surface feature information is required to decide whether an object is desired or not, and spatial–temporal information is required to direct the response. Furthermore, the cortical representation of these two types of information must be sufficiently well developed for accurate integration to occur. We suggest that early in development only visible objects offer the degree of representational precision needed to support an accurate integrated response because cell activations diminish when a target is no longer visible.

One possible explanation is that the lag occurs whenever it is necessary to integrate two potentially imprecise sources of information: spatial–temporal information about the location of the occluded object and featural information about the identity of the occluded object. This explanation predicts that tasks requiring access to only one imprecise source of information or tasks that are performed with a visible object will not result in a developmental lag. In contrast, any task that calls for the integration of cortically separable representations will fail unless performed with a visible object or with precise cortical representations. This account does not attribute the lag to any difficulties the infant might encounter in attempting to remove or circumvent the occluder in manual retrieval tasks. In addition, the lag does not depend on the response modality. Instead, it arises from information processing considerations associated with voluntary, object-directed behaviors. Surprise reflex responses, which may subsequently be manifested by an increased inspection time or spontaneous visual search behaviors, can be elicited by access to only one of the object representations.

Building the Model

Figure 3.10 shows the model in schematic outline. It consists of a modular architecture. Each functional module is enclosed by a dashed line. Some units are shared by two modules (e.g., the 75 hidden units are shared by the response integration and trajectory prediction networks) and serve as a gateway for information between the modules. In accordance with the neurological evidence already reviewed, spatial–temporal information about objects in the world is processed independently of feature information. Information enters the network through a two-dimensional retina homogeneously covered by feature detectors. It is then concurrently funneled into one pathway that processes the spatial–temporal history of the object and another pathway that develops a spatially invariant feature representation of the object.

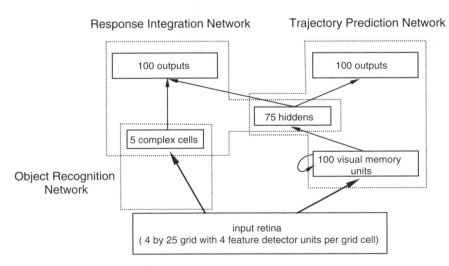

FIG. 3.10. Schema of network architecture for object processing.

The retina consists of a 4×25 cell grid. Each cell contains four feature detectors responding to different properties (e.g. light/dark, high/low contrast, red/green, soft/hard). If a projected object image overlaps with a grid cell, the cell's feature detectors take on the value $+1.0$ if the feature is present and -1.0 if the feature is absent. Cells on which the object image is not projected are quiescent and take on the value 0.0. An occluding screen is also projected onto the retina. The retinal cells corresponding to the screen's image have a constant activation of 1.0.

The network experiences 4 different objects with correlated features (i.e., $\{-1\ 1\ -1\ 1\}$, $\{-1\ 1\ 1\ -1\}$, $\{1\ -1\ 1\ -1\}$, $\{1\ -1\ -1\ 1\}$). All object images are 2×2 grid cells large. For each object presentation, an object moves once back and forth across the retina, either horizontally or vertically. All horizontal movements across the retina involve an interim occluding event, whereas vertical movements across the retina can result in either nonoccluding or partially occluding events. Completely occluded vertical movements are never observed because the occluder height is identical to the height of the retina. At any specific time step, there are four possible next positions for the object: up, down, left, or right. Predicting the next object position can only be resolved by learning to attend to the trajectory of the object.

The object recognition module generates a spatially invariant representation of the object by using a modified version of the unsupervised learning algorithm developed by Foldiak (1991). Initially, a bank of five complex cells is fully and randomly connected to all feature detectors. The algorithm exploits the fact that an object tends to be contiguous with itself at successive temporal intervals. Thus, two successive images will probably be derived from the same object. At the end of learning, each complex cell becomes associated with a particular feature combination wherever it appears on the retina.

The trajectory prediction module uses a partially recurrent, feedforward network trained with the backpropagation learning algorithm. At each time step, information about the position of the object on the retina is extracted from the 100 retinal grid cells and mapped onto the visual memory layer. The retinal grid cells with which the object image overlaps become active ($+1.0$), whereas the other cells remain inactive (0.0). The network is trained to predict the next instantaneous, retinal position of the object. The prediction is output onto a bank of 100 units coding position in the same way as the inputs into the module. The network has a target of $+1.0$ for those units corresponding to the next object position and 0.0 for all other units.

All units in the visual memory layer have a self-recurrent connection (fixed at $\mu = 0.3$). The resulting spatial distribution of activation across the visual memory layer takes the form of a comet with a tail that tapers off in the direction from which the object came. The length and distinctiveness of this tail depend on the velocity of the object. The information in this layer is then forced through a bottleneck of 75 hidden units to generate a more compact, internal rerepresentation of the object's spatial–temporal history. As there are no direct connections from the input to the output, the network's ability to predict the next position is a direct measure of the reliability of its internal object representation. We interpret the response of the trajectory prediction network as a measure of its sensitivity to spatial–temporal information about the object.

The output of the response integration network corresponds to the infant's ability to coordinate and use the information it has about object position and object identity. This network integrates the internal representations generated by other modules (i.e., the feature representation at the complex cell level and spatial–temporal representation in the hidden unit layer) as required by a retrieval response task. It consists of a single layered perceptron whose task is to output the same next position as the prediction network for two of the objects, and to inhibit any response (all units set to 0.0) for the other two objects. This reflects the fact that infants do not retrieve (e.g., reach for) all objects. In general, infants are not asked or rewarded for search. The experimental set-up relies on *spontaneous* search by the infant. Some objects are desired (e.g., sweet) whereas others are not desired (e.g., sour). Any voluntary retrieval response will necessarily require the processing of feature information (to identify the object as a desired one) as well as trajectory information (to localize the object).

The model embodies the basic architectural constraints on visual cortical pathways revealed by contemporary neuroscience: an object-recognition network that develops spatially invariant feature representations of objects, a trajectory-prediction network that is blind to surface features and computes appropriate spatial–temporal properties even if no actions are undertaken toward the object, and a response module that integrates information from the two latter networks for use in voluntary actions. We suggest that surprise can be modeled by a mismatch between the information stored in an internal representation and the new information arriving from the external world. More specifically, in the trajectory prediction module, surprise occurs when there is a discrepancy between the predicted reappearance of an object from behind an occluder and its actual reappearance on the retina. In the object recognition module, surprise occurs when there is a discrepancy between the feature representation stored across the complex units and the new representation produced by the new image.

Model Results

Object Localization. The trajectory prediction network learns very quickly to predict an object's next position when it is visible. However, the hidden unit representations that are developed persist for some time after

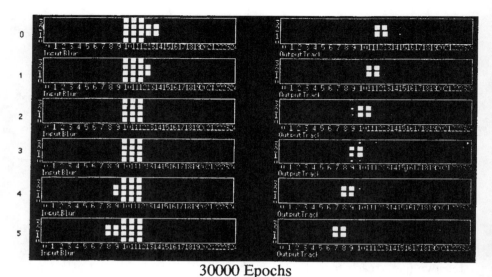

30000 Epochs

FIG. 3.11.   Network tracking of occluded object after 30000 object presentations.

the object has disappeared and allow the network to keep track of the object even when it is no longer directly perceptible. Figure 3.11 shows a graphic representation of the network's ability to predict the next position of an occluded object. The left-hand column shows what is projected onto the retina once feature information has been removed. The right-hand column shows the corresponding object position predicted by the trained trajectory network. The rows (from top to bottom) correspond to successive time steps. This network has seen 30,000 presentations of randomly selected objects moving back and forth in random position and directions at a fixed speed.

   Both the screen and the object are projected onto the retina. The network correctly predicts the next position of the object even when the object is occluded by the screen and not directly perceptible. At $t = 0$, the object is about to disappear behind the occluding screen. At all subsequent time steps, the network correctly predicts that the object will have moved over one position. Note especially step $t = 3$ for which the direct perceptual information available to the network is *exactly the same* as at $t = 2$, in that only the occluding screen is visible. The network is able to predict the subsequent reappearance of the object, taking account of how long it has been behind the screen.

   Feature Monitoring.   The object recognition network also maintains a representation of the features of the object that persist beyond direct per-

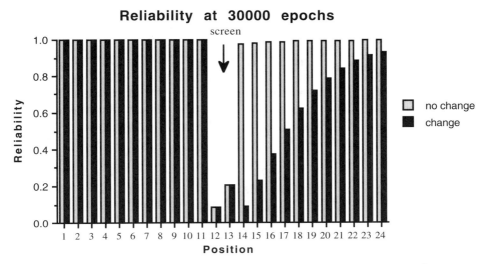

FIG. 3.12.   Maintaining a feature representation of an occluded object.

ception. Figure 3.12 shows the reliability of the internal feature representation developed across the complex cells. The reliability is computed as the dot product between the existing activation across the complex cells and the new activation pattern produced by the incoming feature input. It represents how similar the stored feature representation is to the new feature representation. Each of the columns represents the feature reliability as the object moves horizontally through the 24 positions for which the object image falls entirely on the retina. Positions 12 and 13 correspond to the object being fully hidden behind the screen. The white columns show performance when there are no changes in features, whereas the black columns show the reliability when the object is surreptitiously changed behind the screen. When there are no changes, the reliability drops while the object is behind the screen (because there is no perceptual evidence with which to assess the internal representation) but recovers immediately when the object reappears. However, when the object is surreptitiously changed, there is a delayed recovery in reliability. This reflects the fact that the new object features are different from those that are stored in the recognition module's internal representations. The rate of recovery is directly related to the similarity between the new object features and the original object features. Effectively, delayed recovery corresponds to a surprise reaction.

Developmental Lag in Retrieval Responses.   The model was designed to test the hypothesis that the developmental lag between voluntary retrieval and surprise-based indices arises from the difference in the integration demands of the two tasks. Network responses when presented with an unoccluded desired object, an occluded desired object, and an occluded undesired object are depicted in Figure 3.13. The reliability of a module is computed as (1 - *sum-of-squares-error of outputs*) averaged over the output units and patterns involved in the event. Because the networks begin with random weights, the initial (untrained) output activations are also random. The initial network response is to turn off almost all output units. This results in an immediate increase in reliability (decrease in error) but it only reflects a blanket inhibition of output activity (including some cells which should be active). Hence, this stage of learning does not reflect the acquisition of position-specific knowledge. To normalize for this, the plotted reliabilities are linearly scaled to range between 0.0 and 1.0 with the origin of the scale (the baseline) corresponding to the reliability value obtained when all output units are turned off. Any increase in reliability above this origin corresponds to an increase in the ability to predict the object's next position. The baseline reliability value was 0.863 because on average about 86% of the units will be silent in producing an accurate response.

Figure 3.13a shows the average network performance ($n = 10$) on both the position prediction and retrieval tasks when presented with an unoccluded, desired object. We interpret network behavior by assuming that a threshold of reliability over and above the previously mentioned baseline level is required to control an accurate prediction/response. Consider the case where this threshold is set to 0.8. At this level, it can be seen from Fig. 3.13a that the network learns very quickly (within 1,000 epochs) not just to predict the position of the desired object but also to produce an appropriate retrieval response.

When the object is occluded, the network's behavior is very different (Fig. 3.13b). Predictive localization and retrieval responses are initially equally poor. The internal representations are not adequately mature to support *any* reliable response. However, the reliability of tracking develops faster than that of retrieval. By 10,000 epochs, the prediction response has achieved the requisite level of reliability, whereas the retrieval response does not achieve this level until approximately 20,000 epochs. In other words, the network replicates the well-established finding that infants exhibit a developmental lag between successful predictive tracking of an occluded object and successful retrieval of an occluded object.

The output required for retrieval of a desired, occluded object is identical to that required for predictive localization. Moreover, both sets of output units receive exactly the same information from the hidden units about the spatial–temporal history of the object. The two modules differ only in that the retrieval response module must *also* integrate information coming from the object recognition module. Thus, the developmental lag

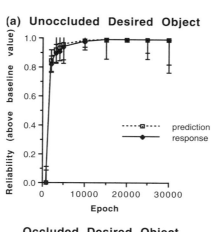

(a) Unoccluded Desired Object

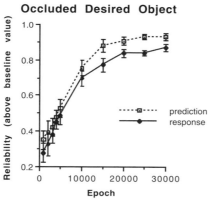

Occluded Desired Object

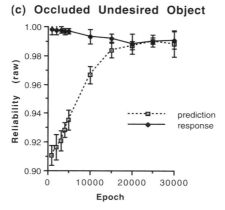

(c) Occluded Undesired Object

FIG. 3.13.   Network performance on tracking and responding to (a) a desired unoccluded object, (b) a desired occluded object, and (c) an undesired occluded object.

in the network arises from the added task demands of integrating information concerning the location and identity of an *occluded* object.

An advantage of modeling is that we can test this hypothesis directly using a manipulation that would not be possible with infants. If the lag is due to the need for information integration concerning the location and identity of an occluded object, then it should disappear on a task that does not require such integration. Undesired objects do not require information integration because it suffices to attend only to the identity representation in order to elicit an appropriate response. An inhibitory output can then be emitted that does not require any spatial–temporal information. Figure 3.13c shows the network's performance when presented with an undesired object. Here, raw reliabilities are plotted because the correct response is to turn all output units off. The network learns to inhibit any attempt at retrieval because it can ignore information from the spatial–temporal channel even though it is still learning to predict the object's position. In short, inspection of Fig. 3.13c shows, as predicted, that the developmental lag disappears on tasks not requiring integration of information across modules.

The model is successful in demonstrating how the requirement to integrate information across two object representations in a voluntary retrieval task can lead to a development lag relative to performance on surprise tasks that only require access to either spatial–temporal information concerning an occluded object or surface feature information accessed separately. Early mastery of surprise tasks that claim to show the coordination of position and feature information (e.g., Baillargeon, 1993) have—on close scrutiny—provided evidence only for the use of positional information in conjunction with size or volume information. Both size and volume are spatial dimensions that are encoded by the dorsal route. Thus processing information in these tasks only requires accessing a single cortical route. Note that early surprise responses can arise from feature violations, from spatial–temporal violations, and even from both types of violation arising concurrently and independently, but not from a violation involving the *integration* of feature and spatial–temporal information concerning an occluded object. The model predicts that infants will show a developmental lag not just on manual search tasks but also on surprise tasks that involve such integration.

In summary, this model shows how specialized modules can emerge through basic constraints in the form of different assumptions about the associative mechanisms that operate in a network and the original architecture of a network. This model also demonstrates that different connectionist modeling techniques can be combined within the same model. Connectionist models are not necessarily synonymous with homogenous processing systems.

THE PERCEPTION OF OBJECT UNITY

This section provides an example of highly constrained learning. High-level behaviors, such as the apparent ability to draw perceptual inferences, can be acquired through the recombination of low-level perceptual abilities. The model in this section differs from previous ones in that there are many built-in constraints. This section describes a model of the developing ability to perceive object unity in displays involving partially occluded objects (described in more detail in Mareschal & Johnson, 1999). An updated version of this model will appear in Mareschal and Johnson (in press), along with commentaries. A network learns to associate the presence of low-level visual cues with the presence of a unified object, and thereby learns to predict when an ambiguous, partially occluded stimulus event arises from one object rather than two distinct partially occluded objects.

A Brief Survey of the Perception of Object Unity

Neonates appear to perceive the moving and partly occluded rod in Fig. 3.14 as consisting of two disjoint objects (Slater, Morison, Somers, Mattock, Brown, & Taylor, 1990). In contrast, 4-month-olds (and adults) perceive such a partly occluded rod as consisting of a single unified object. Early studies of the cues that support the perception of object unity concluded that common motion of the rod parts was the primary visual cue used by infants in determining that the rod parts belonged to a common object (Kellman & Spelke, 1983; Kellman, Spelke, & Short, 1986).

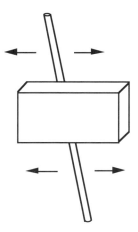

FIG. 3.14.   Partially occluded ambiguous test stimulus.

However, more recent studies called this finding into question by systematically varying the cues available in a display. Three dimensional depth cues were not found to be necessary for the perception of unity as 4-month-olds still perceived a two-dimensional (computer generated) rod-and-box display, in which two rod parts moved above and below a stationary box against a textured background, as a single unified rod (Johnson & Nanez, 1995). However, in the absence of a textured background, there was no systematic preference for a unified over two disjoint rods when tested with a two-dimensional display (Johnson & Aslin, 1996). The relatability of the two rod segments (the fact that, if extended, they would meet behind the screen) was also found to be important in determining the infants' perception of unity (Johnson & Aslin, 1996).

Currently, there are few accounts of how the developmental shift could take place. Spelke (1990; Spelke & Van de Walle, 1993) suggested that young infants' object perception is tantamount to reasoning, in accord with a set of core principles. However, infants' performance on object unity tasks is dependent on the presence or absence of motion, edge alignment, accretion and deletion of background texture, and other cues, implying that low-level perceptual variables strongly influence object perception, rather than reasoning from core principles (Johnson & Aslin, 1996; Kellman & Spelke, 1983). Two-month-olds are found to have an intermediate response between that of neonates and 4-month-olds (Johnson & Nanez, 1995). Whereas neonates perceive the stimulus in Fig. 3.14 as arising from two disjoint objects and 4-month-olds perceive it as arising from a single unified object, 2-month-olds do not show a preference and are equally likely to respond as though the stimulus is unified or disjoint. In this section we explore whether the perception of object unity can be *learned* by experience with objects and events in early infancy.

Building the Model

Figure 3.15 illustrates the basic model architecture. The model receives input via a simple retina. The retinal information is processed by separate encapsulated modules. Each module identifies the presence of one of the following cues: (a) motion, (b) texture deletion and accretion, (c) t-junctions, (d) co-motion (i.e., motion in the upper and lower halves of the retina), (e) common motion in the upper and lower halves of the retina,[2] (f) co-

---

[2]Common motion indicates that the motion in the upper and lower halves of the retina are relatable. In this model, the absence of common motion signifies that the object fragments in the upper and lower halves of the retina are moving in the opposite direction.

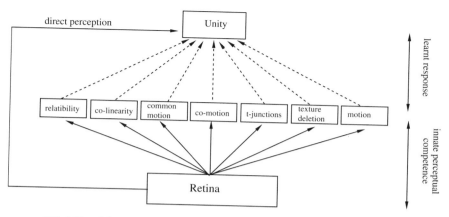

FIG. 3.15. Schema of network architecture for the perception of object unity.

linearity of objects in the upper and lower halves of the retina, (g) the relatability of objects in the upper and lower halves of the retina.

Unity is also a primitive, like the other cues, in that the network can immediately perceive it (via direct perception). Indeed, when testing the perception of unity, all experimental studies assume that (in the test phase) infants can perceive a unified and a broken stick as distinct from one another. In the absence of direct perception (i.e., when the object(s) are partly occluded) the perception of unity (in the network) is mediated by its associations with other (directly perceivable) cues.

We do not wish to make the claim that a mediated route is unique to the perception of unity. There may well be a highly complex and interactive network of connections in the brain that allow any set of not-directly-perceivable cues to be indirectly computed from the activation of other directly perceivable cues. However, in the interest of clarity, we have only considered the one mediated route.

The bottom half of the network embodies innate abilities. We assume that neonates are able to perceive the components of each of these cues. Indirect evidence suggests that this is the case (Slater, 1995). There is no learning in any of these encapsulated modules. The top half of the network embodies the learning that can occur through interactions with the environment.

The network "sees" a series of images from the world and responds with whether a perceived object is unified or not. The response is coded across two output units: $(+1, -1)$ signifies that the object is unified; $(-1, +1)$ signifies that the object is not unified. $(+1, +1)$ or $(-1, -1)$ is interpreted as an ambiguous response.

The input retina consists of a 196-bit vector mapping all the cells on a 14 × 14-unit grid. In the middle of the grid is a 4 × 4-unit occluder. All units corresponding to the position of the screen are given a value of 1. When background texture is required, all other units on the retina are given a value of 0.0 or 0.2, depending on the texture pattern. Units with values of 0.2 correspond to position on which there is a texture element (e.g., a dot). Units corresponding to the position of an object are given a value of 1.0. Figure 3.16 shows a snapshot taken from the "ambiguous" portion of all 26 events in the environment.

An object-event is made up of a series of snapshots like this one in which the rod moves progressively across the retina. All events begin with the object moving onto the retina from the side. We call this the *unambiguous* portion of the event. The object then moves across the retina, passing behind the area occupied by the occluding screen. We call this the *ambiguous* portion of the event. Finally, the object reappears on the other side of the screen and continues off the retina.

All events except 5 and 6 involve motion. The presence of texture, t-junctions, relatability, and co-linearity are varied systematically. All events with motion involve motion in the upper and lower half of the retina (co-motion) but only half of those involve common motion (relatible motion). This leads to a total of 26 possible events. Although alignment has been manipulated as a cue in some infant studies, note that two objects are aligned *if and only if* they are co-linear and relatable. Thus, co-linearity and relatability are more primitive cues than alignment in the sense that the latter cannot be computed without computing (at least implicitly) the former, whereas the converse is not true (i.e., both co-linearity and relatability can be computed independently of alignment).

Learning is driven by direct feedback from the environment. When the object is visible, the environment provides immediate feedback about the unity of the object via the direct perception link. When the object is not completely visible, the environment cannot provide feedback about the unity of the object. The model has a short-term, rapidly decaying memory that encodes unity information obtained while the object was entirely visible. Immediately following occlusion, there is a clear trace of the state of the stick before occlusion (i.e., a kind of short-lived visual memory). After a short delay, that information has decayed away completely and can no longer be used for learning.

The interaction between memory and direct perception is embodied in the target signal used to train the connection weights between the perceptual cue modules and the unity output. This signal has two components. One component arises from direct perception whereas the other component arises from memory. In the absence of direct perception (i.e., when the

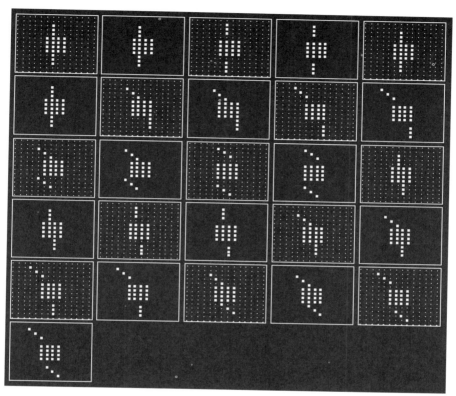

1: motion, texture, t-junction, co-motion, common motion, ,co-linearity, relatibility	2: motion, t-junction, co-motion, common motion, co-linearity, relatibility	3: motion, texture, co-motion, common motion, co-linearity, relatibility	4: motion, co-motion, common motion, co-linearity, relatibility	5: texture, t-junction, co-linearity, relatibility
6: t-junction, co-linearity, relatibility	7: motion, texture, t-junction, co-motion, common motion, relatibility	8: motion, t-junction, co-motion, common motion, relatibility	9: motion, texture co-motion, common motion, relatibility	10: motion, co-motion, common motion, relatibility
11: motion, texture, t-junction, co-motion, common motion, co-linearity	12: motion, t-junction, co-motion, common motion, co-linearity	13: motion, texture, co-motion, common motion, co-linearity	14: motion, co-motion, common motion, co-linearity	15: motion, texture, t-junction, co-linearity
16: motion, texture, t-junction, co-linearity	17: motion, texture, co-linearity	18: motion, co-linearity	19: motion, texture, t-junction	20: motion, t-junction
21: motion, texture	22: motion	23: motion, texture, t-junction, co-linearity	24: motion, t-junction, co-linearity	25: motion, texture, co-linearity
26:motion, co-linearity				

FIG. 3.16.   Complete set of object events with corresponding visual cues.

object is partly occluded), the perceptual component is zero and the memory component determines the value of the training signal.

When direct perception is possible, the model's prediction of unity (via the mediated route) can be compared to the signal coming from direct perception. The degree to which the prediction is correct when direct perception is not possible reflects how well the model's ability to fill in missing information matches that of infants tested on ambiguous events. The degree to which the prediction is corrected when direct perception is possible reflects how well the network has extracted general object occlusion knowledge that applies across its entire learning environment.

Model Results

In the interest of brevity we report only the model's performance in the best condition. Three hidden units were added between the perceptual modules and the output response units. The hidden units provide the power to form an internal rerepresentation of the higher order correlation information between the different cues. The training environment consisted of events 1, 2, and 17 to 22 to capture the fact that there are far more examples of disjoint objects than examples of unified but occluded objects. The results are based on 10 replications with different random initial weights.

The networks very quickly (by 10 epochs) learned to perceived one or two objects on the unambiguous portion of the event. This is when the stick(s) are moving across the retina and have not yet reached a position of partial occlusion or with one stick above and below the occluder.

Figure 3.17 shows the networks' performance based on the computations of the mediated route when tested with the ambiguous portion of the events 1, 3, 5, and 7. Correct performance is obtained when the mediated response correctly classifies whether the test event arises from a single object or two separate objects. These are the events most commonly used to test infants. Note that only event 1 was part of the original training set. The other three events reflect the networks' ability to generalize their knowledge to previously unseen stimuli.

The networks learned quickly (by 100 epochs) to perceive two objects, when the event was produced by two objects. The correct perception of a single unified object took much longer to learn. Over the first 4,000 epochs, these networks perceived event 1 as arising from two disjoint objects. Then, from 5,000 to 8,000 epochs, the majority of networks gradually came to perceive the event as arising from one object.

There is a different developmental profile in the absence of motion. Up to epoch 500, networks perceive this event as arising from two disjoint objects. Then, from 1,000 epochs onwards, the networks consistently per-

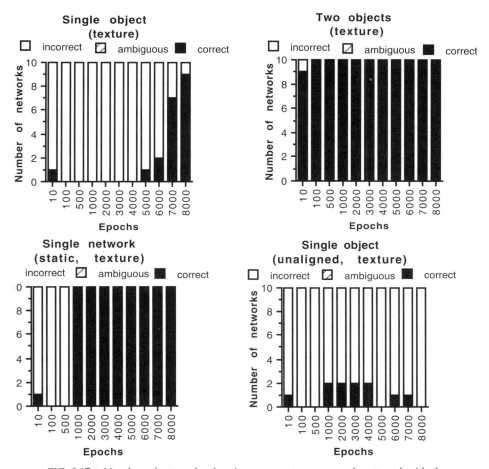

FIG. 3.17.   Number of networks showing a correct response when tested with the ambiguous segment of events 1, 3, 5, and 7.

ceive the event as arising from a single unified object. When the object segments are unaligned but relatable, the pattern of development is rather different. Throughout development, the networks fail to perceive this event as arising from a single object. At different times, up to 20% of networks perceive a unified object whereas the rest perceive two disjoint objects.

Network performance on these four events matches human performance very well. Newborns perceive the single object depicted in Fig. 3.14 (event 1) as two disjoint objects. There is then a transition period in which no distinct preference is obtained. By 4 months, infants perceive this display as arising from a single object. Infants always perceive two separate objects as disjoint (event 3). Finally, unaligned displays have been found to remain ambiguous percepts into adulthood (S. P. Johnson, personal communication, summer, 1999).

These networks do a good job of generalizing their knowledge to the complete set of test events. By the end of training, they respond correctly to 21 of the 26 test events when tested with the *ambiguous* portion of the event. That is, the mediated route makes the wrong prediction on five events. Two of those are events 7 and 8 (which, as described before, matches adult performance). The remaining events for which they fail to predict the correct percept are events 22, 23, and 24. The response to events 23 and 24 are definitely incorrect, whereas half the networks provide the correct response to event 22 and half provide an incorrect response.

Moreover, the model performs very well on the unambiguous, visible segment of the trajectories. The mediated route produces the correct percept on 24 of the 26 events. In particular, they fail to respond appropriately on events 20 and 22. In the former case, four networks correctly predicted two objects and six predicted a single object; in the latter case six networks correctly predicted two objects and four predicted a single object.

This model suggests that perception of object unity can be *learned* rapidly through interaction with the environment. The networks respond to the statistical regularities in the environment—*no prior object representations are required.* Rather than appealing to "core principles" that guide inferences about object unity, the resolution of ambiguous stimuli relies on the previous association of low-level cues with the percept of unity. There is a need for hidden units (the power for internal rerepresentation) for proper generalization of knowledge. A strong prediction of the model is that experience viewing unoccluded objects that *become* occluded lies at the heart of learning to resolve the ambiguous stimuli. The model suggests that there is a differential role for "common motion" and "co-motion" in the displays and that the occluded portions of events 23 and 24 lead to ambiguous percepts or even percepts of unity because of the change in relatability that occurs halfway through the event. The model provides a mechanistic account of how learning to perceive object unity could occur.

In summary, this model has shown how initial wiring constraints coupled with a simple associative learning mechanism results in rapid learning of a complex high-level ability (namely, the apparent perceptual inference of unity). Of course, this remains a preliminary model. For example, the current model does not have access to three-dimensional depth cues and is therefore not a full model of infant behavior. Nevertheless, it illustrates how associative mechanism could drive the developmental profiles observed with infants.

GENERAL DISCUSSION AND FUTURE DIRECTIONS

This chapter presented four connectionist models of infant behaviors. The models increased in complexity. The first was a model of infant categorization that also illustrated the basic connectionist information processing mechanisms. Autoencoder networks were found to develop the same categories as 3-month-olds when presented with the same stimuli used to test these infants. The same network architecture was also found to use feature correlation information to set up distinct categories in the same way as 10-month-olds. Plotting the hidden unit activations in a three-dimensional space revealed how networks separated out exemplars of different categories at the level of internal representations. The second model demonstrated how information from different sources or modalities could be integrated within a single internal representation. Acquiring representations that enabled the networks to learn one task (word learning) constrained their subsequent ability to perform on another task (phoneme discrimination). This illustrates how differences in levels of general experience can explain age differences in performance on a particular task. The third model illustrated how functionally distinct modules can emerge from the same environmental experience. Networks with initially different associative mechanisms differed in the type of object information they came to process. The appearance of object-directed behaviors was related to the ability to integrate information across multiple object representations. Finally, the fourth model showed how complex high-level behaviors could arise from the combination of low-level visual processes. Inferring the continuity of a partially occluded object could be achieved by learning the associations between unity and low-level perceptual cues. This model also illustrated how a variety of mechanisms could be hardwired into a connectionist system to embody initial knowledge constraints.

Together these models illustrate how a range of diverse infant behaviors can be explained in terms of neurally plausible information processing mechanisms. The models provide an *explanation* for these behaviors in terms of the interaction between neural information processing and the characteristics of the infant's environment. Both components are equally important. Because connectionist networks extract statistical regularities, the distribution of features in the environment determines the type of representations developed. Similarly, constraints such as the different initial architectures or different associative learning mechanisms also determine the type of representations developed. Finally, the way these representations interact in a complex multimodule system causes the observed behaviors.

Although there are generally no "innate" representations in connectionist networks, innate knowledge can be implemented through different learning mechanisms and architectures that promote the rapid learning of domain-specific information. Thus, what is interpreted as innate knowledge in very young infants may actually reflect the rapid learning of a highly constrained associative system.

These models provide a mechanistic account of infant behaviors. They allow us to explain behaviors across a range of different domains in terms of a common set of mechanisms. In turn, these mechanisms can be speculatively related to the brain (Johnson, 1996). Of course, these models remain very simple. Nevertheless, they allow us to raise causal questions about *how* learning and development occur rather than simply describing the consequences of learning and development. By showing how the same family of mechanisms can explain behaviors from such a diverse set of domains, these and other connectionist models of infant development (e.g., Munakata, 1998; Munakata, McClelland, Johnson, & Siegler, 1997; Quinn & Johnson, 1997) lay the groundwork for an explanatory synthesis of infant development.

One added advantage of mechanistic accounts of infant development is that they provide a handle with which to start asking how infant competence gets transformed into the abilities of older children and even adults. For example, we have begun to explore how the categorization abilities of young infants can account for 3- and 4-year-olds' performance on inductive reasoning tasks that oppose perceptual category information with label category information (e.g., Loose & Mareschal, 1997).

All the models in this chapter describe networks in which the connectivity is fixed from the onset. Although the weights are adjustable, the initial connectivity provides constraints that guide the rapid learning of basic perceptual and cognitive skills. However, there are networks that develop their own connectivity as part of the learning process (Mareschal & Shultz, 1996). We have argued elsewhere (Shultz & Mareschal, 1997) that networks with fixed connectivity are good models of learning in infancy (during which the basic building blocks of cognition are developing), whereas networks that developed their own connectivity are better models of later learning and development (in which there are fewer *a priori* constraints on what will need to be learned; e.g., learning a particular arithmetic system is culturally specific whereas learning about object unity is universal). This raises the question of how one system (the static connectivity system) develops into the other systems (the dynamic connectivity system).

Finally, although connectionist models aspire to provide explanations of behavior in terms of neurally plausible mechanisms, they are a far cry from the full complexity of the human brain. One direction in which these models need to develop is to incorporate more constraints from the neurosciences. More realistic learning mechanisms need to be considered.

However progress in this direction cannot proceed any faster than our knowledge of brain functioning.

ACKNOWLEDGMENTS

The work reported in this chapter was completed in collaboration with Robert M. French, Paul Harris, Scott P. Johnson, Kim Plunkett, Paul Quinn, and Graham Schafer. The writing of this chapter was supported by ESRC grant R000239112 and by European Commission HP-RTN grant CT-2000-00065.

REFERENCES

Baillargeon, R. (1993). The object concept revisited: New directions in the investigation of infants' physical knowledge. In C. E. Granrud (Ed.), *Visual perception and cognition in infancy* (pp. 265–315). London, UK: Lawrence Erlbaum Associates.

Baillargeon, R., Spelke, E. S., & Wasserman, S. (1985). Object permanence in 5-month-old infants. *Cognition, 20,* 191–208.

Best, C. W., McRoberts, G. W., & Sithole, N. N. (1988). The phonological basis of perceptual loss for non-native contrasts: Maintenance and discrimination among Zulu clicks by English-speaking adults and infants. *Journal of Experimental Psychology: Human Perception and Performance, 14,* 345–360.

Boden, M. A. (1980). Artificial intelligence and Piagetian theory. In M. Boden (Ed.), *Minds and mechanisms: Philosophical psychology and computational models* (pp. 236–261). Ithaca, NY: Cornell University Press.

Broadbent, D. (1985). A question of levels: Comment on McClelland and Rumelhart. *Journal of Experimental Psychology: General, 114,* 189–192.

Changeux, J. P, & Dehaene, S. (1989). Neuronal models of cognitive function. *Cognition, 33,* 63–109.

Charlesworth, W. R. (1969). The role of surprise in cognitive development. In D. Elkind & J. Flavell (Eds.), *Studies in cognitive development. Essays in honor of Jean Piaget* (pp. 257–314). Oxford, UK: Oxford University Press.

Chauvin, Y. (1989). Towards a connectionist model of symbol emergence. In *Proceedings of the 11th annual conference of the Cognitive Science Society* (pp. 580–587). Hillsdale, NJ: Lawrence Erlbaum Associates.

Cohen, L. B. (1973). A two-process model of infant visual attention. *Merrill-Palmer Quarterly, 19,* 157–180.

Cottrell, G. W., Munro, P., & Zipser, D. (1988). Image compression by backpropagation: an example of extensional programming. In N. E. Sharkey (Ed.), *Advances in cognitive science, Vol. 3* (pp. 208–240). Norwood, NJ: Ablex.

Cybenko, G. (1989). Approximation by superpositions of a sigmoidal function. *Mathematics of Control, Signals, and Systems, 2,* 303–314.

Diamond, A. (1991). Neuropsychological insights into the meaning of object concept development. In S. Carey & G. Gelman (Eds.), *The epigenesis of mind: Essays on biology and cognition* (pp. 67–110). Hillsdale, NJ: Lawrence Erlbaum Associates.

Di Lollo, V., & Enns, J. T., & Rensink, R. A. (2000). Competition for consciousness among visual events: The psychophysics of reentrant visual processes. *Journal of Experimental Psychology: General, 129,* 481–507.

Drescher, G. L. (1991). *Made up minds.* Cambridge, MA: MIT press.

Elman, J. L., Bates, E. A., Johnson, M. H., Karmiloff-Smith, A., Parisi, D., & Plunkett, K. (1996). *Rethinking innateness: A connectionist perspective on development.* Cambridge, MA: MIT Press.

Fantz, R. L. (1964) Visual experience in infants. Decreased attention to familiar patterns relative to novel ones. *Science, 164,* 668–670.

Foldiak, P. (1991). Learning invariance from transformation sequences. *Neural Computation, 3,* 194–200.

Fodor, J. (1983). *The modularity of mind.* Cambridge, MA: MIT Press.

Goodale, M. A. (1993). Visual pathways supporting perception and action in the primate cerebral cortex. *Current Opinion in Neurobiology, 3,* 578–585.

Hertz, J., Krogh, A., & Palmer, R. G. (1991). *Introduction to the theory of neural computation.* Reading, MA: Addison Wesley.

Johnson, M. H. (1996). *Developmental cognitive neuroscience.* Oxford, UK: Blackwells.

Johnson, M. H., Mareschal, D., & Csibra, G. (2001). The functional development and integration of the dorsal and ventral visual pathways: A neurocomputational approach. In C. A. Nelson & M. Luciana (Eds.) *The handbook of developmental cognitive neuroscience,* (pp. 339–351). Cambridge MA: MIT press.

Johnson, S. P., & Aslin, R. N. (1996). Perception of object unity in young infants: The roles of motion, depth, and orientation. *Cognitive Development, 11,* 161–180.

Johnson, S. P., & Nanez, J. E. (1995). Young infants' perception of object unity in two-dimensional displays. *Infant Behavior and Development, 18,* 133–143.

Kellman, P. J., & Spelke, E. S. (1983). Perception of partly occluded objects in infancy. *Cognitive Psychology, 15,* 483–524.

Kellman, P. J., Spelke, E. S., & Short, K. R. (1986). Infant perception of object unity from translatory motion in depth and vertical translation. *Child Development, 57,* 72–86.

Klahr, D., & Wallace, J. G. (1976). *Cognitive development: An information processing view.* Hillsdale, NJ: Lawrence Erlbaum Associates.

Loose, J. J., & Mareschal, D. (1997).When a word is worth a thousand pictures: A connectionist account of the percept to label shift in children's inductive reasoning. In G. W. Cottrell (Ed.), *Proceedings of the 19th annual conference of the Cognitive Science Society* (pp. 454–459). London: Lawrence Erlbaum Associates.

Mareschal, D., & French, R. M. (1997). A connectionist account of interference effects in early infant memory and categorization. In M. G. Shafto & P. Langley (Eds.), *Proceedings of the 19th annual conference of the Cognitive Science Society* (pp. 484–489). Mahwah, NJ: Lawrence Erlbaum Associates.

Mareschal, D., & French, R. M. (2000). Mechanisms of categorization in infancy. *Infancy, 1,* 59–76.

Mareschal, D., French, R. M., & Quinn, P. C. (2000). A connectionist account of asymmetric category learning in early infancy. *Developmental Psychology, 36,* 635–645.

Mareschal, D., & Johnson, S. P (1999). Mechanisms of development in the perception of object unity. In Hahn & S. C. Stone (Eds.), *Proceedings of the twenty-first annual conference of the Cognitive Science Society* (pp.343–348). London: Lawrence Erlbaum Associates.

Mareschal, D., Plunkett, K., & Harris, P. (1999). A computational and neuropsychological account of object-oriented behaviors in Infancy. *Developmental Science, 2,* 306–317.

Mareschal, D., & Shultz, T. R. (1996). Generative connectionist networks and constructivist cognitive development. *Cognitive Development, 11,* 571–603.

Mareschal, D., & Johnson, S. P. (in press). Learning to perceive object unity: A connectionist account. *Developmental Science.*

Marr, D. (1982). *Vision.* New York: Freeman.

McClelland, J. L. (1989). Parallel distributed processing: Implications for cognition and development. In R. G. M. Morris (Ed.), *Parallel distributed processing: Implications for psychology and neurobiology* (pp. 8–45). Oxford: Oxford University Press.

McLeod, P., Plunkett, K., & Rolls, E.T. (1998). *Introduction to connectionist modeling of cognitive processes.* Oxford: Oxford University Press.

Milner, A. D., & Goodale, M. A. (1995). *The visual brain in action.* Oxford, UK: Oxford University Press.

Munakata, Y. (1998). Infants perseveration and implication for object permanence theories: A PDP model of the AB task. *Developmental Science, 1,* 161–211.

Munakata, Y., McClelland, J. L., Johnson, M. N., & Siegler, R. S. (1997). Rethinking infant knowledge: Towards an adaptive process account of successes and failures in object permanence tasks. *Psychological Review, 104,* 686–713.

Papert, S. (1963). Intelligence chez l'enfant et chez le robot [Intelligence in the child and the robot]. *Etudes D'Epistemologie Génétiques, 15,* 131–194.

Passingham, R. E. (1993). *The frontal lobes and voluntary action.* Oxford, UK: Oxford University Press.

Piaget, J. (1952). *The origins of intelligence in the child.* New York: International Universities Press.

Piaget, J. (1954). *The construction of reality in the child.* New York: Basic Books.

Plunkett, K., & Elman, J. L. (1997). *Exercises in rethinking innateness.* Cambridge, MA: MIT Press.

Plunkett, K., & Marchman, V. (1991). U-shaped learning and frequency effects in a multi-layered perceptron: Implications for child language acquisition. *Cognition, 38,* 43–102.

Plunkett, K., & Sinha, C. (1992). Connectionism and developmental theory. *British Journal of Developmental Psychology, 10,* 209–254.

Plunkett, K., Sinha, C., Moller, M. F., & Strandsby, O. (1992). Symbol grounding or the emergence of symbols? Vocabulary growth in children and a connectionist net. *Connection Science, 4,* 293–312.

Posner, M. I. (1989). *Foundations of cognitive science.* Cambridge, MA: MIT press.

Pylyshyn, Z. W. (1984). *Computation and cognition: Towards a foundation for cognitive science.* Cambridge, MA: MIT press.

Quinn, P. C., & Eimas, P. D. (1996). Perceptual organization and categorization in young infants. *Advances in Infancy Research, 10,* 1–36.

Quinn, P. C., Eimas, P. D., & Rosenkrantz, S. L. (1993). Evidence for representations of perceptually similar natural categories by 3-month-old and 4-month-old infants. *Perception, 22,* 463–475.

Quinn, P. C., & Johnson, M. H. (1997). The emergence of perceptual category representations in young infants. *Journal of Experimental Child Psychology, 66,* 236–263.

Rosch, E., Mervis, C. B., Gray, W. D., Johnson, D. M., & Boyes-Braem, P. (1976). Basic objects in natural categories. *Cognitive Psychology, 8,* 382–439.

Rumelhart, D. E., & McClelland, J. L. (1986). *Parallel distributed processing: Explorations in the microstructure of cognition, Vol. 1.* Cambridge, MA: MIT Press.

Rumelhart, D.E., Hinton, G.E., & Williams, R.J. (1986). Learning representations by back-propagating errors. *Nature, 323,* 533–536.

Rutkowska, J. C. (1995). *The computational infant.* London, UK: Harvester Wheatsheaf.

Schafer, G., & Mareschal, D. (2001). Modeling infant speech sound discrimination using simple associative networks. *Infancy, 2,* 7–28.

Shultz, T. R., & Mareschal, D. (1997). Rethinking innateness, learning, and constructivism. *Cognitive Development, 12,* 563–586.

Shultz, T. R., Schmidt, W. C., Buckingham, D., & Mareschal, D. (1995). Modeling cognitive development with a generative connectionist algorithm. In T. Simon & G. Halford (Eds.), *Developing cognitive competence: New approaches to process modeling* (pp. 347–362) Hillsdale, NJ: Lawrence Erlbaum Associates.

Simon, H. A. (1962), An information processing theory of intellectual development. *Monograph of the Society for Research in Child Development, 27* (2, Serial No. 82).

Simon, T. J. (1998) Computational evidence for the foundations of numerical competence *Developmental Science, 1,* 71–78

Slater, A. (1995). Visual perception and memory at birth. *Advances in Infancy Research, 9,* 107–162.

Slater, A. M., Morison, V., Somers, M., Mattock, A., Brown, E., & Taylor, D. (1990). Newborn and older infants' perception of partly occluded objects. *Infant Behavior and Development, 13,* 33–49.

Spelke, E. S. (1990). Principles of object perception. *Cognitive Science, 14,* 29–56.

Spelke, E. S., & Van de Walle, G. (1993). Perceiving and reasoning about objects: Insights from infants. In N. Eilan, R. A. McCarthy, & B. Brewer (Eds.), *Spatial representation: Problems in philosophy and psychology* (pp. 132–161). Oxford: Blackwell.

Sokolov, E. N. (1963). *Perception and the conditioned reflex.* Hillsdale, NJ: Lawrence Erlbaum Associates.

Stager, S., & Werker, J.F. (1997). Infants listen to more phonetic detail in speech perception tasks than in word-learning tasks. *Nature, 388,* 381–382.

Trehub, S. (1976). The discrimination of foreign speech contrasts by infants and adults. *Child Development, 47,* 466–472.

Ungerleider, L. G., & Mishkin, M. (1982). Two cortical visual systems. In D. J. Ingle, M. A. Goodale, & R. J. W. Mansfield (Eds.), *Analysis of visual behavior* (pp. 549–586). Cambridge, MA: MIT Press.

Van Essen, D. C., Anderson, C. H., & Felleman, D. J. (1992). Information processing in the primate visual system: An integrated systems perspective. *Science, 255,* 419–423.

Von Hofsten, C. (1989). Transition mechanisms in sensori-motor development. In A. De Ribaupierre (Ed.), *Transition mechanisms in child development: The longitudinal perspective* (pp. 223–259). Cambridge, UK: Cambridge University Press.

Werker, J. F., & Tees, R. C. (1984b). Phonemic and phonetic factors in adult cross-language speech perception. *Journal of the Acoustical Society of America, 75,* 1866–1878.

Werker, J. F., & Lalonde, C. E. (1988). Cross-language speech perception: Initial capabilities and developmental changes. *Developmental Psychology, 24,* 1–12.

Werker, J. F., & Pegg, J. E. (1992). Infant speech perception and phonological acquisition. In C. A. Ferguson, L. Menn, & C. Stoel-Gammon (Eds.), *Phonological development: Models, research, implications* (pp. 285–231). Timonium, MD: York Press.

Werker, J. F., & Tees, R. C. (1983). Developmental changes across childhood in the perception of non-native speech sounds. *Canadian Journal of Psychology, 37,* 278–286.

Werker, J. F., & Tees, R. C. (1984a). Cross language speech perception: Evidence for perceptual reorganization during the first year of life. *Infant Behavior and Development, 7,* 49–63.

Young, R. (1976). *Seriation by children: An artificial intelligence analysis of a Piagetian task.* Basel: Birkhauser.

Younger, B, A. (1985). The segregation of items into categories by ten-month-old infants. *Child Development, 56,* 1574–1583.

Younger, B. A. (1990). Infants' detection of correlations among feature categories. *Child Development, 61,* 614–620.

Flexibility and Specificity in Infant Motor Skill Acquisition

Karen E. Adolph
New York University

Marion A. Eppler
East Carolina University

INTRODUCTION: TRANSFER IN MOTOR SKILL ACQUISITION

A long-standing, unsolved puzzle in motor skill acquisition is the problem of transfer: How does experience in a familiar motor context facilitate performance in a novel situation? Since Thorndike's (1906; Thorndike & Woodworth, 1901) classic work at the turn of the century, researchers have assumed that the solution to the puzzle can be found in a search for identical elements. More specifically, the traditional assumption is that transfer depends on the extent to which elements of the training context—the nature of the environmental stimulus, the patterns characterizing the motor response, or the mental representations that support motor knowledge—are similar to elements of the performance context (e.g., Anderson & Singley, 1993). Concepts like stimulus generalization, motor equivalence, and learning via analogous mental elements have each had their heyday (Adams, 1987). However, after nearly 100 years of study, researchers still lack a satisfactory theory of transfer in motor skill acquisition. One of the impediments to progress is that the identical elements approach and the experiments that stem from it cannot, in principle, explain adaptive, functional motor skills. The notion of identical elements in simple associative learning is far too static and narrow to account for the step-to-step, moment-to-moment variability that characterizes real, everyday motor skills.

Motor skill in the natural environment involves knowing which actions are possible for the given situation. It requires a continual, online decision-making process because the everyday environment and one's physical capabilities are continually changing. Both factors (i.e., properties of the environment and physical abilities of the individual) must be considered together in a relationship that is dynamic rather than fixed. The same slippery slope may be perfectly safe when walking with the arms free and wearing shoes with a sure grip, but completely impossible while carrying a heavy load or wearing leather-soled shoes. Changing the distribution of the load, modifying step length, even raising or lowering the arms change possibilities for action because such step-to-step variations change the physical constraints on keeping balance. Thus, an identical elements approach to transfer based on accretion of static facts about stimuli or responses cannot be sufficient for explaining adaptive control of action. The same elements can have different movement consequences depending on the current status of the actor–environment relationship.

In this chapter, we describe a fresh approach to tackling the old problem of transfer. The question remains of when and how experience facilitates performance in a novel motor context. However, the old search for identical elements has been reformulated into a new program of research aimed at understanding the process of online decision making in infant motor skill acquisition. The ability to generate adaptive solutions in a dynamic and variable real world requires flexibility of action. Motor skills show flexibility when the individual can cope adaptively across a wide range of novel contexts. On the flip side, motor skills show specificity when adaptive action is limited to a narrow range of contexts. As described shortly, the broader focus on flexible, adaptive action leads to a very different way of understanding experience-related changes. Rather than acquiring a repertoire of stimulus–response bonds or any sort of static representations for controlling action, infants may acquire the tools for online decision making. The key to learning and transfer of motor skill may be the wherewithal to plan movements adaptively, from moment to moment and task to task.

The study of flexibility in infants is particularly illustrative because transfer of learning is nested within a larger context of developmental change. Infants' bodies change dramatically over the first 2 years of life and their effective environment expands exponentially. In the midst of all this flux, new skills appear with remarkable regularity and abundance— reaching, sitting, crawling, walking, etc. Changes in the biomechanical constraints of their growing bodies and physical propensities change possibilities for action and introduce infants to new situations. Infants' everyday life poses continual tests of transfer because they must use their current motor skills to respond adaptively to new environmental properties and tasks. However, unlike any traditional test of transfer, babies must also respond adaptively to the same situations and tasks at different periods of development using very different postural control systems. The same environmental property (e.g., a squishy surface, a sloping floor, or a cliff) can have very different consequences for action when a baby is mastering head and trunk control, able to sit up alone, crawling on all fours, or able to walk independently.

OVERVIEW

This chapter describes a program of research aimed at understanding flexibility in infant motor skill. Our primary goal is to illustrate a new way of addressing the old problem of transfer in motor skill acquisition.

Conceptually, both transfer and flexibility deal with novelty. Transfer is the extent to which experience in a familiar motor context facilitates performance in a novel situation. Similarly, flexibility is the extent to which actions are adapted to novel and variable local conditions. Flexibility implies adaptation to a wide range of novel motor contexts. Specificity, on the other hand, implies adaptive responses only in a narrow range of motor contexts, when adaptive action is limited to particular environmental situations, motor responses, or body parts. The next section defines flexibility in more detail, why it is so central for functional motor skills, and how it is achieved in online decision making.

Traditional studies of transfer in motor skill are limited primarily to adult populations performing specialized motor tasks such as tapping out Morse Code (Bryan & Harter, 1897; Bryan & Harter, 1899), typing (Book, 1925), piano playing (Shaffer, 1980), and flying an airplane (Adams & Hufford, 1962); or to sport skills such as skiing (Emmerik, Brinker, Vereijken, & Whiting, 1989), perfecting a golf swing (Adams, 1985), and throwing beanbags at targets (Kerr & Booth, 1978) and basketballs through hoops (Wallace & Hagler, 1979). Outcome measures are typically limited to success/failure and speed/accuracy. In contrast, our studies of flexibility focus on more everyday motor skills (e.g., locomotion over novel terrain) in infants at various stages of motor development. We exploit the variability endemic on both sides of the actor–environment equation and present a wide array of outcome measures designed to provide insights into the online decision-making process. The fourth section shows that the study of flexibility in infants is feasible. Indeed, research paradigms that focus on flexibility may better reflect adaptive responses to novelty under real world constraints than tasks designed to test simpler models of skill acquisition and transfer. Moreover, this section shows that infants are capable of impressive displays of flexibility.

An important conceptual difference between the constructs of transfer and flexibility concerns the role of learning. Transfer, of course, requires learning by definition. In contrast, flexibility does not require learning by definition; in principle, skills could be highly flexible from the start. However, that turns out not to be the case. In the fifth section, we provide empirical evidence that flexibility, like transfer, depends on experience. The tools for online decision-making are the heart of what infants must learn for adaptive action. Additionally, we describe cases where learning does and does not transfer. As outlined later, learning is both remarkably general and surprisingly specific.

In the sixth section, we propose possible mechanisms that may underlie this sort of learning in a system that is itself continually changing. We focus on what infants do and do not learn that promotes flexibility, and on ways in which the developmental context may affect how knowledge is acquired. Finally, in the last section, we conclude with implications of this research program on flexibility for understanding the problem of transfer in motor skill acquisition.

We illustrate each section of the chapter by drawing on recent research from our laboratories and others where infants were challenged to adapt their newly developing locomotor skills to variations in the ground surface. The basic experimental paradigm is to observe the conditions under which infants respond adaptively to potentially risky ground and to examine the processes underlying their perceptual judgments and motor responses.

HALLMARKS OF ADAPTIVE ACTION
AND THE ROLE OF FLEXIBILITY

Skilled actions require flexibility. They cannot be performed in the same way over and over because the biomechanical constraints on movement are continually changing (Bernstein, 1967, 1996; Lashley, 1960; MacKay, 1982). The everyday environment is variable and unpredictable and full of novel situations. The functional, physical propensities of the body change from moment to moment (e.g., raising an arm changes the subtle biomechanics of maintaining balance). Even the most automatized movements such as walking and talking must be continually modified to suit the current demands of the particular motor context. Flexibility refers to the extent to which ongoing movements are adapted to novel changes in local conditions. It is what makes a basketball star able to change his plan mid-jump to land a basket or what makes ordinary pedestrians able to modify their gait or select a new path to navigate a tricky patch of ground. It is the adaptive nature of true motor skill rather than the rote reproducibility.

Prospectivity

Adaptive action has three important characteristics. First, skilled movements must be prospective and planful rather than merely responsive (Hofsten, 1993; Lee, 1993). Prospective control means lifting a leg to clear the curb, rather than recovering balance after tripping. Unexpected, unique motor problems demand online solutions. Because we cannot know all of the relevant parameters ahead of time, flexibility requires exploratory movements to generate the requisite information for planning adaptive responses. Typically, exploration involves subtle movements of eyes, head, and body, and results in multimodal and redundant sources of information. Infants provide a revealing test case for studying prospective control because their exploratory and preparatory movements tend to be larger and more easily observable than those of adults.

Affordance Relationship

Second, adaptive action is relational. It depends on the match, or fit, between the current properties of the environment and the current status of the person's physical abilities—what J. J. Gibson (1979) termed *affordances* (see also Adolph, Eppler, & Gibson, 1993b; Warren, 1984). Walking, for example, is possible only if the ground surface is sufficiently clear of obstacles to permit safe passage, extensive enough to keep balance, rigid enough to support the body's weight, flat enough to keep the body upright, with the necessary friction to counteract shearing forces, and so on (Stoffregen & Riccio, 1988). When there is a mismatch or lack of fit between environmental properties and the person's physical capabilities, normal walking is impossible. We must stop in our tracks, choose a different route, modify walking gait, or select an alternative method of locomotion.

This relational aspect of motor skill is especially important during infancy because babies' bodies and physical constraints on balance control change so dramatically. From birth to 2 years of age, infants' height nearly doubles and their weight more than quadruples (Palmer, 1944; Shirley, 1931; Snyder, Spencer, Owings, & Schneider, 1975). Recent research shows that infants' body growth is episodic, not continuous (Lampl, 1983, 1993; Lampl, Veldhuis, & Johnson, 1992). Height, for example, remains at a constant plateau for days or weeks on end, then spurts .5 cm to 2 cm overnight. As babies' bodies become slimmer and more maturely proportioned, their center of mass lowers from the bottom of the sternum to slightly above the belly button (Palmer, 1944). Such changes in infants' body proportions combined with variations in the ground literally change the physics of keeping balance in sitting, crawling, and walking postures.

Variety of Means

Finally, adaptive action involves a variety of means to achieve similar functional outcomes. On a muscle level, variability is endemic in movement. Because of the viscoelastic properties of the muscles and joints and the inertial forces resulting from ongoing movements, identical muscle forces can generate different outward movement patterns (Bernstein, 1967, 1996). For example, the same muscle forces in the arm generate different movements when the arm is at the side of the body, overhead, or swinging. Reciprocally, the same movement pattern can be performed with different underlying muscle forces (e.g., using only biceps to hold the arm parallel to the floor versus cocontracting biceps and triceps to do the same thing). Furthermore, on a behavioral level, flexible variety of means requires more than motor equivalence or response generalization (MacKay, 1982). Movements must be truly creative (Bruner, 1972, 1973). The changeable nature of infants' bodies, skills, and environments requires that the right movements be selected at the right time. Variety of strategic options is necessary for such a selection process. By observing skill acquisition in infants, we may discover the origins of variable means: where new movement strategies come from, factors that influence strategy selection, and how variety of means is maintained in infants' repertoires.

In sum, flexibility allows infants to cope with a varying body in a varying world by providing the wherewithal to predict the consequences of future movements on a step-to-step basis. Thus, an appropriate research program for studying flexibility in infant skill acquisition must incorporate variation on both sides of the infant–environment equation and maintain the nested structure of experience-related changes—during the course of a single trial, across trials within the session, and across the course of development.

STUDYING FLEXIBILITY IN INFANT LOCOMOTION

Our research focused on tasks where babies must cope with potentially risky ground surfaces. In particular, we challenge babies to descend slopes and stairs, and to cross cliffs and gaps because such changes in the depth of the ground surface provide good motivation for adaptive responding. Falling downward is aversive for infants (they typically fuss after falling) and they are usually loathe to err on the side of recklessness.

This section presents examples of two experiments designed to examine flexibility of responding. In the first study, walking infants were asked to cope with locomotion down shallow and steep—safe and risky—slopes (Adolph, 1995). In the second study, toddlers coped with locomotion down slopes while loaded with lead-weight shoulderpacks (Adolph & Avolio, 2000). As described next, slopes offer an ideal condition for studying flexibility in infant locomotor skill acquisition for several reasons.

The Slope Task

Transfer to a Novel Motor Task.   A primary reason for observing infants' behavior on slopes is to examine how and when infants display flexibility in a novel motor context. Viewing and navigating sloping ground are relatively novel activities for young infants. Although babies have many opportunities to view objects slanting in depth especially around a vertical axis, they rarely see the ground surface slanting downward away from the line of sight around the horizontal axis (Eppler, Adolph, & Weiner, 1996). Most parents in our studies report that they do not allow their young babies to negotiate playground slides independently or to walk down sloping driveways, wheelchair ramps, or hills without an adult's help.

More than half a century ago, McGraw (1935) exploited the novelty of sloping ground to examine how learning and development affect changes in infants' crawling and walking patterns. Fueled by the nature/nurture debate of the day, McGraw's aim was to compare the gait patterns of one infant who received daily training on slopes with the gait patterns of his identical twin for whom the slope task would be truly novel. She reasoned that any differences between the twins would be the result of learning. Unfortunately, the untrained "control" twin refused to cooperate and sat at the base of the slopes weeping. Like McGraw, we appreciate the novelty of slopes as a fruitful testing ground for studying motor learning and development. However, with our focus on flexibility, we aimed to test the adaptiveness of infants' responses rather than biomechanical changes in their gait patterns. We reasoned that if flexibility requires learning, adaptive responses should be linked with infants' locomotor experiences. If such learning transfers across various types of ground surfaces and motor contexts, then locomotor experience outside the laboratory (e.g., on flat ground) should predict the adaptiveness of their responses on novel slopes.

The Biomechanical Relationship Between Surface Slant and Body Propensities. A second reason for observing infants' behavior on slopes is that changes in surface slant have serious biomechanical consequences for balance control during stance and locomotion. Steeper hills are more difficult because more muscle torque is required to counteract destabilizing forces. Coping with downhill slopes is especially difficult because of the configuration of the body relative to the ground surface and the pull of gravity. Toddlers' feet (or crawlers' hands) are at a downward angle, decreasing the base of support. The muscles at the back of the supporting limbs must work to keep the body in an upright position and to brace it against rotating forward. With each walking or crawling step, the moving limb must straighten before contacting the ground surface resulting in a prolonged period with only one foot or hand on the ground. This is especially serious for babies' locomotion because they have trouble keeping balance with only one foot (or one hand and knee) on the floor. The already compromised supporting limb must bend rather than straighten to exert force. Such eccentric muscle actions require more muscle strength for supporting body weight and maintaining balance than a straight limb. The vertical acceleration of the center of mass is negative when the moving foot or hand contacts the surface, meaning that infants are falling downward into each step. This exacerbates the already thorny problem of keeping balance during single limb support. Steeper slopes increase the vertical distance that the body falls. If infants lose control, their hands are in an awkward position to protect their heads.

Reciprocally, differences in infants' physical attributes interact with degree of slant. Developmental changes in physical growth and locomotor experience affect changes in body dimensions, muscle strength, and balance control. These variables, in turn, affect the biomechanics of locomotion down slopes. Babies with more mature body dimensions, more muscle strength, and more advanced gait patterns on flat ground have greater wherewithal to walk or crawl down steeper slopes. More mature body dimensions such as a lower center of mass mean that the body can sway farther forward and backward before toppling over. Like a top-heavy bookcase, top-heavy babies tip over sooner and with less provocation than more maturely proportioned, cylindrically shaped ones. Stronger legs (or arms in the case of crawlers) give greater stability during single leg/arm support and allow infants to generate more muscle torque to counteract destabilizing torque if their body begins to rotate too far forward or backward. More advanced gait patterns on flat ground give infants more options to adapt gait to the slant of a hill. An efficient strategy for coping with downhill slopes, for example, is to shorten step length and decrease step velocity to minimize the vertical distance that the body falls at each step.

Information for Prospective Control.   A third reason why slopes provide a good test case for studying flexibility is that so much multimodal and redundant information is available for prospective control of locomotion. Obtaining the appropriate information requires babies to produce a variety of exploratory movements, allowing us to observe the process of prospective control firsthand. Infants can obtain visual information about surface slant, the height of the drop-off, and visible surface texture by peering over the brink of the hill. Movements of the head and body in depth generate motion parallax and cause changes in visual texture gradients such that the optic texture elements farther away from infants' eyes are denser and flow more quickly across the optic array than the closer elements. Infants can obtain both visual and mechanical information about their own postural stability relative to the slope as they sway back and forth or take small steps to approach the hill. As their bodies sway forward in the course of quiet stance or locomotion, texture elements in the optic array stream backward. As their bodies sway backward, optic texture elements stream forward. The speed of body sway is specified by the speed of the optic flow. Tactile information about surface slant and friction is available by probing the slope with a hand or foot. Most commonly, infants straddle the brink of the slope with their feet or hands and sway back and forth. These movements are extremely rich sources of information about the properties of the ground surface relative to infants' own physical propensities. They generate torque around the ankles or wrists and shearing forces between the extremities and the ground surface, and at the same time, generate concomitant changes in the speed and direction of optic flow.

Variety of Means.   A final virtue of the slope task is that it allows observation of a flexible variety of means. As McGraw (1935) described in her classic co-twin study, there are multiple options for responding adaptively to variations in downhill slopes: walking, crawling on hands and knees, sliding down headfirst prone (like Superman), sliding or crawling backward feetfirst with the head pointing away from the direction of travel, sliding down in a sitting position, and avoiding descent entirely. Moreover, infants can modify walking and crawling gait with subtle changes in locomotor strategy. They can minimize the vertical distance that their body falls by decreasing step length and/or step velocity with increase in degree of slant. They can augment postural control via a form of tool use by holding onto a railing, banister, or adult for additional support. Or, they could modify the joint angles characteristic of normal walking or crawling so as to keep the body in a more upright configuration, limit the range of forward and backward postural sway, or bear the brunt of destabilizing forces at stronger joints such as knees rather than ankles.

How Toddlers Cope With Locomotion Down Slopes

In our initial work, we found that 14-month-old walking infants differentiated 10°, 20°, 30°, and 40° slopes by their method of locomotion and exploratory activity (Adolph, Eppler, & Gibson, 1993a; Eppler et al., 1996).

The study described in this subsection introduced a new, modified psy-chophysical staircase procedure for testing infants over dozens of trials and over a continuous range of slopes (Adolph, 1995). The aim was to as-sess the accuracy of their judgments about safe and risky slopes and to exa-mine the online process underlying their decisions.

Age-Matched Control Design.   Thirty-one infants (17 boys and 14 girls) participated in the study. All were 14 months old ± one week and could walk over a 9-foot path independently, but walking experience, walking skill, and body dimensions varied freely. This age-matched control design allowed comparisons between individuals for the developmental vari-ables of interest, while providing a crude control for general age-related changes.

Walking experience and walking skill varied widely among infants. Walking experience ranged from 10 days to 137 days ($M = 77$ days). Ten infants had prior experience going down playground slides and 17 had prior experience descending stairs independently. Four toddlers had expe-rienced a serious fall after walking onset requiring medical attention.

Walking skill on flat ground was assessed using a footprint method of gait analysis (Adolph et al., 1996, April). Babies walked over a long strip of butcher paper with inked tabs on the soles of their shoes, leaving behind a trail of footprints. Coders used a coordinate grid to identify the x-y coordinates of each heel and toe placement and a computer program transformed these coordinates into kinematic measures of walking skill (linear distance between consecutive steps, lateral distance between the feet, dynamic base of support, and amount of in- or out-toeing). Step lengths ranged from 16 cm to 31 cm, step width from 6 cm to 18 cm, base of support from 100° to 156°, and foot rotation from −14° to 27°. More mature gait patterns are characterized by longer step lengths, smaller step widths, a base of support approaching 180°, and toes pointing straight ahead closer to 0°.

In contrast to the wide range in experience and walking skill, there was a relatively narrow range in infants' body dimensions. Height ranged from 73 cm to 83 cm, weight from 8 kg to 13 kg, head circumference from 45 cm to 50 cm, leg length from 31 cm to 36 cm, and Ponderal Index (an overall chubbiness index) from 1.8 to 2.4.

Sloping Walkway.   A mechanized sloping walkway was constructed to vary the slant of the ground surface along a continuous scale (see Fig. 4.1). The walkway was composed of three wooden sections, each 91 cm long × 84 cm wide, connected by piano hinges: a stationary flat starting plat-form, a middle sloping section, and an adjustable flat landing platform. A hydraulic pump under the landing platform changed its height from 22

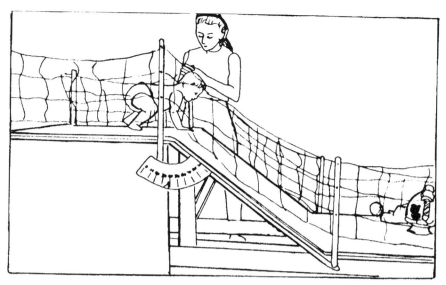

FIG. 4.1. Walkway with adjustable slope (0°–36°). Infants begin on flat starting platform. Parents encourage them from the end of the landing platform. Experimenter follows alongside infants to ensure their safety.

cm to 75 cm, causing the middle section to slant from 0° to 36° in 2° increments. The walkway was covered with soft carpet to cushion infants' falls and safety nets along the sides provided protection from tumbling off the sides of the ramp. All trials were videotaped for later analyses.

Psychophysical Staircase Procedure. The infants' task was to decide whether to walk, slide, or avoid going down slopes. The shallowest slopes were safe for every baby to walk down. The steepest slopes were risky for even the most expert walkers. The viability of the intermediate range of slopes depended on each infant's level of walking skill. Babies began each 60s trial in a standing position on the starting platform. Parents stood at the far side of the landing platform and encouraged their babies to come down using toys and Cheerios as enticements. An experimenter followed alongside infants to ensure their safety. Adults never instructed infants to be careful or to use a particular method of locomotion for traversal.

The experimenter used a modified psychophysical staircase procedure (Adolph, 1995) to estimate the steepest slope each infant could walk down. A staircase procedure is a classic method in psychophysics (Cornsweet, 1962) for estimating a threshold or change point—in this case, a motor threshold rather than a perceptual one—while minimizing the total num-

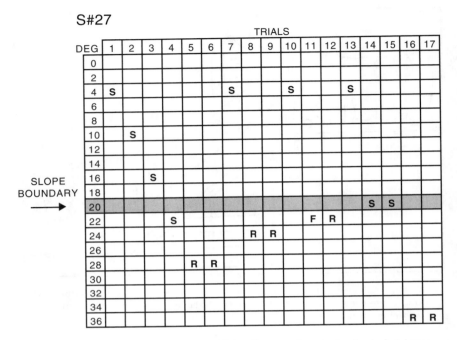

FIG. 4.2. Typical protocol from Baby #27 to illustrate the psychophysical staircase procedure. Each trial was coded online as *success*, S (walked safely), *failure*, F (tried to walk but fell), or *refusal*, R (slid down or avoided going). The experimenter presented steeper slopes after successful trials and shallower slopes after failures or refusals to estimate slope boundary to a 67% criterion. Shaded row indicates the boundary slope.

ber of required trials. Each trial was coded online as either a success (walked safely), failure (tried to walk but fell), or a refusal to walk (slid down or avoided going). Beginning with an easy 4° baseline slope, the experimenter increased slant by 6° after successful trials and decreased slant by 4° after two consecutive failures or refusals. Baseline trials were interspersed with staircase trials to maintain infants' motivation. This process continued until converging on a "slope boundary" to a 67% criterion: the steepest slope infants walked successfully on $\geq 2/3$ trials and failed or refused $\geq 2/3$ trials at the next 2° increment and all steeper slopes. At the end of the session, the experimenter presented babies with the 36° slope to observe how they coped with the steepest increment. Figure 4.2 shows a typical staircase protocol from one infant.

Slope Boundaries.   Just as there was a wide range in walking skill on flat ground, infants showed a wide range of walking abilities on slopes (6° to 28°). Some infants could walk down only the shallowest slopes without falling and others could manage terrifically steep ones. Measures of walking experience and walking skill on flat ground predicted infants' slope boundaries, attesting to the validity of the estimates derived from the staircase procedure. More experienced, skillful walkers on flat ground were also better walkers on slopes. Body proportions were not related to slope boundaries.

Online Decision Making About Relative Risk. To equate relative degree of risk across babies with such different walking abilities, we normalized the definition of safe and risky slopes to each infant's slope boundary. By definition, slopes shallower than infants' boundaries were safe and slopes steeper than their boundaries were increasingly risky. A "go ratio" indexed the accuracy of infants' perceptual judgments about whether slopes were safe for walking: (successes + failures)/(successes + failures + refusals). In the numerator are attempts to walk and in the denominator are both attempts and refusals to walk. (Note, the inverse "no-go ratio" yields the same information). Because successes were rare on risky slopes by definition, the range in go ratios at these increments depended on the difference between failures and refusals. The ratio could vary freely from 0 to 1 on all slopes except the boundary slope, where the ratio was $\geq .67$ by definition. Perfectly adapted decisions would be indicated by scaling perceptual judgments to infants' actual ability (i.e., matching the probability of attempts to the conditional probability of success). Babies should display high go ratios, near 1.0, on safe slopes where the probability of successful walking was high, and low go ratios, near 0, on risky slopes where the probability of success was low. Thus, the slope boundary served as a measure of infants' actual ability to walk down slopes, the go ratio served as a measure of the accuracy of their prospective control of locomotion, and the normalization of go ratios to slope boundaries served as a measure of whether their judgments reflected appreciation of the relationship between their own abilities and environmental properties.

On average, infants' judgments were impressively adaptive. They attempted to walk down safe slopes and refused to walk down increasingly risky ones. Figure 4.3a shows go ratios normalized by relative degree of risk to each infant's slope boundary. The boundary slope is denoted by 0 on the x-axis, slightly easier and slightly harder slopes by $\pm 5°$, slopes in an intermediate range by $\pm 13°$, and impossibly risky slopes by $\geq +18°$. Go ratios decreased steadily from .94 at slope boundary to .11 at $+18°$ and the shape of the go ratio curve closely matched the probability of success. Prospective control involved perceiving the fit between infants' own physical capabilities and the properties of the slope. This sort of prospective control is all the more impressive given the variability in degree of slant from trial to trial. Infants' decisions about whether slopes were safe for

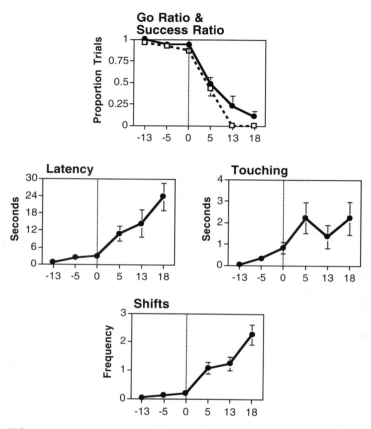

FIG. 4.3. (a) *Top graph.* Accuracy of infants' perceptual judgments on safe and risky slopes. Data are shown normalized to each infant's slope boundary (dotted vertical line). Safe slopes are to the left of the slope boundary and risky slopes are to the right. Perceptual judgments were indexed by a go ratio (Successes + Failures)/(Successes + Failures + Refusals) and walking ability by a success ratio (Successes)/(Successes + Failures). Go ratio = solid curve and filled symbols, success ratio = dashed curve and open symbols. The correspondence between the two curves shows infants' ability to gauge possibilities for walking. (b) *Bottom three graphs.* Three measures of exploratory activity. Latency reflects infants' hesitation before starting down slopes. Touching shows accumulated duration of haptic exploration at the brink of slopes. Shifts reflect a means–ends search for an alternative method of locomotion.

walking had to be based on information they obtained on the starting platform at the beginning of each trial.

The Informational Basis for Infants' Decisions. Infants' activity on the starting platform provided the basis for inferences about the process of prospective control of locomotion. By definition, exploratory movements occurred earlier in the trial than the behaviors used to index perceptual judgments. Trials began only after infants made visual contact with the slope. Parents and the experimenter called infants' attention to the slope and to an attractive lure on the landing platform. Then the experimenter released the babies on the starting platform. For the next 60s, babies had to decide on their own whether and how to descend. Coders scored latency to begin descent as a crude index of visual exploration. Brief latencies reflect quick glances and long latencies reflect longer looking times. Duration of touching slopes was an index of haptic exploration. Coders scored touches only when infants stopped forward locomotion and probed the sloping surface with hands or feet. To examine how infants selected an appropriate descent strategy, coders scored babies' shifts in position. Avoidance required no shifts and the various sliding positions required only one shift. Thus, multiple shifts in position (e.g., standing to backing to standing to prone = 3 shifts) reflected a means–ends search for an alternative method of locomotion to descend. In principle, duration and type of exploratory activity were independent of infants' slope boundaries and go ratios. That is, refusals to walk did not require prolonged exploration (babies could immediately choose an alternative sliding position for descent), and successes and failures did not prohibit prior exploration (babies could engage in prolonged exploration of any type then walk over the brink nonetheless).

Overall, infants' spontaneous exploratory activity neatly mirrored their perceptual judgments. Go ratios decreased and exploratory activity increased with relative degree of risk (compare Fig. 4.3a with Figs. 4.3b, c, and d). On average, babies hesitated longer, touched more, and displayed more shifts in position on increasingly risky slopes. Latencies ranged from 0.1s to 60.0s, but were generally very short (*Mdn* = 0.2s). On safe slopes, infants walked right down after only a brief glance at the surface as the experimenter released them on the starting platform. Long latencies were restricted to riskier slopes where the probability of falling increased. During the time babies hesitated, they peered over the brink of the slope, swayed backward and forward in place, took steps on the starting platform, touched slopes, and tested various sliding positions. The information obtained during the latency period informed infants' decisions about whether and how to descend. If toddlers hesitated, even for a brief moment, they were more likely to refuse to walk than if they descended without hesitation (9% refusals on trials ≤ 0.2s versus 53% refusals on trials > 0.2s).

On a subset of trials where infants hesitated, they obtained additional information by touching slopes (48% trials). Duration of touches ranged from 0.5s to 34.3s but most were relatively brief ($M = 4.3$s). Most touches (77%) were close simulations of walking and were maximally informative. Babies straddled the brink with their feet and rocked back and forth over their ankles or they made small stepping and swaying movements with their feet on the edge of the slope. The remainder of touches were pats and probes with the hands. All touches involved active movement and were accompanied by looking. After touching, infants were more likely to refuse to walk than on trials where they did not touch (61% of touch trials versus 21% of no-touch trials).

Like latency and touching, shifts in position increased on increasingly risky slopes. Overall, number of shifts per trial ranged from 0 to 10. The fact that shifts in position exceeded 1.0 at each slope increment steeper than slope boundary (see Fig. 4.3d) suggests that babies explored various positions rather than selecting a predetermined descent strategy from their repertoires. In contrast to other forms of exploratory activity, shifts in position were nearly always followed by refusals to walk (93% of trials), suggesting that infants had already decided that slopes were too steep to walk safely before they began exploring alternative options.

The systematic relationship between exploratory activity and perceptual judgments is even more evident in the behaviors of individual infants. Figure 4.4 shows four groups of babies, grouped according to the slope increment where their go ratios dropped consistently $\leq .50$. Reading along the top row of graphs in Fig. 4.4, the 17 infants in group A displayed the most conservative and accurate perceptual judgments, most closely geared to the probability of successful walking. Their go ratios dropped to $\leq .50$ at slightly risky slopes ($+5°$ steeper than slope boundary). The two babies in group B refused to walk at intermediate slopes ($+13°$ steeper than slope boundary). The eight infants in group C continued to walk until approaching impossibly risky slopes ($+18°$ steeper than slope boundary). The four infants in group D attempted to walk down every slope indiscriminately. The next three rows of graphs show three measures of exploratory activity for each go ratio group. Reading down columns, we see that children hesitated, touched, and shifted positions at approximately the same slopes where their go ratios decreased. That is, exploratory behavior on the starting platform predicted infants' success at safely navigating slopes. Group A hesitated, touched, and tested alternative descent methods at slope boundary or slightly steeper. Group B began to explore on the intermediate range of slopes. Group C did not explore until challenged with impossibly steep slopes. Finally, the hapless infants in group D never hesitated or tested alternative positions and they touched slopes indiscriminately.

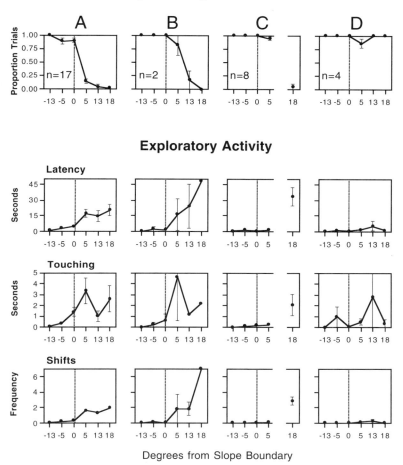

FIG. 4.4. Individual differences in accuracy of perceptual judgments and corresponding measures of exploratory activity for each go-ratio group.

Variety of Means for Descent. Recognizing that some slopes were risky for upright locomotion was only part of the story. Infants also recognized that on risky slopes, various sliding positions could serve as a means for descent. Of 184 trials scored as refusals to walk, on 83% they found an alternative method to achieve their goal: sliding in a sitting position (39%), backing down feetfirst (32%), crawling on hands and knees (9%), and sliding headfirst prone (3%). Although any single sliding strategy would have been sufficient to descend risky slopes, many infants used multiple methods. One infant used three sliding positions, 10 toddlers used two strategies, and 14 babies used only one method (two of the reckless infants in group D never refused to walk on risky slopes).

Prior experience using various descent methods in other contexts was not related to infants' methods of descent in the laboratory slope task. Nearly every child had descended from furniture by scooting backward feetfirst. Slightly more than half had descended stairs in a backing or sitting position, and one third had gone down a toddler slide independently. However, knowing a strategy for getting down did not mean that children knew when to use the strategy. Use of the various descent methods on laboratory slopes was spread randomly across infants with and without prior experience. Similarly, children with previous slide and stair experience were distributed evenly across the four go ratio groups. Moreover, having experienced a serious fall prior to the test session was not related to infants' descent strategies or perceptual judgments. Apparently, infants treated the slope task as novel and they used means–ends exploration (shifting positions on the starting platform) to discover various means for descent online.

Summary: How Toddlers Cope With Slopes. In sum, results of this study showed that young walking infants display impressive flexibility in coping with locomotion over slopes. Rather than a set of prespecified responses acquired prior to testing on slopes, infants' behaviors have all the hallmarks of adaptive action—online prospective control of movements, a tight fit between their own physical propensities and the properties of the environment, and variety of means for solving a novel motor problem. They guide locomotion prospectively by spontaneously generating looking, swaying, and touching movements to differentiate safe from risky slopes. They judge the potential consequences of maintaining their current upright posture based on the relationship between surface slant and their individual physiques and level of walking skill. On risky slopes, they explore and use a variety of sliding positions to navigate descent.

Moreover, this experiment illustrates that the study of flexibility in infant skill acquisition is eminently feasible. A modified psychophysical procedure yields detailed data about the adaptiveness of individual infants' responses. Careful observation of infants' exploratory behaviors sheds light on the informational basis for their perceptual judgments and the online decision-making process underlying prospective control of locomotion. An age-matched control design provides a way to assess the effects of various developmental factors on individual differences in responding. The next study examined the role of developmental changes more closely by experimentally inducing changes in infants' body dimensions and walking skill.

Coping With Changes in Body Dimensions and Walking Skill

Infants' growth during the first 2 years of life represents nearly unparalleled physical changes (the fetal and pubertal periods and women's growth during pregnancy are also dramatic examples of physical changes). Babies undergo sudden, surprisingly large growth spurts, showing no change in body dimensions for days or weeks on end, then spurting forward literally overnight (Lampl, 1983, 1993; Lampl et al., 1992). Moreover, babies don't just get bigger. Their body mass redistributes from the top-heavy dimensions characteristic of newborns to the more slender and cylindrical proportions characteristic of preschoolers, and their ratio of muscle mass to fat increases. It is as if infants' bodies are growing to fit their comparatively large heads.

Changing body dimensions are important because they affect the physical constraints on keeping balance. More babyish top-heavy dimensions, for example, make the body less stable during stance and locomotion. Destabilizing torques build up faster as the body sways back and forth and more muscle torque is required to keep the body within its region of permissible sway. More mature cylindrical dimensions make the body more stable. With a lower center of mass, less muscle strength is required to move the body the same angular distance. Thus, the redistribution of body mass and the rapid replacement of fat tissue with muscle throughout infancy should augment possibilities for action.

Since the 1930s, researchers have assumed that rapid growth in infancy must affect motor skill acquisition (e.g., Shirley, 1931; Thelen, 1984). For example, several studies found modest correlations between children's body proportions and when they began crawling and walking. More maturely proportioned babies with higher muscle-to-fat ratios crawled and walked sooner than more top-heavy, chubbier infants (Adolph, 1997; Adolph, Vereijken, & Denny, 1998; Garn, 1966; Shirley, 1931). However, there is little direct evidence that changes in body dimensions affect how well children crawl or walk, and there is little work examining how children might cope with novel changes in their own bodies. The following study examined whether infants display flexible adaptation to functional changes in body proportions and if so, how they managed it (Adolph & Avolio, 2000).

Walking With Weights. Twenty 14-month-old walking infants (10 girls, 10 boys) participated. All babies could walk at least 12 feet independently; walking experience ranged from 3 to 107 days ($M = 62.55$ days). Three infants had prior experience on playground slides, eight had experience walking down wheelchair ramps or sloping lawns, and nine had experience descending stairs.

To examine how infants recalibrate actions to account for rapid, developmental changes in body dimensions, we experimentally manipulated babies' dimensions via lead-weight shoulderpacks. Then, to exacerbate the problem of keeping balance, we challenged babies to walk down slopes. Infants were fitted into an adjustable, padded vest with removable velcro shoulderpacks (see Fig. 4.5). On some trials, the shoulderpacks were filled with feather-weight polyfill (120g) and on other trials they were filled with lead weights (25% of each infant's body weight). Based on pilot data, 25% of body weight was the maximum infants could tolerate before their knees collapsed. The feather weights only increased the girth of infants' chest dimensions. In contrast, the lead weights added to infants' overall mass and raised their center of mass from an average of 58.7% of standing height to 63% of standing height or by an average of 3.11 cm. The effect of this manipulation was to reduce the angular distance that infants could sway forward and backward before losing balance. When babies stand perfectly upright, the torque acting on their bodes is 0. When infants sway back and forth with their bodies at an angle, the torque acting on their bodies is represented by a sine function. While wearing the lead weights, the sine of the angle of permissible sway was reduced by an average of 25% when infants swayed around their ankles and by 35% when they swayed around their hips.

We tested infants on an adjustable sloping walkway (0° to 88°). As in earlier studies, parents stood at the end of the landing platform and encouraged their infants to descend. An experimenter followed alongside in-

FIG. 4.5.   Infant wearing adjustable vest with removable shoulderpacks for feather-weight and lead-weight conditions on slopes.

fants to ensure their safety if they began to fall. The appropriate shoulder-packs were attached at the start of each trial so that infants would be forced to decide online whether slopes were safe or risky for walking relative to their current body dimensions. We reasoned that the same absolute degree of slope could be safe in the feather-weight condition but risky in the lead-weight condition.

We designed a psychophysical *double* staircase procedure to test each infant in both feather-weight and lead-weight conditions (Adolph & Avolio, 2000). The experimenter ran two independent staircase protocols in tandem so that the weighting conditions were interleaved quasirandomly. Babies began with an easy 4° baseline slope. After each successful trial (walked safely), the experimenter increased slope by 8°. After a failure (tried to walk but fell) or refusal to walk (slid down or avoided descent), the experimenter presented infants with a shallow baseline slope of 4° to provide them with an easy success and to maintain their motivation to continue. Then, the experimenter removed the shoulderpacks for the current condition, attached the shoulderpacks for the other condition, and switched from the current staircase protocol to the other protocol. Upon reentering a staircase protocol, the experimenter presented infants with a slope 4° shallower than the last unsuccessful trial for that condition. This process continued for each protocol until the experimenter identified a slope boundary to a 75% criterion—the steepest slope that infants walked down successfully at least three out of four times and less than three out of four times at the next 4° and 8° increments. On average, each infant had 75 slope trials total.

Slope Boundaries. As predicted, experimental manipulation of infants' body proportions had immediate effects on their walking skill. The lead weights hampered their ability to walk down slopes. Walking boundaries ranged from 4° to 24° in the feather-weight condition and from 0° to 16° in the lead-weight condition. Overall, infants had steeper walking boundaries in the feather-weight condition ($M = 12.0°$) than the lead-weight condition ($M = 7.6°$). Three babies had boundaries 12° steeper in the feather-weight condition, 13 infants had boundaries 4° steeper, and four babies had identical boundaries in both conditions. Infants' walking experience and footprint measures of their walking skill on flat ground predicted their walking boundaries on slopes in both conditions, attesting to the validity of the estimates derived from the staircase procedure. More experienced infants with mature gait patterns on flat ground had steeper walking boundaries on slopes.

Flexible Online Recalibration. Could infants adapt to their altered bodies and skills? The strongest evidence for flexible, online recalibration would be a difference in infants' go ratios based on weighting condition at the same absolute degree of slope. Because the lead weights hampered infants' ability to walk down slopes, the same absolute degree of slope could be safe in the feather-weight condition but risky in the lead. For example, the degree of slant at infants' feather-weight boundary was safer (higher probability of success) while walking with feather-weight shoulderpacks than with lead. Indeed, comparisons between infants' go ratios in the feather-weight and lead-weight conditions at feather-weight and lead-weight walking boundaries showed significant effects for condition and for slope. That is, infants were more likely to walk down the same absolute degree of slope while loaded with feather weights than with lead and they were more likely to walk down their shallower lead-weight slope boundary than their steeper one (see Fig. 4.6). Given the constant switching between weighting conditions from trial to trial, these results could only be obtained if infants recalibrated their judgments to their current body dimensions and degree of slope online, based on information they obtained at the start of the trial.

Despite strong evidence that infants' decisions were affected by weighting condition, recalibration to relative degree of risk was not complete. Perfect recalibration would be indicated if feather- and lead-weight go ratio curves were superimposed after normalizing each curve to its respective slope boundary. If infants responded more cautiously or more recklessly while wearing lead weights, then the lead-weight go ratio curve

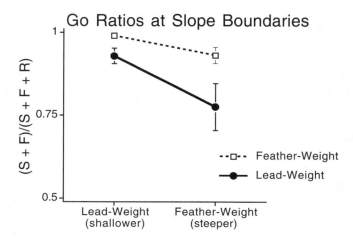

FIG. 4.6.   Go ratios loaded with feather weights and lead weights at the feather- and lead-weight slope boundaries show condition dependant judgments at the same absolute degree of slope.

would be displaced respectively to the left or the right of the feather-weight curve. Figure 4.7a shows infants' go ratio curves normalized to the appropriate slope boundary. Although both go ratio curves decreased with increase in relative degree in risk, the discrepancy between weighting conditions at slightly risky slopes (+4° and +10°) indicates more reckless errors while wearing lead weights.

Exploratory Movements.   As in the earlier studies, duration and type of exploratory movements predicted the functional outcome of each trial. If infants hesitated on the starting platform, even for a few brief moments, they were more likely to refuse to walk (66% and 62% of trials in feather- and lead-weight conditions, respectively) than if they did not hesitate on the starting platform (11% and 6% of trials in feather- and lead-weight conditions, respectively). During the time that they hesitated, infants peered over the brink, stepped and swayed on the starting platform, touched slopes, tested alternative sliding positions, and occasionally appealed to their parents or the experimenter for help. In both weighting conditions, infants touched slopes primarily with their feet (94% of trials in both feather- and lead-weights), by rocking back and forth over the ankles at the brink of the slope. They were more likely to refuse to walk after touching slopes (70% and 78% of trials in feather- and lead-weight conditions, respectively) than if they did not explore the surface by touching (30% and 27% of trials).

Differences in infants' exploratory movements due to weighting condition may explain the discrepancy between go ratio curves. On the same slightly risky slopes where they erred more frequently in the lead-weight condition, babies explored less, not more, while wearing their lead-weight shoulderpacks (see Figs. 4.7b and 4.7c). Latency and touching only diverged at the +4° and +10° slope increments where go ratios diverged—at precisely those increments near slope boundary where extended exploratory movements should prove most useful for distinguishing safe from risky slopes. The differences in exploratory movements between the two weighting conditions suggests that infants were sensitive to their altered body dimensions. However, maintaining upright balance while wearing the lead weights may have interfered with infants' ability to execute exploratory looking, touching, rocking, and swaying movements.

Variety of Means for Descent.   Just as the lead weights may have restricted infants' exploratory movements, the heavy shoulderpacks may have hampered infants from adjusting their gait to walk down slopes. On safe, but increasingly difficult slopes preceding the slope boundary, infants showed more modifications in their walking gait in the feather-weight than lead-weight condition (see Figs. 4.7d and 4.7e). In the feather-

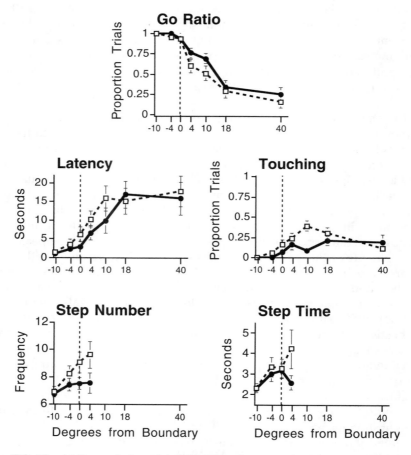

FIG. 4.7. (a) *Top graphs (go ratio)*. Calibration of perceptual judgments to feather-weight (dashed curves) and lead-weight (solid curves) conditions on safe and risky slopes. Data are shown normalized to each infant's slope boundary in each weighting condition (dotted vertical line). Safe slopes are to the left of the slope boundary and risky slopes are to the right. Perceptual judgments were indexed by a go ratio (Successes + Failures)/(Successes + Failures + Refusals). Perfect recalibration would be evidenced by superimposed curves at each increment of slope. (b) *Middle graphs (latency and touching)*. Exploratory activity in feather- and lead-weight conditions. Latency reflects infants' hesitation before starting down slopes. Touching was measured by proportion of trials that involved haptic exploration. (c) *Bottom graphs (step number and step time)*. Gait modifications in feather- and lead-weight conditions. Larger step numbers reflect smaller steps to travel the same distance. Longer step times reflect slower walking velocity.

weight shoulderpacks, they increased step number and step time to walk down steeper slopes (i.e., smaller, slower steps), but in the lead-weight condition, these measures yielded flatter curves.

The problem of coping with altered body proportions affected only decisions about whether and how to walk, not selection of alternative methods of locomotion. In both feather- and lead-weight conditions, infants displayed a flexible variety of means for descending risky slopes. They rarely avoided descent (17% and 19% of refusal trials in feather- and lead-weight conditions, respectively). Instead they slid down backward feet-first (31% and 29%), sitting on their bottoms (34% and 35%), crawling (10% and 11%), sliding headfirst prone (1% in both conditions), and walking while holding the nets for support (5% and 4%). Prior experience with descent in other contexts was not related to infants' methods of descent in the slope task. There were no differences in total number of descent methods or prevalence of any particular method between children with prior experience descending playground slides or stairs and babies with no prior experience. Apparently, infants maintained a high variety of means for descent by drawing on previous methods already in their repertoires and discovering new methods during the course of the session.

Summary: How Toddlers Cope With Changes in Body Dimensions and Skill. Toddlers do flexibly adapt locomotion to experimentally induced changes in body dimensions and walking skill. However, when their body proportions are unpredictable from trial to trial, recalibration to relative degree of risk is not complete. Infants were more likely to refuse to walk at the same absolute degree of slant while wearing the lead weights than the feather, indicating that go ratios did not depend solely on degree of slope. However, infants were also more likely to overestimate their ability on slightly risky slopes in the lead-weight condition compared with the feather. The differences between weighting conditions were not an artifact due to variability in infants' behavior or to fatigue. A control experiment, where two "dummy" feather-weight conditions were interleaved in an identical double staircase procedure showed no differences between dummy conditions for any outcome measures at any degree of slope (Adolph & Avolio, 2000).

Accurate online decisions require updated perceptual information about the current state of affairs. The relevant information can be obtained from a rich variety of exploratory movements—looking, swaying, touching, testing different positions, etc. As in the earlier studies with this age group, exploration tended to mirror perceptual judgments. When infants obtained the requisite information via looking and touching, their judgments were more accurate. When they did not explore slopes, they tended to err. The lead-weight loads in the current study caused infants to keep their bodies in a stiff upright posture, thereby hampering them from performing their usual range of exploratory movements and gait modifications. In contrast, maintaining a wide variety of means was unaffected by physical constraints. After deciding not to walk, infants generated a rich repertoire of alternative descent methods.

FLEXIBILITY AND LOCOMOTOR EXPERIENCE: WHEN LEARNING DOES AND DOES NOT TRANSFER

The question of how experience in one context facilitates performance in a different context is central to the concept of transfer, but learning is not necessarily required for the concept of flexibility. In principle, motor skills could be adaptive across a wide variety of novel contexts without the need for practice or experience. In this section, we present evidence that flexibility in infant locomotor skill acquisition does, in fact, involve learning. Drawing on studies of infants' behavior at the edge of slopes and cliffs, we show that the duration of motor experience is the key to adaptive responding. Flexibility is not apparent at the start of mobility and it does not depend on pure physical maturation or other age-related changes independent of experience.

In addition, we describe cases where learning does and does not transfer. The transfer data support our claim that learning does not entail a fixed repertoire of responses, a set of stimulus–response bonds, knowledge about a body schema or of one's own abilities, or even common sense knowledge about properties of the ground and their consequences for locomotion. Rather, learning entails acquiring the tools for online decision making—prospective control of movements based on relational information about current capabilities vis à vis the properties of the environment, and a variety of means to achieve the desired end state.

Transfer From Flat Ground to Slopes but Not From Crawling to Walking

Longitudinal Design. A longitudinal study was designed to separate the effects of age and locomotor experience in infants' ability to cope with safe and risky slopes (Adolph, 1997). We observed changes in flexibility over the entire course of locomotor skill acquisition, from infants' first crawling steps, over the transition from expert crawler to novice walker, and then for several weeks after walking onset. The study controlled for the duration of infants' everyday crawling and walking experience and allowed age to vary freely within test sessions. Of special interest was what happened over the transition from crawling to walking, when the same experienced crawlers faced the same slopes as novice walkers.

Fifteen infants (seven girls, eight boys) in an experimental group were tested every 3 weeks, from their first week of crawling until several weeks after they began walking. Weekly phone calls, home visits, and lab visits ensured that each child's crawling and walking onsets were identified precisely. Most babies were observed for 22 or more weeks of crawling, although duration of crawling experience was very variable (one infant crawled for only 1 week and another crawled for 37 weeks). Most babies were observed for 13 or more weeks of walking. Fourteen additional infants (seven girls, seven boys) in a control group were tested only three times at matched sessions (first week of crawling, tenth week of crawling, and first week of walking) to control for effects of repeated testing in the laboratory. Across both groups, there was a wide range in the age at which infants began crawling (4.8 to 9.6 months) and walking (9.3 to 14.9 months). Thus, age varied widely (range ~ 5 months) at each test session.

Procedure. Infants were tested using Adolph's (1995) psychophysical staircase procedure. Crawlers began each trial in a prone position on the starting platform and walkers began in an upright position. Parents waited at the bottom of the landing platform and encouraged their babies to descend. An experimenter followed alongside infants to ensure their safety if they began to fall. After successful trials, the experimenter increased slant by 6°, and after consecutive failures or refusals, she decreased slant by 4°. Easy 4° baseline trials were interspersed with staircase trials to maintain infants' motivation. The process continued until converging on a slope boundary to a 67% criterion. After identifying slope boundary, the experimenter presented infants with multiple probe trials at slightly risky slopes (6° steeper than boundary), intermediate slopes (12° steeper), impossibly risky slopes (18° steeper), and the steepest 36° slope. Significant correlations at each test session between infants' crawling and walking skill on flat ground and their slope boundaries attested to the validity of the estimates derived from the staircase procedure.

As in the earlier studies, a go ratio indexed the adaptiveness of infants' responses. Perfectly adaptive responses would be indicated by matching the probability of going to the conditional probability of success (i.e., high go ratios on safe slopes and low go ratios on risky ones). Conversely, high go ratios on risky slopes constitute serious errors and indicate lack of prospective control.

Prospective Control Transfers From Everyday Experience. The longitudinal data from this study provide strong evidence that flexible, prospective control depends primarily on everyday locomotor experience, not age. Of course, age and locomotor experience are normally intercorrelated (older children tend to have more experience). However, in the current study where duration of locomotor experience was held constant, there was no effect for infants' age at any test sessions. That is, older children fared no better than younger ones when matched for duration of crawling or walking experience. At infants' final week of crawling, when both age and experience varied freely, experience was a stronger predictor of adaptive responding than age. Moreover, experience independently explained variance above and beyond that explained by age alone, but age did not explain additional variance after experience was partialled out.

Figure 4.8 shows the primary index of adaptive responding and learning. The solid curves represent changes in experimental-group infants' go ratios (i.e., errors) on risky slopes across the weeks of testing—when crawlers tried to crawl and had to be rescued by the experimenter to prevent injury, and when walkers tried to walk and fell over the brink into the experimenter's arms. Most notably, the pattern of results indicates that the adaptiveness of infants' responses was related to the duration of their everyday crawling and walking experience. In their first week of crawling, infants plunged headlong down impossibly steep slopes on trial after trial (average go ratios were .68). Over weeks of crawling, go ratios decreased steadily until by their 22nd week of crawling, infants' judgments reflected nearly perfectly accurate prospective control of locomotion (average go ratios were .11). Similarly, in their first week of walking, infants walked

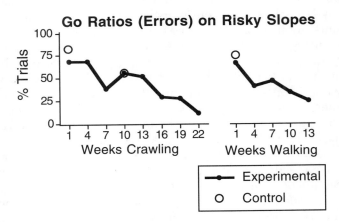

FIG. 4.8. Change in perceptual judgments on risky slopes over weeks of crawling and walking. Perceptual judgments were indexed by a go ratio (Successes + Failures)/(Successes + Failures + Refusals). Risky slopes included all increments steeper than infants' boundary slope. Filled symbols denote infants in the experimental group who were tested weekly on slopes. Open symbols denote infants in the control group who were tested only three times at matched session.

over the brink of impossibly steep slopes (average go ratios were .65). Over weeks of walking, go ratios decreased again. By their 13th week of walking, average go ratios were .24.

A second noteworthy point from the figure is that learning takes a surprisingly long time. Infants required 10 or more weeks of experience before errors on risky slopes decreased below 50% and 20 or more weeks before errors decreased to approximately 10%. Such slow learning curves represent a massive amount of everyday locomotor experience. In fact, preliminary data from an ongoing home diary study (Chan, Lu, Marin, & Adolph, 1999) points to a staggering amount of varied experiences in infants' first months of crawling and walking. New crawlers spend approximately 40% of their waking day on the floor, traverse 5 to 13 different surfaces per day, and log 50 to 350 feet per hour. New walkers spend over 50% of their waking day on the floor and take 500 to 1500 walking steps per hour. These preliminary data suggest that infants may take thousands of crawling or walking steps each day and hundreds of thousands of steps across days before they show adaptive responses in a novel task such as descending risky slopes.

In addition, Fig. 4.8 indicates that learning transferred from everyday locomotor experience on safe, flat ground to coping with the novel task of descending risky slopes. No infants in this study had experience on slopes outside the laboratory. Thus, the critical comparison is between the infants in the experimental group (solid symbols) who experienced more than a dozen test sessions and hundreds of trials on slopes and the infants in the control group (open symbols) who were tested only three times on laboratory slopes. There were no differences between experimental and control groups at any of the matched session times. Learning depended only on the duration of infants' everyday locomotor experience traveling over safe, flat ground at home, not on specific experiences coping with slopes.

Similarly, learning did not depend on specific experiences falling from heights in home accidents or falling down slopes in the laboratory. One child fell down a flight of stairs in a mechanical baby walker and was treated for serious contusions. Another broke his arm in a home accident. Despite these negative experiences in their first weeks of crawling, both babies dragged their bruised bodies over the edge of impossibly steep slopes similar to their inexperienced peers. Likewise, there was no evidence that infants learned to avoid steep hills from falling down laboratory slopes. After falling on one trial, infants were most likely to attempt the same crawling or walking response on the same impossibly steep hill on the very next trial (80% of consecutive trials). When infants slid down or avoided going, they refused outright after a successful trial on a shallower slope (93% of refusals).

*Relational Judgments Transfer Over Changes in Body Dimensions and Loco-
motor Skill.*   Transfer of experience-driven flexibility from flat ground to
slopes was all the more impressive because the definition of safe and risky
slopes changed from session to session for each infant. The procedure of
normalizing safe and risky slopes to each infant's current slope boundary
ensured that babies must take into account the relationship between their
current capabilities and the properties of the ground surface. In fact, infants' bodies and skills changed dramatically from session to session. For
example, average height increased by more than 12 cm across test sessions,
weight by nearly 3 kg, and Ponderal Index (overall chubbiness) decreased
by 17%. As infants' bodies got larger and more maturely proportioned,
their crawling and walking skill improved. On flat ground, average crawling velocity increased more than five-fold across test sessions, and average
walking step length increased by 60%. On slopes, boundaries changed as
infants improved at belly crawling, mastered crawling on hands and
knees, and became more proficient walkers (see Fig. 4.9). Thus, the learning curves in Fig. 4.8 indicate that infants learned to make flexible, adaptive decisions despite weekly changes in their bodies and skills. A safe hill
one week could be risky the next, and vice versa, depending on infants'
current method of locomotion and current level of locomotor skill.

Variety of Means Transfers From Crawling to Walking.   Just as infants
learned to control locomotion prospectively and to base their judgments
on the relationship between their own abilities and the ground surface,
they slowly acquired a variety of means for coping with descent. On average, avoidance appeared first at infants' 4th week of crawling, sliding
headfirst prone like Superman in their 13th week of crawling, sliding in

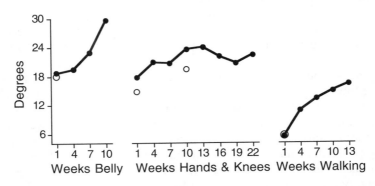

FIG. 4.9.   Developmental changes in slope boundaries across locomotor
milestones. Filled symbols represent infants in the experimental group who
were tested weekly on slopes. Open symbols represent infant in the control
group who were tested only three times at matched sessions.

a sitting position in their 16th week, and sliding backward feetfirst in their 19th week. Nearly every infant demonstrated multiple descent methods for going down slopes. As new options entered their repertoires, infants decreased use of the avoidance response (from 100% to 1% of refusal trials over weeks of crawling) and increased use of the various sliding positions. Most infants maintained all of their newly acquiring sliding positions as viable means of descent within and across crawling sessions. As refusals increased over weeks of walking, infants again used the various sliding positions that they had discovered during crawling. As in crawling, variety of means was maintained within and across walking sessions.

No Transfer From Crawling to Walking. The impressive transfer of prospective, relational control evident over weeks of crawling and walking was matched by equally impressive failure to transfer between crawling and walking. Figure 4.8 shows two parallel learning curves. Apparently, there was no savings from weeks of crawling. Go ratios on risky slopes were just as high in infants' first week of walking as they were in babies' first week of crawling, and learning was no faster the second time around.

In fact, infants' learning was so posture specific that they showed no transfer even from trial to trial. At the end of each walking session, babies were given six back-to-back trials at the steepest 36° slope: two trials in their new upright walking posture, then two trials in their old, familiar crawling posture, then two trials again in their unfamiliar walking posture. As shown in the left panel of Fig. 4.10, infants rarely erred at 36° in their last week of crawling. Similarly, when new walkers were tested in their old familiar crawling posture, they immediately slid down or avoided going. However, when new walkers were tested in their unfamiliar upright posture, they frequently attempted to walk down the same risky 36° slope and fell, requiring rescue by an experimenter.

Summary: Transfer From Flat Ground to Slopes but Not From Crawling to Walking. The longitudinal study of infants' locomotion over slopes shows that the three hallmarks of adaptive action are learned. Transfer of learning is both remarkably general and surprisingly specific. Adaptive action transfers from everyday crawling and walking experience on flat ground to the novel slope task and across changes in body dimensions and locomotor skill. However, learning does not transfer across developmental changes in posture. Infants acquire prospective, relational, varied control of action over weeks of crawling and again over weeks of walking.

How do we account for both the flexibility and specificity of learning in infant motor skill acquisition? Acquiring a body image or a static concept of their own bodies and skills would have been useless because these aspects of self were changeable within each method of locomotion. Recip-

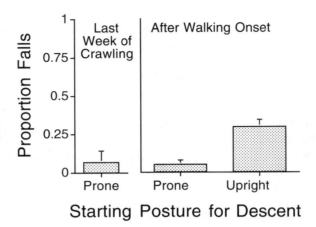

Starting Posture for Descent

FIG. 4.10.   No transfer of learning from crawling to walking on consecutive trials. Height of bars indicates proportion of falls on 36°
slope for prone versus standing postures at the same testing session.

rocally, specific knowledge about slopes or their meaning for locomotion
(e.g., 30° hills are risky) would have been useless because possibilities for
action depended on the fit between babies' propensities and the properties
of the ground surface. Likewise, learning particular stimulus–response
associations (e.g., slide backward down 30° slopes) would not have helped
because the appropriateness of each locomotor method depended on the
changing and dynamic fit between environmental properties and infants'
physical capabilities.

A more plausible explanation is that infants learn a posture-specific
means of controlling balance. As they gain experience keeping balance
and moving in a particular body posture, their actions become more flexible across a wider range of novel motor contexts. However, this flexibility
is limited to the experienced posture. When infants make the transition to
a new mode of locomotion, they must learn how to maintain balance
under a whole new set of constraints. The next section presents studies
that compare adaptive actions across a different pair of experienced and
unfamiliar postures (sitting and crawling) in a new task context (balancing
at the edge of a precipice).

Transfer From Solid Ground to Cliffs but Not From Sitting to Crawling

As degree of slant approaches the most extreme angle, 90°, the surface
becomes a sheer drop-off rather than a gradual slope. Although from a
functional point of view, slopes ranging from 45° to 90° are equally risky

for crawling and walking (0% probability of success), perceptually, slopes and cliffs are very different. A slope has a continuous visible surface texture and a cliff has an abrupt discontinuity in visual texture gradients. A slope has a surface that can be probed and felt with the hands and feet, a cliff does not. Many properties of a sloping surface have practical consequences for locomotion (degree of slant, size of the vertical drop-off, length of the slope itself, rigidity of the surface, frictional properties, surface relief, etc.), but the relevant properties of a cliff involve only its dimensions. Finally, a steep slope has several alternative options for managing descent (sliding down in backing, sitting, or prone positions) but a large cliff is not navigable by human infants and requires avoidance.

Since Gibson and Walk's classic studies (Gibson & Walk, 1960; Walk & Gibson, 1961; Walk, Gibson, & Tighe, 1957), most researchers have tested animals' and babies' responses to a sheer drop-off on a "visual cliff" rather than a real one. To ensure participants' safety, the cliff is covered in invisible glass. In the usual arrangement, a narrow starting platform divides a glass table. On the "shallow" side of the divide, a patterned surface is placed directly beneath the glass so that the surface looks continuous. On the "deep" side of the divide, the same patterned surface is placed far below the glass so that the surface looks like a cliff. The animal or baby is coaxed to cross first one side, then the other, using the parent, food, or a toy as a lure. The primary outcome measures are percent of subjects who avoid crossing the deep side versus the shallow side and their latency to begin traversal.

The Role of Experience in Visual Cliff Avoidance. The young of some precocial (already locomotor) species avoid the apparent drop-off on the visual cliff on their first exposure (e.g., Gibson & Walk, 1960; Walk & Gibson, 1961; Walk et al., 1957). Baby chickens and goats, for example, walk or hop over the shallow side of the visual cliff, but adamantly refuse to go over the deep side. When newborn goats are placed directly on the glass covering the deep side, they splay their legs in a defensive reaction and back up toward the starting platform. In fact, Gibson drew inspiration for the design of the first visual cliff from her observation that baby goats will not step off the edge of a stool moments after birth (Gibson, 1991). (Kids are born in pairs and she needed a way to manage one twin while the other was being birthed.)

In contrast, human infants and other altricial species such as kittens and rabbits require a protracted period of crawling experience before they avoid crossing the deep side of the visual cliff (e.g., Campos, Bertenthal, & Kermoian, 1992; Held & Hein, 1963; Richards & Rader, 1983; Walk, 1966). For example, Bertenthal, Campos, and Barrett (1984) demonstrated that the duration of infants' everyday crawling experience predicts avoidance on the visual cliff, independent of crawling onset age or age at testing (see Fig. 4.11). The curves represent avoidance responses in infants with approximately 6 weeks of crawling experience and babies with approximately 2 weeks of crawling experience. Most impressive, comparison of the curves in the middle section of the x-axis shows that at the very same ages at testing (7.5 to 8.5 months), 60% to 70% of experienced crawlers avoided crossing the deep side of the visual cliff but only 30% to 40% of inexperienced babies did likewise. Bertenthal and Campos (1984) argued that the beneficial effects of everyday crawling experience are likely to be asymptotic rather than strictly linear. Thus, we should expect the strongest effects for experience in the first few months after infants begin crawling before avoidance responses reach asymptote.

Although infants must learn to avoid a precipitous drop-off, their learning does not reflect any sort of simple associative pairing between the depth information for a drop-off and the negative consequences of falling. Rather, avoiding the visual cliff reflects the same sort of flexible, adaptive, online decision making that babies displayed in the slope tasks. For example, negative experiences falling from heights are not related to avoidance on the visual cliff (Scarr & Salapatek, 1970; Walk, 1966); inexperienced crawlers are likely to cross the visual cliff regardless of whether they experienced home accidents falling from a steep place in the course of crawling. Similarly, adaptive avoidance responses do not depend on actual experience with the visual cliff. For approximately 15 days after they become locomotor, kittens and bunnies safely cross the deep side of the visual cliff without incident, then they subsequently avoid it (Walk, 1966). More-

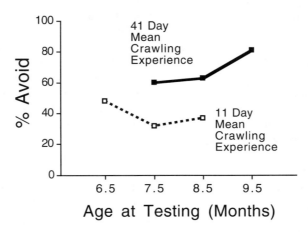

FIG. 4.11.   Percent of infants who avoided the visual cliff as a function of age and crawling experience. Figure adapted from Bertenthal, Campos, and Barrett (1984).

over, like the babies who learned to cope with novel slopes as crawlers but showed no transfer to a new walking posture, adaptive avoidance responses at the edge of a cliff may be specific to the posture in which infants have acquired experience. In a clever within-subject design, Rader, Bausano, and Richards (1980) showed that infants with several weeks of home crawling experience avoided crossing the visual cliff when tested in their experienced crawling posture. However, moments later, the same babies went right over the deep side when supported upright in mechanical baby walkers. The critical experience for promoting visual guidance of locomotion appears to stem from using one's own powers to maintain balance in a particular body posture while moving over various visually patterned ground surfaces.

Of course, the visual cliff is, in fact, perfectly safe for locomotion, and human infants eventually learn that transparent surfaces can provide support for locomotion. Such learning is problematic for studies involving repeated testing but interesting for examining how infants learn about transparency. When babies are tested longitudinally or given multiple trials in cross-sectional studies, avoidance responses actually attenuate in some experienced crawlers after repeated exposure to the glass surface (Campos, Hiatt, Ramsay, Henderson, & Svejda, 1978; Eppler, Satterwhite, Wendt, & Bruce, 1997). Instead of avoiding, infants display long latencies, all the while peering down into the crevice, then cross using ingenious compromise strategies such as detouring along the wooden edge of the glass platform, attempting to back into the precipice, or crawling midway over the glass then stretching out an arm as though trying to bridge the remaining gap with their extremity. Similarly, Titzer (1995, March) found that infants who had been given several weeks of home experience playing with transparent, plexiglass boxes subsequently crossed the visual cliff after long latencies and a strong push on the glass surface with their hands. Although they are uncomfortable locomoting over a surface while they can see the ground far below their bodies, babies can learn about the substantial properties of a transparent surface for supporting their bodies.

Sitting and Crawling at the Edge of an Adjustable Gap.   In two recent studies (Adolph, 2000; Adolph, Avolio, Melton, Arnet, & Eppler, 1998), we expanded on our earlier finding of specificity of learning from crawling to walking in infants' locomotion over slopes and Rader et al.'s (1980) finding of specificity of knowledge from prone to upright postures on the visual cliff. However, rather than testing babies in an experienced crawling posture versus an unfamiliar walking posture, we tested them in an experienced sitting posture versus an unfamiliar crawling posture. And rather than testing babies on slopes or a visual cliff, we tested them at the edge of an actual precipice.

We built an adjustable "gaps" apparatus by constructing a stationary, wooden starting platform (106 cm long × 76 cm wide × 86 cm high) and a moveable landing platform (158 cm long × 76 cm wide × 86 cm high). By sliding the landing platform back and forth along a calibrated track, we could create a gap between the two platforms, varying in 2 cm increments from 0 cm to 90 cm. Both platforms were covered in carpet and the floor of the crevice was padded with foam. As in earlier studies, parents stood at the far side of the landing platform and encouraged their babies to cross the gap. An experimenter followed alongside infants to ensure their safety if they began to fall.

The experimental design capitalized on the overlap in timing of two postural milestones: an earlier developing sitting posture and a later developing crawling posture. Nine-month-old infants were tested in a familiar sitting posture where they had a great deal of experience maintaining balance (approximately 3 months), and in a less familiar crawling posture where they were relative novices at maintaining balance (approximately 1.5 months). In both postures, their task was to decide whether they could lean forward over the gap without falling into the crevice (see Fig. 4.12). In the sitting posture, infants sat at the edge of the gap with their legs dangling into the hole. A toy was suspended at the end of a stick to provide an incentive for babies to lean forward and stretch an arm out over the gap. In the crawling posture, babies began in a prone position on the starting platform. A toy was placed on the landing platform to encourage them to lean forward and stretch an arm out over the gap. This task was relatively

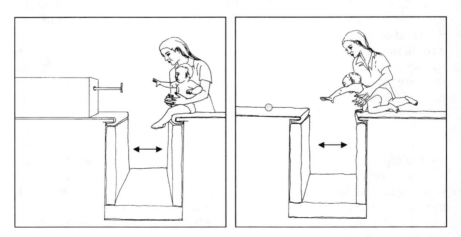

FIG. 4.12. "Gaps" apparatus with adjustable hole (0–90 cm) in the surface of support. Infants were coaxed to stretch their arm out and lean forward over the gap in order to retrieve a toy on the other side. An experimenter spotted infants to prevent injury from falls.

novel. No infants had prior experience crawling over holes in the floor or sitting at the edge of a precipice without external support to strap them in.

Adolph's (1995) psychophysical staircase procedure was used to identify the largest gap each infant could span in each posture—their sitting and crawling gap boundaries. Then the experimenter presented infants with multiple trials on safe and risky gaps (6 cm smaller than gap boundary, 6 cm, 12 cm, and 18 cm larger than gap boundary, and trials at the largest 90 cm gap). The latter 90 cm gap was the same dimensions as the traditional visual cliff, minus the safety glass. We reasoned that if experience precipitates learning something general about ground surfaces, then infants' actions at the edge of an impossibly large gap should be the same regardless of the posture in which they are tested. If, on the other hand, experience facilitates a more specific form of learning how to maintain balance within a specific postural system across a wide variety of situations, then babies should demonstrate more adaptive, prospective, and relational control of action in their more experienced sitting posture.

In two separate experiments, infants exhibited highly adaptive responses in their experienced sitting posture and surprisingly maladaptive responses in their less familiar crawling posture (see Fig. 4.13). In the sitting posture, they consistently matched the probability of avoiding to the probability of falling. That is, they leaned forward to retrieve the toy on safe gaps where the goal was within reach, and avoided leaning forward on increasingly risky gaps where they were likely to fall. In contrast, in the crawling posture, they crawled into impossibly large gaps on trial after trial, requiring rescue by the experimenter. At every risky gap increment, infants made more errors in the crawling posture than the sitting posture. In fact, several infants in both experiments attempted the largest 90 cm gap in the crawling posture, which was tantamount to crawling into thin air. All babies avoided the 90 cm gap in the sitting posture. As in earlier studies, there was no effect for condition order and no evidence of within-session learning from falling on previous trials. Also, as in earlier studies, there was no evidence that prior experiences falling over drop-offs (e.g., edge of bed, changing table, stairs) affected behavior in the novel laboratory task.

Summary: Transfer From Solid Ground to Cliffs but Not From Sitting to Crawling. Like the crawling and walking infants on slopes, findings from sitting and crawling babies on cliffs and gaps provide further evidence that flexibility, like the old concept of transfer, requires learning. Over weeks of everyday experience maintaining balance in particular body postures on safe, solid ground, infants acquire the wherewithal to make adaptive decisions for maintaining balance at the edge of a novel, potentially risky precipice. Experience facilitates flexibility when faced with novel contexts in a familiar body posture, but leads to specificity when faced

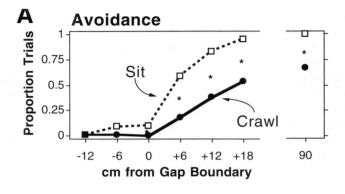

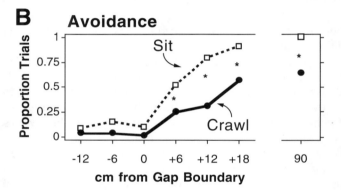

FIG. 4.13.   Accuracy of infants' judgments on safe and risky gaps. Data
are shown normalized to each infants' gap boundary (represented as 0
on the x-axis) in the sitting (dashed curve) and crawling (solid curve)
postures. Safe gaps are to the left of the gap boundary and risky gaps are
to the right. Perceptual judgments were indexed by a go ratio. (a) Experiment I. (b) Experiment II.

with a familiar task in a novel body posture. The following section focuses
on what infants may learn that promotes both flexibility and specificity of
responding.

WHAT INFANTS LEARN THAT PROMOTES
BOTH FLEXIBILITY AND SPECIFICITY

What, then, might infants learn? The empirical results belie several traditional, common-sense explanations. Infants do not learn a set of facts
about surfaces. Although steep slopes and precipitous drop-offs are dan-
gerous in any posture, infants' knowledge was posture-specific. They do

not acquire static concepts of their own abilities. Infants recalibrated to both naturally occurring changes and experimentally induced changes in their body dimensions and locomotor skill. They do not learn fixed associations between specific environmental properties and specific motor responses. Babies adapted their responses to the current status of the actor–environment fit and they displayed a wide variety of alternative locomotor strategies from trial to trial. Their responses are not mediated by acquisition of a fear of heights or fear of falling. Babies rarely displayed negative emotions of any sort in any of the experimental tasks (Adolph & Eppler, 1999; Sorce, Emde, Campos, & Klinnert, 1985; Stergiou, Adolph, Alibali, Avolio, & Cenedella, 1997), and it is unlikely that fear would wax and wane with changes in body postures. Finally, there is no evidence of one-trial learning or of learning from falling within the testing session.

Posture-Specific Learning About Balance Control:
The Region of Permissible Sway

An explanation that can account for both the impressive flexibility and surprising specificity described in this chapter is that infants are learning about balance control. They learn to detect threats to balance and they learn compensatory strategies for when balance is disrupted.

In quiet stance and locomotion, the body is always swaying to and fro in a cyclical process of imminent balance loss and recovery. To prevent themselves from falling over, infants must maintain their bodies within a region of permissible postural sway (Riccio, 1993; Riccio & Stoffregen, 1988). The extent of this region is defined by the available muscle torque relative to destabilizing torque. Babies will lose balance if their bodies move outside their base of support without sufficient muscle strength to pull themselves back into position.

Typically, balance control appears effortless because we keep our bodies well within the region of permissible sway. Balance control is threatened when variations in the ground surface or changes in body propensities increase the ratio of destabilizing torque to muscle torque above tolerable limits. This narrows the region of permissible sway or quickens the body's movement toward the outer limits of reversibility. A downward slant, for example, narrows the sway region by decreasing the base of support and increasing the vertical distance that the body falls during each step. A weighted vest narrows the sway window and increases destabilizing torque by increasing the body mass above the pivot point. A small drop-off or gap in the surface of support requires infants to place their extremity on the far side of the hole before toppling over. On an impossible large cliff, of course, balance is disrupted because there is no floor at all to support the body. In fact, the size of the sway window fluctuates from step to step, with every irregularity in terrain, with every change in the location of the center of mass due to body movements or shifting a load, etc.

Thus, the trick for keeping balance is to continually gauge the region of permissible sway against the available muscle torque for counteracting destabilizing torque. Perceptual information is required to specify the extent of spontaneous swaying motions and the results of compensatory sways to recover balance. Exploratory looking, swaying, and touching movements yield redundant information about the current status of the sway region.

Learning the appropriate exploratory movements to maintain balance might be general with respect to surface properties and body propensities, yet specific with respect to developmental changes in posture because each postural milestone represents a different balance control system (see Fig. 4.14). Each postural milestone has a different set of relevant parameters for gauging the region of permissible sway and keeping the body within tolerable limits. Sitting, crawling, and walking postures, for example, involve different key pivots around which the body rotates (e.g., the hips for sitting, the wrists for crawling, and the ankles for walking). Each posture involves different muscle groups for executing movements and for generating compensatory sway, different vantage points for viewing the ground surface, different frequency and amplitude of optic flow information as the body sways back and forth, different extremities for obtaining haptic information, different correlations between visual, kinesthetic, and vestibular information, and so on. Variations in the ground or in body propensities affect only the settings of the relevant parameters—that is, the size of the sway region. The developmental shift from one postural milestone to another presents a different problem. New postures actually involve new control parameters. Thus, infants may require extensive

Sitting   Crawling

Walking

FIG. 4.14.   Schematic illustration of region of permissible sway around key pivot for maintaining balance in sitting, crawling, and walking postures.

experience with each postural milestone in development to define the relevant parameters for the new balance control system and to facilitate the online calibration of parameter settings.

Step-to-Step Exploration in the Service of Action

How might infants gauge their current region of permissible sway on a step-to-step basis? Our analyses of infants' behavior at the edge of potentially risky surfaces indicate a sequential process of exploration in adaptive online decision making (Adolph, 1997; Adolph & Eppler, 1998, 1999). Visual exploration serves as the first strategy for guiding action. Babies take a quick glance at the ground ahead. If the surface appears similar to the ground beneath their bodies, they continue on their current path without pause. If the surface looks discrepant, they stop, engage in more prolonged visual inspection, and sway back and forth or take small steps in place. Prolonged looking and swaying/stepping movements produce changes in the speed and direction of optic flow and concomitant changes in vestibular and kinesthetic information about postural control. If these movements specify safe going, infants plunge ahead. However, if something seems amiss, they may obtain additional information from coordinated looking and touching. Tactile exploration is limited largely to situations where the probability of falling begins to increase. Typically, infants touch with their leading extremity and use movements that produce similar forces to those involved in locomotion (rocking and stepping at the brink of the questionable surface). When tactile probes of the ground surface reveal adequate support for locomotion, babies proceed forward but modify their gait by shortening step length and decreasing step velocity. If touching specifies undue risk, they seek out alternative methods of locomotion or navigate a detour around the problem site. Means–ends exploration in the service of locomotion involves multiple shifts in position and partial attempts at traversal. If infants discover an alternative course of action to achieve their goal, they use it. Otherwise, they stay put and fuss. Avoidance appears to be the solution of last resort and typically produces very frustrated infants.

NEW ANSWERS TO OLD QUESTIONS: ACQUIRING THE TOOLS FOR ONLINE DECISION MAKING

Understanding Transfer in Motor Skill Acquisition

For nearly a century, research on transfer has concentrated on identifying identical elements in training and performance contexts. Accordingly, traditional experimental paradigms have relied on tasks that involve learning rote routines, stimulus–response associations, fixed contingencies, reinforcement schedules, and so on. For example, dozens of studies (e.g., Kalnins & Bruner, 1973; Rovee-Collier & Gekoski, 1979) have shown that human infants can be operantly conditioned to maintain an experimental contingency between a particular motor response (e.g., sucking, kicking, head-turning) and a particular reinforcer (e.g., the clarity of a visual display, the movement of an overhead mobile). Babies' spontaneous mouth, head, or limb movements quickly take on an exploratory function as they begin to discover the built-in contingency (Thelen & Fisher, 1983). As movements become more instrumental in maintaining the contingency, they can also become more spare and efficient (Rovee-Collier & Gekoski, 1979). With appropriate variations in stimulus displays during training, babies can even demonstrate stimulus generalization to novel displays (e.g., Greco, Hayne, & Rovee-Collier, 1990). However, the empirical evidence presented in this chapter indicates that traditional learning paradigms such as operant conditioning are poor analogues of everyday motor skill acquisition. They fail to capture the rich and continually changing constraints on movement on both sides of the actor–environment relationship.

Harlow's (e.g., Harlow, 1949, 1959) discrimination and oddity problems represented a try at something broader than simple associative learning. His notion of "learning to learn" involved acquiring a rule that spanned multiple problem sets. In the discrimination problems, monkeys were presented with dozens of sets of differently shaped block pairs. A raisin was hidden under one block in the pair for the 10 or so trials that comprised that learning set. After several trials, monkeys learned to track the designated block to retrieve the raisin, but when they were presented with a pair of new shapes in the next problem set, they responded at chance levels. Adult monkeys required dozens of problem sets (and hundreds or thousands of trials) before they abstracted a general rule of "win-stay/ lose-shift" that would allow them to solve the next discrimination problem in only one trial: If the first lifted block reveals the raisin, track it ; otherwise, track the other shape. In the oddity problems, monkeys had to select the shape that was different from three or more blocks. Here, the general rule was to choose the odd one from among a set. Like monkeys, children of normal intelligence and children with mental retardation can learn to solve discrimination and oddity problems (e.g., Levinson & Reese, 1967; Zeaman & House, 1963).

Harlow called this phenomenon *learning to learn* because it allowed for online problem solving. However, his experimental paradigm cannot serve as an adequate model of flexibility in motor skill acquisition. No simple rule to a single class of problem will suffice for coping with a varying body, a varying terrain, and step-to-step variations in biomechanical constraints.

Novelty and Variability Require Flexibility

Theoretically, transfer is an important concept because it highlights our need to understand how behavior is adapted to novel and highly variable contexts. We have argued that novelty and variability characterize the essential nature of everyday motor skill. Even expert, adult performance and highly automatized actions such as walking, talking, and driving require an online decision-making process because the biomechanical constraints on movement are continually changing. We walk through a cluttered environment, over various floor coverings, carrying variable loads. We talk with a mouthful of food, with teeth clenched, while gasping for breath, and through interruptions by our interlocutors. We drive unfamiliar rental cars over varied terrain in changeable weather and traffic conditions. Flexibility is the extent to which we cope adaptively with this sea of novelty. It is marked by prospective, relational control of action, and use of a variety of means to achieve a desired movement outcome.

Flexibility is especially paramount in infancy because motor skill is acquired in the context of developmental change. Babies' bodies change radically and abruptly. They undergo metamorphoses of postural control as they sit up, crawl on all fours, and finally walk upright. They are exposed to new worlds of opportunities for action as their new bodies and skills expose them to an expanded environment. With so much flux, the content of motor knowledge is unlikely to be limited to facts about environmental features, particular motor responses, static mental representations, or fixed associations between stimuli and responses. In fact, such knowledge would be maladaptive in a system that is continually changing. In the experiments described in this chapter—babies locomoting over slopes, walking with weights, and balancing at the edge of gaps and cliffs—infants showed no evidence that their judgments were based on static forms of knowledge. They do not learn particular solutions for particular motor problems or even more general rules for solving a class of motor problems. Instead, they appear to recalibrate online to the changing relationship between environmental properties and their own physical propensities.

In general, the data suggest that infants acquire the tools for online decision making in controlling posture and locomotion. Acquiring flexibility entails the wherewithal to identify novel motor problems and discover viable solutions online. The essential tools are a fluid repertoire of exploratory movements that allow prospective, relational, and varied control of action. The skilled application of these tools across a variety of environmental contexts grows with increasing experience. Surprisingly, these tools are not carried over the transition to new postural milestones. In sum, infant motor skill acquisition is both far more flexible and far more specific than previously recognized.

ACKNOWLEDGMENT

This research was supported by National Institutes of Child Health and Human Development Grant HD33486 to Karen Adolph.

REFERENCES

Adams, J. A. (1985). The use of a model of movement sequences for the study of knowledge of results and the training of experts. *Human Movement Studies, 11,* 223–236.

Adams, J. A. (1987). Historical review and appraisal of research on the learning, retention, and transfer of human motor skills. *Psychological Bulletin, 101,* 41–74.

Adams, J. A., & Hufford, L. E. (1962). Contributions of a part-task trainer to the learning and relearning of a time-shared flight maneuver. *Human Factors, 4,* 159–170.

Adolph, K. E. (1995). A psychophysical assessment of toddlers' ability to cope with slopes. *Journal of Experimental Psychology: Human Perception and Performance, 21,* 734–750.

Adolph, K. E. (1997). Learning in the development of infant locomotion. *Monographs of the Society for Research in Child Development, 62*(3, Serial No. 251).

Adolph, K. E. (2000). Specificity of learning: Why infants fall over a veritable cliff. *Psychological Science, 11,* 290–295.

Adolph, K.E. & Avolio, A. M. (2000). Walking infants adapt locomotion to changing body dimensions. *Journal of Experimental Psychology: Human Perception and Performance, 26,* 1148–1166.

Adolph, K. E., Avolio, A. M., Melton, K. E., Arnet, H. S., & Eppler, M. A. (1998, April). *Infant learning about balance control across changes in body posture.* Poster presented to the International Conference on Infant Studies, Atlanta, GA.

Adolph, K. E., & Eppler, M. A. (1998). Development of visually guided locomotion. *Ecological Psychology, 10,* 303–321.

Adolph, K. E., & Eppler, M. A. (1999). Obstacles to understanding: An ecological approach to infant problem solving. In E. Winograd, R. Fivush, & W. Hirst (Eds.), *Ecological approaches to cognition: Essays in honor of Ulric Neisser* (pp. 31–58). Hillsdale, NJ: Lawrence Erlbaum Associates.

Adolph, K. E., Eppler, M. A., & Gibson, E. J. (1993a). Crawling versus walking infants' perception of affordances for locomotion over sloping surfaces. *Child Development, Special Section on Developmental Biodynamics, 64,* 1158–1174.

Adolph, K. E., Eppler, M. A., & Gibson, E. J. (1993b). Development of perception of affordances. In C. Rovee-Collier & L. P. Lipsitt (Eds.), *Advances in infancy research,* (Vol. 8, pp. 51–98). Norwood, NJ: Ablex.

Adolph, K. E., Vereijken, B., Byrne, K. J., Urspruch, T., Ilustre, I., & Ondrako, A. M. (1996, April). *Footprint Method of Gait Analysis: New Insights into Infant Walking.* Poster presented to the International Conference on Infant Studies, Providence, RI.

Adolph, K. E., Vereijken, B., & Denny, M. A. (1998). Learning to crawl. *Child Development, 69,* 1299–1312.

Anderson, J. R., & Singley, M. K. (1993). The identical elements theory of transfer. In J. R. Anderson (Ed.), *Rules of the mind* (pp. 183–204). Hillsdale, NJ: Lawrence Erlbaum Associates.

Bernstein, N. (1967). *The coordination and regulation of movements.* Oxford: Pergamon Press.

Bernstein, N. (1996). Dexterity and its development. In M. L. Latash & M. T. Turvey (Eds.), *Dexterity and its development* (pp. 3–244). Mahwah, NJ: Lawrence Erlbaum Associates.

Bertenthal, B. I., & Campos, J. J. (1984). A reexamination of fear and its determinants on the visual cliff. *Psychophysiology, 21,* 413–417.

Bertenthal, B. I., Campos, J. J., & Barrett, K. C. (1984). Self-produced locomotion: An organizer of emotional, cognitive, and social development in infancy. In R. N. Emde & R. J. Harmon (Eds.), *Continuities and discontinuities in development* (pp. 175–210). New York: Plenum.

Book, W. F. (1925). *The psychology of skill.* New York: Gregg.

Bruner, J. (1972). Nature and uses of immaturity. *American Psychologist, 27,* 1–22.

Bruner, J. S. (1973). Organization of early skilled action. *Child Development, 44,* 1–11.

Bryan, W. L., & Harter, N. (1897). Studies in the physiology and psychology of the telegraphic language. *Psychological Review, 4,* 27–53.

Bryan, W. L., & Harter, N. (1899). Studies on the telegraphic language: The acquisition of a hierarchy of habits. *Psychological Review, 6,* 345–375.

Campos, J., Hiatt, S., Ramsay, D., Henderson, C., & Svejda, M. (1978). The emergence of fear on the visual cliff. In M. Lewis & L. Rosenblum (Eds.), *The development of affect* (pp. 149–182). New York: Plenum.

Campos, J. J., Bertenthal, B. I., & Kermoian, R. (1992). Early experience and emotional development: The emergence of wariness of heights. *Psychological Science, 3,* 61–64.

Chan, M., Lu, Y., Marin, L., & Adolph, K. E. (1999). A baby's day: Capturing crawling experience. In M. A. Grealy & J. A. Thompson (Eds.), *Studies in perception and action V* (pp. 245–249). Mahwah, NJ: Lawrence Erlbaum Associates.

Cornsweet, T. N. (1962). The staircase-method in psychophysics. *American Journal of Psychology, 75,* 485–491.

Emmerik, R. E. A. v., Brinker, B. P. L. M. d., Vereijken, B., & Whiting, H. T. A. (1989). Preferred tempo in the learning of a gross cyclical action. *The Quarterly Journal of Experimental Psychology, 41,* 251–262.

Eppler, M. A., Adolph, K. E., & Weiner, T. (1996). The developmental relationship between exploration and action on sloping surfaces. *Infant Behavior and Development, 19,* 391–405.

Eppler, M. A., Satterwhite, T., Wendt, J., & Bruce, K. (1997). Infants' responses to a visual cliff and other ground surfaces. In M. A. Schmuckler & J. M. Kennedy (Eds.), *Studies in perception and action IV* (pp. 219–222). Mahwah, NJ: Lawrence Erlbaum Associates.

Garn, S. M. (1966). Body size and its implications. In L. W. Hoffman & M. L. Hoffman (Eds.), *Review of child development research* (Vol. 2, pp. 529–561). New York: Russell Sage Foundation.

Gibson, E. J. (1991). *An odyssey in learning and perception.* Cambridge, MA: MIT Press.

Gibson, E. J., & Walk, R. D. (1960). The "visual cliff." *Scientific American, 202,* 64–71.

Gibson, J. J. (1979). *The ecological approach to visual perception.* Boston: Houghton Mifflin Company.

Greco, A., Hayne, H., & Rovee-Collier, C. (1990). Roles of function, reminding, and variability in categorization by 3-month-old infants. *Journal of Experimental Psychology: Learning, Memory, and Cognition, 16,* 617–633.

Harlow, H. F. (1949). The formation of learning sets. *Psychological Review, 56,* 26–39.

Harlow, H. F. (1959). Learning set and error factor theory. In S. Koch (Ed.), *Psychology: A study of a science* (pp. 492–533). New York: McGraw-Hill.

Held, R., & Hein, A. (1963). Movement-produced stimulation in the development of visually guided behavior. *Journal of Comparative and Physiological Psychology, 56,* 872–876.

Hofsten, C. (1993). Prospective control: A basic aspect of action development. *Human Development, 36,* 253–270.

Kalnins, I. V., & Bruner, J. S. (1973). The coordination of visual observation and instrumental behavior in early infancy. *Perception, 2,* 307–314.

Kerr, R., & Booth, B. (1978). Specific and varied practice of a motor skill. *Perceptual and Motor Skills, 46,* 395–401.

Lampl, M. (1983). Postnatal infant growth: Leaps and bounds (Abstract). *American Journal of Physical Anthropology, 60,* 215–216.

Lampl, M. (1993). Evidence of saltatory growth in infancy. *American Journal of Human Biology, 5,* 641–652.

Lampl, M., Veldhuis, J. D., & Johnson, M. L. (1992). Saltation and statis: A model of human growth. *Science, 258*(5083), 801–803.

Lashley, K. S. (1960). *The neuropsychology of Lashley: Selected papers.* New York: McGraw-Hill.

Lee, D. N. (1993). Body-environment coupling. In U. Neisser (Ed.), *The perceived self: Ecological and interpersonal sources of self-knowledge* (pp. 43–67). Cambridge: Cambridge University Press.

Levinson, B. & Reese, H. W. (1967). Patterns of discrimination learning set in preschool children, fifth graders, college freshmen, and the aged. *Monographs of the Society for Research in Child Development, 32* (Whole Number 7).

MacKay, D. G. (1982). The problems of flexibility, fluency, and speed–accuracy trade-off in skilled behavior. *Psychological Review, 89,* 483–506.

McGraw, M. (1935). *Growth: A study of Johnny and Jimmy.* New York: Appleton Century Co.

Palmer, C. E. (1944). Studies of the center of gravity in the human body. *Child Development, 15,* 99–163.

Rader, N., Bausano, M., & Richards, J. E. (1980). On the nature of the visual-cliff-avoidance response in human infants. *Child Development, 51,* 61–68.

Riccio, G. E. (1993). Information in movement variability about the qualitative dynamics of posture and orientation. In K. M. Newell & D. M. Corcos (Eds.), *Variability and motor control* (pp. 317–357). Champaign, IL: Human Kinetics Publishers.

Riccio, G. E., & Stoffregen, T. A. (1988). Affordances as constraints on the control of stance. *Human Movement Science, 7,* 265–300.

Richards, J. E., & Rader, N. (1983). Affective, behavioral, and avoidance responses on the visual cliff: Effects of crawling onset age, crawling experience, and testing age. *Psychophysiology, 20,* 633–642.

Rovee-Collier, C. K., & Gekoski, M. (1979). The economics of infancy: A review of conjugate reinforcement. In H. W. Reese & L. P. Lipsitt (Eds.), *Advances in child development and behavior* (Vol. 13, pp. 195–255). New York: Academic Press.

Scarr, S., & Salapatek, P. (1970). Patterns of fear development during infancy. *Merrill-Palmer Quarterly, 16*, 53–90.

Shaffer, L. H. (1980). Analyzing piano performance: A study of concert pianists. In G. E. Stelmach & J. Requin (Eds.), *Tutorials in motor behavior* (pp. 443–454). New York: North Holland.

Shirley, M. M. (1931). *The first two years: A study of twenty-five babies.* Minneapolis: University of Minnesota Press.

Snyder, R. G., Spencer, M. L., Owings, C. L., & Schneider, L. W. (1975). *Anthropometry of U.S. infants and children. (Paper No. 750423).* Warrendale, PA: Society of Automotive Engineers.

Sorce, J., Emde, R., Campos, J., & Klinnert, M. (1985). Maternal emotional-signaling: Its effect on the visual cliff behavior of 1-year-olds. *Developmental Psychology, 21,* 195–200.

Stergiou, C. S., Adolph, K. E., Alibali, M. W., Avolio, A. M., & Cenedella, C. (1997). Social expressions in infant locomotion: vocalizations and gestures on slopes. In M. A. Schmuckler & J. M. Kennedy (Eds.), *Studies in perception and action IV* (pp. 215–219). Mahwah, NJ: Lawrence Erlbaum Associates.

Stoffregen, T. A., & Riccio, G. E. (1988). An ecological theory of orientation and the vestibular system. *Psychological Review, 95,* 3–14.

Thelen, E. (1984). Learning to walk: Ecological demands and phylogenetic constraints. *Advances in Infancy Research, 3,* 213–260.

Thelen, E., & Fisher, D. M. (1983). From spontaneous to instrumental behavior: Kinematic analysis of movement changes during very early learning. *Child Development, 54,* 129–140.

Thorndike, E. L. (1906). *Principles of teaching.* New York: A. G. Seiler.

Thorndike, E. L., & Woodworth, R. S. (1901). The influence of improvement in one mental function upon the efficiency of other functions. *Psychological Review, 8,* 247–261.

Titzer, R. (1995, March). *The developmental dynamics of understanding transparency.* Paper presented at the meeting of the Society for Research in Child Development, Indianapolis.

Walk, R. D. (1966). The development of depth perception in animals and human infants. *Monographs of the Society for Research in Child Development, 31* (5, Serial No. 107), 82–108.

Walk, R. D., & Gibson, E. J. (1961). A comparative and analytical study of visual depth perception. *Psychological Monographs, 75*(15, Whole No. 519).

Walk, R. D., Gibson, E. J., & Tighe, T. J. (1957). Behavior of light- and dark-reared rats on a visual cliff. *Science, 126,* 80–81.

Wallace, S. A., & Hagler, R. W. (1979). Knowledge of performance and the learning of a closed motor skill. *Research Quarterly, 50,* 265–271.

Warren, W. H. (1984). Perceiving affordances: Visual guidance of stair climbing. *Journal of Experimental Psychology: Human Perception and Performance, 10*(5), 683–703.

Zeaman, D., & House, B. J. (1963). The role of attention in retardate discrimination learning. In N. R. Ellis (Ed.), *Handbook of mental deficiency* (pp. 159–223). New York: McGraw-Hill.

5

▼▼▼▼▼▼▼

Limitations on Visual Sensitivity During Infancy: Contrast Sensitivity, Vernier Acuity, and Orientation Processing

Ann M. Skoczenski
University of Massachusetts Medical School

INTRODUCTION

Visual Spatial Processes: Building Blocks of Higher Visual Perception

A full understanding of the visual environment requires the ability to discriminate objects that vary along many dimensions, including size, shape, and brightness. Also required are levels of processing sufficient to resolve the fine details that define individual objects. Additionally, in order to manipulate and move through the environment, one must perceive the visual boundaries between self and surroundings. Throughout life, our competence in understanding and manipulating our environment is at least partly limited by our ability to visually discriminate the objects that surround us.

The ability to process visual information is prominently immature in neonates, and develops steadily during infancy and into childhood. Development occurs at different rates for different visual functions; for example, peak contrast sensitivity approaches adult levels earlier than grating acuity, which in turn matures earlier than relative position sensitivity. Visual development depends on experience, combined with maturation of the eyes and development within neural structures of the visual brain. The purpose of this chapter is to describe the development of three facets of *spatial vision*—contrast sensitivity, vernier acuity, and orientation processing—and to discuss different factors that place limitations on them during infant development, from early optical and retinal factors up through complex neural mechanisms. Thus the scope of this chapter is limited to a subset of aspects of visual perceptual development, although other recent review chapters provide additional viewpoints or more comprehensive reviews (e.g., Aslin, 1987; Bertenthal, 1996; Hamer & Mayer, 1994; Mohn & Van Hof-van Duin, 1991).

"Early" Versus "Late" Limitations on Spatial Vision During Development

In an attempt to understand the limitations on spatial vision during infancy, several labs have estimated contributions from different sites in the visual pathways. There are multiple ways to accomplish this. Some labs have studied the anatomy and physiology of the eyes, optic nerves, and brain in humans or in animals (e.g., Blakemore & Vital-Durand, 1986; Huttenlocher, De Courten, Garey, & van der Loos, 1982; Larsen, 1971; Yuodelis & Hendrickson, 1986). Others have used this information to develop models of visual development (e.g., Banks & Bennett, 1988; Wilson, 1988). Still others have designed experiments to isolate different levels of processing (e.g., Kiorpes & Movshon, 1998; Skoczenski & Aslin, 1995; Skoczenski & Norcia, 1998). Finally, because different aspects of vision develop at different rates, some studies used comparisons of developmental sequences to differentiate underlying limitations (e.g., Kiorpes, 1992a, 1992b; Skoczenski & Norcia, 1999; Zanker, Mohn, Weber, Zeitler-Driess, & Fahle, 1992). These factors can be divided into two categories: those that occur "early," that is, in the anterior visual pathways that include the eyes and optic nerves; and "late" limitations that occur in geniculo-striate pathways that include the lateral geniculate nucleus, primary visual cortex, and extrastriate cortex.

Early/Front-End Factors. Properties of visual processing that occur early in the visual pathways are also referred to as *front-end factors* (cf. Banks & Crowell, 1993; Geisler, 1984). These include the optical properties and morphological characteristics of the eye, which have been studied developmentally (Diaz-Araya & Provis, 1992; Larsen, 1971; Hendrickson & Drucker, 1992; Yuodelis & Hendrickson, 1986). The eye undergoes considerable postnatal development. Although the optical properties of the lens and cornea are close to adult levels at birth, the overall size of the eye grows postnatally, affecting focusing power (Larsen, 1971). Postnatal development of the photoreceptors of the retina is even more dramatic: they change size and shape, improving their ability to capture light; and their spacing decreases in the central part of the retina (fovea) during a postnatal period of migration that leads to improved ability to process visual details. Thus at least a portion of the postnatal improvements in visual behavior must be due to development of these early factors. The specific effects of these factors on visual development have been modeled by three different labs (Banks & Bennett, 1988; Brown, 1990; Wilson, 1988), and some of these model predictions are discussed in later sections of this chapter. However, early factors are not sufficient to explain the postnatal changes that occur in infant visual processing.

Late/Central Factors. Postnatal development also occurs in later (*central*) portions of the visual pathway. Anatomically, the number of synapses in the human cortex changes considerably after birth, first increasing and then decreasing (Huttenlocher et al., 1982); and dendritic projections between visual areas develop substantially (Burkhalter, Bernardo, & Charles, 1993). On a physiological level, receptive field properties of neurons in the cat and monkey lateral geniculate nucleus (Blakemore & Vital-Durand, 1986; Hawken, Blakemore, & Morley, 1997) and visual cortex (Blakemore, 1990; Zumbroich, Price, & Blakemore, 1988) develop postnatally to allow processing of progressively higher spatial frequency information (finer details). These factors must also play a role in infants' developing visual behavior. In general, central, particularly cortical, visual mechanisms develop later than front-end mechanisms, consistent with previous hypotheses that perceptual development proceeds from being dominated by subcortical processes to increasing involvement of cortical processing (Atkinson, 1984; Bronson, 1974).

Neural processing of sensory stimuli is noise-limited. This has been demonstrated in the human visual system and is most likely due to spontaneous firing of neurons and associated imperfections in transmitting information along neural pathways. Visual processing in human infants has been characterized by higher levels of neural noise than are estimated in adults (Brown, 1990; Skoczenski & Aslin, 1995; Skoczenski & Norcia, 1998). The result of relatively high neural noise is reduced efficiency in visual processing leading to degraded perception. In this chapter, I describe the developmental sequences of contrast sensitivity and vernier acuity, discuss limitations imposed by early and late factors in the visual pathway, and describe each in terms of neural noise limitations. Then I briefly discuss what is known about the development of orientation processing, its relationship to vernier acuity, and the hypothesis that vernier acuity and orientation processing can be used as markers of cortical processing and cortical integrity during development. First, a brief section describes the two major techniques used to measure visual abilities in young infants. More details on these and additional techniques can be found in previous reviews (e.g., Banks & Salapatek, 1983; Hamer & Mayer, 1994; Mohn & van Hof-van Duin, 1991).

Methods of Measuring Sensory Thresholds in Infants

Behavior. The most widely used method of estimating vision in pre-verbal infants is preferential looking (Fantz, 1958; Teller, 1979), which relies on infants' natural tendency to orient toward visual stimuli that they find interesting. Based on Fantz' early studies of infant visual preferences and adult two-alternative, forced-choice psychophysical techniques, Teller and colleagues developed the *forced-choice preferential-looking* (FPL) technique, a psychophysical method of measuring visual thresholds in infants. In an FPL test, the infant's attention is first attracted to midline, then visual stimuli are presented to the left or right of midline, or on both sides. Figure 5.1 shows examples of stimuli used in FPL tests. As one example, the stimulus might be a grating presented in combination with a grey field that is matched in space average luminance (Fig. 5.1a). If the infant can detect the grating, and finds it interesting, he or she will be more likely to look toward the side on which it is presented. If, however, the grating cannot be detected, both sides will look identical to the infant, and he or she will be equally likely to look left or right. A hidden experimenter, who cannot see the stimulus but is watching the infant, must use the infant's looking behavior to judge the side that contains the stimulus. Characteristics of the stimulus may then be varied—for example, grating contrast or spatial frequency—placing the grating above or below the infant's detection threshold. Over a number of trials, usually at least 20 per stimulus level, a *psychometric function* is determined: the experimenter's percent correct as a function of stimulus level. The infant's threshold is estimated using a criterion percent correct that is significantly above chance, for example, 75%. In a slightly more complex form of FPL, two suprathresh-

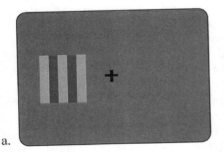 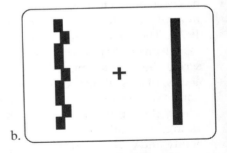

a.   b.

FIG. 5.1.   Forced-choice preferential looking (FPL) stimuli. *a.* Grating detection stimulus. The cross represents a fixation stimulus, which is normally extinguished when the stimulus is presented. On subsequent trials, the spatial frequency of the grating may be varied to measure resolution acuity, or luminance contrast may be varied to measure sensitivity. *b.* Vernier acuity stimulus. Offset detection is assumed if the infant reliably looks toward the side containing a bar or grating with offsets.

old stimuli may be presented, as in Fig. 5.1b. In this case, one parameter is varied, for example, spatial offset size, and infants' tendency to prefer more complex stimuli (bar with offsets vs. bar without offset) is used to determine the smallest offset that can be detected. If the offset cannot be detected, both bars will appear straight, and looking behavior will be at chance.

A general weakness of the FPL technique is that it sets only an upper bound on infants' sensory thresholds. That is, although a positive result (infant looks at the stimulus for a significant proportion of trials) indicates an infant can detect a stimulus, a negative result (the failure of an infant to look toward a given stimulus) could occur because the stimulus is not detected, but also could be because the infant is simply not interested in it. Thus, FPL thresholds may reflect interest/attention rather than pure sensory thresholds.

Electrophysiology. Another established method of measuring infant vision is the noninvasive electrophysiological technique of *visual evoked potentials,* or VEPs. This technique is also widely used to measure adults' visual responses (e.g., Campbell & Maffei, 1970; Regan, 1973, 1989), and is described in detail by Regan (1989). The VEP technique is based on the brain's reflexive generation of electrical potentials in response to temporally modulated or abruptly presented visual stimuli. Examples of steady-state VEP stimuli are shown in Fig. 5.2. Steady-state VEP stimuli are periodically modulated, either by phase reversal or alternating appearance/ disappearance. A stimulus alternating at a rate of 5 Hz between a grating and an unpatterned field with space-average luminance matched to the grating (Fig. 5.2a) will evoke a brain response at that stimulation frequency and its integer multiples. If the grating cannot be detected, both stimulus states appear to be blank grey fields and no brain response is evoked. Most of the VEP data discussed in this chapter were collected using a version of the steady-state technique known as *sweep VEP,* in which the stimulus varies along the dimension of interest during each 10-second trial of presentation. For example, in a contrast sweep, grating contrast is changed in log steps from low to high (Fig. 5.2a), whereas in a vernier acuity sweep, spatial offset size is swept (Fig. 5.2b). In any type of sweep VEP stimulus, while the parameter of interest is varied (swept) throughout the trial, the temporal frequency remains fixed.

Figure 5.3 shows examples of sweep VEP data, collected with surface electrodes placed on the scalp at the occipital pole, over visual cortex. The summed cortical response recorded at the electrodes undergoes spectral analysis to extract the evoked response (for example, the response to a pattern appearing and disappearing at 5 Hz will yield an evoked response at 5 Hz) for each stimulus trial. These responses are coherently averaged

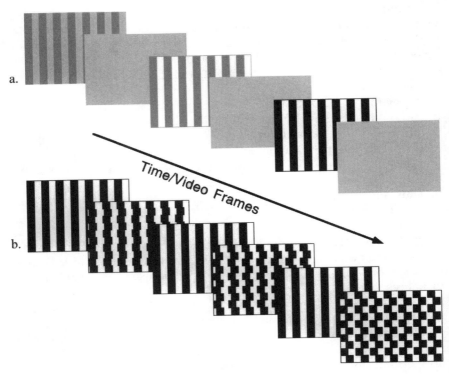

FIG. 5.2. Schematic stimuli for measuring sweep VEP contrast sensitivity (a) and vernier acuity (b). Each box shows a schematic drawing of one video frame of stimulus presentation, to indicate the spatiotemporal characteristics of each stimulus. *a.* The contrast sensitivity stimulus is a grating that alternates with a luminance-matched unpatterned field at a fixed temporal frequency. During each 10-second trial grating contrast "sweeps" from low to high in log steps. *b.* The vernier acuity stimulus is a high-contrast luminance squarewave that alternates between states containing offsets and a collinear state. Alternation occurs at a fixed temporal frequency, and offset size changes in log steps from below to above threshold over a 10-second trial.

over several trials, and compared to background electroencephalogram (EEG) activity. Background EEG is measured as the average amplitude at frequencies near the evoked response—a 5 Hz evoked response is compared to the average background response at 3 Hz and 7 Hz. Evoked response strength decreases linearly as stimulus visibility decreases (e.g., by increasing spatial frequency or decreasing contrast), and threshold is estimated by extrapolating along the linear portion of the VEP amplitude response function to zero microvolts. The phase of the response also can be measured in the VEP and is shown in the lower portion of the graphs in Fig. 5.3. Phase information can be taken into account in VEP threshold extrapolation because it typically remains constant or leads slightly as stimuli become more visible, and is often highly variable when the stimulus is below the sensory threshold.

During a VEP test, an infant is seated on a parent's lap in front of a computer screen on which the visual stimuli appear. An experimenter attracts the infant's attention to the screen with small toys and bells, and by singing or talking during each trial (usually about 10 seconds in length). The infant must attend to the screen during each trial, but unlike in the FPL technique, in the VEP technique the infant is not required to make a behavioral response.

A second type of evoked potential test is known as the *transient* VEP (Regan, 1989). In this technique, the visual stimulus is abruptly and briefly presented, and characteristics of the waveform of the evoked response are recorded, such as amplitude and latency of positive and negative waveform components. Over a series of trials, transient evoked potential amplitude may be recorded as a function of stimulus level to determine a sensory threshold, but transient VEPs are more often used to quantify different components of responses to suprathreshold stimuli. VEP and FPL

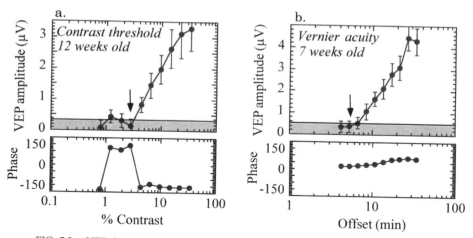

FIG. 5.3. VEP data in response to swept contrast (a) and vernier offset (b) stimuli. *a.* VEP amplitude (top) and phase (bottom) as a function of contrast, with standard errors, from a 12-week-old infant. The horizontal line and shaded area of the amplitude plot shows the level of the background EEG noise, for comparison to the evoked potential amplitude. Amplitude increases linearly with contrast, and threshold (arrow) is estimated by extrapolating along the linear rising portion of the amplitude function to zero microvolts, taking into account phase information and error statistics. *b.* VEP amplitude (top) and phase (bottom) as a function of vernier offset size, from a 7-week-old infant. Amplitude increases as offset size increases, and threshold estimation follows the same procedure as in *a.*

techniques have been used extensively to measure the development of spatial vision, including contrast sensitivity, during infancy.

CONTRAST SENSITIVITY DEVELOPMENT

Contrast sensitivity, the ability to distinguish adjacent pattern elements based on subtle brightness differences, is one of the fundamental components of spatial vision. The capacity to see subtle brightness differences is critical for distinguishing the countless subtle shadings that define objects, and having poor contrast sensitivity is effectively like seeing one's surroundings through heavy fog: differences between light and dark are degraded and sharp edges are blurred.

Contrast sensitivity has been studied extensively during development as well as in adults. Most tests of contrast sensitivity require subjects to detect sinewave gratings that can be described by their spatial frequency (element size) as well as their contrast level. Contrast sensitivity in adults and infants varies with spatial frequency. This is illustrated in Fig. 5.4, which demonstrates the bandpass nature of the contrast sensitivity function (CSF): peak contrast sensitivity occurs at medium spatial frequencies, and it declines at lower and higher spatial frequencies. The low frequency fall-off of the CSF is attributed to lateral inhibition in visual mechanisms selective for low spatial frequencies (Robson, 1966). Sensitivity also falls with increasing spatial frequency; Fig. 5.4 also illustrates grating resolution, the highest visible spatial frequency, at which contrast sensitivity approaches zero. Grating resolution effectively defines the smallest element that can be resolved for a high-contrast pattern. Thus the CSF describes the interactions between element size and sensitivity to relative luminance differences.

Developmental Sequence of Contrast Sensitivity

Behavioral Studies. Preferential-looking (Atkinson, Braddick, & Moar, 1977a; Banks & Salapatek, 1978; Peterzell, Werner, & Kaplan, 1993, 1995) and motion-tracking (Dobkins & Teller, 1996; Hainline & Abramov, 1997) techniques have been used to estimate contrast sensitivity in infants, and some of these data are shown in Fig. 5.5a. CSF development also has been measured in infant monkeys using operant behavioral techniques (Boothe, Kiorpes, Williams, & Teller, 1988), and the general pattern of development is very similar to human development, although the rate of development and time to maturity is faster in monkeys compared to humans, as in other aspects of visual development. Behavioral measures of CSF

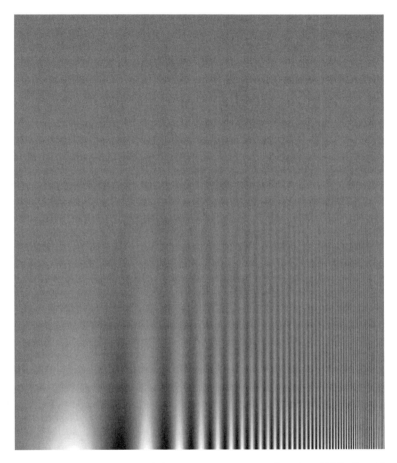

FIG. 5.4. Demonstration of the contrast sensitivity function (CSF). Spatial frequency increases from left to right, and contrast decreases from bottom to top. The original demonstration is from Campbell and Robson (1964), and this image is courtesy of Izumi Ohzawa (http://vsoc.berkeley.edu/izumi/CSF/A_JG_RobsonCSFchart.html).

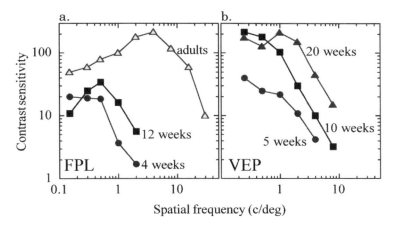

FIG. 5.5. Development of FPL and VEP contrast sensitivity. Both graphs show contrast sensitivity as a function of spatial frequency at three ages. *a.* Forced-choice preferential looking data from Banks and Salapatek (1978). *b.* Visual evoked potential data from Norcia et al. (1990).

development have shown that contrast sensitivity is initially extremely low in neonates, about 50 to 100 times worse than adults' sensitivity at all spatial frequencies (Atkinson et al., 1977a; Banks & Salapatek, 1978). In addition to the overall sensitivity loss, peak sensitivity is shifted to lower spatial frequencies in infants compared to adults. Rapid contrast sensitivity development occurs between birth and 3 months of age, but at the end of this rapid phase of development, peak contrast sensitivity is still considerably immature, more than 10 times worse than adult sensitivity. Because the preferential-looking technique works best with young infants, data from infants older than 3 months is sparse, and these data suggest that only modest improvement occurs between 3 and 8 months of age. (Peterzell et al., 1995).

Behavioral psychophysical techniques have been used to measure CSF development in young children, and these indicate that by 4 years of age, sensitivity at all spatial frequencies is within a factor of three of adult sensitivity, and fully mature sensitivity is reached between 4 and 7 years of age (Atkinson, French, & Braddick, 1981; Bradley & Freeman, 1982; Ellemberg, Lewis, Liu, & Maurer, 1999; Gwiazda, Bauer, Thorn, & Held, 1997).

Visual Evoked Potential Studies. CSF development also has been studied using VEPs (Harris, Atkinson, & Braddick, 1976; Norcia, Tyler, & Hamer, 1988, 1990; Pirchio, Spinelli, Fiorentini, & Maffei, 1978); some of these data are shown in Fig. 5.5b. In accordance with behavioral data, VEP measures indicate that contrast sensitivity is initially quite poor at birth. VEP CSF development is characterized by two phases. A rapid phase of development occurs between 2 and 9 weeks postnatal, in which sensitivity at all frequencies improves by approximately a factor of 5. At the end of this phase, infant contrast thresholds at low spatial frequencies are within a factor of 2 of adult performance. The second phase of development, between 9 and 40 weeks, involves a more gradual development of contrast sensitivity, mainly at higher spatial frequencies. Although there is some evidence of bandpass VEP CSFs (Norcia et al., 1990), the shape of the CSF measured with VEPs tends to be more lowpass than bandpass. That is, rather than sensitivity falling off at low as well as high spatial frequencies (bandpass), VEP CSFs are sometimes uniformly high at low and medium spatial frequencies, then fall at high frequencies. The finding of lowpass CSFs with the VEP has been attributed to a reduction of lateral inhibition, and increase in sensitivity, that is seen for temporally modulated stimuli compared to static stimuli (Robson, 1966). Additional development must occur between 40 weeks and adulthood, inasmuch as the VEP CSF has not reached adult levels by this age. However, no studies exist to document the earliest age at which VEP CSFs reach full maturity.

Methodological Similarities and Differences. Both VEPs and FPL demonstrate that infant contrast sensitivity, like adults', peaks at medium spatial frequencies and falls linearly from the peak to the resolution limit. A low spatial frequency decline in contrast sensitivity is found in behavioral techniques (though not consistently for neonates—compare Banks and Salapatek [1978] with Peterzell et al. [1993]). These similarities suggest that behavioral and VEP measures are tapping into the same sensory mechanisms. However, there is a notable difference between the two techniques in the absolute levels of sensitivity that are observed in infants. Although psychophysical (i.e., "behavioral") and VEP measures yield roughly the same estimates of contrast sensitivity in adults, VEP contrast sensitivity in infants is consistently and markedly higher than behavioral estimates. The difference in some cases is a factor of 10 or more. The exact source of this difference is somewhat controversial, perhaps because there are several different candidate factors from which to choose.

The difference could originate in the stimuli. As noted earlier, VEP stimuli must be temporally modulated, and there is some evidence that infants' contrast sensitivity is higher for moving versus static patterns (Atkinson, Braddick, & Moar, 1977b). Second, luminance varied between studies, being higher in the VEP studies. This could contribute to the differences as well, since there is a positive correlation between stimulus luminance and contrast sensitivity in adults (Van Nes & Bouman, 1967) as well as infants (Shannon, Skoczenski, & Banks, 1996).

The difference could also lie in other factors related to data collection and analysis. FPL and VEP measures use different criteria to estimate threshold, and this could contribute to threshold differences. More compelling is the fact that infants in behavioral tests need to exhibit selective attention in order to generate the responses needed to determine threshold, whereas a similar level of active attention is not needed in VEP measures. Thus, attentional load differences could explain the technique differences. Another compelling possibility is that VEP measures reflect information that, although processed at some level in the visual system, is then somehow filtered out before it reaches the level of consciousness needed to generate a response in a behavioral test (cf. Dobson & Teller, 1978). However, the task remains for both techniques to explain the difference between infant and adult performance. Although this difference is smaller in the VEP technique, even VEPs show considerable postnatal development of contrast sensitivity.

Limitations on Contrast Sensitivity During Development

Optical and Receptoral Factors. As noted earlier, the eye undergoes marked postnatal development, in terms of its overall size (Larsen, 1971) and of the morphology and spacing of the light-capturing photoreceptors that cover the retina (Yuodelis & Hendrickson, 1986). Postnatal photoreceptor migration causes an increase in the fineness of the spatial grain of the retina, and this most likely plays a key role in the development of the high spatial frequency end of the CSF, that is, the resolution limit. Additionally, the overall sensitivity improvement must be due at least in part to the postnatal increase in the photon-collecting efficiency of the photoreceptors (Yuodelis & Hendrickson, 1986). Two labs have performed quantitative analyses to determine the effect of these front-end factors on contrast sensitivity development (Banks & Bennett, 1988; Banks & Crowell, 1993; Wilson, 1988, 1993). Briefly, these analyses determined that some, but not all, of the development of contrast sensitivity during infancy could be explained by development in front-end factors. First, photoreceptor spacing: The Nyquist frequency (the highest spatial frequency resolvable by the photoreceptors, determined by their spacing) suggested by anatomical data (Yuodelis & Hendrickson, 1986) predicts a higher resolution limit than is observed by any of the techniques to test infants. Second, photon-capture efficiency predicts higher overall contrast sensitivity than is observed, on the order of a factor of 10 or more. As noted by Banks and Crowell (1993), an exact quantification of the proportion of infant sensitivity losses explained by front-end factors is impossible because of unknown factors related to infant visual performance (e.g., the precise effect of stimulus luminance). However, these analyses determined that additional post-receptoral factors must play a role in infants' poor contrast sensitivity compared to adults'.

Intrinsic Neural Noise.   Much has been learned about the characteristics of visual information processing from experiments in which visual information is selectively degraded or masked, in order to estimate the degree to which intrinsic imperfections in processing affect visual detection. These take the form of titration experiments, in which the external stimulus is altered by degrees, to determine the importance of the altered information in visual sensory processing.

Figure 5.6 illustrates the effect of visual white noise on grating detection. With added masking noise, it becomes more difficult to detect the lowest contrast gratings. Several groups have hypothesized that two-dimensional dynamic stimulus noise mimics the effects of intrinsic visual system noise. They used broadband visual noise to estimate intrinsic noise, by measuring contrast detection thresholds for gratings masked by increasing levels of visual white noise (Kiorpes & Movshon, 1998; Pelli, 1990; Rose, 1942; Skoczenski, Banks, & Candy, 1993; Skoczenski, Brown, Kiorpes, & Movshon, 1995; Skoczenski & Norcia, 1998; Skoczenski, O'Keefe, Kiorpes, Tang, Hawken, Movshon, 1994).

One developmental hypothesis motivating this type of experiment is that infants have higher levels of intrinsic noise than adults, and that differences in intrinsic noise may account for developmental differences in contrast sensitivity. Skoczenski and Norcia (1998) used the VEP technique to test this hypothesis, because VEPs yield the highest estimates of contrast sensitivity in human infants. A schematic representation of the effect of stimulus noise on contrast threshold, and an illustration of the developmental hypothesis, are shown in Fig. 5.7.

When we measure contrast threshold as a function of stimulus noise contrast, we get a pattern of results like those shown in Fig. 5.7a. The left endpoint of the curve represents contrast threshold for a grating with no added masking noise, known as the unmasked threshold. In the flat region of the function, when masking noise contrast is low, there is no effect on contrast threshold. As higher contrast masking noise is added to the stimulus, there is a point at which threshold becomes proportional to the masking noise contrast. According to the model, in the flat region, the subject's intrinsic noise is greater than the stimulus noise, so intrinsic noise is limiting threshold. In the rising region of the function, stimulus noise exceeds intrinsic noise, so stimulus noise is limiting threshold. And the inflection point that marks the shift between these two regions, indicated by the arrow on the x-axis, is where the stimulus noise has the same effect as intrinsic noise. This point is known as the subject's *equivalent noise.* Thus,

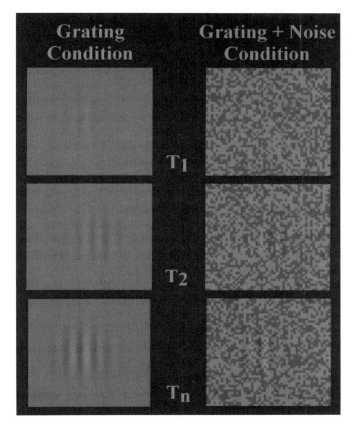

FIG. 5.6.   Sweep VEP stimuli, and a demonstration of the effect of spatiotemporal white noise on grating detection. *Left:* a sinewave grating shown at three levels of luminance contrast. *Right:* the same grating with superimposed spatiotemporally broadband visual white noise. Each box represents one video frame of a sweep VEP stimulus (T_1–T_n). Reprinted by permission from *Nature* (391:697–700) copyright 1998 Macmillan Magazines Ltd.

equivalent noise is a measurable quantity that represents the effect of intrinsic visual noise. Pelli (1990) showed that human adults' psychophysical contrast thresholds follow this pattern, and Kiorpes and Movshon (1998) showed the same pattern of results in monkeys using psychophysical (operant) techniques.

   The hypothetical curves in Fig. 5.7b and Fig. 5.7c represent two possible outcomes if we measure contrast thresholds as a function of masking noise contrast for five cases in which unmasked contrast threshold varies, for

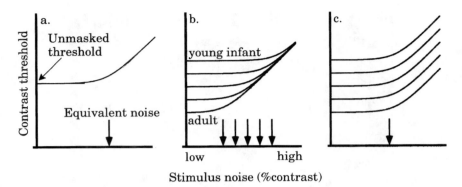

FIG. 5.7.   Hypothetical equivalent noise curves. Each graph shows hypothetical contrast threshold as a function of stimulus noise contrast. *a*. One curve, identifying unmasked contrast threshold and equivalent noise estimation, at the inflection point of the curve. The curve is defined by the equation $T = k\sqrt{(N^2_s + N^2_{eq})}$, in which T is contrast threshold, N_s is external noise, and N_{eq} is equivalent noise (representing the effects of internal neural noise). *b*. Five equivalent noise curves illustrating the developmental hypothesis. *c*. Five equivalent noise curves illustrating the null hypothesis.

example, at five stages of infant development. We predicted that our results would follow the pattern shown in Fig. 5.7b, that is, subjects with high unmasked thresholds would have relatively high equivalent noise, and those with lower unmasked thresholds would have relatively lower equivalent noise. More specifically, we predicted that unmasked contrast threshold would be proportional to equivalent noise, as seen in an inspection of hypothetical unmasked threshold and equivalent noise estimates in Fig. 5.7b. On the other hand, if equivalent noise is the same at all ages, we would see the pattern of results in Fig. 5.7c. Each curve represents a case with a different unmasked contrast threshold, but the curves are simply shifted vertically with respect to one another and the position of the inflection point that estimates equivalent noise is the same in each case. Thus equivalent noise bears no relationship to unmasked contrast threshold in the null hypothesis case shown in Fig. 5.7c.

We tested 32 infants, aged 6 to 30 weeks postnatal, and five adults for comparison. Figure 5.8 shows results, in the form of contrast threshold as a function of masking noise contrast, from two representative infants and one adult. The model curve fit the data from all subjects well. The youngest infant, aged 6 weeks (Fig. 5.8a), had both higher unmasked threshold and higher equivalent noise, compared to the 16-week-old infant (Fig. 5.8b), whose threshold and equivalent noise were in turn higher than those of the adult (Fig. 5.8c). Figure 5.9 shows results from all subjects tested, comparing unmasked contrast threshold and equivalent noise within sub-

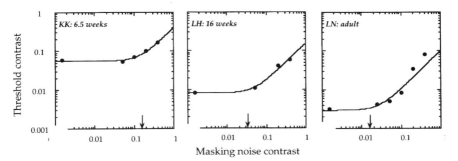

FIG. 5.8. Equivalent noise data and curves of two infants and one adult. Each graph shows one subject's contrast threshold as a function of stimulus noise. Unmasked threshold is the left data point on each graph, and equivalent noise is indicated by the arrow pointing to the x-axis. Reprinted by permission from *Nature* (391:697–700) copyright 1998 Macmillan Magazines Ltd.

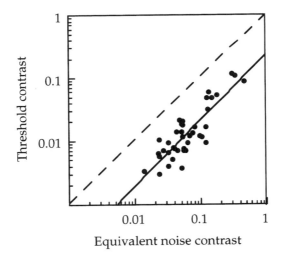

FIG. 5.9. The relationship between contrast threshold and equivalent noise in infants. Each data point is from an individual subject. The line of best fit to the data, with a slope of 1.1, is indicated by the solid line. The dashed line has a slope of 1.0, which would be expected if threshold is limited by equivalent noise. Reprinted by permission from *Nature* (391:697–700) copyright 1998 Macmillan Magazines Ltd.

185

jects. There was a significant correlation between the two measures across two log units of variation in contrast threshold. The slope of the line relating the two measures was 1.04. Although not showing a causative relationship, these results provide support for the hypothesis that intrinsic noise critically limits contrast threshold during development. Specifically, as equivalent noise decreases during development, contrast sensitivity increases.

Theoretically, the intrinsic noise represented by equivalent noise could arise anywhere along the visual pathway, with the only constraint from these data being that it must arise prior to, or within, the cortical generator of the VEP. Thus, the equivalent noise technique does not provide direct evidence for the specific site of intrinsic noise. Indirect evidence suggests that equivalent noise is not simply a reflection of noise within front-end factors, such as the photon-capture efficiency of photoreceptors. Previous studies have shown that neither adults' (Van Nes & Bouman, 1967) nor infants' (Shannon et al., 1996) thresholds are limited by photon capture in the high luminance, low spatial frequency conditions that we used to estimate intrinsic noise in infants. Also, the developmental differences in equivalent noise are not attributed to differences in background EEG noise levels, which were not significantly different between infants and adults. Thus we can tentatively conclude that a large proportion of the equivalent noise measured by our VEP technique arises in the geniculostriate portion of the visual pathway.

Development of Inhibitory Processes. Figure 5.10 illustrates a second finding from Skoczenski and Norcia (1998) that reflects an aspect of suprathreshold contrast processing suggestive of inhibitory processes in the vi-

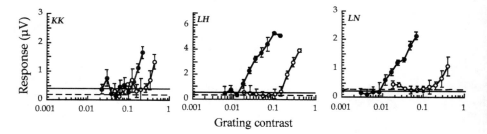

FIG. 5.10.   VEP contrast response functions (response amplitude as a function of grating contrast) for two infants and one adult. In each graph, filled circles represent the unmasked grating condition, and open circles represent a condition with high stimulus noise contrast. The latter condition shifts each subject's response function to the right, while preserving the shape of the function. Reprinted by permission from *Nature* (391:697–700) copyright 1998 Macmillan Magazines Ltd.

sual system. For each of three observers, contrast response functions (VEP amplitude as a function of grating contrast) are shown for the grating presented alone (without any mask), and for the grating presented with a high contrast noise mask. The contrast response function has a stereotypical shape and the effect of the noise mask in all observers was a simple rightward displacement of the function, on log–log axes, with overall shape preserved (although the magnitude of the rightward displacement varied with age). This shift combined with shape preservation is the hallmark of a *contrast gain control* mechanism (Bonds, 1991; Geisler & Albrecht, 1992; Ohzawa, Sclar, & Freeman, 1985). Contrast gain control is a form of visual inhibition that serves "to maximize differential sensitivity (or visual discrimination) over the functional range of contrasts" (Skoczenski & Norcia, 1998, p. 699). In other words, gain control mechanisms shift the dynamic range of visual responses according to the ambient contrast level. Our data suggest that although young human infants have markedly degraded contrast sensitivity and high levels of intrinsic noise, one qualitative aspect of their contrast processing appears nearly adult-like. However, it is not fully mature, as found by a more recent study in our lab. Skoczenski, Candy, and Norcia (1998) tested the orientation-selectivity of contrast gain control in infants. In adults, contrast gain control is highly selective for pattern orientation: sensitivity to a vertical grating is much more degraded in the presence of parallel one-dimensional noise than it is in the presence of orthogonal noise. This pattern specificity suggests that gain control mechanisms play a role in pattern discriminations. However, we found that gain control is not orientation-selective in infants, at least until approximately 11 months of age, suggesting that some aspects of gain control develop quite late. The orientation results are discussed in more detail later in this chapter.

In sum, it appears that the development of sensitivity to luminance contrast is not a single process. At least one aspect (simple contrast gain control) is in place from very early infancy, another (sensitivity at low/medium spatial frequencies) undergoes rapid development during the first months of life, and still others (sensitivity at higher spatial frequencies, and orientation-selectivity of contrast gain control) have a more protracted course of development. This suggests that mechanisms at multiple levels of processing are responsible for mature contrast sensitivity.

As contrast sensitivity develops, the infant's world emerges from the "fog," and more objects and shades of grey can be detected. However, detecting patterns and objects is only the first step toward understanding the visual world. A more complete understanding emerges when different visual stimuli can be discriminated. The development of this ability is the topic of the next section.

VERNIER ACUITY DEVELOPMENT

Definition of Vernier Acuity

Compared to contrast sensitivity, *vernier acuity,* a measure of relative position sensitivity, is a much more complex form of pattern processing. Our ability to interpret patterns and objects in the visual world depends on an accurate representation of the *spatial arrangement of pattern elements.* Without this sense, the world might appear to be a disorganized jumble of lines and shadings, similar to some abstract paintings. Vernier acuity reflects the ability to judge the relative spatial position of pattern elements. This is a critical ability for determining the shape of objects, and for discriminating different objects or patterns—for example, discrimination of different letters of the alphabet. Figure 5.1b shows an example of a vernier acuity stimulus. Observers are required to demonstrate that offsets in a bar (or grating) are detected. For example, the observer may be presented with two bars and must pick the one that contains offsets; or he or she may be presented with one bar containing one or more offsets, and must judge the direction (e.g., left or right) of the offsets with respect to the reference bar. Psychophysical (e.g., Westheimer, 1975) and VEP (Levi, Manny, Klein, & Steinman, 1983; Norcia, Wesemann, & Manny, 1999) techniques have been used to study vernier acuity in adults. These techniques provide good convergence in their estimates of adults' vernier acuity.

Adult Vernier Acuity Is a Hyperacuity. The mature human visual system performs the task of spatial position discrimination not only accurately, but also with elegant precision. Vernier acuity is on the order of 3 to 10 seconds of arc in normal human adults (Westheimer, 1975). This is superior not only to the finest resolvable grating, 40 cycles per degree, but also to the smallest center-to-center spacing between photoreceptors, 30 to 45 seconds of arc (Williams, 1985). This level of precision places vernier acuity in the category of the "hyperacuities," with other forms of spatial position sensitivity (and stereoacuity) that are significantly better than resolution acuity (Westheimer, 1975).

Photoreceptor spacing is likely the major limiting factor of resolution (grating) acuity, because the center-to-center spacing of photoreceptors accurately predicts adults' performance in this task. Vernier acuity, on the other hand, is superior to predictions based on photoreceptor spacing because it is finer than this spacing. Because receptor spacing cannot predict the high precision of position sensitivity, several hypotheses have evolved to explain it. One suggested that high contrast sensitivity at the level of retinal ganglion cells preserves the precise vernier spatial position signal based on a differential weighting of the light distribution at the ganglion cell level (Lee, Wehrhahn, Westheimer, & Kremers, 1995). Other theories suggest that different processing characteristics in the retina (e.g., quantum efficiency and ganglion cell sensitivity, in addition to photoreceptor spacing/density) may be sufficient to explain at least part of the difference between grating acuity and vernier acuity (Banks & Bennett, 1988; Banks, Sekuler, & Anderson, 1991; Geisler, 1984; Kiorpes, 1992a, 1992b). But the majority of data and theory suggests that vernier acuity, like the other hyperacuities, is limited by the information processing characteristics of cortical mechanisms (e.g. Hess & Field, 1993; Hess & Watt, 1990; Kiorpes & Movshon, 1989; Levi, Klein, & Aitsebaomo, 1985; Levi, Klein, & Yap, 1987; Waugh, Levi, & Carney, 1993; Wilson, 1986). They claim that vernier performance depends critically on a cortical substrate that can read the signals from earlier stages and reconstruct the spatial arrangement.

Examples of Degraded Vernier Acuity. Many laboratories have sought to understand the mechanisms of vernier acuity by studying cases in which it is degraded, and these cases provide support for the hypothesis that vernier acuity and grating acuity are limited by different mechanisms. One case of deficiency that can be observed in normal adults is peripheral viewing: Vernier acuity degrades with retinal eccentricity, to a greater degree than the peripheral degradation of grating acuity (Levi & Klein, 1985). Second, patients with amblyopia also have poor vernier acuity compared to the normal adult fovea; as with the normal periphery, amblyopes' vernier acuity deficits are greater than their grating acuity deficits (Levi & Klein, 1982, 1985). Finally, human infants have markedly poor vernier acuity, according to some studies even worse than their grating acuity, which is also quite immature during the first months after birth (e.g., Skoczenski & Norcia, 1999; Zanker, Mohn, Weber, Zeitler-Driess, & Fahle, 1992). Levi and Carkeet (1993) pointed out the dramatic parallels between the normal periphery, amblyopia, and infancy, when discussing potential cortical mechanisms of vernier acuity.

Developmental Studies

Although other aspects of infant visual development have been studied for several decades, vernier acuity development has been studied only since the middle 1980s. Most studies have been descriptive and used versions of the behavioral forced-choice preferential looking technique. The one consistency across developmental studies is the finding that vernier acuity is strikingly poor, compared to adults' vernier acuity, during early infancy. Although some studies have observed a rapid early phase of development, vernier acuity is still far inferior in human infants compared to adults by the end of the first 8 to 12 postnatal months, when many other aspects of visual performance are very close to adult levels (Brown, 1997; Manny & Klein, 1984; Shimojo, Birch, Gwiazda, & Held, 1984; Shimojo & Held, 1987; Skoczenski & Norcia, 1999; Zanker et al., 1992).

Behavioral Studies. The primary developmental tool used to assess the mechanisms of vernier acuity has been a comparison of the *developmental rates* of vernier acuity and grating acuity. The hypothesis motivating these studies was that different underlying mechanisms may lead to different developmental rates. Of the four behavioral studies comparing developmental rates, two found that vernier acuity developed more rapidly than grating acuity, and the other two found similar rates of development during infancy (see Fig. 5.11). Shimojo, Birch, Gwiazda, and Held (1984) found vernier acuity and grating acuity to be at similar levels during early infancy, and vernier acuity to develop to superior levels over the first 9 months (Fig. 5.11a). A later study by Shimojo and Held (1987), using a wider range of stimulus values, found that vernier acuity was actually worse than grating acuity early in infancy, but developed more rapidly and became superior to grating acuity around 4 months (Fig. 5.11b). Manny and Klein (1984) found that vernier acuity was consistently marginally superior to grating acuity between 0.5 and 6 months, and that the two acuities developed at approximately the same rate. Zanker et al. (1992) found that vernier acuity and grating acuity developed at approximately the same rate during the first 1.5 *years* of life and that vernier acuity did not become superior to grating acuity until between 2 and 4 years of age (Fig. 5.11c), and was still markedly immature at 4 years.

Differences in stimuli and experimental techniques may account for these different results. Nonetheless, the within-study vernier/grating acuity developmental sequence comparisons provide no consistent evidence to support or refute the developmental rate hypothesis. The only converging evidence from human developmental studies to support the hypothesis is the finding in children that vernier and grating acuity approach adult levels at different ages (Carkeet, Levi, & Manny, 1997; Zanker et al., 1992). This supports the hypothesis that the two functions are limited by different mechanisms.

The most comprehensive data comparing the development of vernier acuity and grating acuity are from infant monkeys (Kiorpes, 1992a, 1992b; Kiorpes & Movshon, 1989). Kiorpes and Movshon used preferential looking and operant techniques and showed that vernier acuity and grating acuity develop at different rates in infant pigtail macaques, but the two functions reach adult levels at the same age (unlike human performance). Thus Kiorpes and Movshon found data to both support and refute the multiple mechanism hypothesis. Their finding of different developmental

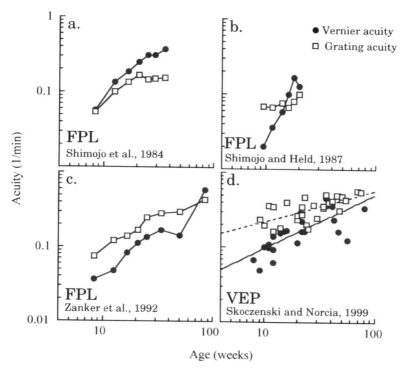

FIG. 5.11.   The development of vernier acuity and grating acuity in human infants, from four published studies. *a*. FPL data from Shimojo et al. (1984). *b*. FPL data from Shimojo and Held (1987). *c*. FPL data from Zanker et al. (1992). *d*. VEP data from Skoczenski and Norcia (1999).

rates supports the hypothesis that vernier and grating acuity are limited by different mechanisms. However, the finding that the two functions reached maturity at the same age, plus the stereotypical relationship between monkeys' vernier acuity and grating acuity seen in a within-subjects comparison, refuted the two-mechanism hypothesis, and led Kiorpes and Movshon (1989) to conclude that different characteristics of a single mechanism might be limiting both vernier acuity and grating acuity during infancy in macaques. They suggested a candidate mechanism at the level of the retinal photoreceptors. This is discussed later in more detail.

Visual Evoked Potential Studies.   Only two studies have used VEPs to examine vernier acuity responses in infants. In an early study, Manny (1988) used a transient VEP technique and measured infant responses to vernier offsets. Rather than the traditional quantitative analysis of the components of the evoked response waveform, Manny used a nonquantitative method of asking observers to discriminate a VEP waveform in response to a ver-nier stimulus, and a record containing only background EEG noise waveforms. Observers failed to distinguish between the two types of waveforms reliably, leading Manny to the conclusion that transient VEPs cannot be used to measure infant vernier responses.

Skoczenski and Norcia (1999) used the quantitative steady-state VEP technique described earlier to examine developmental rates of vernier acuity and grating acuity in human infants. As discussed extensively in the journal report (Skoczenski & Norcia, 1999), we used a control study to verify that infants' VEP responses were selective for the appearance and disappearance of vernier offsets. Thus the VEP waveforms generated by our technique reliably indicated the detection of vernier offsets.

We hypothesized that young infants' poor vernier acuity (relative to adults') as measured by previous behavioral studies might have been due to differences in attentional demands between behavioral vernier acuity and grating acuity tasks. As described earlier, behavioral studies rely on infants' natural tendency to direct their visual attention toward complex patterns, and these studies base threshold estimates on infants' reliability in looking at different patterns. For example, an infant will prefer to look at a sinewave grating when it is paired with an unpatterned luminance-matched field, as long as the infant can resolve the grating, or as long as the difference is large enough to capture his or her attention. To estimate infants' vernier acuity, behavioral studies have paired a grating (or single line) containing vernier offsets with a grating (or single line) with no offsets (see Fig. 5.1b). If the offsets are resolvable, the pattern containing them will be more complex and thus more interesting to an infant. Thus the behavioral vernier acuity task is a *discrimination task* that requires selective attention to one of two suprathreshold patterns, whereas most behavioral grating acuity tasks are simpler *detection tasks* with lower attentional demands. We attempted to overcome these attentional differences by recording steady-state VEPs while infants looked at single patterns in which gratings appeared/disappeared while spatial frequency was increased, or offsets appeared/disappeared in a grating while offset size decreased.

Even using a measure that required the same attentional demands for the two tests, we found that VEP vernier acuity was less mature than VEP grating acuity throughout the first postnatal year (Fig. 5.11d). Thus the attentional load hypothesis of behavioral measures of vernier acuity and grating acuity was not supported. Vernier acuity did develop at a faster rate than grating acuity (while remaining less mature than grating acuity) between 2 and 12 months of age, consistent with the developmental rate difference found by Shimojo and colleagues (1984, 1987), and providing preliminary support for the hypothesis that vernier acuity and grating acuity are limited by different mechanisms.

However, the poor levels of VEP vernier acuity observed by Skoczenski and Norcia (1999), and the observation that vernier acuity was worse than grating acuity in infants, are most similar to the behavioral findings of Zanker et al. (1992), as seen in a comparison of Fig. 5.11a, through Fig. 5.11d. It is notable that the Zanker et al. and Skoczenski and Norcia studies were the only two studies to equate the vernier and grating tasks on temporal information, with the Zanker group using stationary stimuli for both tasks and Skoczenski and Norcia using 3 Hz stimuli for both tasks. The other studies used a moving vernier acuity task and a stationary grating acuity task. This could explain some of the differences among the studies. When all of these developmental studies are taken together, the question of developmental rates and vernier acuity mechanisms remains open. A consideration of the role of temporal sensitivity may shed some light on the differences among studies.

The Role of Temporal Processing in Measures of Infant Vernier Acuity. As already noted, many infant vernier acuity studies used moving stimuli. Although high speed motion can degrade adults' vernier acuity, motion sometimes enhances infant vernier acuity (Dannemiller, 1998; Skoczenski & Aslin, 1992). Behavioral studies use motion to attract and maintain infants' attention, and VEP studies by necessity use temporally modulating stimuli to elicit a measurable brain response. Infant vernier acuity studies have employed two types of motion: gratings or lines that drift along the axis of the carrier grating/line (e.g., Shimojo & Held, 1987; Skoczenski & Aslin, 1992), or offsets that jitter so that they alternate appearance and disappearance in gratings or lines (Dannemiller, 1998; Skoczenski & Aslin, 1992; Skoczenski & Norcia, 1999). Motion adds a layer of complexity to the vernier stimulus, and careful control studies are necessary to ensure that thresholds reflect position sensitivity rather than simply motion sensitivity. Two behavioral studies have addressed the role of motion in measures of infant vernier acuity.

Skoczenski and Aslin (1992), using the preferential-looking technique to study 3-month-old infants, showed that their vernier acuity for single-line stimuli was not enhanced by 2 Hz offset jitter (i.e., offset appearance/disappearance, the type of motion used in VEP vernier stimuli), compared to a stationary condition. However, single-line vernier acuity was superior in conditions containing drifting positional offsets compared to the stationary condition. In these continuous drift conditions, infants' vernier acuity appeared to be governed by a "local motion" mechanism, which incorporated a positional component.

These results were recently extended by Dannemiller (1998), who focused on the offset jitter condition. Dannemiller tested two ages of infants and two different jitter temporal frequencies, and found that 3-month-olds' performance was not enhanced by either 1.2 Hz or 4.8 Hz offset jitter, compared to a stationary flashed condition. However, 5-month-olds' vernier acuity was enhanced in the 4.8 Hz jitter condition, compared to the other two conditions. One interpretation of these results is that age-related increases in temporal sensitivity may govern improvements in vernier acuity when jitter is used. However, the Dannemiller results also may be explained by local flicker sensitivity rather than motion. In any case, these two studies show a clear interaction between motion/flicker sensitivity and pure position sensitivity, which must be considered whenever motion is used in a vernier stimulus.

Skoczenski and Norcia (1999) ruled out motion as a contaminating cue in steady-state VEP measures of infant vernier acuity. Although some components of the vernier VEP represent motion responses, we demonstrated that infants' first harmonic responses (e.g., the 3Hz component of the VEP to a 3Hz stimulus) were specific to a discrimination of spatial offset appearance and disappearance (see also Norcia et al., 1999).

The superiority of vernier acuity for moving versus stationary conditions may explain the results from the behavioral studies that found vernier acuity to be better than grating acuity in infants (Shimojo et al., 1984; Shimojo & Held, 1987; Manny & Klein, 1984). Recall that these studies used moving vernier stimuli and stationary grating acuity stimuli. Thus they may have observed motion-enhanced vernier acuity without analogous enhancement of grating acuity.

Limitations on Vernier Acuity During Development

Front-End Factors. It is important to note that both acuity measures (vernier and grating acuity) in all infant studies to date were worse than would be predicted from even *newborn* photoreceptor spacing (Yuodelis & Hendrickson, 1986). This is in contrast to normal adults, whose vernier acuity is superior to photoreceptor spacing limits, and whose grating acuity is predicted by these limits. Thus, a consideration of photoreceptor spacing as a candidate limiting factor leads to the conclusion that the information for both vernier and grating acuity that is obtained at the level of the infant retina must be lost in later stages of visual processing that lead up to the behavior exhibited in a preferential-looking study or the cortical firing involved in a VEP study.

The light-capturing characteristics of photoreceptors may also contribute to immaturities in vernier acuity. The growth of photoreceptor outer segments that occurs postnatally leads to an increased efficiency in photon catch within individual photoreceptors (Yuodelis & Hendrickson, 1986). This information has been used in computational analyses of vernier acuity development by two labs (Banks & Bennett, 1988; Wilson, 1988). They considered the anatomical evidence of changing photoreceptor morphology during postnatal development to estimate effective light capture (photon efficiency), and determined that changes in photon efficiency may contribute to the qualitative differences between infant vernier and grating acuity, that is, their different rates of development. However, changes in light capture and effective illuminance are insufficient to predict the quantitative differences between infant and adult vernier acuity. Thus front-end factors cannot explain the poor vernier acuity of infants relative to adults.

Is Infant Vernier Acuity Hyperacuity? An interpretation of the adult literature leads to the conclusion that hyperacuity-level processing is a marker of functioning cortical mechanisms. This is based on vernier acuity being superior to both grating acuity and to the Nyquist frequency of the retina, the two latter of which are equal in adults. However, as noted before, infant vernier acuity is not as good as predicted by the infant Nyquist frequency. Because of the discrepancy between infant photoreceptor spacing and spatial acuities, some researchers choose to define hyperacuity in relation to grating acuity measures alone (e.g., Birch & Swanson, 1999). Even by this standard, there is no converging evidence that vernier acuity is hyperacuity, and thus mediated by cortical mechanisms, during the first year of life. The three infant studies that demonstrated "hyperacuity" had confounding temporal cues in their stimuli (Manny & Klein, 1984; Shimojo et al., 1984; Shimojo & Held, 1987), and two other studies, using matched temporal cues, found that vernier acuity was worse than or equal to grating acuity during infancy (Skoczenski & Norcia, 1999; Zanker et al., 1992). Studies of older infants and children have found that vernier acuity develops to the hyperacuity range (superior to grating acuity) around 4 years of age, and at this age vernier acuity is still considerably worse in children compared to adults (Zanker et al., 1992; Carkeet, et al., 1997). This leads to the conclusion that the cortical processing that supports hyperacuity-level performance is still quite immature throughout the first year of life.

Intrinsic Neural Blur and Vernier Acuity Development. The neural noise technique described earlier in this chapter has been adapted to study the mechanisms of vernier acuity in the normal periphery and in patients with amblyopia (Levi & Klein, 1990a, 1990b), as well as during infancy (Skoczenski & Aslin, 1995). These studies masked different cues in vernier stimuli to measure their importance for spatial position sensitivity. For example, the role of positional uncertainty has been tested by adding position noise (Hess & Field, 1993; Hess & Watt, 1990; Levi, Klein & Yap, 1987), and the importance of high spatial frequency information has been assessed by blurring vernier stimuli (Levi & Klein, 1990a, 1990b; Skoczenski & Aslin, 1995; Watt & Morgan, 1984).

Skoczenski and Aslin (1995) tested the hypothesis that infants' poor vernier acuity is due to high levels of "neural blur." We used a preferential-looking technique to measure infants' and adults' vernier acuity for stimuli degraded by Gaussian blur, which removes high spatial frequency information. By measuring vernier acuity for multiple levels of blur, we found the largest amount of stimulus blur that could be tolerated before degrading threshold, for 3-month-olds, 5-month-olds, and adults. Analogous to the equivalent/intrinsic noise experiments described earlier, we used the following equation to calculate equivalent blur for a vernier acuity task:

$$\text{Th} = k\sqrt{(B_s^2 + B_i^2)}.$$

In this equation (Watt & Morgan, 1984), Th is spatial threshold, B_s is stimulus blur, B_i is equivalent intrinsic blur, and k is a constant multiplicative factor describing the slope of the rising portion of the function (see Fig. 5.7a) at stimulus levels that are greater than intrinsic neural blur.

The data from this experiment are shown in Fig. 5.12. Vernier acuity improved between three and five months of age, and the blur data suggested that this improvement can be explained solely by a reduction in neural blur. That is, the relationship between threshold and intrinsic blur was proportional across these two age groups; moreover, 5-month-olds performed at the level of 3-month-olds when the stimulus was blurred enough. However, the additional improvements in vernier acuity that occur between 5 months of age and adulthood cannot be explained solely by a reduction in intrinsic/neural blur. If it were the sole factor, adult thresholds would be equal to infants' thresholds at high levels of blur, as 5-month-olds' thresholds were equal to those of 3-month-olds. However, an extrapolation of the intrinsic blur curve on the adult data shows that at the highest levels of blur, adult performance is still dramatically better than infants. That is, the rising portion of the adult and infant curves do not overlap at high levels of stimulus blur. After eliminating other factors such as accommodative errors and reduced contrast from the stimulus blur, we concluded that, while neural blur decreased significantly during infancy, it accounted for only a portion of infants' vernier acuity deficits compared to adults. Therefore, other factors besides intrinsic blur must account for infant/adult vernier acuity differences.

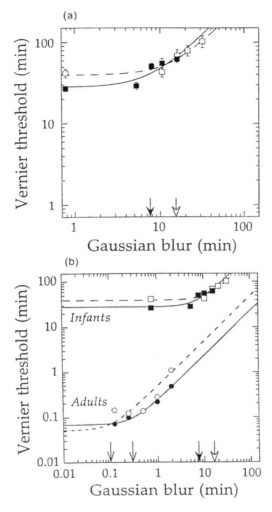

FIG. 5.12. The effect of Gaussian blur on vernier acuity in infants and adults. *a.* Vernier threshold as a function of Gaussian blur for 3-month-olds (open squares) and 5-month-olds (filled squares), showing standard error bars. *b.* Infant data replotted with data from two adults for comparison. Reprinted from *Vision Research,* volume 35, A.M. Skoczenski & R.N. Aslin, pages 1879–1887, copyright 1995, with permission from Elsevier Science.

Vernier Acuity in Clinical Patients.   Further evidence that vernier acuity is limited by cortical mechanisms comes from studies of two clinical populations: amblyopia and cortical visual impairment. *Amblyopia* is a developmental disorder of the visual system that leads to poor vision, usually in one eye, that cannot be corrected optically (Levi, 1988). It is generally caused by strabismus (eye turn) or anisometropia (unbalanced refractive errors between the two eyes), both of which can cause the two eyes to receive conflicting input. If this conflicting input occurs during the critical period of visual development, amblyopia develops. A strong theory about amblyopia that has support from animal models is that imbalanced visual input (between the two eyes) during development leads to an impoverished population of cortical connections serving the weaker eye (Levi, 1988; Levi & Carkeet, 1993; Kiorpes & McKee, 1999).

Vernier acuity has been shown to be more sensitive than grating acuity in detecting vision loss due to amblyopia (Levi & Klein, 1982; McKee, 1998, personal communication). Both vernier acuity and grating acuity correlate well with optotype (e.g., eye chart) acuity, but vernier acuity has a wider range of performance than grating acuity in amblyopes, and a proportional relationship with letter acuity. Thus vernier acuity provides a more reliable predictor of optotype acuity in amblyopic patients. This suggests that vernier acuity measures in infants and children (especially those unable to participate in optotype tests, which require a verbal or pointing response) may serve as more sensitive tests to identify those who are at risk for developing amblyopia, or to track the treatment of those already diagnosed with amblyopia. Furthermore, the selective impairment of vernier acuity in amblyopia provides support for the hypothesis that vernier acuity reflects cortical processing (Levi & Carkeet, 1993).

Cortical visual impairment (CVI) occurs in infants as a result of trauma- or disease-induced brain damage that affects areas of the visual geniculostriate pathway. For example, a hypoxic event during birth may lead to CVI. CVI is now the leading cause of vision loss in children in the western world (Good, Jan, Burden, Skoczenski, & Candy, 2001). Children with CVI may have secondary ocular and oculomotor deficits, but their vision loss cannot be explained by these deficits and is primarily due to their cortical damage. We recently showed in a preliminary study that vernier acuity is more degraded than grating acuity in many infants and children with CVI (Skoczenski & Good, 1999). This is illustrated in Fig. 5.13. The left graph in Fig. 5.13 shows the relationship between vernier acuity and grating acuity in normal human and monkey infants. As originally noted by Kiorpes (1992a, 1992b) and extended by later studies (Carkeet, et al., 1997; Skoczenski & Norcia, 1999), the within-subject relationship between vernier and grating acuity follows a stereotypical relationship during development of humans and monkeys who have normal visual experience. The right graph of Fig. 5.13 compares the VEP vernier–grating acuity relationship of human infants with normal visual experience to infants and children with cortical visual impairment (Skoczenski & Good, 1999). CVI patient data "fall off" the normal sequence, consistent with their vernier acuity being relatively more affected than their grating acuity. Thus, in the presence of cortical damage, vernier acuity is most affected. This provides further support to the hypothesis that vernier acuity is limited by cortical mechanisms, and it also suggests that vernier acuity may be an excellent measure to assess, and track the rehabilitation of, children with CVI.

ORIENTATION PROCESSING DURING DEVELOPMENT

Another form of complex spatial processing is the discrimination of pattern orientation, which makes important contributions to higher order perceptual processes. For example, the processing of edge orientation is critical in the perception of linear perspective, an important cue for depth perception. Initial studies of the development of orientation processing

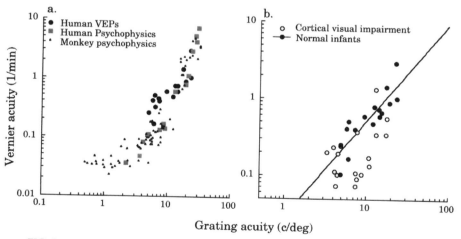

FIG. 5.13. The relationship between vernier acuity and grating acuity. *a.* Data from normal infants tested with VEPs (circles, from Skoczenski & Norcia, 1999) and FPL (squares, from Zanker et al., 1992); and monkeys tested behaviorally (triangles, from Kiorpes, 1992a). *b.* VEP data from normal infants (filled circles) and infants/children with cortical visual impairment (open circles). The solid line and shaded area represent the line of best fit and confidence limits on the normal infant data, defining the normal range of performance.

suggested that it is present in very young infants. However, more recent studies suggest that although some simple aspects of orientation discrimination are in place early in life, more complex orientation interactions develop later.

Development of Orientation Discrimination

Development of Anatomy/Physiology. Orientation-selective neurons, organized into orientation columns, can be found in newborn kittens (Blakemore & van Sluyters, 1975; Bonds, 1979; Hubel & Wiesel, 1963) and primates (Blasdel, Obermayer, & Kiorpes, 1995; Wiesel & Hubel, 1974), suggesting that the machinery to support orientation processing is in place about the time visual experience begins, if not before. Some early postnatal development of orientation-selectivity occurs in single neurons, but neuronal selectivity appears to be adult-like during the first 1 to 2 months of life (Chino, Smith, Hatta, & Cheng, 1997; Thompson, Kossut, & Blakemore, 1983). These studies demonstrated selectivity by serially presenting gratings of different orientation.

In studies that presented multiple orientations simultaneously, Morrone and colleagues (Morrone, Burr, & Maffei, 1982; Morrone, Speed, & Burr, 1991) found that orientation-selective pattern masking developed slightly later in kittens, compared to single-presentation orientation-selective responses. Pattern-masking selectivity developed around 20 to 50 days postnatal, compared to the orientation-selectivity found in newborns in serial-presentation studies (e.g., Bonds, 1979).

Infant Development: Serial Presentations Reveal Early Development. The development of orientation processing in human infants has been studied by several labs using behavioral and electrophysiological techniques. In behavioral measures, infants habituated to a grating at one orientation subsequently show novelty preferences for gratings at different orientations, indicating that the novel orientation can be discriminated from the habituated orientation. For stationary gratings, orientation discriminations have been shown as early 1 week of age (Atkinson, Braddick, Weeks, & Hood, 1990; Atkinson, Hood, Wattam-Bell, Anker, & Tricklebank, 1988; Slater, Morrison, & Somers, 1988), whereas discriminations for temporally modulated gratings develop one to two months later (Hood, Atkinson, Braddick, & Wattam-Bell, 1992), indicating that orientation-selective mechanisms may be present from birth, but their temporal sensitivity increases postnatally.

VEPs studies of orientation-selectivity in infants show similar results, although static stimuli cannot be used in VEP tests. VEPs can be measured in infants as young as 6 weeks of age in response to a grating pattern that periodically switches orientation (Braddick, Wattam-Bell, & Atkinson, 1986; Manny, 1992). Taken together, these studies suggest that very young human infants, like kittens and monkeys, possess orientation-selective neurons.

Infant Development: Simultaneous Masking Reveals Late Development. In a study of the development of the slope of contrast response functions in human infants, Morrone and Burr (1986) reported data from three human infants, suggesting a similarity with their kitten data, described earlier. When gratings of different orientations are presented simultaneously, human infants' orientation-selective responses developed later than in studies of serially presented gratings. We recently extended these results, showing that through the first year of life, infants have a marked immaturity in processing simultaneously presented multiple orientations (Candy, Skoczenski, & Norcia, 1998, 1999; Skoczenski, Candy, & Norcia, 1998). Skoczenski et al. (1998) measured orientation processing and contrast responses in 54 infants ranging in age from 3 to 11 months. Figure 5.14 shows examples of the stimuli used in our experiments. Sinewave gratings were presented alone (baseline) and with superimposed one-dimensional noise oriented parallel or orthogonal to the sinewave grating. Adults showed a response pattern in which the parallel mask elevated threshold considerably more than the orthogonal mask, consistent with the notion that the orthogonal mask is outside the orientation "channel" of the grating, and thus has little effect on the visibility of the grating.

Young infants' responses, however, were masked equally by parallel and orthogonal masks, as shown in Fig. 5.15, which shows contrast response functions for detection of a grating alone (baseline) and with parallel and orthogonal noise masks. Data from 3-month-olds and 5-month-olds (Fig. 5.15: left and center) show that their responses were equally affected by the two mask orientations. It is not until 11 months postnatal

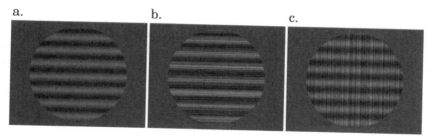

FIG. 5.14. The effect of one-dimensional (oriented) noise on grating detection. A sinewave grating without noise (a), and with simultaneously presented parallel (b) and orthogonal (c) stimulus noise.

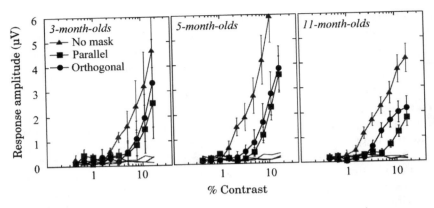

FIG. 5.15.   VEP response amplitude as a function of grating contrast for three groups of infants, 3-month-olds (*a*), 5-month-olds (*b*), and 11-month-olds (*c*). Each graph shows functions for a grating presented alone (triangles) and with parallel (squares) and orthogonal (circles) noise masks.

(Fig. 5.15: right) that infants' responses to the two mask orientations began to differentiate, and this differential response was still immature relative to adults' response. This suggests that *interactions* between different oriented mechanisms develop late, although discrimination of sequentially presented orientation information is in place during early infancy. Similar results using grating masks instead of one-dimensional noise have been reported by Candy, Skoczenski, and Norcia (1998, 1999).

The Relationship Between Orientation Processing and Vernier Acuity

Models and Evidence of Orientation Filters in Vernier Acuity.   Wilson proposed models of normal foveal vision (1986) and peripheral and amblyopic vision (1991) of adults that suggest that vernier signals are processed by mechanisms ("filters") that are optimally tuned for orientation and spatial frequency. Wilson suggested that vernier offsets are coded by the differential signals between filters that are oriented at oblique angles to the offset line, in order to signal the left tilt or right tilt in the line caused by the offset. Figure 5.16 shows how differential responses from such filters could discriminate a line with and without a vernier offset. An optimally oriented filter with an excitatory center and inhibitory surrounds will be differentially excited by an offset bar compared to a straight bar, because a relatively greater portion of the offset will fall into its excitatory region. Wilson's model predicts that optimally oriented filters with spatial frequency tuning in the range of 12 to 16 c/deg detect vernier offsets in the hyperacuity range.

Waugh et al. (1993) also examined the spatial frequency tuning of oriented mechanisms in vernier acuity, by varying the spatial frequency content of their one-dimensional noise masks. Maximum threshold elevation of an optimally oriented mask occurs when the spatial frequency content of the mask is centered at 12 c/deg. These results provide strong support for Wilson's model of optimal filters for vernier acuity.

Several laboratories have investigated the role of orientation processing

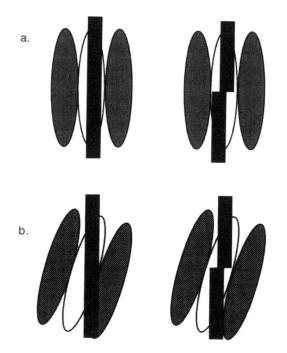

FIG. 5.16.   Hypothetical oriented filters for the detection of vernier offsets (based on Wilson, 1986). The top row (*a*) shows a filter oriented optimally to detect a bar. The bar falls only in the excitatory center region (*white*), not in the inhibitory region (*dark-shaded flanks*). When an offset is introduced (*top, right*), both offset portions still fall within the excitatory region, thus no differential response occurs between offset and no offset stimulation. The bottom row (*b*) shows a filter oriented in an off-axis relative to the offset stimulus. When an offset is introduced (*bottom, right*), it places more of the bar into the filter's excitatory region relative to the case (*bottom, left*) when no offset is present. Differential responses between and within filters such as these could signal the presence of vernier offsets.

in adults' vernier acuity, and have concluded that orientation-tuned filters play a critical role in detecting vernier offsets (Andrews, Butcher, & Buckley, 1973; Fahle & Harris, 1998; Findlay, 1973; Mussap & Levi, 1997; Waugh, Levi, & Carney, 1993; Wilson, 1986, 1988, 1991). When an offset appears in a line, there is orientation information from the carrier line (vertical), the direction of the offset (horizontal), and the implicit tilted (oblique) orientation in the carrier line caused by the offset (Findlay, 1973). Levi's laboratory has made extensive use of the simultaneous masking paradigm to study the importance of orientation information and spatial frequency information for vernier acuity. They measured vernier acuity for stimuli with superimposed one-dimensional noise (Waugh & Levi, 1995; Waugh, Levi, & Carney, 1993), gratings (Mussap & Levi, 1997), or plaid patterns (Mussap & Levi, 1997). The results of these studies can be summarized to suggest that the critical information for adults' vernier acuity occurs at two orientations that straddle the offset orientation, corresponding to the tilt in the line created by the offset. Adult observers showed maximum masking at two orientations, plus or minus 10° to 20° from the offset carrier line (Waugh et al., 1993). Thus specifically oriented filters are critical for vernier hyperacuity in adults.

Hypothesis of Developmental Relationship. The direct relationship between orientation responses and vernier acuity has not been studied in infants, but our data showing that infants' ability to process two simultaneously presented orientations develops quite late (Skoczenski et al., 1998), suggest that the temporal sequence of orientation processing and vernier acuity are similar, and that both develop later than more basic aspects of spatial vision, such as contrast sensitivity and grating resolution. These results, combined with adult data and models suggesting the importance of oriented filters in vernier acuity, provide support for a hypothetical relationship between the development of orientation responses and vernier responses.

Although previous studies have shown that infants have relatively early orientation sensitivity for sequentially presented stimuli (Atkinson et al., 1988, 1990; Braddick et al., 1986; Manny, 1992), studies from adults (e.g., Wilson, 1986, 1991; Waugh et al., 1993) suggest that vernier acuity depends on a *differential* response from two off-axis orientation mechanisms (i.e., filters sensitive to left oblique and right oblique relative to a vertical vernier line). Thus processing of a vernier offset requires communication between separate orientation filters. Because our data show that the interactions between orientation mechanisms are immature, it is plausible that this differential signal is poorly encoded. It is also likely that infants' orientation tuning is broader than adults' tuning (cf. Manny, 1992), thus even if infants do use immature versions of oriented filters in vernier acuity tasks, they may be quite different from those used by adults to perform similar tasks. These could be major factors in infants' poor vernier acuity.

CONCLUSIONS

General Summary of Results

This chapter reviewed recent studies of visual development in a framework designed to determine limitations on different aspects of spatial vision. Figure 5.17 schematically illustrates the development of three components of vision—contrast sensitivity, grating acuity, and vernier acuity—showing the age at which each function develops to within a factor of two of adult performance. This figure represents the best available estimates for each function. Peak contrast sensitivity (for low spatial frequencies) develops earliest. According to VEP estimates, it is within a factor of two of adult sensitivity by 2.5 months postnatal. Although behavioral measures do not show such early development on absolute terms, they do show relatively earlier development of sensitivity for low versus high spatial

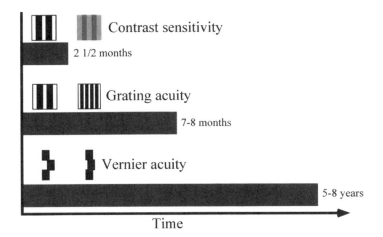

FIG. 5.17. Schematic of normal developmental sequences for spatial vision. This timeline shows the age at which three aspects of spatial vision reach within a factor of two of adult performance. Peak contrast sensitivity (*top*) approaches adult levels earliest, followed by grating acuity (*middle*) and vernier acuity (*bottom*), which reaches adult levels relatively late in visual development.

frequencies. Grating acuity approaches adult levels later than contrast sensitivity, at about 7 to 8 months postnatal by VEP estimates, and behavioral measures also show a relatively rapid phase of development up to this age. Of the three functions shown in Fig. 5.17, vernier acuity develops latest. Although there are as yet no data showing when VEP vernier acuity reaches adult levels, all studies of infants (FPL and VEP) show that it is far worse than adult performance by 12 months postnatal, and psychophysical studies of children show that it is not until between 5 and 8 *years* of age that vernier acuity develops to within a factor of two of adult performance.

In addition to their different developmental sequences, there is evidence that contrast sensitivity, grating acuity, and vernier acuity are constrained differently by front-end and central factors in the visual processing pathways. I have summarized studies that suggest that front-end factors are insufficient to explain fully development in any of these functions. However, evidence suggests that aspects of front-end (retinal) factors can at least partly explain development of contrast sensitivity (photon capture efficiency of photoreceptors) and grating acuity (foveal photoreceptor spacing). The role of front-end factors in the development of vernier acuity is less clear, and there is stronger evidence that vernier acuity is limited primarily by processing in the geniculo-striate portion of the visual pathway. In general, later development occurs in characteristics of visual processing that are dominated by cortical functioning, consistent with previous hypotheses (Atkinson, 1984; Bronson, 1974). Furthermore, the later stages of development of all of the visual functions discussed, even those that can be explained partially by development in front-end factors, must be limited by postnatal refinements in cortical processing.

Development of Connections to Support Pattern Processing

The sensitivity and precision of adult spatial vision must be supported by complex networks of neurons that communicate to compare information from the visual environment. Evidence from studies of contrast sensitivity, grating acuity, vernier acuity, and orientation processing during human and nonhuman development suggest that, although the basic "building blocks" of spatial vision may be in place neonatally or develop early in infancy, complex interactions between visual neurons—both within and between different visual areas—may not develop until substantially later. These interactions likely support the processing of more complex patterns. The data summarized here on vernier acuity and orientation masking in infants and adults points to the development of communication between different cortical oriented mechanisms and/or filters as a main factor in the development of relative position sensitivity.

Also, it is possible that postnatal development in interactions between cortical neurons and neurons in other areas of the visual pathway governs relative position sensitivity. For example, as discussed earlier, it is known that the photoreceptors of the retina undergo considerable postnatal migration, that is, they move into their final positions sometime after birth. By 45 months of age, postnatal migration is not yet complete (Yuodelis & Hendrickson, 1986). By contrast, even though cortical synaptic connections undergo postnatal development (Huttenlocher et al., 1982), cortical neuron (cell body) migration is complete at birth (Conel, 1939). Because of these different developmental sequences of migrations, it is likely that cortical maps of visual space change dramatically during development. For example, a given photoreceptor in a 2-month-old infant will provide information to its associated cortical neurons about a different segment of visual space than the same photoreceptor will at 4 and 6 months of age. As position information from photoreceptors changes developmentally, cortical neurons must undergo some form of recalibration in order to represent spatial position accurately. It is possible that this recalibration is dependent on synaptic proliferation and synaptic pruning (Huttenlocher et al., 1982) and is not precise enough to support hyperacuity-level position sensitivity until well into the period of synaptic pruning that occurs between 10 months and 10 years of age.

Future Directions

The data presented here suggest at least two fruitful directions of future research. First, in the study of neural noise limitations on spatial vision during development, the critical next step is to partition different sites of neural noise. One way to do this is by measuring equivalent noise in single neurons at different stages of visual processing. For example, we have preliminary data suggesting that contrast sensitivity differences between neurons in magnocellular and parvocellular layers of the adult monkey lateral geniculate nucleus can be explained by different levels of equivalent noise (Skoczenski et al., 1994). These results have been extended to developing animals (e.g., Movshon et al., 1997).

A second direction of research would determine the relationship between the cortically limited complex pattern processing described here and higher forms of visual perception and visual spatial cognition. The recent evolution of visual perceptual development research, and the technological innovations that have allowed the study of complex neural processing during infancy, have also—unfortunately—moved visual sensory/perceptual development research away from the core of infant behavioral and psychological development research. Thus, an important task ahead is to meld what we are learning about the limitations on visual sensory development with research on the development of even more complex perceptual and cognitive skills that develop in later infancy and early childhood, such as categorization abilities (e.g., Quinn & Eimas, 1998; Rakison & Butterworth, 1998; Thompson & Markson, 1998).

ACKNOWLEDGMENTS

The author's studies presented here were conducted in four different laboratories with numerous collaborators. In chronological order, they are: University of Rochester, Richard N. Aslin; University of California at Berkeley, Martin S. Banks; New York University, Lynne Kiorpes and J. Anthony Movshon; and The Smith-Kettlewell Eye Research Institute, Anthony M. Norcia, T. Rowan Candy, and William V. Good. These studies were supported by the National Institutes of Health, the Howard Hughes Medical Institute, an American Psychological Association Dissertation Research Award, Fight for Sight/Society to Prevent Blindness, and the Smith-Kettlewell Eye Research Foundation.

REFERENCES

Andrews, D. P., Butcher, A. K., & Buckley, B. R. (1973). Acuities for spatial arrangement in line figures: human and ideal observers compared. *Vision Research, 13,* 599–620.

Aslin, R. N. (1987). Visual and auditory development in infancy. In J. D. Osofsky (Ed.), *Handbook of infant development* (2nd ed.) New York: Wiley.

Atkinson, J. (1984). Human visual development over the first six months of life: a review and a hypothesis. *Human Neurobiology, 3,* 61–74.

Atkinson, J., Braddick, O., & Moar, K. (1977a). Development of contrast sensitivity over the first three months of life in the human infant. *Vision Research, 17,* 1037–1044.

Atkinson, J., Braddick, O., & Moar, K. (1977b). Contrast sensitivity of the human infant for moving and static patterns. *Vision Research, 17,* 1045–1047.

Atkinson, J., Braddick, O., Weeks, F., & Hood, B. (1990). Spatial and temporal tuning of infants' orientation-specific responses. *Perception, 19,* 371.

Atkinson, J., French, J., & Braddick, O. (1981). Contrast sensitivity function of preschool children. *British Journal of Ophthalmology, 65,* 525–529.

Atkinson, J., Hood, B., Wattam-Bell, J., Anker, S., & Tricklebank, J. (1988). Development of orientation discrimination in infancy. *Perception, 17,* 587–595.

Banks, M. S., & Bennett, P. J. (1988). Optical and photoreceptor immaturities limit the spatial and chromatic vision of human neonates. *Journal of the Optical Society of America A, 5,* 2059–2079.

Banks, M. S., & Crowell, J. A. (1993). Front-end limitations to infant spatial vision: examination of two analyses. In K. Simons, (Ed.), *Early visual development: Normal and abnormal.* (pp. 91–116). New York: Oxford University Press.

Banks, M. S., & Salapatek, P. (1978). Acuity and contrast sensitivity in 1-, 2- and 3-month-old human infants. *Investigative Ophthalmology and Visual Science, 17,* 361–365.

Banks, M. S., & Salpatek, P. (1983). Infant visual perception. In M. M. Haith & J. J. Campos (Eds.), *Handbook of child psychology: Vol. II. Infancy and developmental psychobiology* (pp. 435–471). New York: Wiley.

Banks, M. S., Sekuler, A. B., & Anderson, S. A. (1991). Peripheral spatial vision: Limits imposed by optics, photoreceptors, and receptor pooling. *Journal of the Optical Society of America, 8,* 1775–1787.

Bertenthal, B. I. (1996). Origins and early development of perception, action, and representation. *Annual Review of Psychology, 47,* 431–59.

Birch, E. E., & Swanson, W. H. (1999). Maturation of positional hyperacuity during infancy. *Investigative Ophthalmology and Visual Science, 40,* S395.

Blakemore, C. (1990). Maturation of mechanisms for efficient spatial vision. In C. Blakemore (Ed.), *Vision: Coding and efficiency.* (pp. 254–266). Cambridge: Cambridge University Press.

Blakemore C., & van Sluyters, R. C. (1975). Innate and environmental factors in the development of the kitten's visual cortex. *Journal of Physiology (London), 248,* 663–716.

Blakemore, C., & Vital-Durand, F. (1986). Organization and postnatal development of the monkey's lateral geniculate nucleus. *Journal of Physiology (London), 380,* 453–491.

Blasdel, G., Obermayer, K., & Kiorpes, L. (1995). Organization of ocular dominance and orientation columns in the striate cortex of neonatal macaque monkeys. *Visual Neuroscience, 12,* 589–603.

Bonds, A. B. (1979). Development of orientation tuning in the visual cortex of kittens. In R. D. Freeman (Ed.), *Developmental neurobiology of vision* (pp. 31–41). New York: Plenum.

Bonds, A. B. (1991). Temporal dynamics of contrast gain in single cells of the cat striate cortex. *Visual Neuroscience, 6,* 239–255.

Boothe, R. G., Kiorpes, L., Williams, R. A., & Teller, D. Y. (1988). Operant measurements of contrast sensitivity in infant macaque monkeys during normal development. *Vision Research, 28,* 387–396.

Braddick, O., Wattam-Bell, J., & Atkinson, J. (1986). Orientation-specific cortical responses develop in early infancy. *Nature, 320,* 617–619.

Bradley, A., & Freeman, R. D. (1982). Contrast sensitivity in children. *Vision Research, 22,* 953–959.

Bronson, G. W. (1974). The postnatal growth of visual capacity. *Child Development, 45,* 873–890.

Brown, A. M. (1990). Development of visual sensitivity to light and color vision in human infants: A critical review. *Vision Research, 30,* 1159–1188.

Brown, A. M. (1997). Vernier acuity in human infants: Rapid emergence shown in a longitudinal study. *Optometry and Vision Science, 74,* 732–740.

Burkhalter, A., Bernardo, K. L., & Charles, V. (1993). Development of local circuits in human visual cortex. *Journal of Neuroscience, 13,* 1916–1931.

Campbell, F. W., & Maffei, L. (1970). Electrophysiological evidence for the existence of orientation and size detectors in the human visual system. *Journal of Physiology, 207,* 635–652.

Campbell, F. W., & Robson, J. G. (1964). Application of Fourier analysis to the modulation response of the eye. *Journal of the Optical Society of America, 54,* 581A.

Candy, T. R., Skoczenski, A. M., & Norcia, A. M. (1998). Strong temporal frequency dependence of orientation masking in infancy. *Investigative Ophthalmology and Visual Science, 39,* S1089.

Candy, T. R., Skoczenski, A. M., & Norcia, A. M. (1999). Paradoxical orientation masking in human infants. *Investigative Ophthalmology and Visual Science, 40,* S349.

Carkeet, A., Levi, D. M., & Manny, R. E. (1997). Development of vernier acuity in childhood. *Optometry and Vision Science, 74,* 741–750.

Chino, Y. M., Smith, E. L., Hatta, S., & Cheng, H. (1997). Postnatal development of binocular disparity sensitivity in neurons of the primate visual cortex. *Journal of Neuroscience, 17,* 296–307.

Conel, J. (1939). *The postnatal development of the human cerebral cortex: Vol. 1. The cortex of the newborn.* Cambridge, MA: Harvard University Press.

Dannemiller, J. (1998). Temporal modulation enhances the efficiency of spatial offset discrimination by 6-month-olds. *Vision Research, 38,* 2127–2134.

Diaz-Araya C., & Provis J. M. (1992). Evidence of photoreceptor migration during early foveal development: a quantitative analysis of human fetal retinae. *Visual Neuroscience, 6,* 505–514.

Dobkins, K. R., & Teller, D. Y. (1996). Infant contrast detectors are selective for direction of motion. *Vision Research, 36,* 281–294.

Dobson, V., & Teller, D. Y. (1978). Visual acuity in infants: a review and comparison of behavioral and electrophysiological studies. *Vision Research, 18,* 1469–1483.

Ellemberg, D., Lewis, T. L., Liu, C. H., & Maurer, D. (1999). Development of spatial and temporal vision during childhood. *Vision Research, 39,* 2325–2333.

Fahle, M., & Harris, J. P. (1998). The use of different orientation cues in vernier acuity. *Perception and Psychophysics, 60,* 405–426.

Fantz, R. L. (1958). Pattern vision in young infants. *Psychological Record, 8,* 43–47.

Findlay, J. M. (1973). Feature detectors and vernier acuity. *Nature, 241,* 135–137.

Geisler, W. (1984). Physical limits of acuity and hyperacuity. *Journal of the Optical Society of America A, 1,* 775–782.

Geisler, W. S., & Albrecht, D. G. (1992). Cortical neurons: Isolation of contrast gain control. *Vision Research, 32,* 1409–1410.

Good, W. V., Jan, J. E., Burden, S. K., Skoczenski, A. M., & Candy, T. R. (2001). Recent advances in cortical visual impairment. *Developmental Medicine and Child Neurology, 43,* 56–60.

Gwiazda, J., Bauer, J., Thorn, F., & Held, R. (1997). Development of spatial contrast sensitivity from infancy to adulthood: psychophysical data. *Optometry and Vision Science, 74,* 785–789.

Hainline, L., & Abramov, I. (1997). Eye movement-based measures of development of spatial contrast sensitivity in infants. *Optometry and Vision Science, 74,* 790–799.

Hamer, R. D., & Mayer, L. (1994). The development of spatial vision. In D. M. Albert & F.A. Jakobiec (Eds.), *Principles and practice of ophthalmology: Basic sciences* (pp. 578–608). Philadelphia: W. B. Saunders Co.

Harris, L., Atkinson, J., & Braddick, O. (1976). Visual contrast sensitivity in a 6-month-old infant measured by the evoked potential. *Nature, 264,* 570–571.

Hawken, M. J., Blakemore, C., & Morley, J. W. (1997). Development of contrast sensitivity and temporal frequency selectivity in primate lateral geniculate nucleus. *Experimental Brain Research, 114,* 86–98.

Hendrickson, A. E., & Drucker, D. (1992). The development of parafoveal and midperipheral human retina. *Behavioural Brain Research, 49,* 21–31.

Hess, R. F., & Field, D. (1993). Is the increased spatial uncertainty in the normal periphery due to spatial undersampling or uncalibrated disarray? *Vision Research, 33,* 2663–2670.

Hess, R. F., & Watt, R. J. (1990). Regional distribution of the mechanisms that underlie spatial localization. *Vision Research, 30,* 1021–1031.

Hood, B. M., Atkinson, J., Braddick, O., & Wattam-Bell, J. (1992). Orientation selectivity in infancy: behavioural evidence for temporal sensitivity. *Perception, 21,* 351–354.

Hubel, D. H., & Wiesel, T. N. (1963). Receptive fields of cells in striate cortex of very young, visually inexperienced kittens. *Journal of Neurophysiology, 26,* 994–1002.

Huttenlocher, P. R., DeCourten, C., Garey, L. S., & van der Loos, H. (1982). Synaptogenesis in the human visual cortex—evidence for synapse elimination during normal development. *Neuroscience Letters, 33,* 247–252.

Kiorpes, L. (1992a). Development of vernier acuity and grating acuity in normally-reared monkeys. *Visual Neuroscience, 9,* 243–251.

Kiorpes, L. (1992b). Effect of strabismus on the development of vernier acuity and grating acuity in monkeys. *Visual Neuroscience, 9,* 253–259.

Kiorpes L., & McKee S. P. (1999). Neural mechanisms underlying amblyopia. *Current Opinion in Neurobiology, 9,* 480–486.

Kiorpes, L., & Movshon, J. A. (1989). Differential development of two visual functions in primates. *Proceedings of the National Academy of Sciences USA, 86,* 8998–9001.

Kiorpes, L., & Movshon, J. A. (1998). Peripheral and central factors limiting the development of contrast sensitivity in macaque monkeys. *Vision Research, 38,* 61–70.

Larsen, J. S. (1971). The saggital growth of the eye IV: Ultrasonic measurement of the axial length of the eye from birth to puberty. *Acta Ophthalmologica, 49,* 873–886.

Lee, B. B., Wehrhahn, C., Westheimer, G., & Kremers, J. (1995). The spatial precision of macaque ganglion cell responses in relation to vernier acuity of human observers. *Vision Research, 35,* 2743–2758.

Levi, D. M. (1988). The Glenn A. Fry Award Lecture: The "spatial grain" of the amblyopic visual system. *American Journal of Optometry and Physiological Optics, 65,* 767–786.

Levi, D. M., & Carkeet, A. (1993). Amblyopia: A consequence of abnormal visual development. In K. Simons (Ed.) *Early visual development: Normal and abnormal* (pp. 391–408). Oxford: Oxford University Press.

Levi, D. M., & Klein, S. A. (1982). Hyperacuity and amblyopia. *Nature, 298,* 268–270.

Levi, D. M., & Klein, S. A. (1985). Vernier acuity, crowding and amblyopia. *Vision Research, 25,* 979–991.

Levi, D. M., & Klein, S. A. (1990a). Equivalent intrinsic blur in spatial vision. *Vision Research, 30,* 1971–1993.

Levi, D. M., & Klein, S. A. (1990b). Equivalent intrinsic blur in amblyopia. *Vision Research, 30,* 1995–2022.

Levi, D. M., Klein, S. A., & Aitsebaomo, P. (1985). Vernier acuity, crowding and cortical magnification. *Vision Research, 25,* 963–978.

Levi, D. M., Klein, S. A., & Yap, Y. L. (1987). Positional uncertainty in peripheral and amblyopic vision. *Vision Research, 27,* 581–597.

Levi, D. M., Manny, R. E., Klein, S. A., & Steinman, S. B. (1983). Electrophysiological correlates of hyperacuity in the human visual cortex. *Nature, 306,* 468–470.

Manny, R. E. (1988). The visually evoked potential in response to vernier offsets in infants. *Human Neurobiology, 6,* 273–279.

Manny, R. E. (1992). Orientation selectivity of 3-month-old infants. *Vision Research, 32,* 1817–1828.

Manny, R. E., & Klein, S. A. (1984). The development of vernier acuity in infants. *Current Eye Research, 3,* 453–462.

Mohn, G., & van Hof-van Duin, J. (1991). Development of spatial vision. In J. R. Cronly-Dillon (Series Ed.) & D. Regan (Vol. Ed.), *Vision and visual dysfunction: Vol. 10. Spatial vision.* Boca Raton, FL: CRC Press.

Morrone, M. C., & Burr, D. C. (1986). Evidence for the existence and development of visual inhibition in humans. *Nature, 321,* 235–237.

Morrone, M. C., Burr, D. C., & Maffei, L. (1982). Functional significance of cross-orientation inhibition: Part. 1. Neurophysiology. *Proceedings of the Royal Society B (Lond.), 216,* 335–354.

Morrone, M. C., Speed, H. D., & Burr, D. C. (1991). Development of visual inhibitory interactions in kittens. *Visual Neuroscience, 7,* 321–334.

Movshon, J. A., Kiorpes, L., Hawken, M. J., Skoczenski, A. M., Cavanaugh, J. C., & Graham, N. V. (1997). Sensitivity of LGN neurons in infant macaque monkeys. *Investigative Ophthalmology and Visual Science, 38,* S498.

Mussap, A. J., & Levi, D. M. (1997). Vernier acuity with plaid masks: The role of oriented filters in vernier acuity. *Vision Research, 37,* 1325–1340.

Norcia, A. M., Tyler, C. W., & Hamer, R. D. (1988). High visual contrast sensitivity in the young human infant. *Investigative Ophthalmology and Visual Science, 29,* 44–49.

Norcia, A. M., Tyler, C. W., & Hamer, R. D. (1990). Development of contrast sensitivity in the human infant. *Vision Research, 30,* 1475–1486.

Norcia, A. M., Wesemann, W., & Manny, R. E. (1999). Electrophysiological correlates of vernier and relative motion mechanisms in human visual cortex. *Visual Neuroscience, 16,* 1123–1131.

Ohzawa, I., Sclar, G., & Freeman, R. D. (1985). Contrast gain control in the cat's visual system. *Journal of Neurophysiology, 54,* 651–667.

Pelli, D. G. (1990). The quantum efficiency of vision. In C. Blakemore (Ed.), *Vision: Coding and efficiency* (pp. 3–24). Cambridge: Cambridge University Press.

Peterzell, D. H., Werner, J. S., & Kaplan, P. S. (1993). Individual differences in contrast sensitivity functions: The first four months of life in humans. *Vision Research, 33,* 381–396.

Peterzell, D. H., Werner, J. S., & Kaplan, P. S. (1995). Individual differences in contrast sensitivity functions: Longitudinal study of 4-, 6- and 8-month-old human infants. *Vision Research, 35,* 961–979.

Pirchio, M., Spinelli, D., Fiorentini, A., & Maffei, L. (1978). Infant contrast sensitivity evaluated by evoked potentials. *Brain Research, 141,* 179–184.

Quinn, P. C., & Eimas, P. D. (1998). Evidence for a global categorical representation of humans by young infants. *Journal of Experimental Child Psychology, 69,* 151–174.

Rakison, D. H., & Butterworth, G. E. (1998). Infants' attention to object structure in early categorization. *Developmental Psychology, 34,* 1310–1325.

Regan, D. M. (1973). Evoked potentials specific to spatial patterns of luminance and color. *Vision Research, 13,* 2381–2402.

Regan, D. M. (1989). *Human brain electrophysiology: Evoked potentials and evoked magnetic fields in science and medicine.* New York: Elsevier.

Robson, J. G. (1966). Spatial and temporal contrast sensitivity functions of the visual system. *Journal of the Optical Society of America, 56,* 1141–1142.

Rose, A. (1942). The relative sensitivities of television pick-up tubes, photographic film, and the human eye. *Proceedings of the Institute of Radio Engineers, 30,* 293–300.

Shannon, E., Skoczenski, A. M., & Banks, M. S. (1996). Retinal illuminance and contrast sensitivity in human infants. *Vision Research, 36,* 67–76.

Shimojo, S., Birch, E. E., Gwiazda, J., & Held, R. (1984). Development of vernier acuity in human infants. *Vision Research, 24,* 721–728.

Shimojo, S., & Held, R. (1987). Vernier acuity is less than grating acuity in 2- and 3-month-old infants. *Vision Research, 27,* 77–86.

Skoczenski, A. M., & Aslin, R. N. (1992). Spatiotemporal factors in infant position sensitivity: Single-bar stimuli. *Vision Research, 32,* 1761–1770.

Skoczenski, A. M., & Aslin, R. N. (1995). Assessment of vernier acuity development using the "equivalent intrinsic blur" paradigm. *Vision Research, 35,* 1879–1887.

Skoczenski A. M., Banks M. S., & Candy T. R. (1993). Contrast sensitivity and equivalent noise in infants and adults, *Investigative Ophthalmology and Visual Science (Suppl), 34,* 1355.

Skoczenski, A. M., Brown, C., Kiorpes, L., & Movshon, J. A. (1995). Development of contrast sensitivity and visual efficiency in macaque monkeys measured with sweep VEPs. *Investigative Ophthalmology and Visual Science, 36,* S442.

Skoczenski, A. M., Candy, T. R., & Norcia, A. M. (1998). Orientation masking identifies a late immaturity in infant pattern vision. *Investigative Ophthalmology and Visual Science, 39,* S1089.

Skoczenski, A. M., & Good, W. V. (1999). *Selective damage to vernier acuity responses in children with cortical visual impairment.* Paper presented at the meeting of the Child Vision Research Society, Brighton, England.

Skoczenski, A. M., & Norcia, A. M. (1998). Neural noise limitations on infant visual sensitivity. *Nature, 391,* 697–700.

Skoczenski, A. M., & Norcia, A. M. (1999). Development of VEP vernier acuity and grating acuity in human infants. *Investigative Ophthalmology and Visual Science, 40,* 2411–2417.

Skoczenski, A. M., O'Keefe, L. P., Kiorpes, L., Tang, C., Hawken, M. J., & Movshon,

J. A. (1994). Visual efficiency of macaque LGN neurons. *Society for Neuroscience Abstracts, Vol. 1, 7.*

Slater, A., Morrison, V., & Somers, M. (1988). Orientation discrimination and cortical function in the human newborn. *Perception, 17,* 597–602.

Teller, D. Y. (1979). The forced-choice preferential-looking procedure: A psychophysical technique for use with human infants. *Infant Behavior and Development, 2,* 135–153.

Thompson, I. D., Kossut, M., & Blakemore, C. (1983). Development of orientation columns in cat striate cortex revealed by 2-deoxyglucose autoradiography, *Nature, 301,* 712–715.

Thompson, L. A., & Markson, L. (1998). Developmental changes in the effect of dimensional salience on the discriminability of object relations. *Journal of Experimental Child Psychology, 70,* 1–25.

Van Nes, F. L., & Bouman, M. A. (1967). Spatial modulation transfer in the human eye. *Journal of the Optical Society of America A, 57,* 401–406.

Watt, R. J., & Morgan, M. J. (1984). Spatial filters and the localization of luminance changes in human vision. *Vision Research, 24,* 453–469.

Waugh, S. J., & Levi, D. M. (1995). Spatial arrangement across gaps: Contributions of orientation and spatial scale. *Journal of the Optical Society of America A, 12,* 2305–2317.

Waugh, S. J., Levi, D. M., & Carney, T. (1993). Orientation masking and vernier acuity for line targets. *Vision Research, 33,* 1619–1638.

Westheimer, G. (1975). Visual acuity and hyperacuity. *Investigative Ophthalmology and Visual Science, 14,* 570–572.

Wiesel, T. N., & Hubel, D. H. (1974). Ordered arrangement of orientation columns in monkeys lacking visual experience. *Journal of Comparative Neurology, 158,* 307–318.

Williams, D. R. (1985). Aliasing in human foveal vision. *Vision Research, 25,* 195–205.

Wilson, H. R. (1986). Responses of spatial mechanisms can explain hyperacuity. *Vision Research, 26,* 453–469.

Wilson, H. R. (1988). Development of spatiotemporal mechanisms in infant vision. *Vision Research, 28,* 611–628.

Wilson, H. R. (1991). Model of peripheral and amblyopic hyperacuity. *Vision Research, 31,* 967–982.

Wilson, H. R. (1993). Theories of infant visual development. In K. Simons (Ed.), *Early visual development: Normal and abnormal* (pp. 560–572). New York: Oxford University Press.

Yuodelis, C., & Hendrickson, A. E. (1986). A qualitative and quantitative analysis of the human fovea during development. *Vision Research, 26,* 847–855.

Zanker, J., Mohn, G., Weber, U., Zeitler-Driess, K., & Fahle, M. (1992). The development of vernier acuity in human infants. *Vision Research, 32,* 1557–1564.

Zumbroich, T., Price, D. J., & Blakemore, C. (1988). Development of spatial and temporal selectivity in the suprasylvian visual cortex of the cat. *Journal of Neuroscience, 8,* 2713–2728.

6

▼▼▼▼▼▼▼

A Model of the Origins of Autobiographical Memory

Elaine Reese
University of Otago

INTRODUCTION

How and when do infants and young children begin to remember significant events from their lives and communicate them to others? Memory for
personally experienced events, or *autobiographical memory,* is a critical part
of our sense of who we are as adults (Nelson, 1993a). The purpose of this
chapter is to explore the emergence of autobiographical memory in infancy
and early childhood. To accomplish this goal, I first discuss exactly what
counts as autobiographical memory. Then I review historical and current
theories of the development of autobiographical memory and the available evidence supporting each theory. Next I summarize the results of a
longitudinal program of the development of autobiographical memory
from $1^1/_2$ to $3^1/_2$ years of age. Based on these data, I propose a model of the
origins of autobiographical memory development that integrates the existing evidence over this age period.

What Counts as Autobiographical Memory?

Memory research is fraught with definitional controversy. Brewer (1986,
1995) devoted entire chapters to defining autobiographical memory. Most
theorists agree that autobiographical memories are part of the episodic
memory system in that they must consist of memories for one-time, specific events as opposed to memory for procedures or general knowledge ex-

tracted over time (Tulving, 1983). Some theorists, however, think it is not necessary to propose separate memory systems at all. Rovee-Collier and Hayne (1987) proposed a focus on the different functions of memory for the developing infant rather than simply its structure. Uncovering the predictive value of memories, they argued, will help us discover which events are likely to be retained in the long term. Nelson (1993b, 1993c) shared the focus on functional aspects of memory, but proposed a separate autobiographical memory system once children understand the social and cultural reasons for retaining unique past events. Nelson (1996, p. 162) defined autobiographical memories as "enduring chronologically sequenced memory for significant events from one's own life." Under this definition, episodic memories are only autobiographical if they are organized in a culturally appropriate narrative form and make up part of the individual's life story. Pillemer and White (1989, p. 313) added that to count as autobiographical, "recall is intentional; and memory is assessed by verbal performance." Brewer (1986) additionally stipulated that autobiographical memory involves a sense of having been personally experienced. Rovee-Collier and Hayne (1987) and Howe and Courage (1993) countered that the criteria that memories be verbally accessible, and that individuals must possess consciousness of having personally experienced the event to make it autobiographical, essentially preclude infants from being capable of autobiographical memory.

My position in this chapter is to take a middle ground on these issues. I agree that the criterion of a conscious sense of reliving for autobiographical memory may be too strict, but for slightly different reasons than those argued by Howe and Courage (1993). Primarily, this criterion is hard to determine or measure even in adults and may be virtually impossible to ascertain in infancy and early childhood (e.g., Rovee-Collier, 1997). I agree with some theorists that we should focus on verbally accessible memories, but again for slightly different reasons. A verbally accessible memory is the sine qua non of autobiographical memory and underscores the communicative function of such memories. Although adults engage in private reminiscing that may consist primarily of images, one of the most vital functions of autobiographical memory is to relate to others who you are through conversations about what you have experienced and to connect with others through shared past experiences (Hyman & Faries, 1992). This criterion of verbal accessibility does not necessarily preclude autobiographical memory in late infancy and early childhood. Again, it depends on what verbalizations can count as autobiographical memory. Virtually from the time infants begin to talk, they refer to past events (Fenson et al., 1993; Reese, 1999; Sachs, 1983). Thus the working definition of autobiographical memory for this chapter is to retain a focus on specific, one-time events that are verbally accessible. Whether or not these verbal memories count as autobiographical is in part an empirical question that I address further after presenting results from the study. The focus is therefore on the *structure* of emerging autobiographies in infancy. The results of this study do not yet address the *content* of children's early memories, a matter of vital importance for theoretical and practical reasons (see Pillemer, 1997).

A Brief History of Approaches to Autobiographical Memory Development

Historical theories of autobiographical memory development have focused primarily on the presumed absence of autobiographical memory in the first 3 years of life, a deficit approach to memory. Because most adults cannot recall events from the first 3 to 4 years of life, they are termed *amnesic* for personally experienced events during that period (e.g., Dudycha & Dudycha, 1941). Early theories of this phenomenon hypothesized that childhood events were laid down in memory, but for various reasons were unable to be retrieved in adulthood. Freud (1905/1953) claimed that the emotionally and sexually charged nature of early event memories encouraged repression of these events. Schachtel (1947) and Neisser (1962) both proposed that children's categories for encoding and storing life events were qualitatively different from the categories under which adults attempt retrieval; socialization into cultural norms and schemas was responsible for memories eventually becoming accessible into adulthood. Critically, under both of these theories, event memories were initially laid down and could presumably be recovered if the correct retrieval strategy were implemented or a salient cue encountered.

More recently, some theorists proposed that infants and young children are not yet capable of any episodic memories, but have only a procedural or habit memory system in place (e.g., Bachevalier, 1990). This hypothesis is weakened by the now voluminous evidence that the brain structures responsible for long-term memory are in place by at least 8 or 9 months of age (see Nelson, 1995 for a review). Evidence from behavioral tests reveals that infants are capable of declarative or recall memory by at least 6 months of age (Collie & Hayne, 1999), and that under certain conditions, infants and young children can retain events over months and even years during the period of infantile amnesia (e.g., Bauer, Hertsgaard & Dow, 1994; Bauer & Wenner, 1999; Hamond & Fivush, 1991; Myers, Perris, & Speaker, 1994; see Howe & Courage, 1993 for a review). Basic nonverbal, declarative memory abilities certainly increase with age (e.g., Herbert & Hayne, 2000). The capacity for episodic memory, however, is present from very early in life, well before the offset of infantile amnesia.

Current theories instead focus on cognitive and social developments that contribute to the offset of infantile amnesia and the onset of autobiographical memory. The hypothesized critical skill involved, however, varies according to the theory. Hayne and Rovee-Collier (1995) proposed that infantile amnesia can be explained by the limited representational flexibility of infants and young children. Their research with infants demonstrates the extreme specificity of context and cues needed for infants to retrieve memories. Howe and Courage (1993) also proposed a critical change in late infancy as the primary determinant of autobiographical memory, specifically the advent of a cognitive sense of self with the onset of self-recognition between 18 and 24 months of age. Howe and Courage operationalized the necessary development with the classic mirror test of self-recognition (e.g., Amsterdam, 1972), in which a dab of rouge is placed on the child's nose. When placed a few minutes later in front of a mirror, children who reach to touch the mark on the nose instead of the mark in the mirror are said to demonstrate self-recognition. Passing the self-recognition test may indicate that the child has achieved objective self-awareness, and the ability to reflect on self-relevant features and attributes. With the "critical mass" of self-understanding that occurs at this age, infants become capable of encoding and storing memories as self-relevant or autobiographical. After achieving self-recognition, children then vary in the rate at which they acquire further self-knowledge. Individual variation in children's age at passing the self-recognition test and their subsequent rate of acquiring self-knowledge are together claimed to explain variations in the offset of infantile amnesia.

Povinelli (1995) also proposed self-understanding as the critical skill involved in autobiographical memory, but differed in the nature of self-understanding required and in the proposed age of onset. Povinelli proposed that it is not "live" self-recognition, as indexed through the mirror task, that enables autobiographical memory, but a sense of the self as continuous in time, a "proper self." Children's increased representational abilities lead to a proper self in this theory, in that only when they are aware of being aware can they understand that they are the same person now who experienced events an hour, a week, or a year ago. According to Povinelli, this critical development in self-awareness occurs at about $3^1/2$ to 4 years. The task used to index the proper self is described in Povinelli, Landau, and Perilloux (1996). A researcher surreptitiously places a large sticker on the child's head in the course of playing a game. The child is videotaped or photographed with the sticker on the head, and several minutes later is shown the videotape or photograph. Very few 3-year-olds, but most 4-year-olds, immediately reach up to their heads for the sticker when viewing the video or photograph. Povinelli et al. (1996) claim that 3-year-olds' failure to reach for the sticker after such a brief delay, even when these same children can and will touch a mark in the live self-recognition test, demonstrates that they do not yet have a continuous sense of self in time. Once they begin to reach for the sticker, they understand that experiences of the "past self" can be related to properties of the "present self."

Finally, Perner and colleagues (Perner, 1990, 1991; Perner & Ruffman, 1995) also proposed that the fundamental skill involved in autobiographical memory is a change in cognitive capacity. Perner and Ruffman's theory, however, emphasizes children's ability to understand the source of memory as personally experienced as the necessary skill for autobiographical memory. Only when children understand that perceptual access to an event equates to representational access, Perner and Ruffman argued, can they begin to encode events with the necessary source information (i.e., an "episodic trace") for it to be retained as autobiographical. Thus, the ability to understand the origins of knowledge commonly acquired by about age 4 years is the primary determinant of autobiographical memory in this theory.

Although these theories differ in the proposed age of onset of autobiographical memory, and in the nature of the critical skill involved, all propose one primary cognitive influence as contributing to autobiographical memory development and the end of infantile amnesia. Other theories adopt a multifactorial approach, but share with the cognitive theorists the notion that there is a critical skill that children must acquire before they are capable of encoding and retaining events in an autobiographical memory system. Pillemer and White (1989) targeted language skill through social interaction as the critical variable, and especially the ability to organize events in a causal–temporal format upon experience and in later narratives of personal events. Pillemer and White termed this the advent of a socially accessible memory system, in that only at about age $3^1/_2$ to 4 years can children give a relatively coherent and understandable account of a past event to someone who did not initially experience the event.

Nelson (1993b, 1996) also focused on language skill and social interaction as primary influences on autobiographical memory. Specifically, children from about age 4 years can use language as a representational system. At this age, they are beginning to reflect on language and manipulate language in an intentional manner in their conversation and storytelling. Their event memories also become narrativized in the sense that their more advanced language skills encourage encoding in the narrative form of their culture. Narrativized memories are more likely to enter the life story because they are more easily communicated to others. The narrative form is also a mnemonic device that aids long-term retention. Narrativization in Nelson's theory occurs partly as a result of cognitive development, but also as a function of how narrativized are adults' conversations with children about past events.

Hudson (1993) and Fivush and colleagues (Fivush, 1998; Fivush, Haden, & Reese, 1996; Fivush & Reese, 1992) again focused on the importance of social interactions in children's developing narrative skill for talking about the past. Children whose parents are highly elaborative in their talk about the past are predicted to demonstrate richer verbal memory skills later in development than children of less elaborative parents. Social-interaction theorists draw on Vygotsky's (1978) theory that conversations with adults result in the eventual internalization of children's independent cognitive skills. In this application of Vygotsky's theory, children learn the importance and form of talking about the past (but not necessarily the content of specific memories) through their early conversations with adults about past events. By the end of the preschool period, they have internalized adults' "style" of reminiscing, resulting in individual differences in verbal memory that could lead to individual differences in the onset and richness of adult recollections of early childhood experiences. Fivush (1988) additionally proposed that the ability to order self-relevant events in time contributes to the eventual life story. Caregivers are likely to influence this process by providing an evaluative framework for past events (Fivush, in press).

Finally, Welch-Ross and colleagues (Welch-Ross, 1995, 1997, in press; Welch-Ross, Fasig, & Farrar, 1999) proposed a theory that integrates social and cognitive influences on autobiographical memory development. Like Povinelli (1995) and Perner and Ruffman (1995), Welch-Ross (1995) claimed that there are certain cognitive prerequisites for autobiographical memory. For instance, akin to Brewer's (1986) "sense of reliving" criterion, Welch-Ross argued that children must have an understanding of the mental state of remembering for their memories to qualify as autobiographical. The necessary level of source information, however, may be much more implicit than proposed by Perner and Ruffman (1995) and is available by around age 3 years. For example, Custer (1996) demonstrated that 3-year-olds have an understanding of the representational nature of memory prior to their representational understanding of false beliefs. Children's developing ability to reason about conflicting mental representations and to understand the link between experiencing and knowing are proposed to help children engage more fully in reminiscing, as they begin to experience a shared focus with their caregivers on the memory (Welch-Ross, 1997). Social interaction is not necessary for the start of autobiographical memory under this theory, but the verbal reinstatement of personal memories may aid long-term retention, especially once children have the cognitive ability from around age 3 to benefit from verbal reinstatement. Caregivers are also important for the evaluative framework they provide for children's memories: why reminiscing is important and what these events mean for the child's sense of self. Finally, an organized, psychological self concept from around age $3^1/_2$ may lead to the retention of certain memories over others (Welch-Ross, in press; Welch-Ross, Fasig, & Farrar, 1999).

Thus, these theories of autobiographical memory can be grouped first into whether they view autobiographical memory as being caused mainly by one factor or several factors. A second revealing way of grouping these theories of autobiographical memory is with respect to how continuous or discontinuous is the proposed course of development. Hayne and Rovee-Collier (1995) and Rovee-Collier (1997) proposed a highly continuous course of memory development across infancy and early childhood. Rovee-Collier (1997) argued that the constraints on infant memory are the same as those that operate on adult memory (e.g., effects of serial position, timing of practice, and the role of affect). Herbert and Hayne (2000) proposed that the advent of language development in the second year of life does not necessarily result in a qualitative shift in children's memory development, but simply offers children another cue in their repertoire (albeit a particularly powerful cue). Social-interaction theorists also propose a relatively continuous process of development, at least with regard to the gradual transmission of the style and function of autobiographical memory from parent to child during the preschool years. The remaining theories reviewed, however, hypothesize that autobiographical memory is due to a discontinuous development in the child's life (Howe & Courage, 1993; Nelson, 1996; Perner & Ruffman, 1995; Pillemer & White, 1989; Povinelli, 1995; Welch-Ross, 1995). Once a certain cognitive, linguistic, or social skill is achieved, then infants or young children are capable of encoding and maintaining events as autobiographical. Howe and Courage (1993) claimed that their theory does not entail a separate autobiographical memory system, but then proposed that "events that occur before the child develops an independent sense of self at about 18 months of age cannot be organized autobiographically but will probably be coded in memory as a more generalized learning experience" (p. 313). These theories, then, explicitly propose autobiographical memory as a qualitatively different memory system. They differ primarily on what critical skill or skills are involved in jump-starting this separate memory system. I argue instead that the data are better explained by a relatively continuous system in which many social, cognitive, and linguistic factors come together in the development of autobiographical memory, and that the origins of this skill can be seen from infancy.

Recent Research on the Emergence of Autobiographical Memory

Before outlining the current study, however, how well does past research address these various theories of autobiographical memory development? I first review the relevant evidence for the start of autobiographical memory from age $3^{1}/_{2}$ to 6 years because most of the research so far has focused on this age period (see Howe & Courage, 1993, 1997; Nelson, 1996; Pillemer & White, 1989; and Welch-Ross, 1995 for reviews of this literature). Then I go on to review the few studies that have examined autobiographical memory before age $3^1/_2$ years, which is the main focus of the present study.

The studies with preschoolers have demonstrated how children's narratives about past events, with parents and with others, change over the preschool period. Children are capable of producing independent narratives about past events from at least $3^1/_2$ years (e.g., Fivush, Haden & Adam, 1995), but children's past event narratives become more complete and complex with age. Pillemer, Picariello, and Pruett (1994) demonstrated that children who were $3^1/_2$ years old at the time of a significant event (a fire alarm at preschool) were not as accurate in their event retellings as children who were $4^1/_2$ years old at the original event, especially in terms of the event chronology and causal–temporal relationships. By the preschool years, children are already providing a number of evaluatives (emotion words, intensifiers) and orientations (who, when, how) in their past event narratives, but the number and type of evaluatives and orientations increase dramatically over this age period (Peterson & McCabe, 1983; see Fivush & Haden, 1996; Hudson & Shapiro, 1991 for reviews). As children reach the end of the preschool period, they are more likely to include internal state references and to refer the listener to the "when" and the "why" of an event instead of just what happened. Orientations may be particularly important narrative devices for helping the listener understand the chronology of an event; evaluations are important for helping the listener understand why the event was significant to the teller.

These changes in the amount and type of information provided in children's past event narratives over the preschool period may in part be due to the influence of social interaction. A body of research has now demonstrated that parents adopt either a highly elaborative or less elaborative style of conversing about past events with their preschool children (e.g., Fivush & Fromhoff, 1988; Hudson, 1993; McCabe & Peterson, 1991; Reese & Fivush, 1993). Parents who are "high elaborative" or "topic extending" provide a great deal of information about the past event in the course of their questioning; they also tend to confirm their children's responses and in general follow in on their children's interests in the conversation. "Low elaborative" or "topic switching" parents tend to ask the same questions repeatedly and seem to be in search of a particular memory response from the children. These parents tend to switch topics more frequently than do the high elaborative parents. Overall, children of high elaborative parents are exposed to richer memory conversations than children of less elaborative parents. The high elaborative style is associated concurrently and longitudinally with children's past-event narratives with parents (Reese, Haden, & Fivush, 1993) and independently (Hudson, 1993). Recent evidence suggests that parents' elaborative conversational style at encoding of events is also associated with children's recall (Haden, Ornstein, Eckerman, & Didow, in press; Tessler & Nelson, 1994).

The following examples illustrate differences in the strategies of high and low elaborative parents, in this case mothers, and of changes in their children's reminiscing over time (Reese et al., 1993).[1] First, here is a conversation between a low elaborative mother and her son at 40 months. Note that the only memory question the mother asks the child is about the animals they saw at the zoo; she does not follow in and extend on the child's responses.

> **M:** Tell me about the zoo, what do you remember about going to the zoo?
> **C:** I saw animals, good-bye.
> *(three turns in which mother attempts to make child sit down)*
> **M:** What kind of animals did you see, do you remember?
> **C:** Lollipops.
> **M:** Lollipops aren't animals, are they?
> **C:** (unintelligible soundplay)
> **M:** Who, what kind of animals did you see?
> **C:** Giraffe.
> *(two turns of acoustical clarification)*
> **M:** You saw giraffes? Ah. And what else?
> **C:** RRROAR!
> **M:** What's roar?
> **C:** Lion.
> *(two turns in which mother asks child why he is whispering)*
> **M:** What else did you see?
> **C:** ROAR!
> **M:** What else did you see?
> **C:** No, I want to go watch my T.V.
> **M:** Well, you can go back and watch that in a second. What other animals did you see?
> **C:** Um, a monkey.
> *(two turns of acoustical clarification)*
> **M:** Monkeys? And what else?

---

[1] Reprinted from "Mother–child conversations about the past: Relationships of style and memory over time," by E. Reese, C. A. Haden, and R. Fivush, 1993, *Cognitive Development, 8,* 27–56. Copyright 1993 by Elsevier Science. Reprinted with permission.

The same mother and child at 70 months still display a style in which the mother asks the same question repeatedly. Even though the child supplies more information at this age, the mother is not always willing to follow in on the child's interests.

M: Do you remember when we were down in Florida?
C: Yeah.
M: And we were dyeing Easter eggs?
C: Uh huh.
M: What did we do?
C: Hm. Like what?
M: Like remember, well how did we dye the Easter eggs?
C: Oh. Got some little paint something, goes like that?
M: And can you explain more to me what we did?
C: Oh. The Easter bunny came . . .
M: But I mean about dyeing the eggs, remember that day we were all dyeing the eggs?
C: Yes.
M: How did we do it?
C: What's this for?
(two turns in which mother asks for acoustical clarification)
M: A taperecorder. Can you tell me about how we did that?
C: That, what is that stuff called?
M: What we painted the Easter eggs?
M: Dye?
C: No. The little . . . what is that for?
M: It's just a taperecorder, don't worry. I want to know about, how did we do it? Do you remember how we did it and what we did?

In contrast, a high elaborative mother and her child have more harmonious and collaborative conversations about past events. At 40 months, the child does not recall any information but participates readily in the conversation. The mother provides rich information and continues asking elaborative questions even though the child is not recalling any information.

M: Joseph, do you remember a long time ago . . .
C: uh huh.
M: When you and I and some other people got on the MARTA train,
C: Uh huh.
M: And we went to the High Museum.
C: Uh huh.
M: Do you remember what we did there?
C: Uh huh.
M: What did we do?

C: I don't know.
M: Do you remember what we saw that you liked a whole lot?
C: What?
M: Do you remember a helicopter?
C: Uh huh.
M: And, what else did we see there?
C: Um, (long pause). I don't know.
M: I think you and Matthew and Hannah were there.
C: Uh huh.
M: And you all got to get on a bunch of things, like a street sweeper.
C: Um.

By 70 months, the same child and mother are creating together the event conversation.

M: Do you remember something really, really, really special that you and I got to do?
C: Uh uh.
M: Got on the train . . .
C: Yeah.
M: We went to the Omni . . .
C: Uh huh. And we saw Sesame Street Live.
M: Right. Where were our seats?
C: Um, I forget.
M: Way up high. How high?
C: In the balcony.
M: So high we could see all the way over the. . . ? Do you remember? The stage?
C: Yeah.
M: What did we see?
C: We saw Big Bird. We saw, um, the Honkers, we saw Ernie and Bert, we saw Grover.
M: What was the stage set up like?
C: I don't know.
M: It had a bell on top . . .
C: Oh, school.
M: Yeah yeah . . . Do you remember what some of the kids in the audience got to do?
C: uh uh.
M: Go up on the stage.
C: I wish I had got to.
M: Well yeah, but we were up so high, we got to see Big Bird puttin' his head on and stuff like that, remember?
C: Yeah.

M: When we could see before anybody else could see 'cause we
      could see over the top of the stage.

C: Hm.

Mothers who are primary caregivers may play a special role in the internalization of children's past event narrative style. Mothers', but not
fathers', provision of evaluative information to their children at age $3^1/_2$
uniquely predicts children's use of evaluative information at age $5^1/_2$ in
their independent past-event narratives (Haden, Haine, & Fivush, 1997).
Research has also demonstrated that mothers' style of talking about the
past is consistent across siblings (Haden, 1998) and across types of past
events (shared or unshared; Reese & Brown, 2000), although mothers
become more elaborative as children grow older and are contributing
more to conversations (Reese et al., 1993).

Recent research also addresses possible qualitative changes in children's autobiographical memory in conjunction with cognitive changes.
Povinelli et al. (1996) demonstrated that most 3-year-olds do not yet have
a concept of the past self. When surreptitiously marked with a large sticker
on their heads in the course of a game, and then after a brief delay shown
a video of themselves with the sticker on their heads, 75% of 4-year-olds
but only 25% of 3-year-olds immediately reached up to remove the sticker.
Moreover, most 4-year-olds but few 3-year-olds reached for the sticker
after a brief delay (several minutes) but not when they were viewing a
video from the previous week (Povinelli & Simon, 1998), demonstrating
their awareness that events that happened further back in time are less
likely to be causally linked to the present state of affairs. Finally, Povinelli,
Landry, Theall, Clark, and Castille (1999) extended the paradigm by showing videos of an experimenter secretly hiding a puppet in one location
in the target child's presence versus in a different location in another
child's presence. Again, 4-year-olds but not 3-year-olds demonstrated they
understood the causal link between a past event and the present by finding the puppet. A conservative interpretation of these results is that 3-year-
olds are not always capable of understanding causal links between a past
event and the present state of affairs. Perhaps advances in causal–temporal
reasoning serve both to clarify children's thinking about an event as it
occurs and to improve narrative structure in their later recall, although the
link between the past self tasks and children's past-event narratives has
yet to be made. Perner and Ruffman (1995) demonstrated that 3- to 6-year-
olds' episodic memory on a free recall task was uniquely related to their
performance on a task measuring the origins of knowledge, and specifically that visual access was required to "know" about an event. Although
the results of this study do point to a relation between children's understanding of the origins of knowledge and their episodic memory, the free

recall task in Perner and Ruffman's study, a picture recall task, may not comprise autobiographical memory in terms of being a self-relevant past event. Welch-Ross (1997) examined two aspects of children's theory of mind abilities in relation to mother–child conversations about shared past events with $3^1/_2$- to $4^1/_2$- year-old children. Children's memory responding differed as a function of their theory of mind abilities. Specifically, children with more advanced theory of mind skills were more likely to provide unique information and less likely to give nonmemory information (e.g., "I don't know") in response to mothers' elaborative questions in the conversations, regardless of age or syntactic abilities. Thus, Welch-Ross was able to relate directly children's theory of mind skills to their autobiographical memory. At present, then, a relation has been established between children's theory of mind skills and their episodic and autobiographical memory. Furthermore, children are making advances in their causal–temporal understanding over the same time period. It is possible that causal–temporal understanding of events and theory of mind make independent contributions to children's past event narrative skills, although this hypothesis has not yet been tested directly. To make a convincing case for qualitative changes in children's autobiographical memories as a function of cognitive advances, however, longitudinal research would need to demonstrate changes in causal–temporal and theory of mind skills that precede and/or uniquely predict changes in children's autobiographical memory.

To summarize, the research on autobiographical memory during the preschool period shows that children already have quite impressive capabilities for talking about the past by age $3^1/_2$ years. Their narrative responding is related to their theory of mind, although causal and temporal links between theory of mind and autobiographical memory have not yet been established. What are the forces that contribute to this skill by age $3^1/_2$ years? The remainder of this review focuses on the emergence of autobiographical memory from infancy to the start of the preschool period.

Until the present study, most research examining the emergence of autobiographical memory in infancy focused exclusively on children's growing ability to talk about the past. Children refer to past events from about 18 months of age (Sachs, 1983). By 19 months, 52% of American children refer to past events, according to a parental report language instrument (MacArthur Communicative Development Inventory (CDI); Fenson et al., 1993). These first verbal memories usually consist of one or two words and often are a simple reference to an absent object or person as opposed to a true conversation about the past (Nelson & Ross, 1980; Sachs, 1983). Adults feature prominently in this early past-event talk. In a longitudinal study of two children's past-event talk from its inception, Eisenberg (1985) noted that the children progressed from dependence on adults' cues and structure in the conversation (from age 2 years) to independent initiation of talk about one-time past events from around age 2;5 years. Hudson (1991) also described how one child was initiated into conversations about the past. Rachel's mother asked a high preponderance of general prompts ("Tell me about the beach") and yes–no questions ("Did you see Aunt Gail?") initially at age $1^1/_2$ years, then gradually asked more specific memory questions ("What did you see?"). By the end of the recording period at age 2;4 years, Rachel was initiating past-event conversations on her own and was less interested in participating in mother-initiated conversations about the past. Reese (1999) noted how one child moved from mentioning association memories ("choo-choo" in reference to an absent train) to referring to whole events ("Hand. Door." when telling his uncle about pinching his hand in the door) in his first 6 months of talking about the past. Over that 6-month period, Benjamin also became more flexible in his references to the past and could initiate past-event references even when there was no obvious physical cue in the environment reminding him of the past event.

These early references to the past are of interest because they demonstrate that children are willing and capable of talking about the past from infancy. Their verbal memories, although sparse, appear to be accurate and can occur at least one year after the occurrence of the original event (Fivush, Gray, & Fromhoff, 1987; Reese, 1999). Thus, children are capable of verbal displays of long-term memory even within the period of infantile amnesia. Yet adults heavily scaffold these early references to the past. When the children themselves bring up the past event, their references often do not appear to have a narrative or communicative function (Nelson, 1989; Reese, 1999; although cf. Miller & Sperry, 1988 for evidence of early past-event narrative abilities in $2^1/_2$-year-olds). In addition, the "events" children focus on are often quite mundane and routine by adult standards (Nelson, 1989; Reese, 1999). The memories that children bring up on their own at this age are generally not events that adults would consider part of the life story. In this sense, perhaps Schachtel (1947) and Neisser (1962) were on the right track in proposing that children's and adults' storage categories are so disparate that later retrieval is impeded. The disparity may have more to do with what children and adults find interesting rather than fundamental differences in encoding (Reese, 1999). When interviewed about the same events at age $2^1/_2$ and 4 years, older children mentioned more distinctive as opposed to typical aspects of events, whereas $1^1/_2$ years earlier, the same children had focused on routine, mundane aspects of those same events (Fivush & Hamond, 1990). These findings suggest that events are richly encoded in late infancy and early childhood, but that children retrieve different aspects of event representations as they get older. In essence, they may be learning what aspects of events are reportable. However, the seeds of a life story, even in its verbal form, are already present from as early as $1^1/_2$ years of age. From age $2^1/_2$ years, some children can tell a primitive story about a past event (Hudson, 1990).

An obvious question, especially with this younger age group, is the degree to which verbal memory is synonymous with children's language development. How much of the life story is dependent on children's sheer ability to talk, whether about the past or about the present? Surprisingly little research has addressed this fundamental question. Nelson and Ross (1980) acknowledged that it was unclear to what degree children's advances in verbal memory were due to general advances in language development. Neither did Hudson (1990) collect independent measures of language development in her case study. With older children, several studies have included measures of children's syntactic skills and receptive vocabulary, but only one of these studies to date has found an association between preschoolers' language abilities and their talk about the past (Welch-Ross, 1997). Critically, measures of children's expressive language development independent of the past-event conversations have only rarely been collected. In one exception, MacDonald (1997) found few relationships between children's expressive vocabulary levels at the time of retrieval and their verbal memories from 24 to 40 months of age. Reese (1999) demonstrated that although children's expressive vocabulary levels at time of retrieval were correlated with their spontaneous talk about the past, language development was not synonymous with verbal memory development. The growth in frequency and type of children's spontaneous verbal memory talk occurred independently of children's vocabulary development. On the other hand, Bauer and Wewerka (1995) found that $1^1/_2$-year-olds' productive vocabulary at the time of encoding an event uniquely predicted their later verbal memory. Thus, two issues have emerged in this debate. The first is whether language is indeed related to verbal memory. If so, is expressive language a stronger predictor of verbal memory than receptive language? The second is whether language in general might be a stronger factor in verbal memory in the late infancy period than in the preschool period. The present study addresses the issue of whether language in late infancy, utilizing a measure of expressive vocabulary, indeed predicts verbal memory. If so, can verbal memory be completely accounted for by language development?

A related question is the degree to which maternal reminiscing style is a function of children's language development. To what degree is mothers' style of talking about the past simply in response to children's language levels? Until the current research program, this question had not been addressed explicitly, although Welch-Ross (1997) found correlations between children's syntactic skill and mothers' contingent elaborative replies in past-event conversations. The possibility of maternal style of talking about the past being completely accounted for by children's language development is unlikely, however, given the stability in maternal style across siblings and across contexts.

Relationships between these early verbal memories and other cognitive changes have also been neglected until the present research program. Research had not yet investigated the way that various cognitive and linguistic factors in infancy together contribute to autobiographical memory in the same children over time. Most importantly, Howe and Courage's (1993, 1997) hypothesis that autobiographical memory depends on self-recognition in the second year of life had not been addressed empirically. Another important question motivating this research had to do with the larger social origins of maternal style and children's autobiographical memory. Prior research has largely ignored social and personality factors that may be contributing to a high elaborative maternal style of reminiscing and eventually to children's autobiographical memory. Specifically, both maternal style and children's autobiographical memory may arise in part from the prior attachment relationship between mother and child that develops from the first year of life (Ainsworth, Blehar, Waters, & Wall, 1978). Children who are securely attached are able to engage in more harmonious problem-solving interactions with their mothers than children who are insecurely attached (see de Ruiter & van Ijzendoorn, 1993 for a review). Meins (1997) explored extensively the social origins of cognitive skills in the mother—child attachment relationship. Although Meins did not examine autobiographical memory as a cognitive outcome in her study, she did find that securely attached children experienced more rapid language acquisition than insecurely attached children. In addition, mothers of securely attached children had different language styles with their children than mothers of insecurely attached children. Mothers of securely attached children were more likely to attribute intentionality to their children's speech, a stance Meins has labelled *maternal mind-mindedness*. Mothers of securely attached children also responded contingently to children in a more sensitive and constructive manner than mothers of insecurely attached children during a problem-solving task. No research to date has investigated the origins of autobiographical memory from the very early attachment relationship, although Farrar, Fasig, and Welch-Ross (1997) found that attachment security was concurrently related to the emotional content of past event narratives for 3- to 4-year-old children. Mother-daughter dyads with insecurely attached girls initiated negative talk more frequently, but once initiated, mother-daughter dyads with securely attached girls discussed negative aspects in more depth. The present study seeks to examine the social origins of autobiographical memory in the attachment relationship that has developed over the first year of life. Mothers may be more elaborative in their conversations about past events with securely attached young children, especially when discussing events at which both partners were present. Securely attached children may also show more interest in reminiscing, as measured by their attention to mothers during the conversation, and may benefit more from mothers' questioning techniques than insecurely attached children.

The Present Research

The present study was designed as a prospective longitudinal study of children's autobiographical memory. A host of social, linguistic, and cognitive contributors were measured in 58 children from $1^1/_2$ years to predict verbal memory up to $3^1/_2$ years of age. Specifically, at age $1^1/_2$ children's self-recognition was assessed via the mirror test (Lewis & Brooks-Gunn, 1979). Children's productive vocabulary was measured with the MacArthur CDI (Fenson et al., 1993) at this age. Also at age $1^1/_2$, attachment security was measured with the Attachment Q-set (Version 3.0, Waters, 1987). Children's interest in reminiscing was operationalized by their levels of attention to mothers during past-event conversations. Maternal style of talking about the past was also measured throughout the study. The main goal was to predict children's verbal memory with mothers and independently at the end of this period, which typically marks the offset of infantile amnesia and the onset of autobiographical memory. The aim was thus to fill the gap in research relating to multiple contributors to the emergence of autobiographical memory in infancy.

This study is the first to test Howe and Courage's (1993) hypothesis that self-recognition predicts autobiographical memory. It is also the first study to assess the role of attachment security in children's early talk about the past. Finally, it is the first study to integrate various social, cognitive, and linguistic contributors from infancy to the beginning of autobiographical memory.

Summary of Findings From the Project to Date. Harley and Reese (1999) demonstrated that children's self-recognition skill at age $1^1/_2$ indeed predicted children's verbal memory with mothers and others at 2 and $2^1/_2$ years of age. Self-recognition was not the only contributor to later verbal memory; mothers' style of talking about the past and children's language skill also contributed uniquely, especially to children's verbal memory with their mothers at these ages. Moreover, self-recognition and language interacted in predicting children's verbal memory. Language played a greater role in verbal memory for later recognizers in comparison to early recognizers. Children's nonverbal memory, in the form of a deferred imitation task, was also measured in this study but did not contribute uniquely to children's later verbal memory. Other work from this study focused on the process of mother–child reminiscing from $1^1/_2$ to $3^1/_2$ years of age (Farrant & Reese, 2000). Although Reese et al. (1993) suggested that maternal style of talking about the past has a unidirectional influence on children's early reminiscing, mediation analyses used in this study revealed that children play a role in shaping maternal style from a very young age. Specifically, children's early interest in reminiscing at age $1^1/_2$ years, as measured by attentiveness during past-event conversations, mediated the effect of maternal style on children's own later memory. Mothers' style of talking about the past played a more direct role in children's verbal memory from when children were aged 2 years. Finally, children's attachment security predicted children's verbal memory skills and maternal style of talking about the past (Farrant, 1999). The more securely attached the children at age $1^1/_2$ years, the better their verbal memory skills at later ages and the more elaborative their mothers were in talking about the past. Mothers of securely attached children also responded in a more sensitive manner by elaborating more often, given children's willingness to participate in the conversations, compared to mothers of insecurely attached children, who were more likely to repeat their previous questions given children's willingness to participate. Children's temperament was also assessed but did not turn out to be a strong predictor of children's memory performance. To date, there has been no evidence in this sample of marked gender differences. This absence of gender differences is in contrast to other research demonstrating that parents provide richer past-event narratives with girls than boys, and that girls talk in more elaborative ways than boys about past events from as early as $3^1/_2$ years of age (e.g., Haden et al., 1997; Reese & Fivush, 1993; Reese, Haden, & Fivush, 1996). The strongest gender-of-child differences in previous research, however, have been found with regard to narrative analyses (particularly parents' and children's use of evaluative devices) and the emotional content of autobiographical memories (e.g., Haden et al., 1997; Kuebli, Butler, & Fivush, 1995). These domains have not been addressed with the present sample.

The goal of the present chapter is thus to present new analyses, drawing together all the contributors studied to date in this program, to predict autobiographical memory at age $3^1/_2$ years. The most important contributors from these previous analyses appear to be children's self-recognition, language, interest in memory conversations, and attachment security at age $1^1/_2$ years, and maternal style at age 2 years. Do these contributors play unique roles in children's later verbal memory? Or are they interconnected predictors of autobiographical memory?

METHOD

Participants

Fifty-eight children (30 boys and 28 girls) and their primary caregiver mothers took part in the study. The children were on average 19.2 months of age at the first datapoint (SD = 11.3 days), 25.3 months of age at the second datapoint (SD = 12.1 days), 32.1 months of age at the third datapoint (SD = 9.3 days), and 40.2 months of age at the fourth datapoint (SD = 18.1 days). An additional seven children (5 boys and 2 girls) initially took part but failed to complete all datapoints (five families moved, and two withdrew for personal reasons). Children were recruited through birth records and posters placed in the local community of Dunedin, New Zealand. Fifty-two of the children were of New Zealand European ethnicity; five children had one or both parents who were New Zealand Maori; one child had one parent who was of Asian descent. All mothers identified English as the primary language spoken in the home. Children came from middle- and working-class families, according to Elley and Irving's (1976) scale of fathers' occupational status. The children's mothers had an average of 13.2 years of education (SD = 2.35 years) at the beginning of the study. Children received small gifts at each datapoint for their participation.

Procedure

All researchers involved in the study were women. At each visit, one of two primary researchers, accompanied by a secondary researcher (responsible for videotaping and audiotaping the sessions) visited children and their mothers in their homes for three sessions, 1 week apart, at each of the four datapoints. The primary researcher remained the same within each datapoint, but changed for the children across datapoints. At the first session of each datapoint, mothers filled in a consent form. Table 6.1 contains a list of the relevant tasks performed at each datapoint and their order in the session.

Self-Understanding. Children's self-recognition at 19 months was measured with the mirror test (e.g., Lewis & Brooks-Gunn, 1979). In the second session at this datapoint, the researcher surreptitiously wiped odorless blue face paint on the child's nose with a tissue. Two minutes later, the child was placed 50 cm in front of a 40 cm by 60 cm mirror and videotaped for 2 minutes. The main researcher performed online coding of mark-directed behavior. Although children's looking behavior to the mirror has

TABLE 6.1
Order of Tasks at Each Datapoint and Session

19 Months	25 Months	32 Months	40 Months
Session 1	Session 1	Session 1	Session 1
Consent form CDI*	Consent form CDI*	Consent form* Memory interview	Consent form* Memory interview*
Session 2	Session 2	Session 2	Session 2
* Self recognition*	Memory interview*	*	Memory interview*
Session 3	Session 3	Session 3	Session 3
Memory interview* Attachment security Demographic form	Memory interview* Demographic form	* Memory interview* Demographic form	* Demographic form

Note. *Followed by task not relevant to this study.

sometimes been used as an index of self-awareness (Asendorpf, Warkentin & Baudonnier, 1996), mark-directed behavior is the most conservative measure of self-recognition. Usually, self-recognition is operationalized as nose-touching (Lewis & Brooks-Gunn, 1979). If the child touched within 2 cm of the mark on his or her nose at any point in the 2-minute observation period, he or she was coded as passing the mirror test. A second researcher later coded 25% of the tasks from videotape and established 100% reliability with the main coder on children's mark-directed behavior. Using this criterion, 28 children were coded as early recognizers and 30 children coded as later recognizers. Figure 6.1 displays a child demonstrating mark-directed behavior in the mirror test of self-recognition.

Language. Mothers completed the MacArthur CDI: Words and Sentences (CDI:WS; Fenson et al., 1993) over 1-week periods at 19 and 25 months to assess children's productive vocabulary. The CDI:WS was revised slightly for New Zealand English by substituting 6% of the words on the checklist for their New Zealand equivalents (NZ CDI:WS; Reese & Read, 2000). Children's language scores at 19 and 25 months were highly correlated ($r = .82$, $p < .01$); thus only children's language at 19 months was used as a predictor variable.

Attachment Security. Mothers completed the Attachment Q-set Version 3.0 (Waters, 1987) at the last session when children were 19 months old. The researcher was available to answer mothers' questions and to supervise the sorting. The researcher had given mothers a list of relevant be-

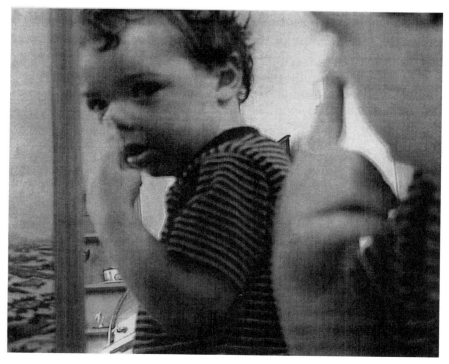

FIG. 6.1.   Mark-directed behavior in the mirror test of self-recognition.

haviors to observe 1 week prior to the sort. The Attachment Q-set consists of 90 cards listing typical child behaviors that mothers sort into a continuum of most characteristic to least characteristic of their child. Their sort is then scored via a computer program in comparison to a criterion sort for a hypothetical securely attached child. The correlation between the mother's sort and the criterion sort makes up the child's final score. Teti and Mc-Gourty (1996) found that mothers were reliable sorters of their children's attachment security, compared to unfamiliar observer sorters, when two conditions were met. The first condition is that the mothers had to be familiar with the items to be sorted in relation to their children's behavior; the second condition is that a trained observer was present during the sort. Both conditions were met in the present study.

Memory Conversations.   Memory conversations were of two types: mother–child conversations about past events (19 to 40 month datapoints) and researcher–child conversations about past events (25 to 40 month datapoints). These conversations took place in separate sessions in counterbalanced order within each datapoint. For each conversation, mothers were encouraged to select one-time, unique events for discussion. All conversations were also about events at which both mother and child were present initially, because these events are the best candidates for shared reminiscing between mother and child. Typical events were feeding the ducks at the park, feeding a baby lamb, riding in an airplane the first time, and going to visit the mudpools. Two researchers independently coded events for emotional tone, with reliability of 96.4% on 25% of the mother–child transcripts and reliability of 98.5% on 25% of the researcher–child transcripts. Events for both mother–child and researcher–child conversations were primarily positive in tone (89% and 91%, respectively; Farrant & Reese, 2000). The average time between the event and the event discussion was 51.1 days for mother–child conversations and 47.9 days for researcher–child conversations. The difference between average time since event for mother–child and researcher–child conversations was not significant ($t(1,57) = .78$, n.s.). All conversations were audiotaped and videotaped.

Mothers and children discussed two events at the 19-month datapoint and three events at each subsequent datapoint. For these conversations, mothers and children were seated on a couch. Researchers asked mothers to discuss the events in whatever way they normally would, for as long as they wished. Researchers left the room during the conversations. Researchers and children discussed two events at each of the 25- and 32-month datapoints, and three events at the 40-month datapoint. At the 25- and 32-month datapoints, researchers asked mothers to provide them with four cues about each event (e.g., four significant things that happened at the event that might cue the child's memory, such as what they ate and who was there). Then, researchers questioned children about each event. The first phase for each event at 25 and 32 months was a free recall phase, in which researchers asked open-ended prompts (e.g., "Tell me what happened when you visited the mudpools") and confirmed children's responses, but did not provide any information or ask any questions containing additional information. In the cued recall phase at these ages, researchers then questioned the child about each of the four cues for each event in turn (e.g., "Your mum said you ate something when you went there. Tell me more about that."). At the 40-month datapoint, the researcher–child interview consisted solely of free recall about the three events, in accord with past research at this age (e.g., Haden et al., 1997). All conversations were transcribed in full from audiotape, with the assistance of the videotape when necessary. Transcripts were masked for the identity and gender of the child prior to coding.

Mothers' and children's utterances in the mother–child conversations (hereafter called *shared memory conversations*) were coded for children's participation and new information provided by mother and child (see Farrant & Reese, 2000 for details of the full coding scheme). Reliability estimates (kappa) between two independent coders on 25% of the shared memory conversations across partner and time ranged from .85 to .90. Researcher–child conversations (hereafter called *independent memory conversations*) were coded for the number of researcher prompts and children's provision of unique information. Reliability estimates (kappa) between two independent coders on 25% of the independent memory conversations across partner and time ranged from .84 to .91. All verbal memory variables were averages of the number of events discussed at each datapoint, because different numbers of events were discussed across conversations and datapoints.

Farrant and Reese (2000) isolated the critical codes for children's long-term memory development. Specifically, children's interest in participating in the conversations at 19 months (*placeholders*) was related to their own later unique memory provisions and to their mothers' later conversational style. Placeholders occurred when children were attending to mothers' conversation and took an appropriate conversational turn but did not provide unique event information (e.g., saying "Mmmmm" and looking attentively to mother after she asked a question). Children's behaviors during the conversations were transcribed from videotape prior to coding because it was necessary to note the direction of the child's gaze and to see the context of the child's utterance in order to determine its function. The following example illustrates that at 19 months, placeholders function as a measure of children's interest in participating in the conversations. Children's placeholder codes are in italics.

M: . . . What happened at Sarah's birthday?
C: (sitting on Mum's knee, listening) *Ah.*
M: Eh? What did we do?
C: (sitting on Mum's knee, still attentive) *Ah.*
M: We sing happy birthday? Eh?
C: Yeah.

Although the child in this conversation is not providing any memory responses, he is listening attentively to his mother's questions and taking conversational turns. As noted in Farrant and Reese (2000), children's placeholders may also allow mothers to ask elaborative questions instead of spending their time persuading children to attend to the conversation. Indeed, children's use of placeholders at 19 months predicted mothers' later use of elaborative questions.

For mothers, the critical component of their conversation for children's later memory turned out to be their rate of open-ended questions offering new information *(memory-question elaborations)* when children were 25 months old (Farrant & Reese, 2000). This maternal variable mediated children's later provision of unique memory information in the shared conversations. Mothers' memory-question elaborations require more than simply a yes or no response from children. The following example illustrates one mother's use of memory-question elaborations with her 25-month-old daughter when discussing a ride in a glass-bottomed boat in Vanuatu. Mothers' memory-question elaboration codes are in italics.

M: *. . . What happened when you looked through the glass in the bottom of the boat? What could you see?*

C: A fish.

M: And was it pretty colours?

C: Mm.

M: *Do you remember what colours the fish were?*

C: Red pish [fish].

M: Red fish?

C: Yeah.

M: And yellow spots.

C: Uh mmm.

M: And do you remember feeding the fish?

C: Mmm.

M: *What did we feed the fish with?*

C: Ah some bread.

M: Bread. That's right. We fed the fish with bread. And Mummy and Daddy and Kate all had a swim in the water too. *And what happened when we were swimming?*

C: Aye ate a uh uh jelly shoe.

M: Your jelly shoe. *What happened to your jelly shoe?*

C: I got some um backa uh a backa boat.

M: On the back of the boat. And your jelly shoe fell in the water, didn't it?

C: Mmm.

Mothers' memory-question elaborations may be important for long-term memory because they are not as directive as yes–no questions and encourage children to give an elaborative response. In responding appropriately to memory-question elaborations, children become active contributors to the re-creation of the past event.

The most important child outcome variable in the shared memory conversations was children's provision of unique information *(shared memory elaborations)*, which they became statistically reliable on between the ages of 25 and 32 months (Farrant & Reese, 2000). Children's 19-

month placeholders and mothers' 25-month memory-question elaborations both uniquely predicted children's 32-month memory elaborations (Farrant & Reese, 2000). The following example illustrates one child's memory responses at 32 months when discussing a visit to a park. Shared memory elaborations are in italics.

> **M:** Do you remember going to Glenfalloch for lunch? (pause) Yes. And what did you do at Glenfalloch? You needed to go and use the potty, didn't you? And what did you need, what what did you do?
> **C:** *Wees in the toilet.*
> **M:** Wees in the toilet at Glenfalloch, and I thought you were a very very clever girl, didn't I? And did Mummy and Daddy have some lunch?
> **C:** *And Beth (sister), Beth had da rusks.*
> **M:** Beth had a rusk, that's right. And what did you have?
> **C:** *But Beth had (pause) a dried apricot.*
> **M:** So she did. She had a dried apricot. I'd forgotten about that. That's right. And what did you have?
> **C:** *Cause I ate a tot [lot] too.*
> **M:** That's right.

Notice that the child in this example is volunteering memory information beyond that asked for by her mother. She initiated the conversation about what she and her sister ate, and even brought up an aspect of the event that her mother had forgotten. Her own initial interest in attending to memory conversations at 19 months, coupled with her mothers' use of open-ended questions at 25 months, probably together contributed to her verbal memory skill by age $2^1/_2$ years.

In researcher–child conversations, the critical child outcome variable was the child's provision of unique information during recall as a function of the researcher's prompts (*independent memory elaborations*), which children became statistically reliable on between 32 and 40 months (Farrant & Reese, 2000). Children's ability at this age to provide independent memory information was predicted by their previous skill in providing shared memory information with their mothers at 32 months of age. The following example illustrates one child's provision of independent memory elaborations (in italics) at 40 months when discussing a parade at a local park with a researcher (R).

> **R:** Do you know what else your mum told me about? She said you went to Forbury Park. Could you tell me about that?
> **C:** *We saw um, a big um dragon going round with people on it and it—*

R: (simultaneously) Ohhh. Good boy.
C: *But I didn't go on it.*
R: Oh, okay.
C: *Because there was too many people on it.*
R: Oh.
C: *Only was only have to be lots of people on because there's lots of seats.*
R: Oh, I see. That was pretty good. And what else?
C: Umm.
R: What else happened at Forbury Park?
C: *We saw a plane* and sometime when we got back there um and the people um the plane will um shoot people out of the plane.
R: Oh. Yeah? Hey, you're telling me lots, aren't you? Anything else happen?
C: *We um um we saw um um horses going past.*
R: Oh yeah.
C: *Lots and lots and lots and lots and lots.*
R: Were there?
C: Mmm. *And one kicked so mum taked me off the gate.*
R: Oh, yeah?
C: Cause one kicked.
R: Oh, no good, is it?
C: *And it nearly got me.*
R: Oh dear. You don't want that, do you?
C: No.
R: No. And what else happened?
C: *Um, and the fire brades [brigades] go first and then some big big horses come past.*
R: Oh yeah. Good boy. Anything else?
C: *And them all going brrmm brrmm brrmm brrmm brrmm.*
R: Yeah? What was that?
C: *We didn't go on thing that goes way up high cause it's real scary.*
R: Oh, is it? Yeah.
C: *When I'm a bit older.*

Notice that this 40-month-old child does not require a great deal of prompting from the researcher to provide memory information. Indeed, he ends up telling an interesting and fairly coherent account of the parade, replete with sound effects and evaluative information.

Figure 6.2 summarizes the course of mother–child and independent reminiscing across this age period. The proposed temporal sequence starts with children's interest in participating at 19 months in the form of placeholders, to maternal style in the form of memory-question elaborations at 25 months, to shared memory elaborations at 32 months, and finally gen-

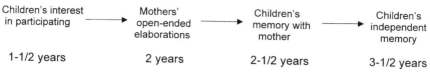

FIG. 6.2. Temporal sequence of mother–child reminiscing to independent verbal memory.

eralizing to independent memory elaborations at 40 months. This model of bidirectional influences between mother and child is based on mediation analyses presented in Farrant and Reese (2000).

RESULTS

The goal of this chapter is to integrate previous analyses on this sample in order to isolate the unique and interacting predictors of children's verbal memory. To accomplish this goal, regression analyses were conducted on the five predictor variables (children's self-recognition, language, interest and attachment variables at 19 months, and maternal reminiscing style at 25 months) in relation to the three outcome variables (children's shared memory responses at 25 and 32 months and independent memory at 40 months). A total of six memory conversations across datapoints were not recorded due to equipment failure (one each at 19 and 32 months; two each at 25 and 40 months). One mother did not complete the CDI at the 19-month datapoint. Mean substitution was used for all missing scores. In addition, some conversational variables and the language variable were positively skewed. Logarithmic transformations were performed as needed to adjust for skewness, and transformed variables were used in all analyses (Tabachnick & Fidell, 1996). Untransformed means for all variables are shown in Table 6.2.

Specifically, mediator and moderator relations among the predictor and outcome variables were explored (Baron & Kenny, 1986). Mediator analyses assess the possibility that a significant predictor of an outcome may actually be an indirect cause of that outcome and instead leads to an intermediate variable that is the direct cause of the outcome. The primary interest in this respect was that some of the initially significant predictor variables in previous analyses might no longer be significant when the full set of variables was entered in a regression equation. If so, the possibility exists that the predictor variable is related to another predictor variable, which acts as a mediator that is more directly related to the outcome variable. For instance, previous analyses suggested that maternal reminiscing style at 25 months mediated the relation between children's 25-month and 32-month memory responding (Farrant & Reese, 2000).

TABLE 6.2
Means, Standard Deviations and Ranges of Predictors and
Outcome Variables ($N = 58$)

Variable	Mean	Standard Deviation	Range
Predictors:			
Children's Language (19 months)	105.19	107.48	4 to 458
Children's Interest (19 months)	1.31	1.79	0 to 7.5
Attachment Security (19 months)	.38	.19	−.11 to .67
Maternal Style (25 months)	3.69	2.18	.67 to 8.67
Outcomes:			
Children's Shared Memory (25 months)	2.15	2.10	0 to 8.50
Children's Shared Memory (32 months)	3.55	2.65	0 to 10.67
Children's Independent Memory (40 months)	.24	.30	0 to 1.39

Another way in which predictor variables might interact is in the form of a moderator relationship. Moderator relationships occur when a relationship between predictor and outcome is only present, or is especially strong, for a subgroup formed by the interaction of two predictor variables. For instance, previous analyses suggested that self-recognition acted to moderate the relation between children's language skill and their verbal memory. The relation between language and verbal memory was stronger for later recognizers than for early recognizers (Harley & Reese, 1999).

Conducting all possible tests for mediation and moderation was not feasible, theoretically or statistically. Conceptually, the primary interest was in the mediator analyses, which assess paths of potential influence and thus contribute to an understanding of the process of development. These analyses first addressed the question of which of the five predictor variables was uniquely related to later verbal memory through standard regression analyses on the three outcome variables. Predictor variables that did not remain significant once all five variables were entered were assessed further for mediation paths through other predictor variables. Then, based on previous analyses, self-recognition and language status were explored further as possible moderator variables of verbal memory. Significant interactions between the two predictor factors would indicate a moderator effect on later verbal memory.

Mediator Analyses

The five predictor variables were entered as a set in standard regression analyses for each of the three outcome variables. The resulting significant beta weights illustrate the unique contributions each predictor variable made to children's shared verbal memory skills (see Table 6.3) and independent verbal memory skills (see Table 6.4). As might be expected, the total amount of variance accounted for by the model of early predictors decreased with children's age. Most interesting, however, are the individual unique predictors. In line with previous analyses, children's early language skill and maternal reminiscing style were unique predictors of children's shared memory at 25 and 32 months. Attachment security uniquely predicted children's shared memory, but only at 25 months. Children's early interest in participating in memory conversations also uniquely pre-

TABLE 6.3
Predicting Children's Shared Memory Skills

Predictor Variable	25-month Shared Memory			32-month Shared Memory		
	B	SE B	β	B	SE B	β
Children's Self-Recognition	.15	.12	.12	.16	.14	.13
Children's Language	.13	.05	.23*	.14	.06	.26*
Children's Interest	−.04	.10	−.04	.27	.13	.27*
Attachment Security	.78	.31	.22*	.07	.38	.02
Maternal Style	.86	.13	.61**	.41	.16	.31*
			$R^2 = .64**$			$R^2 = .41**$

Note.   **$p < .01$; *$p < .05$.

TABLE 6.4
Predicting Children's Independent Memory Skills

Predictor Variable	40-month Independent Memory		
	B	SE B	β
Children's Self-Recognition	−.05	.09	−.08
Children's Language	.04	.04	.17
Children's Interest	.01	.07	.01
Attachment Security	−.01	.23	−.01
Maternal Style	.11	.10	.17
			$R^2 = .06$

dicted their shared memory, but only at 32 months. All significant beta weights were positive, indicating that children with higher language skills, those who are interested in past events, those with highly elaborative mothers, and those who are securely attached provide more memory information later with their mothers. In contrast to the wealth of significant predictors of shared verbal memory, none of the early social, cognitive, or linguistic variables uniquely predicted children's independent memory at 40 months. Farrant and Reese (2000) previously demonstrated that children's 32-month shared memory generalized to their 40-month independent memory. Indeed, when a standard regression was computed on children's 40-month independent memory including children's 32-month shared memory elaborations as a sixth term in the model, only children's earlier shared verbal memory uniquely predicted later independent memory ($\beta = .48$, $p < .01$). Thus, early social and linguistic experiences coalesce into children's shared verbal memory by $2^1/_2$ years, which then generalizes to independent verbal memory by $3^1/_2$ years.

Unexpectedly, children's self-recognition did not uniquely predict any of the verbal memory outcomes. Harley and Reese (1999) demonstrated that self-recognition uniquely predicted children's later shared and independent verbal memory when paired with maternal reminiscing style at 19 months as a predictor. A more in-depth analysis of mother–child relationships revealed maternal reminiscing style at 25 months rather than 19 months to be a better predictor of children's later verbal memory (Farrant & Reese, 2000). Therefore, the possibility of a mediator relationship between self-recognition, later maternal reminiscing style, and later shared memory was investigated.

In order to test for mediation, three conditions must be present (Baron & Kenny, 1986). First, the hypothesized independent variable (self-recognition) must significantly predict the hypothesized mediator variable (maternal style). In our models this condition was tested by regressing mothers' memory-question elaborations at 25 months on self-recognition at 19 months, with a resulting $\beta = .33$, $p < .05$. Second, the hypothesized independent variable (self-recognition) must significantly predict the dependent variable (children's shared memory elaborations at 25 and 32 months). Self-recognition significantly predicted shared memory elaborations at 25 months ($\beta = .33$, $p < .05$) and 32 months ($\beta = .34$, $p < .05$). If these two initial conditions are met, the test for mediation involves regressing the dependent variable (shared memory elaborations at 25 and 32 months) on both the independent (self-recognition) and mediator (maternal style) variables. If the independent variable ceases to be a significant predictor, or if its prediction is substantially decreased from the univariate case, and the mediator variable still predicts the dependent variable, then a mediator model best accounts for the relation between independent and dependent variables. In these cases, the independent variable is hypothesized to

TABLE 6.5
Maternal Style as a Mediator of the Relation Between
Self-Recognition and Children's Shared Memory

Predictor Variable	25-month Shared Memory			32-month Shared Memory		
	B	SE B	β	B	SE B	β
Children's Self-Recognition	.14	.13	.11	.25	.15	.20
Maternal Memory-Question Elaborations	.21	.03	.68**	.12	.04	.41**

Note. Beta weights represent entry as final variable in model.
        **$p < .01$.

affect the dependent variable indirectly, through the mediator variable. When self-recognition and maternal style were entered simultaneously to predict children's shared memory elaborations, maternal style remained a significant predictor but self-recognition ceased to be a significant predictor of both 25- and 32-month shared memory elaborations (see Table 6.5). These analyses thus revealed a mediator role for maternal reminiscing style at 25 months. Self-recognition is positively correlated with maternal reminiscing style at 25 months, and it is maternal style that then contributes uniquely to children's later shared verbal memory.

Moderator Analyses

Because preliminary analyses suggested that self-recognition and language might interact in their effect on verbal memory skills (Harley & Reese, 1999), a moderator relationship was formally analyzed for self-recognition and language. Language skill was dichotomized for these analyses by conducting a median split on 19-month vocabulary and creating a between-subjects factor of children with high and low language levels (n = 29 at each level). Then, between-subjects ANOVAs [self-recognition (2) × language skill (2)] were conducted on the three verbal memory outcome variables (Baron & Kenny, 1986). One moderator relationship emerged. Language and self-recognition interacted in their contribution to 32-month shared verbal memory, with early recognizers reporting more than later recognizers only if they started out in the low language group ($F(1,54) = 4.24, p < .05$; see Fig. 6.3). Therefore, language moderated the effect of self-recognition on children's later shared verbal memory. In other words, self-recognition only made a difference for later verbal memory of children who had initially low language levels. No differences as a function of self-recognition were present in the verbal memory of children who initially had high language levels.

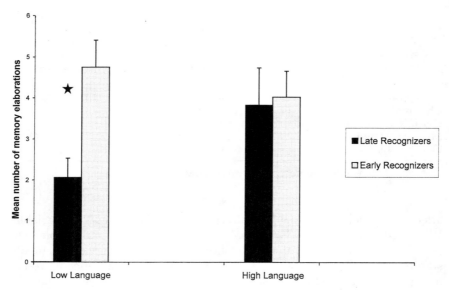

FIG. 6.3.   Language skill as a moderator of self-recognition on children's 32-month shared memory elaborations.

CONCLUSIONS

The results of these analyses culminate in a model of the origins of autobiographical memory that is illustrated in Fig. 6.4. Social and linguistic contributors shape early shared verbal memory at ages 2 and $2^1/_2$ years. Between ages $2^1/_2$ and $3^1/_2$ years, shared verbal memory then generalizes to independent memory. Maternal reminiscing style mediates the contribution of self-recognition to children's later shared verbal memory. Language skill also moderates the contribution of self-recognition to shared verbal memory, with early recognizers only having higher shared verbal memory skills than later recognizers if they had lower language levels initially. I discuss each of these contributors in more depth before proposing a theory of autobiographical memory development.

Cognition as a Predictor of Verbal Memory

One goal of this research was to assess the role of self-recognition in children's autobiographical memory as an empirical test of Howe and Courage's (1993, 1997) theory. Although early analyses suggested that children's self-recognition skill uniquely predicted autobiographical memory

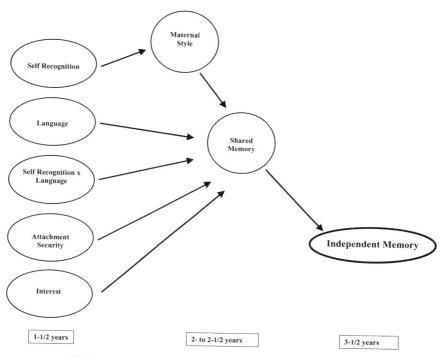

FIG. 6.4. A model of the origins of autobiographical memory.

(Harley & Reese, 1999), analyses incorporating later datapoints revealed that the role of self-recognition was not as straightforward as first appeared. Instead, the mediation and moderation tests suggested that self-recognition may be only an indirect contributor to later shared memory, and then primarily for children with lower language skills. Mothers may notice at some level the cognitive changes in their children that accompany mirror self-recognition. Mothers appear to respond to these cognitive changes by, for one thing, increasing their rate of elaborative questions in the memory conversations. This highly elaborative maternal style is the more direct contributor to children's advances in shared memory skills. Future research during the 19- to 32-month age period could focus on how, and how specifically, self-recognition relates to later maternal style. Harley (2000) noted that self-recognition was correlated with children's receptive vocabulary and their deferred imitation sequencing scores, indicating that self-recognition may serve as an index of nonverbal cognition. Are mothers able to detect (at some level) the self-understanding aspect of this skill specifically? Or is self-recognition simply a good indicator of broader, more general cognitive change? The neurological basis for mirror self-recognition is not yet well specified, but certainly the task incorporates skills of motor control, inhibition, and temperament as well as self-understanding (e.g., Lewis & Ramsay, 1997). Determining what exactly the mirror test of self-recognition measures is a prerequisite to understanding its relationship to maternal behavior in this study.

Language skill also moderated the role of self-recognition on children's later shared verbal memory. As suggested in Harley and Reese (1999), this interaction effect implies that children can enter the verbal memory system in different ways: through the more traditional linguistic routes, or through a more autonomous, nonverbal route when their language skills are initially lower. By age $2^{1}/_{2}$ years, children who initially had lower language skills but who were early recognizers had shared verbal memory skills equivalent to those children who were initially high in their language skills.

Linguistic and Social Contributors to Verbal Memory

The linguistic and social contributors instead acted in a straightforward and positive manner on children's later shared verbal memory, and eventually, on their independent memory skills. Language skill and maternal reminiscing style were the strongest of the contributors, significantly predicting shared memory at both 2 and $2^{1}/_{2}$ years. As expected from prior research with this age group (Bauer & Wewerka, 1995), language did play a role in verbal memory. The relative role of expressive and receptive language was not tested with the present analyses, but other analyses on this dataset at older ages suggest that both expressive and receptive language are highly correlated with verbal memory (Farrant & Reese, 2000). However, bearing out earlier investigations from this same project (Farrant & Reese, 2000; Harley & Reese, 1999), language skill and maternal reminiscing style did not overlap completely in their prediction of shared verbal memory. Therefore, children's verbal memory is not just a function of their language; nor is maternal reminiscing style simply a function of children's language. Past research supports this notion by demonstrating that maternal reminiscing style, although clearly adapted to children's developmental level, also has a stable component across time, context, and child (Haden, 1998; Reese & Brown, 2000; Reese et al., 1993). Recent experimental work also underscores the causal role of maternal conversational style in children's later narrative skill. Peterson, Jesso, and McCabe (1999) trained mothers to talk in a topic-extending style with their $3^{1}/_{2}$-year-old children about past events over a year-long intervention period. The topic-extending style consisted of increasing mothers' open-ended questions (similar to maternal question elaborations in this study) and confirmations of children's utterances. Children were initially matched on their receptive language and narrative skill. Dyads were then randomly assigned to a training or control condition. Immediately after the intervention, children in the training condition had higher receptive language skills than did children in the control condition. One year after the end of the intervention, children in the training condition also had better narrative skills than did children in the control condition. It is possible that the effect of maternal reminiscing style on children's narrative abilities is a function of a more general eliciting conversational style that mothers adopt across a variety of contexts. Haden and Fivush (1996), however, found that mothers' conversational style when reminiscing with their children was not related to their conversational style in a free-play setting. Therefore, maternal conversational style, specifically when reminiscing, may be affecting children's verbal memory skills and then generalizing to children's broader language and narrative skills. The implication of this effect is that children who can effectively organize and communicate past events to others verbally at an earlier age might eventually have earlier and more enduring memories of their childhood. The direct link, however, between verbal memory skill in early childhood and adult memories of early childhood has yet to be demonstrated empirically.

Attachment security and children's interest in participating in memory conversations were significant but somewhat weaker contributors to verbal memory. Notably, each remained a significant predictor even when entered simultaneously in the regression, indicating that children's interest in the conversation did not completely mediate the relation between attachment security and children's memory, as suggested in the introduction. Attachment security was only a significant predictor of shared verbal memory at age 2 years, however, but in the expected direction, with securely attached children producing higher levels of shared verbal memory. Farrant (1999) conducted a more fine-grained analysis of mothers' contingent replies in these conversations as a function of attachment security and found that attachment security at age $1^{1}/_{2}$ primarily acted to set the stage for mothers' later reminiscing style, which in turn contributed more directly to children's autobiographical memory. These findings are in line with Meins (1997), who found that attachment security led to more rapid language acquisition in children, perhaps through more sensitive teaching strategies by mothers. Attachment security could work to affect the tone of early mother–child conversations, which might in turn allow mothers of securely attached children to become more elaborative and to have a more specific effect on their children's memory development. The present results clearly indicate, though, that maternal reminiscing style at age 2 years is not the sole mediator of the relation between attachment security and children's autobiographical memory. Attachment security was still a significant factor in children's verbal memory even after maternal reminiscing style was entered into the equation.

Children's interest in participating in the conversations became a factor in verbal memory by age $2^1/_2$ years. Because this is the age at which shared verbal memory is consolidated and starts to generalize to independent memory, the role of children's interest can be considered quite important. Obviously, mothers' style cannot have as much of an effect if children are not willing to listen and participate in the conversations. The interplay between mother and child in memory conversations is dialectic from the start, not unidirectional from mother to child. Farrant and Reese (2000) suggested that the children's interest measure in this study may be tapping into joint attentional processes between mother and child at 19 months. Joint attention indexes the degree to which mother and child share each other's focus on an external object. In the context of a memory conversation, shared attention is focused on absent objects, people, and places. Welch-Ross (1997) has also viewed children's shared focus on memories with caregivers as an act of joint attention, although in Welch-Ross's theory, the joint attention is an outcome of theory of mind skill. As Baldwin (1995) noted in a review of the literature, levels of joint attention strongly predict the rate of children's language acquisition. In this case, it may be that joint attention predicts acquisition of the verbal form of autobiographical memory.

Limitations

The present study has provided an interesting index of the variables that are likely to be important in accounting for children's autobiographical memory development, and an indication of the timeline of these predictors in relation to children's later memory. However, the present study can only serve as a sketch of the process and not the process of development itself. It should open the way for more focused studies of shorter time periods that can enlighten us about the process of memory development. In addition, the variable set is still limited, both in breadth and depth, both for predictors and outcomes of autobiographical memory. For instance, only the structure or richness, not the content or emotional quality, of autobiographical memories was measured. Additional datapoints with these children will address the vital question of which of these early verbal memories, if any, survive the period of infantile amnesia. In addition, language development was only measured in terms of vocabulary, and autobiographical memory measured only in verbal form. To adequately address Nelson's (1996) theory of the advent of language as a representational system, narrative and pragmatic aspects of children's language development will be analyzed. Howe and Courage (1993) also noted that autobiographical memory might eventually be measured via non-verbal methods, although others have argued that verbal expression is a prerequisite for determining the autobiographical nature of memory (e.g., Pillemer & White, 1989). Finally, the study was conducted on a Western, primarily White sample, albeit of a broad range of socioeconomic status. These patterns may not replicate within other cultures. Cultural differences exist in adults' estimates of the age of earliest memory (MacDonald, Uesiliana, & Hayne, 2000; Mullen, 1994) and in the way mothers from different cultures talk with their children about the past (Mullen & Yi, 1995).

A Theory of the Origins of Autobiographical Memory

This pattern of findings leads to a theory of autobiographical memory that looks considerably different from other theories proposed to date. First, the results support a model of autobiographical memory that is composed of multiple contributing factors, some of which interact but others of which are unique contributors. In contrast to current theories of autobiographical memory, no single development is seen as primary in the present theory; indeed, each may contribute simultaneously to the refinement of children's verbal memory skill. This study is the first examination of a multitude of possible contributors in the same children over time beginning in infancy. Many of the contributors that have previously been proposed as primary are, in fact, just one independent part of the whole picture. This principle is especially true in relation to Howe and Courage's (1993, 1997) theory of infantile amnesia. Howe and Courage proposed that the advent of self-recognition is the primary force in the beginning of autobiographical memory. These results instead suggest that self-recognition is just one piece of the puzzle, and then mainly for children who are starting out with lower language skills.

Better support is provided for linguistic and social interactionist theories (Fivush & Reese, 1992; Hudson, 1993; Nelson, 1993b). Language skill and maternal reminiscing style were the strongest and most straightforward contributors to autobiographical memory in this study. Importantly, they were also independent contributors. Simple socialization explanations, however, do not best account for the data. Children's interest in participating in the conversations was also an inherent part of their later shared memory skill. From near the beginning, then, children are a significant factor in shaping their own autobiographical memory development. This pattern of findings is in accord with Vygotsky's (1978) theory of cognitive development, in that children eventually displayed aspects of adults' earlier conversational style in their independent reminiscing. Moreover, the present study incorporated the bidirectionality that was part of Vygotsky's original proposal when he stated, "But if we ignore the child's needs, and the incentives which are effective in getting him to act, we will never be able to understand his advance from one developmental stage to the next" (p. 92).

Children's autobiographical memory development also appears to be highly buffered. The large number of significant, independent contributors to its development insures that all normally developing children can eventually tell stories of past events they have experienced. This buffering means that children can enter the system in different ways. For instance, children with lower language skills enter the system through a less verbal and more autonomous route, but end up in the same place eventually if they are supported by strong self-recognition skills. Children whose mothers are not highly elaborative, but who themselves have a strong interest in memory conversations, shape both their mothers' conversational style and their own later memory skills. These individual differences in the formation of autobiographical memories may go a long way in accounting for the individual differences in adults' earliest memories of childhood. Retrospective studies of infantile amnesia with adults focus on the average age of earliest memory at around 3 to $3^{1}/_{2}$ years (e.g., Mullen, 1994). However, this focus on the group mean tends to overshadow the tremendous variability among adults in their age of earliest memory—in most of these studies, from around 2 to 6 years (and sometimes even as early as 6 months and as late as 8 years; see Pillemer, 1997 for a review). Theories proposing a single, or even a primary, influence simply cannot account for these dramatic individual differences (see also Herbert & Hayne, 2000; Newcombe & Fox, 1994; Pillemer, 1997 for similar arguments). Again, the empirical link between these individual differences in the onset of autobiographical memory and adults' earliest memories has yet to be made.

Second, the process I propose on the basis of these data is also more continuous than many current theories of infantile amnesia. Children participate in verbally accessible memories from the time that they can refer to past events in conversations at around 18 to 24 months of age. Their verbal memory with caregivers is consolidated by $2^{1}/_{2}$ years, which then results in their eventual independent memory at $3^{1}/_{2}$ years (see Fig. 6.2 again). Memories may well have been personally encoded before this point, but only with verbal references are researchers able to access these memories, at least with present methodologies. The encoding and retrieval of autobiographical memories from infancy progresses gradually and is continuously being refined through various cognitive, social, and linguistic developments. Thus, at least when following children's verbal memory from $1^{1}/_{2}$ to $3^{1}/_{2}$ years, abrupt qualitative change does not appear to characterize children's development. Children's verbal memory does change over this period. Their accounts become less prompted and more self-initiated, more focused on tellable aspects, and reported in a richer narrative format. However, these appear to be primarily quantitative changes that are present in some form from the beginning of verbal memory. Older infants and toddlers spontaneously initiate talk about the past, sometimes about distinctive events (Reese, 1999), and even sometimes in an evaluative format (Miller & Sperry, 1988). I argue that autobiographical memory development seems discontinuous mainly when viewed from the perspective of an adult's memory of early childhood.

Admittedly, the end of the present study at age $3^1/_2$ years limits these speculations. Three and a half years is exactly the average onset of autobiographical memory when viewed retrospectively. It is fully possible that a period of reorganization occurs between $3^1/_2$ and $4^1/_2$ years of age, consistent with the metalinguistic and metacognitive theories of autobiographical memory (e.g., Nelson, 1996; Perner & Ruffman, 1995; Povinelli, 1995; Welch-Ross, 1995). Notably, in this study children's independent memory was consolidated by 40 months, prior to the age of the metalinguistic and theory of mind developments proposed as prerequisites in these theories. Possible indicators of a qualitative shift across this age period might be interruptions in the consistency of children's shared and independent memory, children's initiations of memory talk for purely social rather than informational reasons, and the sudden emergence of children's negotiation in memory talk. These more pragmatic and qualitative measures of children's verbal memory in relation to cognitive changes will be assessed in continuing analyses on this sample between $3^1/_2$ and $5^1/_2$ years of age.

Implications for Theory and Practice in Autobiographical Memory Development

My focus in this chapter has been on the emergence of autobiographical memory in infancy. Is there in fact a separate autobiographical memory system, as many theorists have proposed? It is first necessary to decide what is meant by the word "system" before answering this question. Pillemer (1997) noted that his use of the word "system" is more akin to levels of representation and does not necessarily imply that the imagistic and narrative forms of autobiographical memory are governed by different underlying brain mechanisms. Analogously, Schacter (1987) and Schacter and Tulving (1994) stated that the distinction between implicit and explicit memory does not connote separate memory systems, but simply different expressions of memory. If, indeed, theorists are invoking systems rather than Systems in their explanations, perhaps the continuous and discontinuous theorists in this field are not as at odds as they appear to be on the surface. I would like to propose a focus on continuities as well as discontinuities in autobiographical memory with development. This debate has unnecessarily polarized research on children's memory development. As novelist Ellen Gilchrist (1989) reminds us, "Light can be both wave and particle." Perhaps it is time to acknowledge that both continuous and discontinuous influences may coexist in the growth of children's autobiographical memory, and that the pattern of growth may be different for individual children. Only with longitudinal study of children at more than two points in time—and past the average infantile amnesia offset at age $3^1/_2$ years—is there a hope of seeing continuity *or* discontinuity in the growth of autobiographical memory.

ACKNOWLEDGMENTS

I would like to thank all the families who have participated, and are still participating, in this longitudinal study. I am also grateful to Stephanie Read, Rebecca Brookland, Sandy Powell, Bridget Sly, and Sallie Dawa for their contributions to data collection, transcribing, and coding. Thanks to Harlene Hayne and her lab for their gracious help in recruiting participants for this research. Portions of this project were included in Kate Farrant's and Keryn Harley's PhD theses. I appreciate their permission to reanalyze the data here. This research was supported by a grant from the Marsden Fund of the Royal Society of New Zealand.

REFERENCES

Ainsworth, M. D. S., Blehar, M. C., Waters, E., & Wall, S. (1978). *Patterns of attachment: A psychological study of the strange situation.* Hillsdale, NJ: Lawrence Erlbaum Associates.

Amsterdam, B. (1972). Mirror self-image reactions before age two. *Developmental Psychobiology, 5,* 297–305.

Asendorpf, J. E., Warkentin, V., & Baudonniere, P. (1996). Self-awareness and other-awareness II: Mirror self-recognition, social contingency awareness, and synchronic imitation. *Developmental Psychology, 32,* 313–321.

Bachevalier, J. (1990). Ontogenetic development of habit and memory formation in primates. In A. Diamond (Ed.), *Annals of the New York Academy of Sciences: Vol. 608. The development and neural bases of higher cognitive functions* (pp. 457–477). New York: New York Academy of Sciences.

Baldwin, D. (1995). Understanding the link between joint attention and language. In C. Moore & P. J. Dunham (Eds.), *Joint attention: Its origins and role in development* (pp. 131–158). Mahwah, NJ: Lawrence Erlbaum Associates.

Baron, R. M., & Kenny, D. A. (1986). The moderator-mediator variable distinction in social psychological research: Conceptual, strategic, and statistical considerations. *Journal of Personality and Social Psychology, 51,* 1173–1182.

Bauer, P. J., Hertsgaard, L. A., & Dow, G. A. (1994). After 8 months have passed: Long-term recall of events by 1- to 2-year-old children. *Memory, 2,* 353–382.

Bauer, P. J., & Wenner, J. A. (1999). Developments in long-term recall: Results of a large-scale investigation in one-to two-year-olds. In M. L. Howe (Chair), *Converging perspectives on the nature of early memory development.* Symposium conducted at the Biennial Meetings of the Society for Research in Child Development, Albuquerque, NM.

Bauer, P. J., & Wewerka, S. S. (1995). One- to two- year-olds' recall of events: The more expressed, the more impressed. *Journal of Experimental Child Psychology, 59,* 475–496.

Brewer, W. F. (1986). What is autobiographical memory? In D. C. Rubin (Ed.), *Autobiographical memory* (pp. 25–49). Cambridge, UK: Cambridge University Press.

Brewer, W. F. (1995). What is recollective memory? In D. C. Rubin (Ed.), *Remembering our past: Studies in autobiographical memory* (pp. 19–66). Cambridge, UK: Cambridge University Press.

Collie, R., & Hayne, H. (1999). Deferred imitation by 6- and 9-month-old infants: More evidence for declarative memory. *Developmental Psychobiology, 35,* 83–90.

Custer, W. L. (1996). A comparison of young children's understanding of contradictory representations in pretense, memory, and belief. *Child Development, 67,* 678–688.

Dudycha, G. J., & Dudycha, M. M. (1941). Childhood memories: A review of the literature. *Psychological Bulletin, 38,* 668–682.

Eisenberg, A. R. (1985). Learning to describe past experiences in conversation. *Discourse Processes, 8,* 177–204.

Elley, W. B., & Irving, J. C. (1976). Revised socio-economic index for New Zealand. *New Zealand Journal of Educational Studies, 11,* 25–36.

Farrant, K. (1999). *A tale of autobiographical memory development: New Zealand style.* Unpublished Ph.D. thesis, University of Otago, Dunedin, New Zealand.

Farrant, K., & Reese, E. (2000). Maternal reminiscing style and dyadic quality: Stepping stones in children's autobiographical memory development. *Journal of Cognition and Development, 1,* 193–225.

Farrar, J. M., Fasig, L. G., & Welch-Ross, M. K. (1997). Attachment and emotion in autobiographical memory development. *Journal of Experimental Child Psychology, 67,* 389–408.

Fenson, L., Dale, P. S., Reznick, J. S., Thal, D., Bates, E., Hartung, J. P., Pethick, S., & Reilly, J. S. (1993). *MacArthur Communicative Development Inventories.* San Diego: Singular Publishing Group.

Fivush, R. (1988). The functions of event memory: Some comments on Nelson and Barsalou. In U. Neisser & E. Winograd (Eds.), *Remembering reconsidered: Ecological and traditional approaches to the study of memory* (pp. 277–282). Cambridge, UK: Cambridge University Press.

Fivush, R. (1998). The stories we tell: How language shapes autobiography. *Applied Cognitive Psychology, 12,* 483–487.

Fivush, R. (in press). Owning experience: Developing subjective perspective in autobiographical narratives. In C. Moore & K. Skene (Eds.), *The self in time: Developmental issues*. Mahwah, NJ: Lawrence Erlbaum Associates.

Fivush, R., & Fromhoff, F. A. (1988). Style and structure in mother–child conversations about the past. *Discourse Processes, 11*, 337–355.

Fivush, R., Gray, J. T., & Fromhoff, F. A. (1987). Two-year-olds talk about the past. *Cognitive Development, 2*, 393–409.

Fivush, R., & Haden, C. A. (1996). Narrating and representing experience: Preschoolers' developing autobiographical recounts. In P. van den Broek, P. J. Bauer, & T. Bourg (Eds.), *Developmental spans in event comprehension and representation: Bridging fictional and actual events*. Mahwah, NJ: Lawrence Erlbaum Associates.

Fivush, R., Haden, C. A., & Adam, S. (1995). Structure and coherence of preschoolers' personal narratives over time: Implications for childhood amnesia. *Journal of Experimental Child Psychology, 60*, 32–56.

Fivush, R., Haden, C. A., & Reese, E. (1996). Remembering, recounting, and reminiscing: The development of autobiographical memory in social context. In D. Rubin (Ed.), *Remembering our past: Studies in autobiographical memory* (pp. 341–359). Cambridge: Cambridge University Press.

Fivush, R., & Hamond, N. (1990). Autobiographical memory across the preschool years: Toward reconceptualizing childhood amnesia. In R. Fivush & J. A. Hudson (Eds.), *Knowing and remembering in young children* (pp. 223–248). New York: Cambridge University Press.

Fivush, R., & Reese, E. (1992). The social construction of autobiographical memory. In M. A. Conway, D. C. Rubin, H. Spinnler, & W. A. Wagenaar (Eds.), *Theoretical perspectives on autobiographical memory* (pp. 115–132). Dordrecht, The Netherlands: Kluwer Academic Publishers.

Freud, S. (1905/1953). Three essays on the theory of sexuality. In J. Strachey (Ed.), *The standard edition of the complete psychological works of Sigmund Freud. Vol. 7* (pp. 135–243). London: Hogarth Press.

Gilchrist, E. (1989). *Light can be both wave and particle*. New York: Little, Brown & Co.

Haden, C. A. (1998). Reminiscing with different children: Relating maternal stylistic consistency and sibling similarity in talk about the past. *Developmental Psychology, 34*, 99–114.

Haden, C. A., Ornstein, P. A., Eckerman, C. O., & Didow, S. M. (In press). Mother–child conversational interactions as events unfold: Linkages to subsequent remembering. *Child Development.*

Haden, C.A., & Fivush, R. (1996). Contextual variation in maternal conversational styles. *Merrill-Palmer Quarterly, 42*, 200–227.

Haden, C. A., Haine, R. A., & Fivush, R. (1997). Developing narrative structure in parent–child reminiscing across the preschool years. *Developmental Psychology, 33*, 295–307.

Hamond, N. R., & Fivush, R. (1991). Memories of Mickey Mouse: Young children recount their trip to Disneyworld. *Cognitive Development, 6*, 433–448.

Harley, K. (2000). *Origins of autobiographical memory: The beginning of the story.* Unpublished Ph.D. thesis, University of Otago, Dunedin, New Zealand.

Harley, K., & Reese, E. (1999). Origins of autobiographical memory. *Developmental Psychology, 35*, 1338–1348.

Hayne, H., & Rovee-Collier, C. (1995). The organization of reactivated memory in infancy. *Child Development, 66,* 893–906.

Herbert, J., & Hayne, H. (2000). The ontogeny of long-term retention during the second year of life. *Developmental Science, 3,* 50–56.

Howe, M. L., & Courage, M. L. (1993). On resolving the enigma of infantile amnesia. *Psychological Bulletin, 113,* 305–326.

Howe, M. L., & Courage, M. L. (1997). The emergence and early development of autobiographical memory. *Psychological Review, 104,* 499–523.

Hudson, J. A. (1990). The emergence of autobiographical memory in mother–child conversation. In R. Fivush & J. Hudson (Eds.), *Knowing and remembering in young children* (pp. 166–196). Cambridge, UK: Cambridge University Press.

Hudson, J. A. (1991). Learning to reminisce: A case study. *Journal of Narrative and Life History, 1,* 295–324.

Hudson, J. A. (1993). Reminiscing with mothers and others: Autobiographical memory in young two-year-olds. *Journal of Narrative and Life History, 3,* 1–32.

Hudson, J. A., & Shapiro, L. R. (1991). From knowing to telling: The development of children's scripts, stories, and personal narratives. In A. McCabe & C. Peterson (Eds.), *Developing narrative structure* (pp. 89–136). Hillsdale, NJ: Lawrence Erlbaum Associates.

Hyman, I. E., & Faries, J. M. (1992). The functions of autobiographical memory. In M. A. Conway, D. C. Rubin, H. Spinnler, & W. A. Wagenaar (Eds.), *Theoretical perspectives on autobiographical memory* (pp. 207–221). Dordrecht, The Netherlands: Kluwer Academic Publishers.

Kuebli, J., Butler, S., & Fivush, R. (1995). Mother–child talk about past event emotions: Relations of maternal language and child gender over time. *Cognition and Emotion, 9,* 265–283.

Lewis, M., & Brooks-Gunn, J. (1979). *Social cognition and the acquisition of the self.* New York: Plenum.

Lewis, M., & Ramsay, D. S. (1997). Stress reactivity and self recognition. *Child Development, 68,* 621–629.

MacDonald, S. D. (1997). *The role of socialisation in autobiographical memory in children and adults: A Vygotskian perspective.* Unpublished Ph.D. thesis, University of Otago, Dunedin, New Zealand.

MacDonald, S. D., Uesiliana, K., & Hayne, H. (2000). Cross-cultural and gender differences in childhood amnesia. *Memory, 8,* 365–376.

McCabe, A., & Peterson, C. (1991). Getting the story: A longitudinal study of parental styles in eliciting narratives and developing narrative skill. In A. McCabe & C. Peterson (Eds.), *Developing narrative structure* (pp. 217–253). Hillsdale, NJ: Lawrence Erlbaum Associates.

Meins, E. (1997). *Security of attachment and the social development of cognition.* Hove, UK: Psychology Press Ltd.

Miller, P. J., & Sperry, L. L. (1988). Early talk about the past: The origins of conversational stories of personal experience. *Journal of Child Language, 15,* 293–315.

Mullen, M. K. (1994). Earliest recollections of childhood: A demographic analysis. *Cognition, 52,* 55–79.

Mullen, M. K., & Yi, S. (1995). The cultural context of talk about the past: Implications for the development of autobiographical memory. *Cognitive Development,* *10,* 407–419.

Myers, N. A., Perris, E. E., & Speaker, C. J. (1994). Fifty months of memory: A longitudinal study in early childhood. *Memory, 2,* 383–415.

Neisser, U. (1962). Culture and cognitive discontinuity. In T. E. Gladwin & W. Sturtevant (Eds.), *Anthropology and human behavior* (pp. 54–71). Washington, D.C.: Anthropological Society of Washington.

Nelson, C. A. (1995). The ontogeny of human memory: A cognitive neuroscience perspective. *Developmental Psychology, 31,* 723–738.

Nelson, K. (1989). *Narratives from the crib.* Cambridge, MA: Harvard University Press.

Nelson, K. (1993a). Developing self-knowledge from autobiographical memory. In T. K. Srull & R. S. Wyer (Eds.), *The mental representation of trait and autobiographical knowledge about the self* (pp. 111–121). Hillsdale, NJ: Lawrence Erlbaum Associates.

Nelson, K. (1993b). The psychological and social origins of autobiographical memory. *Psychological Science, 4,* 1–8.

Nelson, K. (1993c). Events, narratives, memory: What develops? In C. A. Nelson (Ed.), *Memory and affect in development: The Minnesota Symposia on Child Psychology* (Vol. 26, pp. 1–25). Hillsdale, NJ: Lawrence Erlbaum Associates.

Nelson, K. (1996). *Language in cognitive development: The emergence of the mediated mind.* Cambridge: Cambridge University Press.

Nelson, K., & Ross, G. (1980). The generalities and specifics of long-term memory in infants and young children. *New Directions for Child Development, 10,* 87–101.

Newcombe, N., & Fox, N. A. (1994). Infantile amnesia: Through a glass darkly. *Child Development, 65,* 31–40.

Perner, J. (1990). Experiential awareness and children's episodic memory. In W. Schneider & F. E. Weinert (Eds.), *Interactions among aptitudes, strategies, and knowledge in cognitive performance* (pp. 3–11). New York: Springer Verlag.

Perner, J. (1991). *Understanding the representational mind.* Cambridge, MA: MIT Press.

Perner, J., & Ruffman, T. (1995). Episodic memory or autonoetic consciousness: Developmental evidence and a theory of childhood amnesia. *Journal of Experimental Child Psychology, 59,* 516–548.

Peterson, C., Jesso, B., & McCabe, A. (1999). Encouraging narratives in preschoolers: An intervention study. *Journal of Child Language, 26,* 46–67.

Peterson, C., & McCabe, A. (1983). *Developmental psycholinguistics: Three ways of looking at a child's narrative.* NY: Plenum.

Pillemer, D. B. (1997). *Momentous events, vivid memories.* Cambridge, MA: Harvard University Press.

Pillemer, D. B., Picariello, M. L., & Pruett, J. C. (1994). Very long-term memories of a salient preschool event. *Applied Cognitive Psychology, 8,* 95–106.

Pillemer, D. B., & White, S. H. (1989). Childhood events recalled by children and adults. In H. W. Reese (Ed.), *Advances in child development and behavior* (Vol. 21, pp. 297–340). San Diego: Academic Press.

Povinelli, D. J. (1995). The unduplicated self. In P. Rochat (Ed.), *Advances in psychology, Vol. 112. The self in infancy: Theory and research* (pp. 161–192). Amsterdam: North Holland-Elsevier.

Povinelli, D. J., Landau, K. R., & Perilloux, H. K. (1996). Self-recognition in young children using delayed versus live feedback: Evidence of a developmental asynchrony. *Child Development, 67,* 1504–1554.

Povinelli, D. J., Landry, A. M., Theall, L. A., Clark, B. R., & Castille, C. M. (1999). Development of young children's understanding that the recent past is causally bound to the present. *Developmental Psychology, 35,* 1426–1439.

Povinelli, D. J., & Simon, B. B. (1998). Young children's understanding of briefly versus extremely delayed images of the self: Emergence of the autobiographical stance. *Developmental Psychology, 34,* 188–194.

Reese, E. (1999). What children say when they talk about the past. *Narrative Inquiry, 9,* 1–27.

Reese, E., & Brown, N. (2000). Reminiscing and recounting in the preschool years. *Applied Cognitive Psychology, 14,* 1–17.

Reese, E., & Fivush, R. (1993). Parental styles of talking about the past. *Developmental Psychology, 29,* 596–606.

Reese, E., Haden, C. A., & Fivush, R. (1993). Mother–child conversations about the past: Relationships of style and memory over time. *Cognitive Development, 8,* 403–430.

Reese, E., Haden, C. A., & Fivush, R. (1996). Mothers, fathers, daughters, sons: Gender differences in autobiographical remembering. *Research on Language and Social Interaction, 29,* 27–56.

Reese, E., & Read, S. (2000). Predictive validity of the New Zealand MacArthur Communicative Development Inventory: Words and Sentences. *Journal of Child Language, 27,* 255–266.

Rovee-Collier, C. (1997). Dissociations in infant memory: Rethinking the development of implicit and explicit memory. *Psychological Review, 104,* 467–498.

Rovee-Collier, C., & Hayne, H. (1987). Reactivation of infant memory: Implications for cognitive development. In H. W. Reese (Ed.), *Advances in child development and behavior, Vol. 20* (pp. 185–238). New York: Academic Press.

de Ruiter, C. & van Ijzendoorn, M. H. (1993). Attachment and cognition: A review of the literature. *International Journal of Educational Research, 19,* 525–540.

Sachs, J. (1983). Topic selection in parent–child discourse. *Discourse Processes, 2,* 145–153.

Schachtel, E. G. (1947). On memory and childhood amnesia. *Psychiatry, 10,* 1–26.

Schacter, D. L. (1987). Implicit memory: History and current status. *Journal of Experimental Psychology: Learning, Memory, and Cognition, 13,* 501–518.

Schacter, D. L., & Tulving, E. (1994). What are the memory systems of 1994? *Memory systems 1994* (pp. 1–38). Cambridge, MA: MIT Press.

Tabachnick, B. G., & Fidell, L. S. (1996). *Using multivariate statistics* (2nd ed.). New York: Harper Collins.

Tessler, M., & Nelson, K. (1994). Making memories: The influence of joint encoding on later recall by young children. *Consciousness and Cognition, 3,* 307–326.

Teti, D. M., & McGourty, S. (1996). Using mothers versus trained observers in assessing children's secure base behavior: Theoretical and methodological considerations. *Child Development, 67,* 597–605.

Tulving, E. (1983). *Elements of episodic memory.* NY: Oxford University Press.

Vygotsky, L. S. (1978). *Mind in society.* Cambridge, MA: Harvard University Press.

Waters, E. (1987). *Attachment Behavior Q-set (Version 3.0)*. Unpublished instrument, State University of New York at Stony Brook, Department of Psychology.

Welch-Ross, M. K. (1995). An integrative model of the development of autobiographical memory. *Developmental Review, 15,* 338–365.

Welch-Ross, M. K. (1997). Mother–child participation in conversation about the past: Relationships to preschoolers' theory of mind. *Developmental Psychology, 33,* 618–629.

Welch-Ross, M. K. (in press). Personalizing the temporally extended self: Evaluative self-awareness and the development of autobiographical memory. In C. Moore & K. Skene (Eds.), *The self in time: Developmental issues.* Hillsdale, NJ: Lawrence Erlbaum Associates.

Welch-Ross, M. K., Fasig, L. G., & Farrar, M. J. (1999). Predictors of preschoolers' self-knowledge: Reference to emotion and mental states in mother–child conversation about past events. *Cognitive Development, 14,* 401–422.

7

▼▼▼▼▼▼▼

Categorization of Infant-Directed Speech

Melanie J. Spence
The University of Texas at Dallas

David S. Moore
Pitzer College and Claremont Graduate University

Observations of caregiver–infant interactions have consistently revealed that adult caregivers begin talking to infants during the newborn period and continue this form of interaction throughout the infancy period. Caregivers engage in these interactions even though young infants themselves can neither reciprocate with language nor comprehend the language that they hear. The type of language adults produce when talking to infants has been labeled *infant-directed* (ID) speech and is different from the type they use for communicating with other adults on several dimensions, but primarily in its prosodic properties. These rhythmic and melodic modifications in speech to infants have been found in a number of languages, and they are produced by children, adults, parents, and nonparents.

This prevalence of ID speech during interactions with infants has led researchers to question if ID speech serves special functions within these interactions. That is, because young infants cannot understand the complete linguistic content of the signal, perhaps the prosodic or melodic properties of the signal serve functions within early social interactions such as regulating infant behavior and communicating speaker affect and intent. Support for this idea has been provided by observations that adult caregivers produce different patterns of ID speech prosody in different interactive or pragmatic contexts—for example, comforting a distressed infant versus eliciting the attention of an infant during play. However, if these ID speech patterns are to serve the functions that have been proposed, it is important that infants be capable of categorizing ID utterances. Infants must detect the acoustic properties that are regularly present in ID utterances produced within one pragmatic context despite acoustic differences across exemplars. Our recent research examined the development of infants' categorization of ID speech, focusing on 4- and 6-month-old infants' categorization of comforting and approving ID utterances.

Our goals for this chapter are threefold. First, we review the evidence in the literature that documents the types of caregiver ID speech to which young infants are exposed, the evidence that infants respond differently to ID speech than to *adult-directed* (AD) speech, and the evidence that infants respond differently to ID speech produced in different interactive contexts. We also discuss the hypotheses that ID speech may function to regulate infant affect and communicate speaker affect and intent to young infants. Second, we review our research that investigated if 4- and 6-month-old infants categorize ID speech produced to convey different communicative intents, specifically, comforting and approving ID utterances. Finally, we discuss hypotheses for explaining the developmental effect revealed by our data as well as the potential significance of infants' ID speech categorization. We conclude by considering the implications of ID speech categorization for infants' social–cognitive development and their developing understanding of vocal communicative intent.

INFANTS' ID SPEECH EXPERIENCE AND ID SPEECH RESPONSIVENESS

ID speech is produced by adults—parents and nonparents alike (Jacobson, Boersma, Fields, & Olson, 1983)—and by children (Sachs & Devin, 1976) speaking to infants. ID speech is distinguished from typical AD speech primarily on the basis of its distinctive prosody. *Prosody* refers to the melodic quality of speech that is imparted by the rise and fall of pitch, modulation of amplitude, and stress and rhythm patterns. ID speech is higher in average frequency, contains more variable pitch excursions, and is slower in tempo than AD speech (Fernald & Kuhl, 1987; Fernald et al., 1989). ID speech has been documented in interactions with infants ranging in age from newborn through 12 months of life and beyond (Fernald & Simon, 1984; Jacobson et al., 1983; Stern, Spieker, Barnett, & MacKain, 1983). What is interesting about these observations is that during much of the first year of life, infants do not understand the linguistic content of the speech they hear.

Both the use of ID speech and prosodic differences between ID and AD speech have been documented in a number of different languages, including French, German, Italian, Mandarin Chinese, and English (Fernald et al., 1989; Grieser & Kuhl, 1988; Papousek, 1992). Because ID speech occurs in a number of cultures and linguistic environments, researchers have questioned whether ID speech serves any particular functions for prelinguistic infants.

Several researchers have suggested that the prosody of ID speech might aid language acquisition by providing cues to syntactic structure. Evidence for such a role of ID speech prosody is provided by research that has demonstrated that pauses between phrases and clauses facilitate infants' parsing of the speech stream (Hirsh-Pasek et al., 1987; Jusczyk, Kemler Nelson, et al., 1992), that syllable stress patterns facilitate segmentation (Echols, 1996), and that pitch and sentence position are used to highlight individual words (Fernald & Mazzie, 1991). One model, proposed by Fernald (1992), posits that there are multiple functions of ID speech and that ID speech tends to serve different functions for infants of differing ages across the first year of life. During the later months of the first year and beyond, ID speech prosody may facilitate infants' detection of linguistic structure by highlighting syntactic structure (see Morgan & Demuth, 1996). However, during the first months of life, ID speech prosody may serve functions that are nonlinguistic in nature, such as regulation of infant behavior and affect and communication of the caregiver's emotion to the infant.

In this chapter, we focus on the characteristics of ID speech prosody that do not facilitate detection of linguistic structure per se, but that may have social and/or prelinguistic functions such as regulating infant behavior and arousal or conveying caregiver emotion and intent. One potential function of ID speech is regulation of attention and arousal during the first months of life. Evidence for this hypothesis is provided by the finding that ID speech is much more effective than AD speech at maintaining the attention of 1-, 4- and 9-month-old infants (Cooper & Aslin, 1990; Fernald, 1985; Pegg, Werker, & McLeod, 1992). Some recent evidence suggests that 4-month-olds might also find ID speech more arousing than AD speech (Kaplan, Goldstein, Huckeby, & Cooper, 1995; Kaplan, Goldstein, Huckeby, Owren, & Cooper, 1995). Behaviors indicative of positive affect (e.g., smiling and cooing), also occur more frequently in 4- to 5.5-month-old English-hearing infants in response to English ID speech (Werker & McLeod, 1989) and Cantonese ID speech (Werker, Pegg, & McLeod, 1994) than in response to AD speech.

A second function hypothesized for speech directed to younger infants is that it communicates the speaker's affect and consequently provides information about the communicative intent of the speaker (Fernald, 1992). Consistent with this hypothesis is evidence that adult-directed speech varies acoustically as a function of speaker affect and that these varying acoustic properties are perceived by adults as reflecting different emotional states of the speaker. Acoustic analyses of adult speech produced in different emotional states have shown that there are distinctive acoustic speech qualities produced when speakers experience fear, anger, joy, and sadness (Scherer, 1986). Additionally, adult listeners' attribution of emotional arousal varies continuously with the frequency range of the voice independent of verbal content and speaker identity (Ladd, Silverman, Tolkmitt, Bergmann, & Scherer, 1985). Studies with infants have also shown that different acoustic properties elicit certain emotional responses from infants. Low-frequency acoustic stimuli soothe infants (Birns, Blank, Bridger, & Escalona, 1965), whereas high-frequency stimuli arouse them (Hutt, Hutt, Lenard, Bernuth, & Muntejewerff, 1968).

Additional evidence consistent with the hypothesis that ID speech may function to communicate speaker affect to infants is provided by observations that caregivers from many language environments vary ID-speech prosody as a function of interactive context, for example, playing, feeding, and/or comforting (Fernald et al., 1989; Grieser & Kuhl, 1988). Specifically, ID utterances produced in different contexts or directed to infants in different affective states have characteristic frequency contours, frequency variation, rhythm, and intensity (Fernald & Simon, 1984). Acoustic analyses of ID speech typically examine average fundamental frequency (F_0), which is correlated with vibration rate and size of the vocal cords, modulation or range of F_0, and the shape of F_0 contours across individual utterances. These analyses have revealed that comforting utterances are characterized by falling frequency contours (Papousek, Papousek, & Bornstein, 1985; Stern, Spieker, & MacKain, 1982), lower mean F_0 (Fernald, 1989), and lower F_0 variability (Katz, Cohn, & Moore, 1996; Papousek, Papousek, & Symmes, 1991) relative to approving utterances. Approving utterances, in addition to having higher mean F_0 and F_0 variability than comforting utterances, are longer in duration (Fernald, 1989) and are characterized as wave-shaped (Katz et al., 1996). Utterances produced with the intention of attracting infants' attention are characterized by rising frequency contours, whereas those produced with the intention of maintaining infant attention have frequency contours that are bell-shaped (Stern et al., 1982).

Stronger evidence that ID speech has the potential to communicate speaker affect to infants is provided by studies demonstrating that young infants exhibit appropriate responses to approving and disapproving ID utterances. Fernald (1993) reported that 5-month-olds showed more behaviors indicative of positive affect in response to approving ID speech than in response to prohibiting ID speech and that they showed more behaviors indicative of negative affect in response to prohibiting ID speech than in response to approving ID speech. Similarly, Papousek, Bornstein, Nuzzo, Papousek, and Symmes (1990) found that 4-month-olds fixated a visual stimulus longer in order to hear prototypical approving nonlinguistic ID contours than prototypical disapproving nonlinguistic ID contours. In these studies, infants were most likely responding to acoustic properties that varied as a function of communicative intent and that are characteristic of utterances conveying these particular intents.

Adults modify their speech as a function of an infant's behaviors and affective state as well as their own affective state and intent. Thus, experiences with caregiver speech provide opportunities for infants to associate certain ID speech prosody patterns with their caregivers' behaviors and emotions. In addition, these interactions provide opportunities for infants to associate their own emotions with their caregivers' ID speech patterns. Consequently, several researchers have suggested that ID utterances may serve as the first vocal communicative signals for prelinguistic infants and may acquire the function of contextual reference for young infants (Fernald, 1992; Papousek, 1992; Stern et al., 1982).

In order for these ID utterances to most effectively serve as communicative signals, however, infants must first be capable of categorizing them. Because any two utterances produced with similar communicative intent (e.g., to comfort the infant) typically vary in verbal content as well as on prosodic dimensions such as mean F_0 and frequency range, categorization of the utterances is essential for perceiving the similarity of their communicative intents, and hence for perceiving them as meaningfully different from utterances with different communicative intents. Categorization is dependent on ignoring detectable physical properties that are not shared across the exemplars from within a single ID utterance class, and that are irrelevant for their assignment to a category. Categorization also requires detecting the properties of exemplars that are characteristic of a single ID utterance class. For example, in order for infants to categorize and subsequently respond appropriately to the communicative intent of a comforting utterance, infants must ignore varying and/or irrelevant verbal content and variations in overall frequency range and mean F_0, and instead attend to the lower-frequency, falling frequency contours that characterize all comforting utterances. Data addressing if and when infants categorize ID utterances are important to consider in the ongoing debate about the proposed function of ID speech as communicating speaker affect and intent. Infants' categorization of ID speech would provide an important piece of evidence in this debate, because this ability would indicate that infants have perceptual processing skills that are important for and may be necessary for their comprehension of ID utterances as meaningful signals. In order to address this issue, we conducted a series of experiments examining 4- and 6-month-olds' categorization of approving and comforting ID utterances. This research is discussed in the following section.

ID SPEECH CATEGORIZATION RESEARCH

Seven experiments investigating infants' categorization of ID speech are described in this chapter. First, however, a brief overview of the specific manipulations conducted in each experiment, as well as a review of the general procedure used in all the experiments, is detailed in this section. The first two experiments examined 6-month-old infants' ability to categorize approving and comforting ID utterances. In these experiments, each ID speech stimulus that infants heard was produced by a different female. Experiment 1 tested infants' categorization of low-pass filtered ID speech, and Experiment 2 examined infants' categorization of natural, unfiltered ID speech. The next three experiments examined 4-month-old infants' categorization of the same ID speech stimuli. Experiments 3 and 5 tested 4-month-olds' categorization of low-pass filtered and unfiltered ID speech stimuli, respectively. Experiment 4 was a control study that assessed whether the experimental method used in this research was appropriate for assessing 4-month-olds' response recovery to a novel stimulus following a series of familiarization trials. Finally, we conducted two additional experiments using a different set of ID speech stimuli that were all produced by one female. The purpose of this change in stimuli was to decrease the variability across stimuli introduced by the speaker-specific differences that characterized the stimuli used in Experiments 1 through 5. Again, 4-month-old (Experiment 6) and 6-month-old (Experiment 7) infants' categorization of comforting and approving ID speech stimuli was assessed.

General Procedure and Design

Speech Stimuli. ID utterances produced by caregivers in approving and comforting contexts were presented as stimuli for three reasons: these classes of utterances are frequently produced in caregiver–infant interactions containing ID speech (Fernald, 1992); these two utterance classes have been shown to be quantitatively discriminable on several variables, including F_0 and frequency contour (Fernald, 1992; Katz, Cohn, & Moore, 1996; Papousek et al., 1991); and utterances of these types were not expected to be aversive to the infants.

The first five experiments discussed used speech stimuli analyzed and described in Katz, Cohn, and Moore (1996). These stimuli were maternal utterances to 4-month-old infants produced in approving or comforting contexts. Utterances were obtained during a laboratory visit in which mother and infant were outfitted with wireless microphones and were recorded during a structured set of interactions. Approving interactions required the mother to indicate approval when her infant reached for and grasped a red ring. Comforting interactions required the mother to speak to her infant as if he or she were distressed. From these stimuli, we selected eight approving utterances and eight comforting utterances, each spoken by a different person. The mean F_0 of approving utterances was significantly higher than the mean F_0 of comforting utterances (Mann-Whitney $U = 1, p < .01$), and the F_0 variability of approving utterances was significantly greater than the F_0 variability of comforting utterances (Mann-Whitney $U = 13, p < .05$). These differences between comforting and approving ID utterances are typical of the prosodic distinctions that have been previously reported in the literature (Fernald et al., 1989). Additionally, a combination of mean F_0 and F_0 variability distinguished the set of approving utterances from the set of comforting utterances; five of eight comforting utterances were below the median value on both F_0 and F_0 variability measures (binomial $p = .0231$), and five of eight approving utterances were above the median value on both measures (binomial $p = .0231$). These analyses reveal that differences between ID utterance classes on either F_0, F_0 variability, or both, were available in the stimuli to support infants' discrimination and categorization. The speech stimuli presented in Experiments 6 and 7 are described later in the section detailing those studies.

Design and Procedure.   A modification of an infant-controlled, familiarization-test procedure (Ferland & Mendelson, 1989) was used in all experiments. In this procedure, an infant's fixations of a visual display are reinforced with contingent presentation of an auditory stimulus, effectively giving the infant control over the presentation of the stimuli. By looking at the display, the infant can initiate playback of the auditory stimulus; by looking away, the infant can terminate it. Because availability of the auditory stimulus depends on their visual behavior, fixation of the display can then be used as an index of interest in the auditory stimulus.

Each infant experienced at least seven familiarization trials followed by at least one test trial; trials eliciting less than 2 s of fixation were repeated (see Moore, Spence, & Katz, 1997 for more details). Infants heard a *different* randomly selected utterance in each trial (unless a trial elicited less than 2 s of fixation, in which case the utterance heard during that trial could be repeated in a later trial). Infants were randomly assigned to one of four groups, with boys and girls equally distributed across these conditions. Half of the infants initially heard seven different comforting utterances, one during each familiarization trial; the other half heard seven different approving utterances during these trials. Half of the infants within each of these two groups were controls who subsequently heard a randomly chosen novel stimulus from the familiar category during a test trial; the rest were experimental infants who heard a randomly chosen novel stimulus from the novel category following familiarization. Visual fixation of the visual displays on the computer monitors was used as the index of attention to the auditory stimulus. If, as we hypothesized, infants are able to categorize ID speech utterances, following familiarization with stimuli from one category, we should see recovery of response (in this case, fixation) to novel stimuli from the unfamiliar class but *not* to novel stimuli from the familiar class.

Each infant was assessed while seated in a caregiver's lap in a dimly lighted testing room. The infant was seated approximately 1 m in front of two computer monitor screens, each of which was surrounded by a black curtain. The experimenter unobtrusively observed the infant through a small hole in the curtain (above and centered between the monitors) and a video camera recorded the infant's behavior through a second hole (centered below the monitors). Caregivers and the experimenter were fitted with headphones through which played a loud, continuous audiotape recording of simultaneous presentations of four randomly chosen experimental stimuli. This recording prevented either adult from hearing or determining which specific utterance or type of utterance the infant heard on any given trial.

To capture the infant's attention and begin each trial, a string of minilights centered between the monitors was flashed on and off. Once the infant fixated the lights, the lights were extinguished and visual stimuli were presented on the monitors. Each monitor displayed identical images of three black and white random checkerboards (Karmel, 1969) on a gray background. During a trial, the color values of the squares changed, so that black squares could become white and vice versa. These color changes made the checkerboards appear to flash and served the purpose of increasing infants' attention to the displays (see Moore et al., 1997, for a detailed description of the visual stimuli). Identical visual stimuli were presented on the two monitors because pilot research had demonstrated that infant attention was more effectively maintained throughout the task when two monitors rather than one were used. These stimuli were displayed continuously until the end of the trial, which occurred either 30 s after the onset of the trial, or when the infant looked away from the stimuli for 2.5 consecutive seconds, whichever came first. Intertrial intervals were typically less than 3 s. These checkerboard stimuli were presented during familiarization trials as well as the test trial.

Whenever an infant was judged by the experimenter to have begun fixating either one of the monitors, a randomly chosen speech stimulus from the predetermined category was played through a speaker (located between the two computer screens at the infant's midline). As long as the infant continued to fixate a monitor, the utterance was heard. Any time the end of the utterance was reached, it was replayed from the beginning after a 1-s pause. Whenever the infant was judged to have terminated fixation of the monitors (or at the end of 30 s), the playback of the utterance ended. If, before the end of the trial, the infant refixated either one of the visual displays, the utterance was replayed from the beginning. Total duration of looking at the monitors was recorded on-line during each trial by a trained experimenter. Inter-rater reliability of experimenters was .98 (phi coefficient computed on two experimenters' interval-by-interval records of infant's fixation behavior).

The primary dependent variable of interest was fixation or looking time (s) at the visual displays during specific trials. Each infant's data were divided into three trial blocks. Block 1 consisted of average fixation data from trials 1 and 2, block 2 consisted of average fixation data from trials 6 and 7 (the final two familiarization trials), and block 3 consisted of fixation data from trial 8 (the test trial). Because complete habituation rarely occurred across seven trials, but we thought it necessary to ensure that infants exhibited some looking decrement across familiarization, 6-month-old infants' data were included in subsequent data analyses only if their looking decreased by a minimum of 5% from block 1 to block 2 (see Moore et al., 1997 for a discussion of the process by which this criterion was selected). A more stringent decrement criterion of 25% was set for 4-month-olds to afford them conditions that maximized recovery on the test trial.

In all studies except Experiment 1A, infants' response recovery to novel ID utterances was tested using a mixed ANOVA in which familiarization class (approval and comfort) and group (experimental and control) served as between-subjects factors, and block (2 and 3) was the repeated factor. We have consistently found no effects of familiarization class. For Experiment 1A, a mixed ANOVA of familiarization class (approval and comfort) and block (2 and 3) was performed. Our conclusions regarding infants' categorization were based on the criteria that a significant interaction of group and block was necessary, in conjunction with either significant group differences in test trial (block 3) fixation, or a significant increase in average fixation from block 2 to block 3 for the experimental group but not for the control group.

Six-Month-Olds' Categorization of ID Speech

Experiment 1: Six-Month-Old Infants' Categorization of Low-Pass Filtered ID Speech. We decided to begin by testing 6-month-old infants' categorization of ID utterances because infants in this age range have been shown to categorize a number of different types of stimuli (Bornstein, 1984; Cohen & Strauss, 1979; Miller, Younger, & Morse, 1982; Younger & Cohen, 1986).

Approving and comforting ID utterances that were low-pass filtered at 650 Hz (98 dB/octave attenuation) were presented to 6-month-old infants in Experiment 1 (Moore et al., 1997). This filtering manipulation preserved the prosodic features of the stimuli, such as F_0 contour, rhythm, and amplitude modulation, but attenuated cues that signal phonetic distinctions so that the linguistic content of the utterances was not identifiable by adult listeners (see footnote in Moore et al., 1997 for a description of this assessment). Inasmuch as prosodic differences distinguish ID speech utterances produced in different interactive contexts and ID speech prosody is salient for infants, then it seemed likely that infants would be capable of using prosodic information to categorize approving and comforting utterances. If infants are able to categorize ID speech stimuli using prosodic information, then after the response decrement characteristic of familiarization, we should see recovery of response to novel stimuli from the unfamiliar class of utterances but *not* to novel stimuli from the familiar class of utterances.

Consistent with our hypothesis, 6-month-olds who heard a stimulus from a novel category on the test trial increased looking from the final familiarization trials to the test trial, whereas infants tested with a novel stimulus from a familiar category did not (Moore et al., 1997). As illustrated in Fig. 7.1, after infants steadily decreased looking in response to a series of seven approving stimuli, they increased looking on the test trial

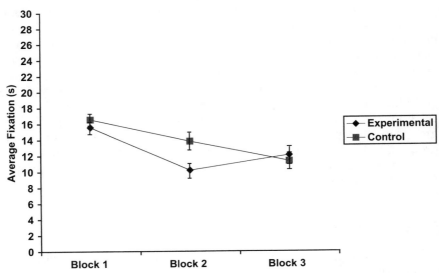

FIG. 7.1.   Experiment 1. Average fixation (s) (means and standard errors) of 6-month-old infants presented low-pass filtered ID speech for each trial block. Experimental infants increased fixation from block 2 (last 2 familiarization trials) to block 3 (test trial), whereas control infants did not.

when a comforting stimulus was presented. In contrast, infants who were familiarized with the same series of approving stimuli but tested with a novel approving stimulus did not increase looking on the test trial. The same looking patterns were found for infants familiarized with either comforting or approving stimuli.

Experiment 1A: Six-Month-Olds' Discrimination of Same-Category ID Speech. In Experiment 1A, we used comparable methods and stimuli to establish that similar stimuli *within* each class were in fact discriminable from one another, which is a necessary condition for categorization (Ferland & Mendelson, 1989; Olson & Sherman, 1983). From the 16 stimuli used in Experiment 1, we selected a pair of comforting and a pair of approving stimuli, such that the exemplars constituting a pair had similar frequency contours, durations, and F_0 characteristics. Each infant first heard one of the speech stimuli in each of seven familiarization trials, and subsequently heard the other (novel) stimulus from the same category during a test trial. Infants recovered fixation from the end of familiarization (block 2) to test (block 3), indicating that they were able to discriminate between very similar stimuli chosen from within a single class of utterances. Thus, although infants in Experiment 1 were able to discriminate between a variety of comforting utterances and a variety of approving utterances, they *disregarded the discriminable differences* among stimuli from within classes, treating all instances from a class similarly. Taken together, the results of these studies suggest that 6-month-old infants are able to categorize comforting and approving ID speech stimuli using only prosodic cues.

Experiment 2: Six-Month-Old Infants' Categorization of Unfiltered ID Speech. We next tested if 6-month-olds categorize *unfiltered* approving and comforting ID utterances (Moore & Spence, 1996; Spence & Moore, submitted). The low-pass filtered utterances used in Experiments 1 and 1A did not contain the higher frequencies that infants normally hear in ID speech. In order to test directly if infants categorize *naturalistic* ID utterances, 6-month-olds' categorization of *unfiltered* ID stimuli was examined in this experiment. Relative to low-pass filtered stimuli, unfiltered stimuli contain higher frequencies that signal phonetic distinctions and convey linguistic content to adults. We expected the presence of this additional acoustic information to have one of three possible effects on the infants' categorization. First, the prosodic properties that distinguish comforting and approving utterances—those that likely supported categorization in Experiment 1—may have been relatively more obscure within the context of this additional acoustic information. Thus, the presence of this additional information could have interfered with the infants' categorization of the unfiltered utterances. Alternatively, 6-month-olds could have categorized the unfiltered ID speech stimuli just as readily as they categorized the low-pass filtered stimuli, inasmuch as the prosodic properties that subserved categorization in Experiment 1 still characterized the stimuli presented in the current experiment. Finally, the high-frequency acoustic information in the unfiltered stimuli could have provided additional cues for the infants that actually *facilitated* their categorization.

In this experiment, we tested 6-month-old infants' categorization of unfiltered versions of the comforting and approving ID utterances presented in Experiment 1. If infants categorize the unfiltered ID utterances, they should respond just like the infants studied in Experiment 1. Specifically, infants in the experimental group should recover fixation on hearing a test stimulus from the novel category, whereas control infants should not recover responding on hearing a novel test stimulus from the familiar category.

As shown in Fig. 7.2, the two groups again produced different fixation patterns across trial blocks 2 and 3; experimental infants increased looking from the end of familiarization to test, whereas the control infants did not. Together, the results of these first two experiments indicate that 6-month-old infants categorize exemplars of comforting and approving ID utterances. In particular, they categorize both low-pass filtered ID utterances, for which prosodic properties are salient, and unfiltered ID utterances, which

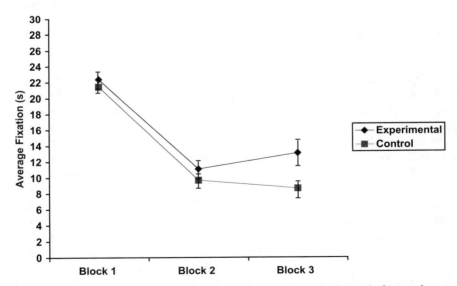

FIG. 7.2. Experiment 2. Average fixation (s) (means and standard errors) of 6-month-old infants presented unfiltered ID speech for each trial block. Experimental infants increased fixation from block 2 (last 2 familiarization trials) to block 3 (test trial), whereas control infants did not.

contain both prosodic and segmental information. Additionally, inasmuch as the two classes of ID utterances presented to these infants are both associated with caregiver intent to evoke positive affect, these results reveal that infants can discriminate utterance categories that have similar affective valence. As discussed in more detail later in the General Discussion, our demonstrations that infants can categorize ID speech suggest that by 6 months of age, they might be learning that caregivers' ID utterances, produced in distinct contexts and characterized by different sets of acoustic properties, signify different communicative intents. Thus, these results provide particularly important support for assertions that ID speech may serve as the first vocal communication of meaningful information (Fernald, 1992; Papousek, 1992; Stern et al., 1982).

Four-Month-Olds' Categorization of ID Speech

Six-month-old infants recovered responding to an ID speech stimulus from a novel category both when the stimuli conveyed only the prosodic properties of the utterance (i.e., when they were low-pass filtered) as well as when they conveyed both prosodic and phonetic information (i.e., when they were unfiltered). In order to explore the developmental trajectory of this ability, we subsequently tested 4-month-old infants' categorization using the same procedure and stimuli used in the studies with 6-month-olds.

Experiment 3: Four-Month-Old Infants' Categorization of Low-Pass Filtered ID Speech. Four-month-olds, like 6-month-olds, have been exposed to and are attentive to ID speech, and they prefer ID to AD speech (Cooper & Aslin, 1994; Cooper, Abraham, Berman, & Staska, 1997). Similarly, the utterances directed at 4-month-olds by caregivers in different pragmatic contexts (and/or in the presence of different infant states) have the characteristic prosodic properties discussed earlier (Fernald & Simon, 1984; Papousek, Papousek, & Haekel, 1987; Stern et al., 1982). However, whether or not 4 months of experience with contextualized ID speech is enough to support infants' categorization of utterances from different ID speech classes is unknown, but an empirical question. Although 4-month-old infants readily discriminate ID and AD speech (Cooper & Aslin, 1990; Fernald & Kuhl, 1987), discrimination of exemplars from different classes of ID speech requires detection of physical differences that are much subtler than those distinguishing ID and AD speech. Consequently, discrimination of utterances from different ID classes presents a more difficult task than discrimination of AD and ID utterances. Categorization would presumably be even more difficult for 4-month-old infants.

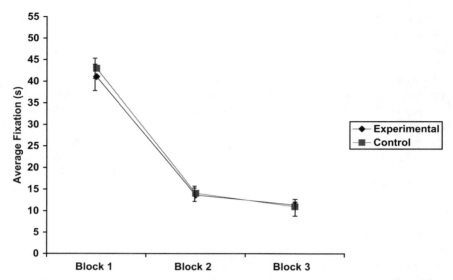

FIG. 7.3. Experiment 3. Average fixation (s) (means and standard errors) of 4-month-old infants presented low-pass filtered ID speech for each trial block. Neither group increased fixation from block 2 (familiarization) to block 3 (test).

We first examined 4-month-olds' categorization of low-pass filtered ID utterances (Spence, Moore, & Longest, 1995) both because speech prosody is very salient for infants at this age and because prosodic properties are particularly salient in low-pass filtered speech. The design, procedure, and stimuli were identical to those used in our work with 6-month-olds, with the exception that longer trials were used with 4-month-olds in order to provide them with sufficient familiarization time (Colombo & Mitchell, 1990). For all experiments with 4-month-olds, a trial ended when stimuli had been presented for a total of 60 s (rather than 30 s) or when the infant looked away from the visual stimuli for 2.5 consecutive s. As in Experiments 1 and 2, control and experimental-group infants were tested—following familiarization—with an ID speech stimulus from the familiar or novel category, respectively.

Neither group of infants recovered responding on the test trial. As seen in Fig. 7.3, the response patterns of the control and experimental groups did not differ. Most importantly, infants tested with a stimulus from the unfamiliar category did not increase looking in response to that stimulus.

Experiment 4: Assessment of the Ability of Our Experimental Method to Induce Response Recovery in 4-Month-Olds.   The results of Experiment 3, in conjunction with a very high attrition rate for 4-month-olds, caused us to question whether the experimental method used in this research was appropriate for this younger age group. Specifically, we hypothesized that failure to recover responding on the test trial could have occurred if the infants were fatigued by the end of the session. The longer familiarization times given 4-month-olds might have contributed to such fatigue or lack of interest in the auditory stimuli so that they were no longer attentive by the end of the session. This concern was addressed with an experiment in which we tested if 4-month-olds would recover responding on the test trial if the auditory stimulus presented was more discrepant than novel ID speech. As in the previous experiments, infants heard either approving or comforting ID utterances during familiarization. Then on the test trial, they heard an 8-s segment of instrumental music played by a full orchestra. We reasoned that if, during the test trial, infants failed to recover responding to a highly discrepant musical stimulus, this would imply that the infants in Experiment 3 were fatigued by the end of familiarization and incapable of demonstrating a novelty response. However, if infants increased their fixation of the visual stimuli in response to hearing music on the test trial, then this result would strengthen our confidence that the infants' failure in Experiment 3 to recover to a stimulus from an unfamiliar ID class means that they did not categorize the stimuli with which they had been familiarized.

Infants' response recovery on the test trial was assessed as in the other experiments. As can be seen in Fig. 7.4, the experimental group increased

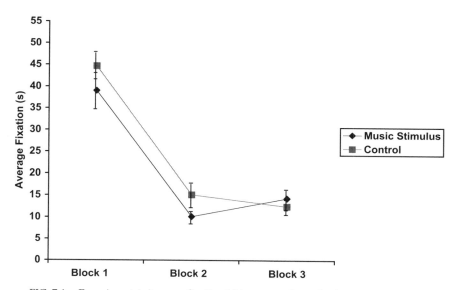

FIG. 7.4.   Experiment 4. Average fixation (s) (means and standard errors) of 4-month-old infants tested with music following ID speech familiarization. Infants tested with music increased fixation from block 2 (familiarization) to block 3 (test) whereas control infants tested with a same-category ID stimulus did not.

looking from block 2 to block 3, whereas the control group did not. That 4-month-olds tested with a musical stimulus recovered looking following familiarization with a series of ID utterances indicates that the procedure used in Experiment 3 is capable of revealing young infants' discrimination of auditory stimuli. It also implies that the experimental-group infants in Experiment 3 failed to recover responding on the test trial not because they were fatigued or bored to inaction, but rather because they did not discriminate between the approving and comforting ID utterances.

Experiment 5: Four-Month-Olds' Categorization of Unfiltered ID Speech. We next examined 4-month-olds' categorization of unfiltered ID utterances (Spence & Moore, submitted). Although we did not find that 6-month-olds differentially processed filtered and unfiltered ID utterances, it is possible that younger infants might only be capable of categorizing ID speech stimuli if they are highly similar to those they hear in their naturalistic environment. Infants were tested with unfiltered versions of the comforting and approving stimuli presented in Experiment 3. Again, 4-month-olds failed to recover responding to the ID speech stimuli that were presented on the test trials. As shown in Fig. 7.5, neither experimental nor control infants increased attention on the test trial in response to presentation of the novel stimuli.

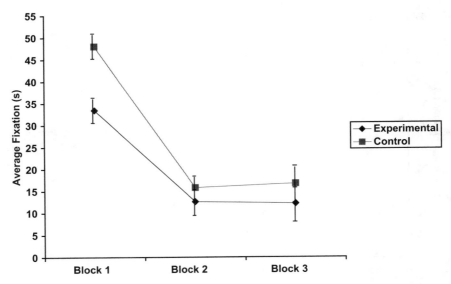

FIG. 7.5.   Experiment 5. Average fixation (s) (means and standard errors) of 4-month-old infants presented unfiltered ID speech for each trial block. Neither group increased fixation from block 2 (familiarization) to block 3 (test).

Our evidence that 4-month-old infants fail to categorize ID speech adds to a growing body of conflicting data on infants' auditory categorization skills. For example, infants under 4 months of age have been shown to be able to categorize both phonetically different syllables despite speaker variation (Jusczyk, Pisoni, & Mullennix, 1992), and different vowels produced with irrelevant variation in frequency contour (Kuhl & Miller, 1982) and voice gender (Marean, Werner, & Kuhl, 1992). In contrast, 1- to 4-month-olds do not categorize falling and monotone synthesized frequency contours despite irrelevant variation in vowel identity (Kuhl & Miller, 1982). These results, which were produced within a variety of experimental paradigms and using a variety of auditory stimuli, imply that the ability to demonstrate auditory categorization in young infants depends on both the experimental method used as well as on the nature and complexity of the stimuli presented in the task. These observations led us to ask: If the ID speech stimuli were changed so as to decrease the complexity of the stimulus set, would 4-month-olds then categorize approving and comforting utterances?

Four- and Six-Month-Old Infants' Categorization of ID Speech With Reduced Interstimulus Variability

Experiments 6 & 7: Four- and 6-Month-Olds' Categorization of ID Speech Produced by One Female. The stimulus set presented to infants in all the research presented thus far consisted of eight ID utterances, each produced by a different female. In order to categorize these stimuli, it was necessary for infants to attend to the properties that characterize ID utterances expressed in a given context (e.g., comforting) while ignoring properties that are irrelevant for inclusion in the pragmatic category. Included among these irrelevant properties are variations in physical attributes such as F_0 and tempo, as well as variations in phonetic content and variations that characterize individual speakers' voices. Studies of adults' speech perception have shown that performance on a variety of tasks is influenced by speaker variability (Pisoni, 1993). For example, adults have longer latencies for identifying words produced by multiple speakers compared with words produced by a single speaker (Mullennix, Pisoni, & Martin, 1989). Identification of words presented amidst noise is also less accurate when the words are spoken by multiple speakers rather than by only one speaker (Mullennix et al., 1989). Speaker variability also appears to interfere with infants' encoding and retention of speech: 2-month-old infants can remember a word for a 2-min interval if it is spoken by one person during familiarization, but they do not remember the word if multiple people produce it during familiarization (Jusczyk, Pisoni, & Mullennix, 1992).

Similarly, infants also require more time to habituate to or encode a familiarization word when it is produced by multiple speakers as opposed to a single speaker (Jusczyk, Kemler Nelson, et al., 1992).

Given this literature on the effects of speaker variability on both adults' and infants' speech perception, we hypothesized that young infants may have more difficulty categorizing comforting and approving ID utterances when the stimuli are produced by multiple speakers than when similar utterances are produced by a single speaker. We tested this hypothesis by examining 4-month-olds' categorization of various approving and comforting utterances produced by a single female (Wambacq, Spence, & Marchman, 1998).

The ID speech stimuli used in this study were produced by one female saying a variety of things to her 6-month-old infant. The stimuli were gathered in procedures similar to those used by Katz et al. (1996). Utterances were classified as comforting when (a) the utterance was produced as a response to the infant's distress, and (b) the content of the utterance indicated the mother's intent to comfort her baby. Utterances were classified as approvals when (a) the utterance was a praising reaction to the infant's behavior, and (b) the content of the utterance indicated that the mother was approving of her infant's behavior. In keeping with descriptions of comforting and approving ID utterances found in the ID speech literature (Fernald, 1992; Katz et al., 1996), our single-speaker comforting stimuli had a lower mean F_0 (Mann Whitney $U = 6$, $p = .006$), and F_0 variability (Mann Whitney $U = 8$, $p = .012$) than our single-speaker approving stimuli. These acoustic characteristics also accord well with the acoustic characteristics of the multiple-speaker utterances we used in Experiments 1 through 5 (Moore et al., 1997).

Four-month-old infants were familiarized with low-pass filtered versions of either comforting or approving ID speech stimuli, each of which was unique, but all of which were produced by one female speaker. The stimulus presented during the test trial was also produced by the same speaker, and was either a novel stimulus from the unfamiliar category (experimental group) or a novel stimulus from the familiar category (control group). The procedure and analyses were otherwise identical to those used for Experiments 1 through 5.

The results are shown in Fig. 7.6. Infants' fixation patterns failed to meet the criteria established for categorization (i.e., interaction of block and group). More specifically, experimental infants did not significantly increase fixation on the test trial when an exemplar from the novel category was presented, nor did group differences occur for test trial (block 3) fixation.

Four-month-olds failed to recover responding to an ID utterance from a novel category even though the set of utterances used in the current study

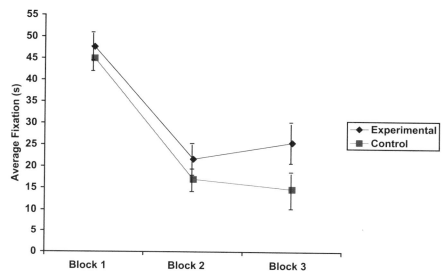

FIG. 7.6. Experiment 6. Average fixation (s) (means and standard errors) of 4-month-old infants presented single-speaker low-pass filtered ID speech. Neither group increased fixation from block 2 (familiarization) to block 3 (test).

was considerably less variable than the set of utterances produced by multiple speakers. However, this null effect might also reflect characteristics of the stimulus set. Although the acoustic attributes of this stimulus set were characteristic of those reported in the literature, the mean F_0 of the speaker was relatively high in frequency (M approval $= 428$ Hz, M comfort $= 302$ Hz) compared to the mean F_0 of the multiple-speaker stimuli used in Experiments 1 through 5 (M approval $= 361$ Hz, M comfort $= 225$ Hz). Given this possibly important difference and the fact that we had not previously studied the ability of older infants to categorize ID speech produced by a single speaker, we conducted a final experiment in which these same stimuli were presented to 6-month-old infants.

Six-month-old infants did provide evidence of categorization of the single-speaker stimuli. Specifically, experimental infants significantly increased fixation from familiarization to test, as illustrated in Fig. 7.7. In contrast, control infants did not increase fixation when presented with a novel exemplar from the familiar category. Thus, 6-month-olds categorized the ID speech stimuli produced by a single speaker. Apparently, the 4-month-olds did not fail to categorize these stimuli because of a property or properties inherent to the stimuli. Rather, 4-month-olds' failure to categorize the single-speaker stimuli mirrored their failure to categorize the multiple-speaker stimuli. This failure was presumably influenced

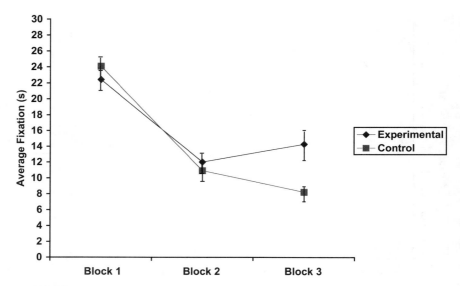

FIG. 7.7.   Experiment 7. Average fixation (s) (means and standard errors) of 6-month-old infants presented single-speaker low-pass filtered ID speech. Experimental infants increased fixation from block 2 (last 2 familiarization trials) to block 3 (test trial), whereas control infants did not.

by the same factors that influenced their failure on each of the other tasks reported in this chapter.

GENERAL DISCUSSION AND IMPLICATIONS

These results reveal age-related changes in infants' categorization of ID speech from 4 to 6 months of age. Six-month-olds categorized filtered and unfiltered utterances produced by multiple speakers as well as filtered utterances produced by a single speaker. In contrast, four-month-olds invariably failed to categorize ID speech exemplars from the two classes. They failed to recover responding to an exemplar from the novel category regardless of whether the stimuli were filtered or unfiltered and regardless of whether the stimuli were complex (produced by different speakers) or simplified (produced by one speaker). Is this developmental difference consistent with other findings in the categorization literature? The answer to this question depends, in part, on the type of category the 6-month-olds in our studies are taken to be forming.

The ID utterance categories formed by the 6-month-olds in our studies most closely resemble sensory conceptual equivalence categories (Bornstein, 1984). These types of categories are formed when infants directly perceive similar physical stimulus attributes—or relations between attributes—across exemplars from one category, even though the exemplars are highly variable on a number of other physical attributes. Infants' categorization of the gender of faces (Cornell, 1974; Fagan, 1979) and facial expressions (Nelson, Morse, & Leavitt, 1979) are cited by Bornstein (1984) as examples of sensory conceptual equivalence categorization, because to form these categories, infants must abstract the relations among the physical attributes that characterize the varying exemplars constituting these categories. Similarly, the categories formed by the 6-month-olds in our studies were sensory conceptual equivalence categories; the ID utterances within each category varied on a number of category-irrelevant attributes (e.g., linguistic content, frequency contour, rhythm, and speaker-specific characteristics such as timbre and speaking rate). However, in spite of this irrelevant variability, 6-month-olds—but not 4-month-olds—detected the co-occurring prosodic properties that characterize the exemplars within each category. Thus, our findings *are* consistent with other findings in the categorization literature; from 4 to 7 months of age, infants have been shown to be increasingly capable of abstracting relations among stimulus attributes (Caron & Caron, 1981), and of processing more complex stimuli (Cohen, 1998; Cohen & Strauss, 1979; Younger & Cohen, 1986).

Hypotheses for Developmental Differences and Future Research Directions

Our studies consistently found that 4-month-olds fail to recover responding to novel-category exemplars. Given the difficulties of interpreting null results, we must emphasize that we cannot be sure that 4-month-olds are completely incapable of categorizing ID speech. Nevertheless, only 6-month-olds—not 4-month-olds—were able to provide evidence of categorization in the specific conditions that characterized our test. Additionally, 4-month-olds did recover responding to music following familiarization with ID speech, suggesting that the experimental procedure we used is capable of detecting discrimination of some contrasts by 4-month-olds. Thus, although 4-month-olds might be capable of categorizing some ID utterances in certain (as yet unspecified) ideal circumstances, our data clearly indicate that their ID speech categorization skills are not yet comparable to those evidenced by slightly older infants. These data suggest that infants' categorization of ID speech changes as a function of age. This developmental difference in ID speech categorization cannot reflect a general deficit in 4-month-olds' categorization, inasmuch as 4-month-old and younger infants do indeed categorize some types of auditory as well as visual stimuli (Eimas & Quinn, 1994; Kuhl & Miller, 1982; Marean, Werner,

& Kuhl, 1992). Therefore, in an effort to explain this phenomenon, we have generated several hypotheses about factors that might mediate such a change.

The developmental difference we observed in ID speech categorization could be due to differences between 4- and 6-month-olds that are not specific to experience with ID speech but that nonetheless influence normal infant functioning (Gottlieb, 1991). Changes in neural structure and/or function that are not dependent on specific ID speech experience but that occur via reciprocal interactions among components of the hierarchical developmental system—ranging from the level of the genes to the level of experience— potentially contribute to the development of categorization (Gottlieb, 1991). Unfortunately, however, we cannot yet offer any more specific hypotheses bearing on this potential source of change.

Infants' specific experiences with ID speech presumably also contribute to the developmental difference we observed in ID speech categorization. More specifically, 6-month-olds' experiences with ID speech may differ qualitatively and/or quantitatively from 4-month-olds' experiences with ID speech. For example, 4-month-olds may not have had sufficient experience with ID speech to be able to categorize ID utterances from two different classes. Their daily experiences might also involve exposure to different distributions of ID utterance types than those to which older infants are typically exposed. It is possible, for example, that infants' exposure to comforting ID speech remains constant or even decreases between 4 and 6 months, whereas their exposure to approving utterances increases across this period due to changes in infants' behavioral and social repertoires (e.g., increased grasping and vocalization). Although we know of no evidence for this hypothesized change in the distribution of ID speech types across this age range, such differences could impact infants' ability to categorize utterances from two different ID speech classes.

Another hypothesis is that 4-month-olds failed to categorize due to the nature of the stimuli presented. Two suggestions relevant to this hypothesis are described now. First, 4-month-old infants may have failed to distinguish the two categories because the acoustic attributes that characterized the categories tested were not sufficiently distinct from one another. In both our multiple- and single-speaker studies reported here, there was considerable acoustic variability among exemplars within each of the two ID speech categories. In addition, there was overlap in the mean F_0 and F_0-variability distributions associated with each category. Although our 6-month-olds' categorization of ID speech was not impeded by the naturally variable, overlapping distributions of the two categories, 4-month-olds' categorization might have been. Second, 4-month-olds may have failed to categorize because the complexity of the ID speech stimuli taxed their information-processing capacity (Cohen, 1998). This suggestion is consistent with previous findings that older infants are more likely than younger infants to categorize stimuli with multiple components or features (Younger & Cohen, 1986). For infants to categorize the ID utterances used in this research, they had to detect the similarities between exemplars within a category while ignoring irrelevant differences between them. Although our experiments with single-speaker stimuli were conducted to address this issue, the ID stimuli used in these experiments still were quite variable and complex (insofar as they were characterized by a number of acoustic dimensions). Given that our stimuli were representative of naturalistic ID utterances, 4-month-olds might have difficulty categorizing the highly variable and complex ID utterances normally heard in their natural environments.

Yet another possibility is that younger infants might require a human facial stimulus to support their categorization of ID utterances (Lewkowicz, 1996; Walker-Andrews & Lennon, 1991). Support for this hypothesis is provided by research demonstrating that 5-month-olds discriminate happy, angry, and sad vocal expressions in the presence of a facial stimulus, but not when the available visual stimulus is a checkerboard (Walker-Andrews & Lennon, 1991). Four-month-old infants may have failed to categorize ID speech in our studies because a facial stimulus was not available to provide them with a needed social context. Without such a context, infants may not have perceived the auditory stimuli as ID speech, or they may not have attended to the "affective quality of the voice" (p. 140), as Walker-Andrews and Lennon (1991) suggested when trying to explain their results. Why, then, were our 6-month-old participants able to categorize the ID utterances without the context provided by a face? Perhaps as infants develop, they become less reliant on contextual cues for ID speech categorization. This idea is consistent with numerous demonstrations that younger children sometimes require greater contextual support than older children to perform successfully on a variety of tasks (for discussion, see Bjorklund, 1995).

Finally, the developmental difference we observed might reflect the fact that both approving and comforting ID utterances are produced by caregivers in an effort to evoke positive affective responses from infants. It is possible that younger infants may be able to categorize ID utterances, but only if they convey contrasting affect. This possibility is supported by the findings of previous studies that have shown that 4- and 5-month-olds can discriminate vocal stimuli with contrasting affect (e.g., approving vs. disapproving, or sad vs. happy utterances; Fernald, 1993; Papousek et al., 1990; Walker-Andrews, 1997). Thus, infants' ID speech categories may initially be broad—containing exemplars produced in a variety of pragmatic contexts but that all possess the same affective valence (e.g., approving and comforting utterances)—and only subsequently become narrower, exclusively containing exemplars produced within particular pragmatic contexts (e.g., approving utterances). Such a progression would be consistent with evidence that perceptual differentiation of finer and subtler details increases as a function of increasing experience with specific perceptual events (Gibson, 1969). To explore this possibility, we plan to test the breadth of 4-month-olds' ID speech categories using another procedure that may be more sensitive to the discriminative and categorization abilities of younger infants, the Observer-based Psychoacoustic Procedure (OPP) (Werner & Marean, 1991). This procedure insures that infants discriminate the task-relevant features of the stimuli and tests their transfer of this discrimination to novel but categorically similar exemplars.

Implications for Infants' Developing Communicative
and Social–Cognitive Skills

Much more research is necessary in order to understand the developmental differences discovered in our research. However, our current results do suggest that 6-month-olds, but not 4-month-olds, can categorize naturalistic, variable ID speech. We think that categorization of ID speech may play a significant role in infants' communicative development. Several researchers have argued that ID speech may communicate speaker affect and intent. Fernald (1992) suggested that ID speech might begin to serve this function toward the end of the first year. Infants' perceptual categorization of ID speech, which occurs at about 6 months of age, may be essential for their processing of ID communicative intent later in the first year, for the following reason. For infants to respond appropriately to vocalizations produced with differing communicative intents, they must categorize the utterances, recognizing and attending to those acoustic attributes that are characteristic of utterances produced within a given pragmatic context while simultaneously disregarding those acoustic attributes that are irrelevant for correct categorization. At a minimum, in the absence of such categorization, the functional meaning of utterances would be lost. Infants would be equally likely to produce appropriate and inappropriate responses to utterances, reacting differently to utterances intended to produce identical responses and similarly to utterances intended to produce different responses.

Our data do not allow us to address whether 6-month-old infants might actually process the communicative intent of ID speech. (They do, however, suggest that younger infants cannot access this information). Inasmuch as 6-month-olds categorize ID speech, it is possible that infants begin processing ID communicative intent in naturalistic interactions during the second half of the first year. If infants do process ID communicative intent, this ability most likely develops from their association of particular patterns of ID speech with other parental and contextual stimuli, including their own affective and/or behavioral state. As detailed next, the opportunity to associate specific feelings and/or behaviors with the perception of specific ID utterances might facilitate infants' detection of correspondences between forms and functions of utterances.

Infants probably learn to associate particular ID sound patterns with particular classes of interactive contexts by being repeatedly exposed to these sound patterns in these contexts. As we described earlier, caregivers modify the forms of ID speech they produce as a function of infants' behaviors and affective state, providing infants with opportunities to associate sound patterns with different contexts. This association is likely enhanced by the fact that ID speech is one component of multimodal, interactive experiences that infants and their caregivers share. Specifically, caregiver facial expressions, gestures, tactile and kinesthetic stimulation, and ID speech all covary as a function of context. This configuration of covarying cues should facilitate infants' initial association of particular ID utterances with particular interactional contexts.

Another set of stimuli that may influence infants' association of prosody with context is the set of vocalization behaviors infants hear themselves produce. Infants produce vocalizations that vary as a function of social-interactive context and infant state (D'Odorico & Franco, 1991; Legerstee, 1991). For example, infants ranging from 4 to 8 months of age have been found to produce vocalizations characterized by rising melodic patterns and high pitch when engaged in social interaction with, and when looking at, an adult. This pattern is not observed when infants are engaged in object manipulation (D'Odorico & Franco, 1991). Caregivers also frequently mirror infants' vocalizations and facial expressions (Papousek et al., 1985; Rochat & Striano, 1999; Trevarthen, 1979), providing additional response-contingent experiences for infants (Gergely & Watson, 1999). Thus, the vocalizations infants hear themselves produce, as well as those they hear others produce, are both correlated with their own affective and/or behavioral states.

Finally, to the extent that caregivers' ID vocalizations—which are often produced specifically to regulate infant affect and arousal—are effective in modulating infants' behaviors and/or states, then changes in these behaviors and/or states occur as a consequence of hearing ID sound patterns. Thus, the contingencies that typically exist between ID utterances, infants' and caregivers' affective and behavioral states, and other contextual variables could together provide a means by which infants could begin to associate ID speech forms with functions.

Learning that different sound patterns communicate distinctive meanings is an important component in the development of comprehension.

Quite a few researchers have argued that consistent relations between prosodic patterns and communicative functions may provide infants their first experiences with sound-meaning correspondences (Fernald, 1984; Flax, Lahey, Harris, & Boothroyd, 1991; Lewis, 1936; McRoberts, Fernald, & Moses, in press; Stern et al., 1982). Specifically, Lewis (1936) proposed that form–function correspondences that are conveyed by the intonation of ID speech provide a foundation for the infant's later comprehension of words. There are no data available to support the validity of this proposal. However, if this continuity hypothesis is correct, then ID categorization would be quite important for the development of comprehension. Because categorization allows infants to detect classes of ID speech, it affects infants' initial learning about prosody–function pairings. Failure to categorize utterances would result in infants' matching individual prosodic forms with functions, rather than classes of forms with functions. Mismatching of form–function relations would also occur, leading infants to respond inappropriately to ID utterances. An associative process such as that just discussed, in conjunction with categorization processes like those observed in our research, could provide a mechanism by which infants could form associations among classes of forms, functions, and contexts. Infants' processing of vocal communicative intent may also be relevant for their later-developing knowledge that people are intentional agents, organisms who perform behaviors in order to reach specific goals (Tomasello, 1995). A major theme in current developmental literature is that infants' developing understanding of intentionality is important for skills in cognitive, social, and linguistic domains, and is a precursor to the appearance of a "theory of mind," that is, young children's understanding that people's actions are influenced both by desires (emotions) and beliefs (thoughts; Wellman, 1993). Behaviors such as social referencing, joint engagement, imitation, and the use of communicative gestures, all begin between 9 and 12 months of age and are believed by Tomasello and colleagues to reflect an emerging social-cognitive understanding of persons as intentional agents (Carpenter, Nagell, & Tomasello, 1998). Other researchers adopt a more conservative stance, arguing instead that these behaviors form the foundation for an understanding of human intentional activity that develops sometime after 18 months of age (Moore, 1998; Wellman, 1993; for discussion of other views and relevant abilities see Rochat, 1999).

ID speech categorization may be an earlier-appearing *perceptual* ability that, like these other behaviors, may contribute to infants' developing understanding that humans are intentional agents. Although most of the research examining infants' knowledge of others as intentional agents has studied infants' understanding of persons' actions (Carpenter et al., 1998), it is also likely that vocalizations that are either directed toward specific persons or produced in specific situations also serve as cues that humans are intentional beings. There is evidence, for example, that pragmatic intent conveyed by adults' vocalizations, performed in conjunction with specific actions on objects, affects 14- to 18-month-olds' interpretations of those actions as accidental or intentional. Specifically, infants are more likely to imitate actions on objects when the adult model performs those actions in conjunction with the expression "there!" rather than "woops!" (Carpenter, Akhtar, & Tomasello, 1998). These results suggest that the pragmatic intent of a person's vocalizations influences infants' perceptions of the goal-directedness of that individual's actions. Similarly, for infants in the later months of the first year, categorization of ID speech may influence their perception of object-directedness of actions, which is thought to be a precursor to understanding that actions are goal-directed (Wellman, 1993). Additionally, the association of specific classes of vocalizations with specific actions may facilitate infants' knowledge that utterances are produced by people to obtain specific goals. If infants fail to detect the perceptual similarities across different utterances of the same type, then this failure to categorize could be expected to interfere with their ability to link specific types of utterances with specific actions. To the extent that categorization is involved in this process, then it would contribute to infants' knowledge that vocalizations provide information about a speaker's intentions and emotions (Wellman, 1993). If processing and comprehension of vocal communicative intent contribute to or are indicative of competencies constituting an understanding of intentionality and/or a later-developing "theory of mind," then data on the phenomena we have been studying will likely be of interest to those reading and writing the literature in these areas.

Our conjectures about the possible relation between ID speech categorization and the development of infants' comprehension skills or processing of communicative intent are speculative, inasmuch as we know of no data that address the nature of these relations or the mechanisms underlying their development. Our goal here has been to evoke further discussion and research in this area. We have described a set of experiments that, taken together, suggest that infants categorize approving and comforting ID speech at 6 months of age, but not at 4 months of age. The developmental effect observed warrants further investigation to learn which factors contribute to this change in infants' processing. Additionally, these data contribute to our knowledge of young infants' perception of and responsiveness to ID speech. Finally, they represent an important step toward the goal of evaluating assertions that one function of ID speech may be to communicate speaker affect and intent. One function of categorization per se is that it allows individuals to more efficiently process information in their environments (Bruner, Olver, & Greenfield, 1967). We have suggested that infants' categorization of ID speech may facilitate processing of communicative intent, which in turn has implications for the development of communicative and social-cognitive abilities.

ACKNOWLEDGMENTS

Collection, preparation, and analyses of the multiple-speaker auditory stimuli used in this research were supported by NSF Grant #BNS-8919711 to Jeffrey F. Cohn and Christopher A. Moore. Data collection was supported by awards to David S. Moore by the Research and Awards Committee of Pitzer College, and funding of Melanie J. Spence by UTD Faculty Research Initiative Awards.

We gratefully acknowledge the assistance of Jeffrey Cohn, Christopher Moore, and Gary Katz for providing auditory stimuli used in this research. Thanks are extended also to Ilse Wambacq, Miriam Longest, Catherine Stephens, Lucia Ramirez, Karen Thierry, and Karen Gove, who contributed to data collection and analysis, and to Virginia Marchman for her collaboration on collection and preparation of the single-speaker stimuli. Special thanks go to the parents and infants who participated in these studies.

REFERENCES

Birns, B., Blank, M., Bridger, W. H., & Escalona, S. K. (1965). Behavioral inhibition in neonates produced by auditory stimuli. *Child Development, 36,* 639–645.

Bjorklund, D. F. (1995). *Children's thinking: Developmental function and individual differences* (2nd ed.). Pacific Grove, CA: Brooks/Cole.

Bornstein, M. H. (1984). A descriptive taxonomy of psychological categories used by infants. In C. Sophian (Ed.), *Origins of cognitive skills* (pp. 313–338). Hillsdale, NJ: Lawrence Erlbaum Associates.

Bruner, J. S., Olver, R. R., & Greenfield, P. M. (1967). *Studies in cognitive growth.* New York: Wiley.

Caron, A. J., & Caron, R. F. (1981). Processing of relational information as an index of infant risk. In S. L. Friedman & M. Sigman (Eds.), *Preterm birth and psychological development* (pp. 219–237). New York: Academic Press.

Carpenter, M., Akhtar, N., & Tomasello, M. (1998). Fourteen- through 18-month-old infants differentially imitate intentional and accidental actions. *Infant Behavior and Development, 21,* 315–330.

Carpenter, M., Nagell, K., & Tomasello, M. (1998). Social cognition, joint attention, and communicative competence from 9 to 15 months of age. *Monographs of the Society for Research in Child Development, 63.* (4, Serial No. 255).

Cohen, L. B. (1998). An information-processing approach to infant perception and cognition. In F. Simion & G. Butterworth (Eds.), *The development of sensory, motor and cognitive capacities in early infancy* (pp. 277–300). West Sussex, UK: Psychology Press.

Cohen, L. B., & Strauss, M. S. (1979). Concept acquisition in the human infant. *Child Development, 50,* 419–424.

Colombo, J., & Mitchell, D. W. (1990). Individual differences in early visual attention: Fixation time and information processing. In J. Colombo & J. Fagen (Eds.), *Individual differences in infancy: Reliability, stability, prediction* (pp. 193–227). Hillsdale, NJ: Laurence Erlbaum Associates.

Cooper, R. P., Abraham, J., Berman, S., & Staska, M. (1997). The development of infants' preference for motherese. *Infant Behavior and Development, 20,* 477–488.

Cooper, R. P., & Aslin, R. N. (1990). Preference for infant-directed speech in the first month after birth. *Child Development, 61,* 1584–1595.

Cooper, R. P., & Aslin, R. N. (1994). Developmental differences in infant attention to the spectral properties of infant-directed speech. *Child Development, 65,* 1663–1677.

Cornell, E. H. (1974). Infants' discrimination of photographs of faces following redundant presentations. *Journal of Experimental Child Psychology, 18,* 98–106.

D'Odorico, L., & Franco, F. (1991). Selective production of vocalization types in different communication contexts. *Journal of Child Language, 18*(3), 475–499.

Echols, C. H. (1996). A role for stress in early speech segmentation. In J. L. Morgan & K. Demuth (Eds.), *Signal to syntax: Bootstrapping from speech to grammar in early acquisition* (pp. 151–170). Mahwah, NJ: Lawrence Erlbaum Associates.

Eimas, P. D., & Quinn, P. C. (1994). Studies on the formation of perceptually based basic-level categories in young infants. *Child Development, 65,* 903–917.

Fagan, J. F. (1979). The origins of facial pattern recognition. In M. H. Bornstein & W. Kessen (Eds.), *Psychological development from infancy: Image to intention* (pp. 83–113). Hillsdale, N. J.: Lawrence Erlbaum Associates.

Ferland, M. B., & Mendelson, M. J. (1989). Infants' categorization of melodic contour. *Infant Behavior and Development, 12,* 341–355.

Fernald, A. (1984). The perceptual and affective salience of mothers' speech to infants. In L. Feagans, C. Garvey, & R. Golinkoff (Eds.), *The origins and growth of cognition* (pp. 5–29). Norwood, NJ: Ablex.

Fernald, A. (1985). Four-month-old infants prefer to listen to motherese. *Infant Behavior and Development, 8,* 181–195.

Fernald, A. (1989). Intonation and communicative intent in mothers' speech to infants: Is the melody the message? *Child Development, 60,* 1497–1510.

Fernald, A. (1992). Meaningful melodies in mothers' speech to infants. In H. Papousek, U. Jurgens, & M. Papousek (Eds.), *Nonverbal communication: Comparative and developmental approaches* (pp. 262–282). New York: Cambridge University Press.

Fernald, A. (1993). Approval and disapproval: Infant responsiveness to vocal affect in familiar and unfamiliar languages. *Child Development, 64,* 657–674.

Fernald, A., & Kuhl, P. K. (1987). Acoustic determinants of infant preference for motherese speech. *Infant Behavior and Development, 10,* 279–293.

Fernald, A., & Mazzie, C. (1991). Prosody and focus in speech to infants and adults. *Developmental Psychology, 27,* 209–221.

Fernald, A., & Simon, T. (1984). Expanded intonation contours in mothers' speech to newborns. *Developmental Psychology, 20,* 104–113.

Fernald, A., Taeschner, T., Dunn, J., Papousek, M., Boysson-Bardies, B., & Fukui, I. (1989). A cross-language study of prosodic modifications in mothers' and fathers' speech to preverbal infants. *Journal of Child Language, 16,* 477–501.

Flax, J., Lahey, M., Harris, K., & Boothroyd, A. (1991). Relations between prosodic variables and communicative functions. *Journal of Child Language, 18,* 3–19.

Gergely, G., & Watson, J. (1999). Social–cognitive development in the first year. In P. Rochat & T. Striano (Eds.), *Early social cognition: Understanding others in the first months of life* (pp. 101–136). Mahwah, NJ: Lawrence Erlbaum Associates.

Gibson, E. J. (1969). *Principles of perceptual learning and development.* Englewood Cliffs, NJ: Prentice-Hall.

Gottlieb, G. (1991). Experiential canalization of behavioral development: Theory. *Developmental Psychology, 27,* 4–13.

Grieser, D. L., & Kuhl, P. K. (1988). Maternal speech to infants in a tonal language: Support for universal prosodic features in motherese. *Developmental Psychology, 24,* 14–20.

Hirsch-Pasek, K., Kemler Nelson, D. G., Jusczyk, P. W., Wright Cassidy, K., Druss, B., & Kennedy, L. (1987). Clauses are perceptual units for young infants. *Cognition, 26,* 269–286.

Hutt, S. J., Hutt, C., Lenard, H. G., Bernuth, H. V., & Muntejewerff, W. J. (1968). Auditory responsivity in the human neonate. *Nature, 218,* 888–890.

Jacobson, J. L., Boersma, D. C., Fields, R. B., & Olson, K. L. (1983). Paralinguistic features of adult speech to infants and small children. *Child Development, 54,* 436–442.

Jusczyk, P. W., Kemler Nelson, D. G., Hirsch-Pasek, K., Kennedy, L., Woodward, A., & Piwoz, J. (1992). Perception of acoustic correlates of major phrasal units by young infants. *Cognitive Psychology, 24,* 252–293.

Jusczyk, P. W., Pisoni, D. B., & Mullennix, J. (1992). Some consequences of stimulus variability on speech processing by 2-month-old infants. *Cognition, 43,* 253–291.

Kaplan, P. S., Goldstein, M. H., Huckeby, E. R., & Cooper, R. P. (1995). Habituation, sensitization, and infants' responses to motherese speech. *Developmental Psychology, 28,* 45–57.

Kaplan, P. S., Goldstein, M. H., Huckeby, E. R., Owren, M. J., & Cooper, R. P. (1995). Dishabituation of visual attention by infant- versus adult-directed speech: Effects of frequency modulation and spectral properties. *Infant Behavior and Development, 18,* 209–223.

Karmel, B. Z. (1969). The effect of age, complexity, and amount of contour density on pattern preferences in human infants. *Journal of Experimental Child Psychology, 7,* 339–354.

Katz, G. S., Cohn, J. F., & Moore, C. A. (1996). A combination of vocal F_0 dynamic and summary features discriminates between three pragmatic categories of infant-directed speech. *Child Development, 67,* 205–217.

Kuhl, P. K., & Miller, J. D. (1982). Discrimination of auditory target dimensions in the presence or absence of variation in a second dimension by infants. *Perception & Psychophysics, 31,* 279–292.

Ladd, D., Silverman, K., Tolkmitt, F., Bergmann, G., & Scherer, K. (1985). Evidence for the independent function of intonation contour type, voice quality and F_0 range in signaling speaker affect. *Journal of the Acoustical Society of America, 78,* 435–444.

Legerstee, M. (1991). Changes in the quality of infant sounds as a function of social and nonsocial stimulation. *First Language, 11,* 327–343.

Lewis, M. M. (1936). *Infant speech: A study of the beginnings of language.* London: Routledge & Kegan Paul.

Lewkowicz, D. J. (1996). Infants' response to the audible and visible properties of the human face: 1. Role of lexical-syntactic content, temporal synchrony, gender, and manner of speech. *Developmental Psychology, 32,* 347–366.

Marean, G. C., Werner, L. A., & Kuhl, P. K. (1992). Vowel categorization by very young infants. *Developmental Psychology, 28,* 396–405.

McRoberts, G. W., Fernald, A., & Moses, L. J. (in press). An acoustic study of prosodic form–function relations in infant-directed speech: Cross language similarities. *Developmental Psychology.*

Miller, C. L., Younger, B. A., & Morse, P. A. (1982). The categorization of male and female voices in infancy. *Infant Behavior and Development, 5,* 143–159.

Moore, C. (1998). Social cognition in infancy. In M. Carpenter, K. Nagell, & M. Tomasello (Eds.), Social cognition, joint attention, and communicative competence from 9 to 15 months of age (pp. 167–174). *Monographs of the Society for Research in Child Development, 63.* (4, Serial No. 255).

Moore, D. S., & Spence, M. J. (1996). *Infants' categorization of unfiltered infant-directed utterances.* Poster presented at the International Conference on Infant Studies, Providence, RI.

Moore, D. S., Spence, M. J., & Katz, G. S. (1997). Six-month-olds' categorization of natural infant-directed utterances. *Developmental Psychology, 33,* 980–989.

Morgan, J. L., & Demuth, K. (1996). *Signal to syntax: Bootstrapping from speech to grammar in early infancy.* Mahwah, NJ: Lawrence Erlbaum Associates.

Mullennix, J. W., Pisoni, D. B., & Martin, C. S. (1989). Some effects of talker variability on spoken word recognition. *Journal of the Acoustical Society of America, 85,* 365–378.

Nelson, C. A., Morse, P. A., & Leavitt, L. A. (1979). Recognition of facial expressions by seven-month-old infants. *Child Development, 50,* 1239–1242.

Olson, G. M., & Sherman, T. (1983). Attention, learning, and memory in infants. In P. H. Mussen (Series Ed.) and M. M. Haith & J. J. Campos (Vol. Eds.), *Handbook of child psychology: Vol. 2. Infancy and developmental psychobiology* (4th ed., pp. 1001–1080). New York: Wiley.

Papousek, M. (1992). Early ontogeny of vocal communication in parent–infant interactions. In H. Papousek, U. Jurgens, & M. Papousek (Eds.), *Nonverbal vocal communication: Comparative and developmental approaches* (pp. 230–261). Cambridge: Cambridge University Press.

Papousek, M., Bornstein, M. H., Nuzzo, C., Papousek, H., & Symmes, D. (1990). Infant responses to prototypical melodic contours in parental speech. *Infant Behavior and Development, 13,* 539–545.

Papousek, M., Papousek, H., & Bornstein, M. H. (1985). The naturalistic vocal environment of young infants: On the significance of homogeneity and variability in parental speech. In T. M. Field & N. A. Fox (Eds.). *Social perception in infants* (pp. 269–295). Norwood, NJ: Ablex.

Papousek, M., Papousek, H., & Haekel, M. (1987). Didactic adjustments in fathers' and mothers' speech to their 3-month-old infants. *Journal of Psycholinguistic Research, 16,* 491–516.

Papousek, M., Papousek, H., & Symmes, D. (1991). The meanings of melodies in motherese in tone and stress languages. *Infant Behavior and Development, 14,* 415–440.

Pegg, J. E., Werker, J. F., & McLeod, P. J. (1992). Preference for infant-directed over adult-directed speech: Evidence from 7-week-old infants. *Infant Behavior and Development, 15,* 235–245.

Pisoni, D. B. (1993). Long-term memory in speech perception: Some new findings on talker variability, speaking rate and perceptual learning. *Speech Communication, 13,* 109–125.

Rochat, P. (1999). *Early social cognition: Understanding others in the first months of life.* Mahwah, NJ: Lawrence Erlbaum Associates.

Rochat, P., & Striano, T. (1999). Social-cognitive development in the first year. In P. Rochat (Ed.), *Early social cognition: Understanding others in the first months of life* (pp. 3–34). Mahwah, NJ: Lawrence Erlbaum Associates.

Sachs, J., & Devin, J. (1976). Young children's use of age-appropriate speech styles in social interaction and role-playing. *Journal of Child Language, 3,* 81–98.

Scherer, K. R. (1986). Vocal affect expression: A review and a model for future research. *Psychological Bulletin, 99,* 143–165.

Spence, M. J., & Moore, D. S. (2001). *Categorization of infant-directed speech: Development from 4 to 6 months.* Manuscript submitted for publication.

Spence, M. J., Moore, D. S., & Longest, M. (1995). *Categorization of infant-directed utterances develops between 3 and 6 months of age.* Poster presented at the International Society for Developmental Psychobiology, San Diego, CA.

Stern, D. N., Spieker, S., Barnett, R. K., & MacKain, K. (1983). The prosody of maternal speech: Infant age and context related changes. *Journal of Child Language, 10,* 1–15.

Stern, D. N., Spieker, S., & MacKain, K. (1982). Intonation contours as signals in maternal speech to prelinguistic infants. *Developmental Psychology, 18,* 727–735.

Tomasello, M. (1995). Joint attention as social cognition. In C. Moore & P. Dunham (Eds.), *Joint attention: Its origins and role in development* (pp. 103–130). Hillsdale, NJ: Lawrence Erlbaum Associates.

Trevarthen, C. (1979). Instincts for human understanding and for cultural cooperation: their development in infancy. In M. von Cranach, K. Foppa, W. Lepenies, & D. Ploog (Eds.), *Human ethology: Claims and limits of a new discipline* (pp. 530–571). Cambridge: Cambridge University Press.

Walker-Andrews, A. S. (1997). Infants' perception of expressive behaviors: Differentiation of multimodal information. *Psychological Bulletin, 121,* 437–456.

Walker-Andrews, A. S., & Lennon, E. (1991). Infants' discrimination of vocal expressions: Contributions of auditory and visual information. *Infant Behavior and Development, 14,* 131–142.

Wambacq, I. J., Spence, M. J., & Marchman, V. A. (1998). *Infants' categorization of infant-directed utterances produced by a single speaker.* Poster presented at the Eleventh International Conference on Infant Studies, Atlanta, GA.

Wellman, H. M. (1993). Early understanding of mind: the normal case. In S. Baron-Cohen, H. Tager-Flusberg, & D. Cohen (Eds.), *Understanding other minds: Perspectives from autism* (pp. 10–39). Oxford: Oxford University Press.

Werker, J. F., & McLeod, P. J. (1989). Infant preference for both male and female infant-directed talk: A developmental study of attentional and affective responsiveness. *Canadian Journal of Psychology, 43,* 230–246.

Werker, J. F., Pegg, J. E., & McLeod, P. J. (1994). A cross-language investigation of infant preference for infant-directed communication. *Infant Behavior and Development, 17,* 323–333.

Werner, L. A., & Marean, G. C. (1991). Methods for estimating infant thresholds. *Journal of the Acoustical Society of America, 90,* 1867–1875.

Younger, B. A., & Cohen, L. B. (1986). Developmental change in infants' perception of correlations among attributes. *Child Development, 57,* 803–815.

Author Index

Subject Index